WORD
Spell

WORD
Spell

A spelling dictionary

Editors:
Bud Wileman
Robin Wileman

HARRAP'S *REFERENCE*

First published in this edition by
HARRAP Ltd, 19-23 Ludgate Hill
London EC4M 7PD

ISBN 0 245-54656-1 (cased)
ISBN 0 245-54635-1 (plastic cover)

Typeset in Australia by
Abb-typesetting Pty Ltd
126 Oxford Street
Collingwood, Victoria

Printed and bound in Great Britain by
Richard Clay Ltd, Bungay, Suffolk

In gratitude to all those children and adults who helped with the spelling in this dictionary.

Foreword

This is a book that deals with an age old problem.

> "Please, how do you spell 'inconceivable'?"
> "Why don't you look it up in the dictionary?"
> "I did, but it's not there!"

Of course it was there, but not in the form sought by the puzzled inquirer, who was trying to find "inconseavable".

In English, there is no simple relationship between speech sounds and their graphic representation: a single sound may be written in a number of different ways. However, far from being a haphazard arrangement, English spelling is based on a complex system of rules which govern the interrelationship of a word's visual appearance, sound and meaning. Sometimes, as in the K sound in *skip* (Scandinavian) and *schizoid* (Greek), the word's origin determines the spelling. On other occasions it is the grammatical function, as in "there" and "their", which both derive from Old English.

The visual patterns also impose limitations on meaning, and they may give readers significant clues. For example, the homonyms "to", "too", and "two" have differing syntactic and semantic functions; "night" and "knight" are both nouns, but mean different things.

For struggling readers and writers, the whole system can be bewildering, and the rules difficult to learn. What can be done to help? One possibility is to reform spelling so that it becomes phonetically regular. G.B. Shaw left a legacy to that end, and some beginning reading and writing schemes such as the Initial Teaching Alphabet have attempted the task. However, such alleged reforms would result in considerable problems for those who have already learnt to read and write, and would deprive all readers of the valuable clues to meaning inherent in the present system.

The alternatives are, firstly, to find more efficient ways of teaching spelling in context as a system of auditory and visual patterns that contribute to our understanding of the printed word and, secondly, to provide writers with a key to correct spellings of incidental words as they need them.

Word Spell provides such a key. It consists of a lexicon of words commonly used in Australia, containing not only their correct spelling but also common misspellings, so that the reader can look up "inconseavable" or "inconceivable" and find the accepted form of the word. The incorrect spellings are easily identified both by indention and a pale blue lettering.

The misspellings have been drawn from a range of spelling tests, lists of commonly misspelt words, and the editors' own experience. An additional advantage is the provision of a set of simple guidelines to help inexperienced or erratic spellers to improve their mastery of written language.

Word Spell is desinged to help those people who, although their oral conversation is adequate, may not be able to spell all the words they know. It will be an invaluable reference for the many children and adults with problems in this area, as well as for the teachers who are endeavouring to help them.

Dr. Patricia Long,
Chairperson
Special Education Department,
Melbourne College of Advanced Education.

Introduction

How To Find a Word.

If possible, write down what you think is the spelling of the word you wish to find. Decide what are the first two or three letters.

Find these in the dictionary by looking at the left hand column. If you have the correct spelling you will find the word printed in **black**.

If you have the incorrect spelling you will find the word printed in **blue**, in the second left hand column. You will then find the correct spelling in **black** in the right hand column.

If you do not find the word, check any directions that may be given e.g.

> Look under **de-** if the
> word is not under **di**.

Then proceed as above. Check how close you were to the correct spelling and if necessary learn the correct spelling.

How To Learn the Correct Spelling.

Say the word and the letters.
Look at the word carefully.
Write the word three times.
Close your eyes and think of the word. **Write it down** with your eyes closed.
Check to see you are correct.
Write the word in a sentence so that you will remember its meaning as well as its spelling.
Consult a standard dictionary if you are unsure of the meaning.

About the Dictionary.

You will see that all the words, correct spellings and incorrect spellings are listed in alphabetical order.

Nouns

To form the plural of most nouns add "**s**" to the word.

    e.g. rabbit, rabbits.

Where the plural may be difficult, you are given help.

    e.g. injury, -ries (for 'injuries')
         goose, geese
         piano, pianos

You will find hints to help you with plurals on page ix.

Verbs

Verbs listed in the dictionary give the endings for the past tense, the past participle and the present participle. Most verbs have the same word for the past tense and the past participle.

    e.g. reach, -ed, -ing for reach, **reached**, reaching.

Where difficulty could occur with the spelling, you are given further help.

    e.g. collide, -lided, -liding for collide, collided, colliding.
         erase, erased, erasing

Where the past tense and the past participle are different, the words are given in full.

    e.g. sing, sang, sung, singing.

You will find hints to help you with verbs on page ix.

Adjectives

Where there may be difficulty in spelling the comparative and superlative forms, further help is given.

    e.g. dizzy, dizzier, dizziest.

Adverbs
Where the ending -**ly** is given, it is added to the word.
    e.g. mythical, -ly for '**mythically**.'
Where there is a change in spelling, further help is given.
    e.g. haste, -tily for '**hastily**'.
        palpable, -bly for '**palpably**'.

SOME SPELLING HINTS

1. For short sounding words (one syllable words) *that do not end in* **e**, double the last letter when adding -ed, -er or -ing, e.g. ban, banned; jog, jogger; fit, fitting.

2. In short words *that end in* **e** where the central vowel sound is said the same way as the letter name — e.g. make — drop the **e** when -ed, -er or -ing are added, e.g. cope, coped; make, maker; bite, biting.
   Short words keep the **e** when -ly is added, e.g. tame, tamely; time, timely.

3. Short words (one syllable) ending in **y**, preceded by a vowel, keep the **y** when -ed, -er or -ing are added, e.g. key, keyed; buy, buyer; toy, toying. If the **y** is preceded by a consonant, when -ed, or -er are added, the **y** is changed to **i**, e.g. try, tried; fly, flier.
   The **y** is kept when adding -ing, e.g. try, trying.

4. Longer words ending in **y**, change the **y** to **i** when adding other parts, e.g. berry, berries; marry, marriage; happy, happiness; hurry, hurried; funny, funnily; heavy, heavier and heaviest.
   However, when adding -ing, the **y** is kept, e.g. hurry, hurrying; bury, burying.

5. Vowels that can be doubled are **e** (been) and **o** (moon) and sometimes **u** (vacuum); **a** and **i** are not doubled in English words.

6. Letters that can be doubled in the middle of a word are **b**, **d**, **f**, **g**, **m**, **n**, **r**, **s**, **t**, and **z**.

7. In short words, **f**, **l**, **s** and **z** at the end of a word are doubled, e.g. cuff, doll, pass, buzz.

8. If **full** is added to the end of a word, one **l** is dropped, e.g. helpful, until.

9. When **all-** or **well-** are added to the front of a word, one **l** is dropped, e.g. already, welcome.

10. When **dis-** and **mis-**, meaning 'not', are placed in front of a word, the **s** is not doubled — e.g. disable, misbehave — unless the main word begins with **s**, e.g. disservice, misspell.

    Also when **un-** is placed in front of a word, the **n** is not doubled — e.g. unmade — unless the main word begins with **n**, e.g. unnecessary.

    Similarly, when **in-** is placed in front of a word, the **n** is not doubled — e.g. insane — unless the main word begins with **n**, e.g. innumerable.

PLURALS

1. Most words ad **s** to form the plural — e.g. cat, cats, but words that end in a sibilant sound (-s, -sh, -ss, -tch, -x) add **es**, e.g. gases, wishes, masses, catches, foxes.

2. Most words ending in **f** change the **f** to **v** and add **es**, e.g. thief, thieves. There are some exceptions, so check the word.

3. Most words ending in **o** add **es**, e.g. potato, potatoes. Exceptions are foreign words, so check the word if you are unsure.

4. Words ending in **y**, *preceded by a consonant*, change the **y** to **i** and add **es** — e.g. ferry, ferries, but words ending in **y**, *preceded by a vowel*, add **s**, e.g. day, days; monkey, monkeys.

5. Words ending in **ful** usually put the **s** after the stem word, e.g. cupful, cupsful. However the placement of **s** at the end of the word is now becoming acceptable, e.g. cupful, cupfuls.

6. Some words add **en** or **ren** to the stem word, e.g. ox, oxen; child, children.

7. Some foreign words change the ending and add **a**, **ae**, **i**, e.g. compendium, compendia; formula, formulae; bacillus, bacilli.

POSITION OF LETTERS

1. In '**ee**' sound words, **c** is always followed by **ei**, e.g. receive, ceiling. Most others have **ie**, e.g. believe, priest. However, there are many exceptions so check the word if you are unsure.

2. **q** is always followed by **u** in English words.

3. No English words end in **j** or **v**.

4. If **g** and **h** come together, **g** is always before **h**, e.g. eight, enough.

5. **ck** never starts a word.

SOUND

1. If a long word (more than one syllable) ends in the sound '**shun**', it could be spelt -tion, -sion, -cion.

2. **ti**, **si** and **ci** make the '**sh**' sound, but not at the beginning of a word.

3. A long word ending in the '**j**' sound could be -age, -ege, -ige, -dge. Check the word if you are not sure.

4. A long word ending in the '**ree**' sound could be -ary, -ery, -ory, -ury or -ry. Check if you are not sure.

5. Very short words (one syllable) ending in **y** make the '**i**' sound as in sly, pry, sky.

6. Words ending in the '**ul**' sound could be spelt -ble, -al, -el, -il, -ol, -le. Check if you are not sure.

7. Most words ending in the '**ize**' sound are usually spelt -**ise**, e.g. analyse, paralyse. Some exceptions are capsize, prize.

Aa

aback
abacus, abaci, abacuses
  abait   abate
  abakus   abacus
abalone
  abalonie   abalone
abandon, -ed, -ing
abandonment
abase, abased, abasing
abasement
abashed
abate, abated, abating
abatement
  abators   abattoirs
abattoirs
  abatwaz   abattoirs
  abayance   abeyance
abbess (nun)
  abbess   abyss (hole)
abbey, -beys
  abbie   abbey
abbot
abbreviate, -ated, -ating
abbreviation
  abcence   absence
  abdacate   abdicate
abdicate, -cated, -cating
abdication
abdomen
  abduckshun   abduction
abduct
abduction
abductor
  abel   able
  aberation   aberration
aberrant
aberration
abet, abetted, abetting

abeyance
  abeyense   abeyance
abhor, abhorred, abhorring
  abhore   abhor
  abhorent   abhorrent
abhorrent, -ly
abidance
  abidanse   abidance
abide, abode, abided, abiding
  abilitee   ability
  abilitey   ability
ability, -ties
  abismal   abysmal
  abiss   abyss
abject, -ly
  abjective   objective
  abjekt   abject
abjure, -jured, -juring
ablaze
able, abler, ablest
able-bodied
  ablushun   ablution
ablution
  abnegashun   abnegation
abnegate, -gated, -gating
abnegation
abnormal, -ly
abnormality, -ties
aboard
abode
abolish
abolishment
  abolishun   abolition
abolitionary
abolitionist
  abollish   abolish
A-bomb
  abominabel   abominable
abominable
abominably
abominate, -nated, -nating
abomination
  abord   aboard
aboriginal
Aborigine
  aborshun   abortion
abort, -ed, -ing

abortion
abortive, -ly
abound, -ed, -ing
about
above
aboveboard
abowt   about
abracadabra
abradant
abrade, abraded, abrading
abrasion
abrasive
abreast
abrest   abreast
abridge, abridged, abridging
abridgment
abrige   abridge
abroad
abrogate, -gated, -gating
abrupt, -ly
abruptness
absail   abseil
abscess
abscond, -ed, -ing
absconder
abseil, -ed, -ing
absence
absense   absence
absent, -ed, -ing
absentee
absenteeism
absent-minded
absess   abscess
absinth
absolushun   absolution
absolute, -ly
absolution
absolutism
absolutist
absolve, -solved, -solving
absorb, -ed, -ing
absorbency
absorbensy   absorbency
absorbent
absorbshun   absorption
absorption
absorptive

abstain, -ed, -ing
abstane   abstain
abstemious, -ly
abstemius   abstemious
abstenshun   abstention
abstention
abstinence
abstinense   abstinence
abstinent, -ly
abstract, -ed, -ing
abstraction
abstrakshun   abstraction
abstrakt   abstract
abstruse, -ly
absurd, -ly
absurdity
abundance
abundant, -ly
abundence   abundance
abundent   abundant
abusave   abusive
abuse, abused, abusing
abusive, -ly
abut, abutted, abutting
abuttal
abysmal, -ly
abyss (hole)
acacia
academic
academician
academishun   academician
academy, -mies
accacia   acacia
accademic   academic
accademy   academy
accede, -ceded, -ceding (agree)
accede   exceed
                    (surpass)
accelerate, -rated, -rating
acceleration
accelerator
accent, -ed, -ing
accentual, -ly
accentuate, -ated, -ating
accept, -ed, -ing
acceptabel   acceptable
acceptability

acceptable, -bly
acceptance
  acceptense   acceptance
access
  accessable   accessible
accessary, -ries (crime)
  accessibel   accessible
accessibility
accessible, -bly
  accessibul   accessible
accession
accessory, -ries (extra)
accident
accidental, -ly
acclaim, -ed, -ing
acclamation
acclimatise, -tised, -tising
accolade
accommodate, -dated, -dating
accommodation
  accomodation   accommodation
accompaniment
accompanist
accompany, -nied, -nying
  accompanyment   accompaniment
accomplice
accomplish, -ed, -ing
accomplishment
  accompliss   accomplice
accord, -ed, -ing
accordance
  accordanse   accordance
accordant, -ly
accordingly
accordion
accordionist
accost, -ed, -ing
account, -ed, -ing
  accountabel   accountable
accountability
accountable
accountably
  accountabul   accountable
accountancy
accountant
  accoustic   acoustic
accredit, -ed, -ing

accreditation
  accreshun   accretion
accretion
  accrew   accrue
  accross   across
accrual
accrue, -crued, -cruing
  accult   occult
  accumen   acumen
accumulate, -lated, -lating
accumulation
accumulative
accumulator
accuracy
  accurasy   accuracy
accurate, -ly
accurateness
accursed
accusation
accuse, -cused, -cusing
accuser
accustom, -ed, -ing
  accute   acute
ace
  acelerate   accelerate
  acerage   acreage
  acerbait   acerbate
acerbate, -bated, -bating
acerbic
acerbity
  acerige   acreage
acetate
acetic (acid)
  acetic   ascetic (hermit)
  acetilene   acetylene
acetylene
ache, ached, aching
  acheivable   achievable
  acheive   achieve
  achievabel   achievable
achievable
  achievabul   achievable
achieve, achieved, achieving
achievement
achiever
acid
acidic

acidify, -fied, -fying
acidity
ackers
acknowledge, -edged, -edging
acknowledgment

For other **ack-** words,
look under **ac-** or **acc-**.

---

aclaim   acclaim
aclamation   acclamation
acme
acne
acolade   accolade
acommodate   accommodate
acommodation   accommodation
acompanist   accompanist
acompany   accompany
acomplice   accomplice
acomplish   accomplish
acord   accord
acordion   accordion
acorn
acost   accost
acount   account
acoustic
acoustical, -ly
acoustics
acquaint, -ed, -ing
acquaintance
acquaintanse   acquaintance
acquiesce, -esced, -escing
acquiescence
acquiescent, -ly
acquiess   acquiesce
acquire, -quired, -quiring
acquisition
acquisitive, -ly
acquit, -quitted, -quitting
acquittal
acre
acreage
acredit   accredit
acrid, -ly
acrimonious, -ly
acrimony, -nies
acrobat
acrobatic

acrobatically
acrobatics
acrofobia   acrophobia
acrophobia
acropolis
across
acrylic
acryllic   acrylic
act, -ed, -ing
acter   actor
acting
action
actionabel   actionable
actionable
actionabul   actionable
activate, -vated, -vating
active
activism
activist
activity, -ties
actor
actress
actual, -ly
actuality, -ties
actually
actuarial, -ly
actuary, -ries
actuate, -ated, -ating
acuity
acumen
acupuncture
acupuncturist
acupunshur   acupuncture
acute, -ly
acuteness
adage
adagio
adajio   adagio
adamant
adament   adamant
adapt, -ed, -ing
adaptabel   adaptable
adaptability
adaptable
adaptabul   adaptable
adaptation
adaption

adaptive, -ly
adaptor
adda   adder
addendum, -da
adder
addicshun   addiction
addict, -ed, -ing
addiction
addictive
addishun   addition
addition (add)
addition   edition (book)
additional, -ly
additive
addled
address, -ed, -ing
adduce, -duced, -ducing
adducibel   adducible
adducible

For other **add-** words,
look under **ad-**.

adenoid
adept, -ly
adeptness
adequacy
adequasy   adequacy
adequate, -ly
adherant   adherent
adhere, -hered, -hering
adherence
adherense   adherence
adherent, -ly
adheshun   adhesion
adhesion
adhesive, -ly
adjacent, -ly
adjasent   adjacent
adjectival, -ly
adjective
adjetival   adjectival
adjetive   adjective
adjoin, -ed, -ing
adjourn, -ed, -ing
adjournment
adjudicate, -cated, -cating
adjudication

adjudicative, -ly
adjudicator
adjunct
adjure, -jured, -juring
adjurn   adjourn
adjurnment   adjournment
adjust, -ed, -ing
adjustabel   adjustable
adjustable, -bly
adjustabul   adjustable
adjustment
admeral   admiral
administer, -ed, -ing
administrabel   administrable
administrable
administrabul   administrable
administrate, -trated, -trating
administrater   administrator
administration
administrative, -ly
administrator
admirable, -bly
admiral
admiralty, -ties
admiration
admire, -mired, -miring
admirer
admishun   admission
admissable   admissible
admissibel   admissible
admissible, -ly
admissibul   admissible
admission
admit, -mitted, -mitting
admittance
admittanse   admittance
admittedly
admonish, -ed, -ing
admonishun   admonition
admonition
ad nauseam
ado
adobe
adolescence
adolescent
adolesense   adolescence
adolesent   adolescent

adopshun adoption
adopt, -ed, -ing
adoption
adoptive, -ly
adorabel adorable
adorable
adorably
adorabul adorable
adoration
adore, adored, adoring
adorn, -ed, -ing
adornment
adorrable adorable
adorre adore
adrenalin
adress address
adrift
adroit, -ly
adroyt adroit
adulate, -lated, -lating
adulation
adulatory
adult
adulterate, -rated, -rating
adulteration
adulterer
adulteress
adulterous
adultery, -teries
adulthood
adultry adultery
advacate advocate
advance, -vanced, -vancing
advancement
advanse advance
advansement advancement
advantage, -taged, -taging
advantageous, -ly
advantaje advantage
advenscher adventure
advenshur adventure
advent
adventure, -tured, -turing
adventureous adventurous
adventurer
adventuresome
adventurous, -ly

adverb
adverbial, -ly
adversary, -saries
adverse, -ly
adversery adversary
adversity, -ties
advert, -ed, -ing
advertise, -tised, -tising
advertisement
advertiser
advertisment advertisement
advice (opinion)
advice advise (give advice)
advisabel advisable
advisability
advisable, -bly
advisabul advisable
advise, -vised, -vising (give advice)
advise advice (opinion)
advised, -ly
adviser
advisery advisory
advisory
advocacy
advocasy advocacy
advocate, -cated, -cating
advokate advocate
adze
aegis
aeon
aerate, -rated, -rating
aerator
aerial, -ly
aerobatics
aerobics
aerodrome
aerodynamics
aeronautical, -ly
aeronautics
aeronortics aeronautics
aeroplain aeroplane
aeroplane
aerosol
aerospace
aesthetic

aetiologist
aetiology
afable — affable
afadavit — affadavit
afair — affair
afar
afasia — aphasia
afect — affect (pretend)
afect — effect (result)
afectation — affectation
afected — affected
afected — effected
afection — affection
afectionate — affectionate
afective — affective
afeild — afield
affabel — affable
affability
affable
affableness
affably
affabul — affable
affadavit — affidavit
affair
affare — affair
affecshun — affection
affect, -ed, -ing (pretend)
affectation
affection
affectionate, -ly
affective, -ly (emotion)
affective — effective (actual)
affidavit
affiliate, -ated, -ating
affiliation
affilliation — affiliation
affinity, -ties
affirm, -ed, -ing
affirmation
affirmative, -ly
affix, -ed, -ing
afflicshun — affliction
afflict, -ed, -ing
affliction
afflictive, -ly
affluence

affluense — affluence
affluent, -ly
afford, -ed, -ing
affordable
affordabul — affordable
affraid — afraid
affray
affresh — afresh
affro — afro
affront, -ed, -ing
afield
afinity — affinity
afirm — affirm
afirmative — affirmative
afix — affix
aflict — afflict
afliction — affliction
afloat
afluent — affluent
aford — afford
afraid
afray — affray
afresh
afro
afront — affront
aft
after
afterbirth
afterglow
afterlife
aftermath
afternoon
afters
afterthought
afterwards
again
against
agape
agate
age, aged, ageing or aging
agency, -cies
agenda, -das
agensy — agency
agent
agghast — aghast
aggrandise, -dised, -dising
aggrandisement

aggrandiser
aggravate, -vated, -vating
aggravation
aggravator
  aggreeved — aggrieved
aggregate, -gated, -gating
aggregation
aggregative
  aggreived — aggrieved
  aggreshun — aggression
aggression
aggressive, -ly
aggressor
  aggreved — aggrieved
aggrieved
aggro
  agground — aground
aghast
agile, -ly
agility
  agis — aegis
agist, -ed, -ing
agistment
agitate, -tated, -tating
  agitater — agitator
agitation
agitative
agitator
agnostic
agnosticism
ago
agog
agonise, -nised, -nising
agonisingly
agony, -nies
  agorafobia — agoraphobia
agoraphobia
  agraculture — agriculture
agrarian
  agravate — aggravate
  agravation — aggravation
agree, agreed, agreeing
  agreeabel — agreeable
agreeable, -bly
agreeableness
  agreeabul — agreeable
agreement

  agregate — aggregate
  agression — aggression
  agressive — aggressive
  agressor — aggressor
agricultural, -ly
agriculturalist
agriculture
  agrieved — aggrieved
agronomist
agronomy
aground
ahead
  ahed — ahead
ahoy
aid (help)
aide (assistant)
ail, -ed, -ing
  ail — ale (beer)
aileron
  ailias — alias
ailment
aim, -ed, -ing
aimless, -ly
aimlessness
ain't (am not)
  aint — ain't
air, -ed, -ing
  air — hair
  airate — aerate
  airborn — airborne
airborne
air-brake
  air-break — air-brake
airbus
  air condishun — air-condition
air-condition, -ed, -ing
aircraft, -craft
  airfeild — airfield
airfield
airforce
airgun
air hostess
  aireal — aerial
  airial — aerial
airily
airlift
airline

airliner
airlock
airmail
airman, -men
   airobatics   aerobatics
   airobics   aerobics
   airodrome   aerodrome
   airodynamics   aerodynamics
   airoplane   aeroplane
   airosol   aerosol
air-pocket
airport
air-pressure
airship
airspace
airspeed
airstream
airstrip
air terminal
airtight
   airtite   airtight
airwaves
airy, airier, airiest
airy-fairy
aisle (path)
aitch
ajar
   ajis   aegis
akimbo
akin
alabaster
   alabi   alibi
   alacart   à la carte
à la carte
   alackrity   alacrity
alacritous
   alacritus   alacritous
alacrity
   Alah   Allah
alarm, -ed, -ing
alarmist
alas
alaska
   albatros   albatross
albatross, albatrosses
   albeeit   albeit
albeit

albino, -nos
albinism
album
albumen (egg white)
albumin (protein)
albuminous
   albuminus   albuminous
   alcali   alkali
   alcaline   alkaline
alchemist
alchemy
alcohol
alcoholic
alcoholism
alcove
alderman, -men
ale (beer)
   ale   ail (ill)
   alege   allege
alert, -ed, -ing
   alfa   alpha
   alfabet   alphabet
alfalfa
alfresco
alga, -gae
algebra
algebraic, -ally
alias, aliases
alibi, -bis
alien
alienate, -nated, -nating
alienation
alienator
alight, alighted, alighting
align, -ed, -ing
alignment
alike
aliment (food)
   aliment   element (part)
alimentary (food)
   alimentary   elementary
                    (basic)
alimony
alive
   alkaholic   alcoholic
alkali, -lis, -lies
alkaline

alkalinity
  alkeline   alkaline
  alkohol   alcohol
  alkoholic   alcoholic
  alkoholism   alcoholism
  alkove   alcove
all (every)
  all   awl (tool)
  allabaster   alabaster
Allah
allay, -layed, -laying
  allbatross   albatross
  alledge   allege
allegation
allege, -leged, -leging
allegiance
  allegianse   allegiance
allegorical, -ly
allegory, -ries
allegro
alleluia
allergic
allergy, -gies
  allert   alert
alleviate, -ated, -ating
alleviation
alleviator
alley, alleys
alliance
allied
  alliense   alliance
allies
alligator
all-in
alliteration
alliterative, -ly
  allmanac   almanac
  allmost   almost
allocate, -cated, -cating
allocation
  alloft   aloft
  allone   alone
allot, -lotted, -lotting
allotment
all-out
allow, -ed, -ing
  allowabel   allowable

allowable
  allowabul   allowable
allowance
  allowense   allowance
alloy
all right
  allrite   all right
all-rounder
  allso   also
allude, -luded, -luding (refer)
  allude   elude (avoid)
allure, -lured, -luring
  allushun   allusion
allusion (mention)
  allusion   illusion (trick)
allusive, -ly (mentioned)
  allusive   elusive (avoid)
alluvial
ally, -lies
ally, -lied, -lying
  ally   alley
almanac
almanack
almightily
almightiness
almighty
almond
almoner
almost
alms (gifts)
  alocate   allocate
aloe
aloft
alone
along
alongside
  alood   allude
aloof
  alot   a lot (of)
  alot   allot (give)
aloud (speak)
  aloud   allowed
               (permit)
  alow   allow
  alowable   allowable
  alowance   allowance
  aloy   alloy

alp		amaize	amaze	
alpaca		amalgam		
alpacka	alpaca	amalgamate, -mated, -mating		
alpha		amalgamation		
alphabet		amalgum	amalgam	
alphabetical, -ly		amass, -ed, -ing		
alphebet	alphabet	amassabel	amassable	
alpine		amassable		
already		amassabul	amassable	
alredy	already	amatcher	amateur	
Alsatian		amatchur	amateur	
also		amater	amateur	
altar (church)		amateur		
altatude	altitude	amatory		
altenate	alternate	amaze, -mazed, -mazing		
alter (change)		amazement		
alterable, -bly		Amazon		
alteration		ambaguity	ambiguity	
altercation		ambassader	ambassador	
altercative		ambassador, -ial		
alter ego		ambel	amble	
alternate, -nated, -nating		amber		
alternately		ambiance	ambience	
alternation		ambiant	ambient	
alternative, -ly		ambidexterity		
alternator		ambidextrous, -ly		
alterration	alteration	ambience		
although		ambiense	ambience	
altimeter		ambient		
altitude		ambiguity, -ties		
alto, -tos		ambiguous, -ly		
altogether		ambiguus	ambiguous	
altrooism	altruism	ambishen	ambition	
altrueism	altruism	ambishus	ambitious	
altruism		ambit		
altruistic, -ally		ambition		
alturnate	alternate	ambitious, -ly		
alude	allude	ambivalence		
alumina		ambivalense	ambivalence	
aluminium		ambivalent		
aluminum	aluminium	amble, -bled, -bling		
alumminum	aluminium	ambul	amble	
alure	allure	ambulance		
alurt	alert	ambulanse	ambulance	
alushun	allusion	ambush, -ed, -ing		
alusive	allusive	ame	aim	
always		ameanable	amenable	

ameba	amoeba
ameliorate, -rated, -rating	
amelioration	
amen	
amenabel	amenable
amenable, -bly	
amenabul	amenable
amend, -ed, -ing	
amendment	
amends	
amenity, -ties	
America	
ameter	ammeter
amethist	amethyst
amethyst	

For **amf-** words, look under **amph-**.

amiabel	amiable
amiability	
amiable, -bly	
amiabul	amiable
amicabel	amicable
amicability	
amicable, -bly	
amicabul	amicable
amid	
amidst	
amigo	
amiss	
amity, -ties	
ammeter	
ammonia	
ammunition	

For other **amm-** words, look under **am-**.

amnesia, -iac	
amnesty, -ties	
amnesty, -tied, -tying	
amoeba, -bae, -bas	
amoebic	
amok	
among	
amongst	
amoral, -ly	
amorfous	amorphous

amorous, -ly	
amorphism	
amorphous, -ly	
amorphus	amorphous
amortise, -tised, -tising	
amount, -ed, -ing	
amownt	amount
ampair	ampere
ampel	ample
amperage	
ampere	
amphetamine	
amphibian	
amphibious, -ly	
amphitheatre	
ample, -pler, -plest (enough)	
amplefy	amplify
amplification	
amplifier	
amplify, -fied, -fying	
amplitude	
amply	
ampoule (bottle)	
ampul	ample (enough)
ampul	ampoule (bottle)
amputate, -tated, -tating	
amputation	
amuck	
amuk	amok
amuk	amuck
amulet	
amung	among
amungst	amongst
amunition	ammunition
amuse, amused, amusing	
amusement	
anachronism	
anachronistic	
anackronism	anachronism
anackronistic	anachronistic
anaconda	
anaemia	
anaesthesia	
anaesthetic	
anaesthetisation	
anaesthetise, -tised, -tising	

anaesthetist
anagram
  anaky — anarchy
anal
analgesia
analgesic
  analise — analyse
  analisis — analysis
  analist — analyst
analog (electric)
  analog — analogue (similar)
analogous, -ly
analogue (similar)
  analogue — analog (electric)
analogy, -gies
analyse, -lysed, -lysing
analysis, -ses
analyst
analytical, -ly
anarchical, -ly
anarchism
anarchist
anarchy
anathema, -mas
anatomical, -ly
anatomist
anatomy, -mies
ancestor
ancestral, -ly
ancestry, -tries
anchor, -ed, -ing
anchorage
anchorman, -men
anchovy, -vies
ancient
ancillary, -aries
anecdotal
anecdote
  anemia — anaemia
  anemic — anaemic
  anesthesia — anaesthesia
  anesthetic — anaesthetic
  anesthetise — anaesthetise
  anesthetist — anaesthetist
aneurism

anew
  anewity — annuity
angel (spirit)
  angel — angle (fishing)
angelic
  angellic — angelic
anger, -ed, -ing
angina
angle, angled, angling (fishing)
  angle — angel (spirit)
angler
Anglican
Anglicanism
Anglo-Catholic
  Anglo-Sacksen — Anglo-Saxon
Anglo-Saxon
angora
  angree — angry
  angrie — angry
angrily
angry, angrier, angriest
  angsiety — anxiety
anguish, -ed, -ing
angular, -ity
  anguler — angular
  angwish — anguish
  anigma — enigma
animal
animate, -mated, -mating
animatedly
animation
  animel — animal
animosity, -ties
aniseed
  aniversary — anniversary
  anjel — angel
  anjelic — angelic
  anjina — angina
  anker — anchor
  ankerage — anchorage
  ankeridge — anchorage
  ankerije — anchorage
ankle
anklet
annals
anneal, -ed, -ing
annex, -ed, -ing (join)

annexation
annexe (building)
  annialate   annihilate
annihilate, -lated, -lating
anniversary, -ries
Anno Domini
annotate, -tated, -tating
annotation
announce, announced, announcing
announcement
annoy, annoyed, annoying
annual, -ly
annuity, -ties
annul, annulled, annulling
annulment
annulus, -li, or -luses
annunciate, -ated, -ating
annunciation

For other ann- words, look under an-.

anode
  anodine   anodyne
anodyne
anoint, -ed, -ing
  anomaley   anomaly
anomaly, -lies
anon
  anonimity   anonymity
  anonimous   anonymous
anonymity
anonymous, -ly
anorak
  anorecksia   anorexia
anorexia
another
  anoynt   anoint
  anser   answer
  anserable   answerable
  anserabul   answerable
  ansestor   ancestor
  ansestral   ancestral
  ansestrul   ancestral
  ansestry   ancestry
  ansilary   ancillary
answer, -ed, -ing
  answerabel   answerable

answerable, -bly
  answerabul   answerable
antacid
antagonise, -nised, -nising
antagonism
antagonist
antagonistic, -ally
Antarctic
  antasid   antacid
  anteak   antique
anteater
antecedent
antechamber
  anteclimax   anticlimax
  antecyclone   anticyclone
antedate, -dated, -dating
  antediloovian   antediluvian
antediluvian
  anteek   antique
antelope, antelopes
  antena   antenna
antenatal
  antenatel   antenatal
  antenatul   antenatal
antenna, -tennae, -tennas
anterior
anteroom
anthem
anthill
anthology, -gies
anthracite
  anthracks   anthrax
  anthrasite   anthracite
anthrax, -thraces
anthropoid
  anthropologey   anthropology
anthropologist
anthropology
antibiotic
antibody, -bodies
antic
  anticeptic   antiseptic
  antichamber   antechamber
Antichrist
  anticiclone   anticyclone
anticipate, -pated, -pating
anticipation

anticipatory		antonim	antonym
anticlimacks	anticlimax	antonym	
anticlimactic		anus	
anticlimax		anuther	another
anticlockwise		anvil	
anticyclone		anvul	anvil
anticyclonic		anxiety, -ties	
antidate	antedate	anxious, -ly	
antidepressant		any	
antidotal		anybody	
antidote		anyhow	
antifon	antiphon	anyone	
antifreeze		anything	
antigen		anyway	
antihisstamine	antihistamine	anywear	anywhere
antihistamine		anywere	anywhere
antikwarian	antiquarian	anywhere	
antikwated	antiquated	Anzac	
antikwitey	antiquity	aorta, -tas, -tae	
antilope	antelope	apace	
antimony		apart	
antinatal	antenatal	apartheid	
antinatul	antenatal	apartied	apartheid
antinewklear	antinuclear	apartite	apartheid
antinuclear		apartment	
antipathy, -pathies		apase	apace
antiperspirant		apathetic, -ally	
antiphon		apathy	
antipodes		ape, aped, aping	
antipodies	antipodes	apeace	apiece
antiquarian		apease	apiece
antiquary, -quaries		apeice	apiece
antiquated		apeks	apex
antique		apercher	aperture
antiquity, -quities		apergee	apogee
antiroom	anteroom	apergey	apogee
anti-Semitic		aperitif	
anti-Semitism		aperture	
antiseptic, -ally		apex, apexes, apices	
antisiclone	anticyclone	aphasia	
antisipation	anticipation	aphid	
antisocial, -ly		aphorism	
antithesis, -theses		aphrodisiac	
antithisis	antithesis	apiary, apiaries	
antitoksic	antitoxic	apiece	
antitoksin	antitoxin	apissul	epistle
antler		apistle	epistle

aplom — aplomb
aplomb
aply — apply
apocalipse — apocalypse
apocalypse
apocalyptic
apocrifal — apocryphal
apocryphal, -ly
apogee
apologetic, -ally
apologey — apology
apologise, -gised, -gising
apologist
apology, -gies
apoplectic
apoplexy
aposle — apostle
apostasy, -sies
apostel — apostle
apostle
apostolate
apostolic
apostrofy — apostrophe
apostrophe
aposul — apostle
apothecary, -ries
apoynt — appoint

> For other **ap-** words,
> look under **app-**.

appal, -palled, -palling
apparatus, -tus, -tuses
apparel
apparent, -ly
apparishun — apparition
apparition
appart — apart
appeal, -ed, -ing
appealing, -ly
appear, -ed, -ing
appearance
appearense — appearance
appease, -peased, -peasing
appeasement
appelant — appellant
appellant
appellate

appellation
append, -ed, -ing
appendacitis — appendicitis
appendage
appendectomy, -mies
appendicitis
appendige — appendage
appendiks — appendix
apperatus — apparatus
appertain, -ed, -ing
apperture — aperture
appetiser
appetite
applaud, -ed, -ing
applause
applawd — applaud
applaws — applause
apple
appliance
applianse — appliance
applicability
applicable, -bly
applicant
application
applie — apply
applied
applique
apply, -plied, -plying
appoint, -ed, -ing
appointment
apporshun — apportion
apportion, -ed, -ing
apportionment
apposishun — apposition
apposite, -ly
apposition
appraisal
appraise, -praised, -praising
appraysal — appraisal
apprayse — appraise
appreciabel — appreciable
appreciable, -bly
appreciabul — appreciable
appreciate, -ated, -ating
appreciation
appreciative, -ly
apprehend, -ed, -ing

apprehenshun	apprehension	arable	
apprehensibel	apprehensible	arabul	arable
apprehensible		araign	arraign
apprehensibul	apprehensible	arain	arraign
apprehension		arange	arrange
apprehensive, -ly		aray	array
apprentice		arber	arbour
apprenticeship		arbiter	
apprentise	apprentice	arbitrary	
appricot	apricot	arbitrate, -trated, -trating	
apprise, -prised, -prising		arbitration	
approach, -ed, -ing		arbor (axis)	
approachabel	approachable	abor	arbour (shade)
approachable		arboreal	
approbation		arboricultural	
approch	approach	arboriculture	
approchabul	approachable	arbour (shade)	
approove	approve	arbour	arbor (axis)
appropos	apropos	arc, arced, arcing (curve)	
appropriate, -ated, -ating		arc	ark (boat)
appropriation		arcade	
approval		arcane	
approve, -proved, -proving		arch	
approvel	approval	archaeological, -ly	
approximate, -mated, -mating		archaeologist	
approximately		archaeology	
approximation		archaic	
apricot		archaism	
April		archangel	
apron		archary	archery
apropos		archbishop	
apt, -ly		archer	
aptitude		archerfish	
aptley	aptly	archery	
aqualung		archetypal	
aquamarine		archetype	
aquaplane		archipelago, -gos, -goes	
aquarium		architect	
Aquarius		architectural, -ly	
aquatic		architecture	
aqueduct		architrave	
aqueous		archival	
aquiline		archives	
arabel	arable	archivist	
arabesk	arabesque	arcipelago	archipelago
arabesque		arcipeligo	archipelago
Arabic numerals		arcitect	architect

arcitectural	architectural	arival	arrival
arcitecture	architecture	arive	arrive
arcives	archives	ark (boat)	
arc light		ark	arc (curve)
arctic			
Arctic Circle			

For other **ark-** words, look under **arc-**.

ardent, -ly		arm	
arder	ardour	armacher	armature
ardour		armachur	armature
arduous, -ly		armada	
arduus	arduous	armadillo, -los	
are		Armageddon	
area		armament	
arears	arrears	armature	
arena		armchair	
aren't		armed	
arent	aren't	armer	armour
arest	arrest	armey	army
argent		armistice	
argew	argue	armistise	armistice
argon		armoner	almoner
arguabel	arguable	armour	
arguable, -bly		armoured	
arguabul	arguable	armourer	
argue, -gued, -guing		armoury, -ries	
arguement	argument	armpit	
argument		arms (weapons)	
argumentation		arms	alms (gifts)
argumentative, -ly		army, -mies	
argus		arogance	arrogance
arguw	argue	aroganse	arrogance
argy-bargy, -bargies		arogant	arrogant
aria (melody)		aroma	
aria	area (piece)	aromatic	
arial	aerial	arora	aurora
arid, -ly		arose	
aridity		around	
Aries		arousal	
arina	arena	arouse, aroused, arousing	
arise, arose, arisen, arising		arow	arrow
aristocracy, -cies		arownd	around
aristocrasy	aristocracy	arowroot	arrowroot
aristocrat		arowse	arouse
aristocratic		arpeggio	
arithmetic		arpejio	arpeggio
arithmetical, -ly		arraign, -ed, -ing	
arithmetician			

arraignment
arrange, -ranged, -ranging
arrangement
arrant, -ly
arras
array, -ed, -ing
arrears
arrest, -ed, -ing
arrival
arrive, -rived, -riving
arrogance
  arroganse   arrogance
arrogant, -ly
arrogate, -gated, -gating
  arrouse   arouse
arrow
arrowroot
arsenal
arsenic
arsenical
  arsnic   arsenic
arson
art
  artachoke   artichoke
artefact
arterial
artery, -teries
artesian bore
artful, -ly
arthritic
arthritis
  articel   article
artichoke
article, -cled, -cling
  articul   article
articulate, -lated, -lating
articulation
artifact
artifice
artificer
artificial, -ly
artificiality
  artifise   artifice
  artifishial   artificial
artillery
artisan
artist (painter)

artiste (actor)
artistic
artistry
  artizan   artisan
artless, -ly
arvo (afternoon)
  arwry   awry
asbestos
ascend, -ed, -ing
ascendancy
ascendant
  ascenshun   ascension
ascension
ascent (upward)
  ascent   assent (agree)
ascertain, -ed, -ing
  ascertainabel   ascertainable
ascertainable, -bly
  ascertainabul   ascertainable
ascertainment
ascetic, -ally
asceticism
ascribe, ascribed, ascribing
  ase   ace
  asend   ascend
  asendancy   ascendancy
  asendansy   ascendancy
  asendant   ascendant
  asenshun   ascension
  asent   ascent (upwards)
  asent   assent (agree)
aseptic, -ally
  asershun   assertion
  asertain   ascertain
  asertane   ascertain
  asertayne   ascertain
  asetic   ascetic
  aseticism   asceticism
asexual, -ly
  asfalt   asphalt
  asfelt   asphalt
  asfixia   asphyxia
  asfixiate   asphyxiate
ash
ashamed, -ly
  ashaymed   ashamed

ashfelt	asphalt
ashore (beach)	
ashore	assure (certain)
aside	
asidity	acidity
asign	assign
asilum	asylum
asimetrical	asymmetrical
asimetry	asymmetry
asine	assign
asinement	assignment
asinine, -ly	
asininity	
asitic	ascetic
ask, -ed, -ing	
askance	
askanse	askance
askew	
askue	askew
asleep	
asma	asthma
asmatic	asthmatic
asp	
asparagus	
aspect	
aspen	
aspershun	aspersion
aspersion	
asphalt	
asphyxia	
asphyxiate, -ated, -ating	
asphyxiation	
aspic	
aspirant	
aspirate, -rated, -rating	
aspiration	
aspirator	
aspirayte	aspirate
aspire, aspired, aspiring	
aspirin	
asprin	aspirin
ass, asses	
assail, -ed, -ing	
assailant	
assassin	
assassinate, -nated, -nating	
assassination	

assault	
assaulter	
assay, -ed, -ing (analyse)	
assay	essay (try)
assayer	
assemblage	
assemble, -bled, -bling	
assembly, assemblies	
assembul	assemble
assend	ascend
assendancy	ascendancy
assendansy	ascendancy
assendant	ascendant
assenshun	ascension
assension	ascension
assent (agree)	
assent	ascent (upward)
assention	ascension
assershun	assertion
assert, -ed, -ing	
assertion	
assertive, -ly	
assess, -ed, -ing	
assessabel	assessable
assessable	
assessabul	assessable
assessment	
assessor	
asset, assets	
assiduous, -ly	
assign, -ed, -ing	
assignable, -bly	
assignation	
assignee	
assignment	
assine	assign
assinment	assignment
assist, -ed, -ing	
assistance	
assistant	
associate, -ated, -ating	
associashun	association
association	
associayte	associate
assonance	
assonanse	assonance

assonant
assort, -ed, -ing
assortment
  assoshiate   associate
assuage, -suaged, -suaging
assume, -sumed, -suming
assumption
  assumshun   assumption
assurance
  assuranse   assurance
assure, -sured, -suring (certain)
  assure   ashore (beach)
aster
asterisk
astern
asteroid
asthma
asthmatic
astigmatism
astir
astonish, -ed, -ing
astonishment
astound, -ed, -ing
  astownd   astound
astral
astray
astride
astringency
astringent, -ly
astrologer
astrological, -ly
astrology
  astronaught   astronaut
astronaut
astronautics
  astronort   astronaut
  astrul   astral
  astur   astir
  asturn   astern
astute, -ly
astuteness
asunder
asylum
  asymetry   asymmetry
asymmetric
asymmetrical, -ly
asymmetry

ate (food)
  ate   eight (number)
  ateen   eighteen
  atey   eighty
atheism
atheist
atheistic
  athiesm   atheism
  athiest   atheist
  athiestic   atheistic
  athleet   athlete
athlete
athletic
atlas
  atmosfear   atmosphere
  atmosfere   atmosphere
  atmosferic   atmospheric
atmosphere
atmospheric
  atol   atoll
atoll
atom
atomic
atomiser
atone, atoned, atoning
atonement
atrocious, -ly
atrocity, -ties
atrophy, -phied, -phying
  atroshus   atrocious
attach, -ed, -ing
attaché
attachment
attack, -ed, -ing
attain, -ed, -ing
attainable
attainment
attempt, -ed, -ing
attend, -ed, -ing
attendance
attendant
attention
attentive, -ly
attenuate, -ated, -ating
attest, -ed, -ing
attic
attire, -tired, -tiring

attitude
attorney
attract, -ed, -ing
attraction
attractive, -ly
attribute, -uted, -uting
attrishun — attrition
attrition
attune, -tuned, -tuning
atune — attune
aturney — attorney

> For other at- words,
> look under att-.

atypical, -ly
aubergine
auburn
aucshun — auction
auction, -ed, -ing
auctioneer
audacious, -ly
audacity
audasity — audacity
audeo — audio
audibel — audible
audibility
audible
audibly
audibul — audible
audience
audiense — audience
audio
audiometer
audiometric
audiometry
audiovisual
audishun — audition
audit, -ed, -ing
audition
auditor
auditorium, -toriums, -toria
auditory
auditree — auditory
auditry — auditory
auger (tool)
auger — augur (foretell)
aught (any part)

aught — ought (should)
augment, -ed, -ing
augmentation
augur (foretell)
augur — auger (tool)
augural
august (majestic)
August
aukward — awkward
aunt
auntie
aunt sally
aunty
aura
aural, -ly (hearing)
aural — oral (spoken)
aureole
auricle
auricular
auriferous
auriole — aureole
aurora
auspice, auspices
auspicious, -ly
auspise — auspice
Aussie
austeer — austere
austere, -ly
austerity, -ties
austral
Australasia
Australia
Australian
Australiana
Australien — Australian
australight — australite
australite
Australorp
autamatic — automatic
autamobile — automobile
authentic
authenticate, -cated, -cating
authentication
authenticity
authentisity — authenticity
author
authoress

authorisation
authorise, -rised, -rising
authoritarian
authoritative, -ly
authority, -ties
autism
auto
autobiographical, -ly
autobiography, -phies
autocracy
   autocrasy   autocracy
autocrat
autocratic
autocue
   autograf   autograph
autograph
automatic
automation
automative
automobile
automotive
   autonomee   autonomy
autonomous, -ly
   autonomus   autonomous
autonomy
autopilot
autopsy, -sies
   autum   autumn
autumn
autumnal, -ly
auxiliary, -ries
avail, -ed, -ing
   availabel   available
availability
available
   availabul   available
   avalable   available
   avalanch   avalanche
avalanche
   avale   avail
   avaliable   available
avant-garde
   avarey   aviary
avarice
avaricious, -ly
   avaris   avarice
   avarishus   avaricious

   avenew   avenue
avenge, avenged, avenging
avenger
avenue
aver, averred, averring
average, -raged, -raging
   avericious   avaricious
   averidge   average
   averige   average
   averishus   avaricious
   averiss   avarice
averse, -ly
   avershun   aversion
aversion
avert, -ed, -ing
   avery   aviary
avgas
aviary, aviaries
   aviater   aviator
aviation
aviator
avid, -ly
   avinue   avenue
   avlanch   avalanche
avocado, avocados
avoid, -ed, -ing (evade)
   avoid   ovoid (egg)
avoidable, -ably
avow, -ed, -ing
avowal
   avoyd   avoid
   avridge   average
   avrije   average
   avud   avid
   avur   aver
   avurse   averse
   avurshun   aversion
   avursion   aversion
   avurt   avert
await, -ed, -ing
awake, awoke, awaking
awaken, -ed, -ing
award, -ed, -ing
aware
awareness
away
   awayte   await

awb	orb	azalia	azalea
awe, awed, awing (fear)		azure	
awe	oar (boat)	azury	
awear	aware		
awesome, -ly			
awful, -ly			
awgy	orgy		
awksilary	auxiliary		
awkward, -ly			
awkwud	awkward		
awl (tool)			
awl	all (every)		
awning			
awoke			
awry			
axe, axes			
axe, axed, axing			
axel	axle		
axial, -ly			
axident	accident		
axidental	accidental		
axiom			
axiomatic			
axis, axes			
axle			
axsede	accede		
axseed	accede		
axsel	axle		
axsellerate	accelerate		
axsent	accent		
axsentuate	accentuate		
axsept	accept		
axseptable	acceptable		
axseptabul	acceptable		
axseptance	acceptance		
axsesary	accessary		
axsesory	accessory		
axsess	access		
axsessable	accessible		
axsessabul	accessible		
axsessible	accessible		
axsessibul	accessible		
ay, ayes (yes)			
ayatollah			
aye (ever)			
aysure	azure		
azalea			

Bb

babbel	babble (chatter)
babble, -led, -ling (chatter)	
babboon	baboon
babbul	babble (chatter)
babe	
babel (confusion)	
babel	babble (chatter)
babey	baby
babie	baby
baboon	
babul	babble (chatter)
baby, babies	
baby-sitter	
baccarat	
bach	batch
bacheler	bachelor
bachelor	
bacillus, bacilli	
back, -ed, -ing	
backbencher	
backblocks	
backbone	
back-burn	
backer	
backfire, -fired, -firing	
backgammon	
background	
backhand	
backing	
backlash	
back-pedal, -alled, -alling	
backroom	
back-seat driver	
backstage	

backstitch, -ed, -ing	
backstop, -stopped, -stopping	
backstroke, -stroked, -stroking	
back-to-back	
backwards	
backwash	
backyard	
bacon	
bacteria	
bad, worse, worst (not good)	
bade (ask)	
badge	
badger	
badly	
badminton	
baffel	baffle
baffle, -fled, -fling	
bag, bagged, bagging	
bagatelle	
baggage	
baggidge	baggage
baggy, baggier, baggiest	
bagman, -men	
bagpipes	
baige	beige
bail (court)	
bail	bale (bundle)
bailif	bailiff
bailiff	
bairn	
bait (fishing)	
bait	bate (hold)
baize, baized, baizing	
baje	badge
bake, baked, baking	
bakelite	
baker	
bakery	
bakshee	
balaclava	
balad	ballad
balalaika	
balance, -anced, -ancing	
balanse	balance
balast	ballast
balay	ballet
balcony, -conies	

bald (hairless)
  bald — bawled (cried)
balderdash
balding
baldness
bale, baled, baling (bundle)
  bale — bail (court)
baleful, -ly
  balefull — baleful
  balerina — ballerina
  balero — bolero
  balet — ballet
  baliff — bailiff
ball (round)
  ball — bawl (cry)
ballad
ballast
ball-bearing
ballerina
ballet
ballistics
balloon
balloonist
ballot, balloted, balloting
ballpoint
  ballsa — balsa
  ballsam — balsam
ballyhoo
balm
balmy, balmier, balmiest (good)
  balmy — barmy (stupid)
  balonee — baloney
baloney
  baloon — balloon
  balot — ballot
balsa
balsam
balustrade
  balyhoo — ballyhoo
bamboo
bamboozle, -zled, -zling
ban, banned, banning
banal, -ly
banana
banana republic
band, banded, banding (strip)
band (group)

band — banned (forbidden)
bandage, -daged, -daging
bandanna
  bandey — bandy
bandicoot
  bandige — bandage
bandit
  bandoleer — bandolier
bandolier
bandsaw
bandwagon
bandy, -died, -dying
bandy-legged
  baner — banner
bangalow
  bangel — bangle
banger
bangle
bang-on
banish, -ed, -ing
banishment
banister
banjo, banjos
bank, -ed, -ing
bankbook
banker
banknote
  bankrupcy — bankruptcy
  bankrupsy — bankruptcy
bankrupt
bankruptcy
banksia
  bankwet — banquet
banned (forbidden)
  banned — band (strip)
banner
banns (notices)
banquet, -queted, -queting
bans (forbids)
  bans — banns (notices)
bantam
bantamweight
banter, -ed, -ing
  bantum — bantam
banyan
  baonet — bayonet

bap

baptise, -tised, -tising

baptism

baptismal

Baptist

bar, barred, barring

   barack   barrack

   baracouta   barracouta

   barage   barrage

barb

barbarian

barbaric

barbarism

barbarous, -ly

   barbarus   barbarous

barbecue, -cued, -cuing

barbed wire

barbell

barbeque, -qued, -quing

barber

barbiturate

bard (poet)

   bard   barred

                  (stopped)

bare, bared, baring (uncover)

bare, barer, barest

   bare   bear (animal)

bareback

barefaced

barefoot

bareheaded

   barel   barrel

barely

   baren   baron (noble)

   baren .   barren (sterile)

   bareskin   bearskin

bargain, -ed, -ing

bargainer

   bargan   bargain

barge, barged, barging

bargee

   bargen   bargain

   baricade   barricade

   barier   barrier

baring (uncovering)

   baring   barring (stop)

   baring   bearing (hold)

   barister   barrister

baritone

barium

bark, -ed, -ing

barley

   barlie   barley

   barm   balm

   barmade   barmaid

barmaid

barman, -men

barmy, barmier, barmiest (stupid)

   barmy   balmy (good)

barn

   barn   bairn

   barnacel   barnacle

barnacle

barnacled

   barnacul   barnacle

barney

   barnicul   barnacle

barnstorm

barometer

barometric

baron (noble)

   baron   barren (sterile)

baronet

baronial

baroque

   barow   barrow

barrack, -ed, -ing

barracker

barracouta

barracuda

barrage, -raged, -raging

barramundi

barrel, -relled, -relling

barren (sterile)

   barren   baron (noble)

barrenness

barricade, -caded, -cading

barrier

barring (stop)

   barring   baring

              (uncovering)

barrister

barrow

   barrul   barrel

barter, -ed, -ing
  barul   barrel
basal, -ly
basalt
base, based, basing (support)
base, baser, basest
  base   bass (low tone)
baseball
basement
  baset   basset
bash, -ed, -ing
bashful, -ly
basic
basilica
  basillus   bacillus
basin
  basinette   bassinette
basis, bases
  basit   basset
bask, -ed, -ing (enjoy warmth)
  bask   basque (garb)
basketball
  baskit   basket
  basoon   bassoon
basque (garb)
bas-relief
bass (low tone)
  bass   base (support)
bass clef
basset
bassinette
bassoon
bastard
  bastardisashun   bastardisation
bastardisation
bastardry
baste, basted, basting
  basterd   bastard
bastion
bat, batted, batting
batch
bate, bated, bating (hold breath)
  bate   bait (fishing)
  baten   baton (stick)
  baten   batten (timber)
  bater   batter
  baterey   battery

bath
bathe, bathed, bathing
bathers
bathroom
batik
  batle   battle
  batler   battler
batman, -men
baton (stick)
  baton   batten (timber)
batsman, -men
batt (insulating)
  batt   bat (cricket)
battalion
  battaliun   battalion
  battel   battle
batten (timber)
batter
battering ram
battery, -ries
battle, battled, battling
battleaxe
battledress
battler
battleship
batty, battier, battiest
  batul   battle
  baty   batty
  baubel   bauble
bauble
  baubul   bauble
baulk, -ed, -ing
bauxite
  bawble   bauble
  bawdie   bawdy
bawdiness
bawdy, -dier, -diest
bawl, -ed, -ing (cry)
  bawl   ball (round)
  bawlsa   balsa
bay
  bayliff   bailiff
  baynet   bayonet
bayonet
  baythe   bathe
bazaar (market)
  bazaar   bizarre (odd)

bazar   bazaar
bazooka
be, been, being (exist)
     be   bee (insect)
beach, -ches (shore)
     beach   beech (tree)
beachcomber
     beachcomer   beachcomber
beacon
bead, -ed, -ing
beady, beadier, beadiest
     beaf   beef
     beafeater   beefeater
     beafy   beefy
     beagel   beagle
beagle
beak
beaker
beam, -ed, -ing
bean (vegetable)
     bean   been (be)
beanie
beano
bear (animal)
bear, borne, bearing (carry)
     bear   bare (uncover)
     bearback   bareback
beard
bearer
     bearfaced   barefaced
     bearfoot   barefoot
     bearheaded   bareheaded
bearing (hold)
     bearing   baring
                          (uncovering)
bearskin
beast
beastliness
beastly, beastlier, beastliest
beat, beaten, beating (strike)
     beat   beet (food)
     beatel   beetle
beater
beatific
beatify, -fied, -fying
beatitude
     beatle   beetle

beatnik
     beatroot   beetroot
     beatul   beetle
beau, beaus, beaux (suitor)
beaut
beauteous, -ly
beautician
     beautie   beauty
beautiful, -ly
beautify, -fied, -fying
     beautishun   beautician
beauty, beauties
beaver
becalmed
became
     becarmed   becalmed
because
beck
beckon, -ed, -ing
become, became, becoming
     becon   beacon
     becos   because
bed, bedded, bedding
bedeck, -ed, -ing
     bedevel   bedevil
bedevil, -illed, -illing
     bedevul   bedevil
bedlam
bedouin
     bedowin   bedouin
bedpan
bedraggled
     bedraguled   bedraggled
bedridden
     bedriden   bedridden
bedrock
bedside
bed-sitting room
bedspread
     bedspred   bedspread
bedstead
     bedsted   bedstead
bed-wetting
bee (insect)
     bee   be (exist)
beech (tree)
     beech   beach (shore)

beechcomber	beachcomber
beechcomer	beachcomber
beecon	beacon
beed	bead
beef	
beefeater	
beefy, beefier, beefiest	
beegel	beagle
beegle	beagle
beehive	
beeline	
beem	beam
been (be)	
been	bean (food)
beenie	beanie
beep	
beer (ale)	
beer	bier (coffin)
beerd	beard
beest	beast
beeswaks	beeswax
beeswax	
beet (food)	
beet	beat (strike)
beetel	beetle
beetle	
beetle off	
beetroot	
beetul	beetle
beever	beaver
befall, -fell, -fallen, -falling	
befit, -fitted, -fitting	
befor	before
before	
beforehand	
befuddle, -dled, -dling	
befudul	befuddle
beg, begged, begging	
began	
begar	beggar
beger	beggar
beggar	
beggarly	
begger	beggar
begile	beguile
begin, began, begun, beginning	
beginner	

begone	
begonia	
begrudge, -grudged, -grudging	
begruge	begrudge
beguile, -guiled, -guiling	
begun	
behalf	
beharf	behalf
behave, -haved, -having	
behavior	behaviour
behaviour	
behavioural	
behead, -ed, -ing	
behed	behead
beheld	
behest	
behind	
behive	beehive
beige	
beije	beige
being	
bekos	because
bekweath	bequeath
bekwest	bequest
bel	bell (ring)
bel	belle (girl)
belabor	belabour
belabour, -ed, -ing	
belated, -ly	
belay, -layed, -laying	
belbird	bellbird
belch, -ed, -ing	
beleaf	belief
beleavabul	believable
beleave	believe
beleif	belief
beleive	believe
belfrey	belfry
belfry, -fries	
Belgian	
beli	belie
belicose	bellicose
belie, -lied, -lying	
belief	
believable, -bly	
believe, -lieved, -lieving	
beligerence	belligerence

beligerency belligerency
beligerense belligerence
beligerent belligerent
beline beeline
belittel belittle
belittle, -tled, -tling
bell (ring)
bellbird
belle (girl)
bellicose, -ly
belligerence
belligerency
belligerent, -ly
bellow, -ed, -ing (roar)
   bellow below (under)
bellows
belly, bellies
belly, bellied, bellying
bellyache
belong, -ed, -ing
belongings
   belose bellows
beloved
   belovid beloved
below (under)
   below bellow (roar)
   belows bellows
belt, -ed, -ing
belt-up, belted-up, belting-up
   bely belly
bemoan, -ed, -ing
bemused
bench, benches
benchmark
bend, bent, bending
bender
beneath
benediction
benefactor
benefactress
benefice
beneficence
beneficent, -ly
beneficial, -ly
beneficiary, -aries
   benefis benefice
   benefisense beneficence

benefisent beneficent
benefishal beneficial
benefisharey beneficiary
benefit, -fited, -fiting
benevolence
   benevolense benevolence
benevolent, -ly
benign, -ly
   benine benign
bent
   benum benumb
benumb
benzene (coal tar)
benzine (petroleum)
bequeath
   bequeeth bequeath
bequest
berate, -rated, -rating
   beray beret
bereave, -reaved, -reaving
   bereeve bereave
bereft
beret
   bereve bereave
   berglar burglar
   beri berry (fruit)
   beri bury (in earth)
   berial burial
beri-beri
   berie berry (fruit)
berley (bait)
   berley burly (large)
   berli berley (bait)
   berli burly (large)
berry, berries (fruit)
   berry bury (in earth)
berserk
berth (ship)
   berth birth (born)
   bery berry (fruit)
   bery bury (in earth)
   beseach beseech
beseech, -seeched, -seeching
   beseige besiege
beset, -set, -setting
beside
besides

besiege, -sieged, -sieging
besotted
best
bestial, -ly
bestiality
bestir, -stirred, -stirring
bestow, -ed, -ing
bestowal
bet, bet, betting
beta
beta particle
betel nut

| betel | beetle |
| betle | beetle |

betoken, -ed, -ing
betray, -ed, -ing
betrayal
betrayer
betrothal
better
betterment

| betul | beetle |

between
betwixt
bevel, -elled, -elling
beverage

beveridge	beverage
bevarije	beverage
bevie	bevy

bevy, bevies
bewail
beware

bewayl	bewail
bewear	beware
bewhere	beware
bewhich	bewitch

bewilder, -ed, -ing
bewilderment
bewitch

| bewty | beauty |

beyond

| bezerk | berserk |

biannual, -ly (twice a year)

| biannual | biennial (every two years) |

bias, biased, biasing
bias binding

biass	bias
biassed	biased
Bibel	Bible

Bible

| bibliografy | bibliography |

bibliographer
bibliography, -phies

| Bibul | Bible |
| bicame | became |

bicameral
bicarbonate

| bicarmed | becalmed |

bicentenary
bicentennial
biceps

| bich | bitch |
| bicicle | bicycle |

bicker, -ed, -ing
bicycle
bid, bade, bidding

| biday | bidet |

biddy, -dies
bide, bided, biding
bidet

| bidevil | bedevil |

biennial, -ly (every two years)

| biennial | biannual (twice a year) |

bier (coffin)

| bier | beer (ale) |
| bifell | befell |

bifocal
bifurcate, -cated, -cating
big, bigger, biggest
bigamist
bigamy

| bigan | began |
| biggot | bigot |

bight (bay)

bight	bite (cut)
bight	byte (computer)
bigile	beguile
bigin	begin
biginer	beginner
bigining	beginning
bigon	begone

bigone	bygone	billycan	
bigot		billygoat	
bigoted, -ly		bilong	belong
bigotry		bilow	below (under)
bigrudge	begrudge	bilow	billow (wave)
bigun	begun	bilyards	billiards
		bilyon	billion

<table>
<tr><td colspan="2">For bih- words, look under
beh-.</td><td>bilyus</td><td>billious</td></tr>
</table>

		bimoan	bemoan
bikameral	bicameral	bimuse	bemuse
bike		bin, binned, binning	
bikini		bin	been
bikweath	bequeath	binary	
bikwest	bequest	bind, bound, binding	
bil	bill	binder	
bilaber	belabour	bineath	beneath
bilated	belated	binevolent	benevolent
bilateral, -ly		binge	
bilaw	by-law	bingo	
bilay	belay	binine	benign
bild	build	binoculars	
bilding	building	binomial, -ly	
bile		binumb	benumb
bileavabul	believable	biochemist	
bileave	believe	biochemistry	
bileif	belief	biodegradable	
bilet	billet	biografer	biographer
bilge		biografical	biographical
biliards	billiards	biografy	biography
bilief	belief	biographer	
bilingual, -ly		biographical, -ly	
bilingwal	bilingual	biography, -phies	
bilion	billion	biokemist	biochemist
bilious, -ly		biologey	biology
biliousness		biological, -ly	
bilittul	belittle	biologist	
bilius	bilious	biology	
bilk, -ed, -ing		biopsey	biopsy
bill, -ed, -ing		biopsy	
billabong		biorhythm	
billet, -eted, -eting		bipartisan	
billiards		bipartite	
Billingsgate		bipartizen	bipartisan
billion		bipass	by-pass
billit	billet	biped	
billow (wave)		biplane	
billy, billies		biproduct	by-product

birate	berate	bisy	busy
birch		bit	
bird		bitch, -ches	
birdie		bitchiness	
bird's-eye		bitchumen	bitumen
bireave	bereave	bitchy	
bireft	bereft	bite, bitten, bit, biting (cut)	
biro		bite	bight (bay)
birth (born)		bite	byte
birth	berth (ship)		(computer)
birthday		biter	bitter
birthrate		bitoken	betoken
biscet	biscuit	bitray	betray
biscuit		bitrayal	betrayal
biscut	biscuit	bitrothal	betrothal
bisecshun	bisection	bitser	
bisect, -ed, -ing		bitten (bite)	
bisection		bitten	bittern (bird)
bisector		bitter, -ly	
biseech	beseech	bittern (bird)	
biseege	besiege	bitterness	
biseige	besiege	bitters	
biseksual	bisexual	bitumen	
bisen	bison	bituminous	
bisentenary	bicentenary	bitween	between
bisentenyal	bicentennial	bitwixt	betwixt
biseps	biceps	biuld	build
biset	beset	bivalve	
bisexual, -ly		bivouac, -acked, -acking	
bisexuality		bivuac	bivouac
bishop		biwail	bewail
bishopric		biway	byway
bisicle	bicycle	biwear	beware
biside	beside	biwich	bewitch
bisier	busier	biwilder	bewilder
bisily	busily	biwitch	bewitch
biskit	biscuit	biword	byword
bismuth		bizar	bazaar (fair)
bisness	business	bizar	bizarre (odd)
bison, -son		bizarre, -ly (odd)	
bisotted	besotted	bizier	busier
bistander	bystander	bizily	busily
bistir	bestir	bizmuth	bismuth
bistow	bestow	bizness	business
bistowal	bestowal	bizy	busy
bistro		blab, blabbed, blabbing	
bisun	bison	blabber, blabbered, blabbering	

blabbermouth
  blaber   blabber
black
blackberry, -ries
blackbirding
blackboard
  blackbord   blackboard
blackbutt
blackcurrant
  blackcurrent   blackcurrant
blacken, -ed, -ing
blackfellow
blackguard
blackhead
blackjack
blackleg
blackmail
  blackmale   blackmail
blackout
blackshirt
blacksmith
blacktracker
bladder
blade
  blader   bladder
  blaggard   blackguard
  blaid   blade
  blaim   blame
  blaimless   blameless
  blair   blare
  blaise   blaze
  blaiser   blazer
blame, blamed, blaming
blameless, -ly
blameworthy
  blamonge   blancmange
blanch, -ed, -ing
blancmange
bland, -ly
blandish
blandishment
blank
blanket
blare, blared, blaring
blarney, -neyed, -neying
  blarny   blarney
  blasay   blasé

blasé
  blasfeem   blaspheme
  blasfemus   blasphemous
  blasfemy   blasphemy
blaspheme, -phemed, -pheming
blasphemous, -ly
blasphemy, -mies
blast, -ed, -ing
blast-off
blatancy
blatant, -ly
blather
blaze, blazed, blazing
blazer
blazon
bleach, -ed, -ing
bleachers
  blead   bleed
bleak, -ly
bleakness
blear, -ed, -ing
blearily
bleary, blearier, blearist
bleat, -ed, -ing
  bleech   bleach
bleed, bled, bleeding
bleeder
  bleek   bleak
bleep
  bleer   blear
  bleet   bleat
blemish, -ed, -ing
blench, -ed, -ing
blend, -ed, -ing
blender
  blert   blurt
bless, blessed, blessing
blew (to blow)
  blew   blue (colour)

> For other blew- words, look
> under **blue-**.

blight, -ed, -ing
blighter
Blighty
blimey
blimp

blind, -ed, -ing
blind, -ly
blindfold
blindman's buff
blindness
blink, -ed, -ing
blinker
blip
bliss
blissful, -ly
blister, -ed, -ing
blistery
blite   blight
bliter   blighter
blithe, -ly
blithering
blits   blitz
blitz, -ed, -ing
blizard   blizzard
blizzard
blo   blow
bloat, -ed, -ing
bloater
blob
bloc (group)
block, -ed, -ing (stop)
blockade, -kaded, -kading
blockage
blockaid   blockade
blockbuster
blockidge   blockage
blok   bloke
bloke
blond, blonde
blone   blown
blood
bloodbath
bloodcurdling
blooded
bloodless
blood-poisoning
blood pressure
bloodshed
bloodshot
bloodstream
bloodthirsty
bloody, bloodied, bloodying

bloody, bloodier, bloodiest
bloom, -ed, -ing
bloomers
blosom   blossom
blossom
blot, blotted, blotting
blot   bloat
blotch, -ed, -ing
blotchy
bloting   blotting
blouse
blow, blew, blown, blowing
blower
blowfly
blowhole
blowlamp
blow-out
blowpipe
blowse   blouse
blow-up
blu   blue (colour)
blu   blew (to blow)
blubber
blubbery
bluber   blubber
bludge, bludged, bludging
bludger
bludgeon

> For all other blud- words, look
> under **blood-**.

blue (colour)
blue   blew (to blow)
blue, bluer, bluest
bluebird
bluebottle
blue-collar
blueprint
blue-ribbon
blues
blue-tongue
bluey
bluf   bluff
bluff, -ed, -ing
bluish
blummers   bloomers
blunder, -ed, -ing

blunt, -ed, -ing
blur, blurred, blurring
blurb
blurt, -ed, -ing
blush, -ed, -ing
bluster, -ed, -ing
blustery

blustry · blustery

boa
boa constrictor
boar (pig)

boar · boor (rude)
boar · bore (drill)

board, -ed, -ing
board (wood)

board · bored (drill)

boarder (lodger)

boarder · border (edge)

boast, -ed, -ing
boastful, -ly
boat
boater
boat-house
boating
boat people
boat-race
boatswain
bob, bobbed, bobbing

bobbel · bobble
bobbie · bobby

bobbin
bobble

bobbul · bobble

bobby, -bies
bobby-dazzler
bobby pin, bobby pins
bobcat

bobie · bobby
bobin · bobbin
boble · bobble
bobslay · bobsleigh

bobsled
bobsleigh

boby · bobby
boch · botch
boddy · body

bodgie

bodice

bodie · body
bodigard · bodyguard
bodiley · bodily

bodily

bodis · bodice

body, bodies
body, bodied, bodying
body corporate
bodyguard
body language
bodywork
boffin
bog, bogged, bogging
bogey, bogies (golf)

bogey · bogy (evil)
boggel · boggle

boggle, -gled, -gling

bogul · boggle

bogus
bogy, bogies (evil)

bogy · bogey (golf)

bohemian

boi · boy (male)
boi · buoy (afloat)
boiancy · buoyancy
boiant · buoyant
boicot · boycott

boil, -ed, -ing
boiler
boilermaker
boilersuit
boisterous, -ly

boisterus · boisterous
boks · box
bolairo · bolero
bolard · bollard
bolaro · bolero

bold, -ly (brave)

bold · bowled (ball)

bolder (braver)

bolder · boulder (rock)

bole (trunk)

bole · bowl (ball)

bolero
bollard
Bolshevik

Bolshevism

bolshie

bolster, -ed, -ing

bolt

   bom   bomb

bomb, -ed, -ing

bombardier

bombardment

bombastic

bomber

   bomberdeer   bombardier

bombora

bombshell

   bomer   bomber

bona fide

bonanza

bonbon

bonce

bond, -ed, -ing

bondage

bone, boned, boning

   bonet   bonnet

bonfire

   bonie   boney

   bonie   bonny

   bonit   bonnet

bonk, -ed, -ing

bonny, bonnier, bonniest

bonsai

bonus

bony, bonier, boniest

bonzer

boo, booed, booing

boob

   boobie   booby

boo-boo

booby, -bies

   boodwar   boudoir

   boofant   bouffant

boogie-woogie

book, -ed, -ing

   bookay   bouquet

bookcase

   bookeeping   bookkeeping

bookie

bookish, -ly

bookkeeping

bookmaker

bookstall

bookworm

   boolevard   boulevard

boom, -ed, -ing

boomer

boomerang

boon

boor (rude)

   boor   boar (pig)

   boor   bore (drill)

   boorjwah   bourgeois

   boorjwahzey   bourgeoisie

boost, -ed, -ing

booster

boot

bootee (shoe)

   bootee   booty (plunder)

   booteek   ,boutique

booth

   bootie   bootee (shoe)

   bootie   booty (plunder)

   bootik   boutique

bootleg, -legged, -legging

bootlegger

bootstrap

booty, -ties (plunder)

   booty   bootee (shoe)

booze, boozed, boozing

boozer

bora

boracic

   boraks   borax

   borasic   boracic

borax

   borbon   bourbon

   bord   board (plank)

   bord   bored (tired)

border (edge)

   border   boarder

               (lodger)

border, -ed, -ing

borderline

   bording   boarding

   bordom   boredom

   bordy   bawdy

bore, bored, boring (drill)

bore	boar (pig)	bottom -ed, -ing	
bore	boor (rude)	bottomless	
boredom		botul	bottle
boree		botulism	
borer		boudoir	
born (birth)		bouffant	
born	borne (carry)	bougainvillea	
born	bourn (limit)	bough (branch)	
borne (carry)		bough	bow (bend)
borne	born (birth)	bought	
borne	bourn (limit)	bouillon	
boronia		boukay	bouquet
borough (town)		boulder (rock)	
borough	burrow (hole)	boulder	bolder (braver)
borow	borrow	boulevard	
borrow, -ed, -ing		bounce, bounced, bouncing	
borrower		bouncer	
Borstal		bound, -ed, -ing	
bort	bought	boundary, -ries	
bos	boss	boundry	boundary
bosie	bossy	bounteous, -ly	
bosily	bossily	bountiful, -ly	
bosn	bosun	bountious	bounteous
bosom		bounty, -ties	
boss, -ed, -ing		bouquet	
bossom	bosom	bourbon	
bossy, bossier, bossiest		bourgeois	
bosun		bourgeoisie	
bosy	bossy	bourgwah	bourgeois
bot	boat	bourgwahzey	bourgeoisie
botaney	botany	bourn (limit)	
botanical, -ly		bourn	born (birth)
botanist		bourn	borne (carry)
botany		bout	
botch, -ed, -ing		bouteek	boutique
botchy		boutique	
boter	boater	bovine	
both		bow, -ed, -ing (bend)	
bother		bow	bough (branch)
bothersome		bow	beau (dandy)
bothersum	bothersome	bowel	
botom	bottom	bower	
bottel	bottle	bowerbird	
bottle, -tled, -tling		bowie knife	
bottlebrush		bowl (ball)	
bottleneck		bowl	bole (trunk)
bottler		bowleg	

bowler
bowline
bownce	bounce
bownd	bound
bowndary	boundary
bownse	bounce
bouwnser	bouncer
bownteous	bounteous
bowntiful	bountiful
bowt	bout

bowyang
box, -ed, -ing
boxer
box-frame
boy (child)
boy	buoy (float)
boyansy	buoyancy
boyant	buoyant
boycot	boycott

boycott, -ed, -ing
boykot	boycott
boyle	boil
boysterus	boisterous

bra, bras (brassiere)
brace, braced, bracing (clamp)
bracelet
bracken
bracket, -ed, -ing
brackish
brackit	bracket
braclete	bracelet
brade	braid

brag, bragged, bragging
| bragart | braggart |

braggart
bragger
Brahma
Brahman, -mans
braid
| brail | braille |

braille
brain
brainstorm
brainwash, -ed, -ing
brainy, brainier, brainiest
braise, braised, braising (cook)
| braise | braze (solder) |

braisen	brazen
brakage	breakage
brakaway	breakaway
brakdown	breakdown

brake, braked, braking (stop)
brake	break (divide)
braken	bracken
brakeneck	breakneck
braker	breaker
brakewater	breakwater
brakidge	breakage
braking	breaking
brakish	brackish
brale	braille
brambel	bramble

bramble
brambly
| brambul | bramble |
| bramin | Brahman |

bran
branch, -ches
branch, -ed, -ing
brand, -ed, -ing
brandish, -ed, -ing
brand-new
brandy, -dies
| brane | brain |
| braney | brainy |

bras (brassieres)
| bras | brass (metal) |
| brase | brace (clamp) |

brash
brasier	brassiere (bra)
brasier	brazier (burner)
braslet	bracelet

brass
brassiere (bra)
brassy, brassier, brassiest
| brasy | brassy |

brat
bravado, -does, -dos
brave, braver, bravest
bravely
bravery, -ries
| bravly | bravely |

bravo, -voes, -vos
| bravrey | bravery |

brawd   broad
brawl, -ed, -ing
brawn
brawny, brawnier, brawniest
bray, -ed, -ing
    brayd   braid
    brayn   brain
braze, brazed, brazing (solder)
    braze   braise (cook)
brazen, -ly
brazenness
brazier (burner)
    brazier   brassiere (bra)
brazil nut
breach, -ed, -ing (break)
    breach   breech (gun)
bread (food)
    bread   bred
                 (produced)
breadline
breadth
breadwinner
break, broke, broken, breaking
(divide)
    break   brake (stop)
    breakabel   breakable
breakable
    breakabul   breakable
breakage
breakaway
breakdown
breaker
breakfast
break-in
breakthrough
breakwater
bream (fish)
breast
breastbone
breastfeed, -fed, -feeding
breastplate
breast stroke
breath (air)
    breath   breadth (wide)
    breathaliser   breathalyser
breathalyser
breathe, breathed, breathing

breather
breathless, -ly
breathtaking
bred (produced)
    bred   bread (food)
    bredth   breadth
    bree   brie
breech, -ches (gun)
    breech   breach (break)
breed, bred, breeding
breeder
breeding
    breef   brief
breeze, breezed, breezing
breezily
breezy, breezier, breeziest
    breif   brief
    brest   breast
    brest stroke   breast stroke
    breth   breath (air)
    breth   breadth (wide)
    brethalyser   breathalyser
    brethless   breathless
brethren
    brethtaking   breathtaking
breve
brevity, -ties
brew, -ed, -ing (beer)
    brewed   brood (worry)
brewer
brewery, -ries
    brews   bruise (hurt)
    breze   breeze
    brezy   breezy
briar
bribe, bribed, bribing
bribery, -ies
bric-a-brac
brick, -ed, -ing
brickbat
    brickette   briquette
bricklayer
brick veneer
brickyard
bridal (marry)
    bridal   bridle (horse)
bride

bridegroom
~~bridel~~ bridal (marry)
~~bridel~~ bridle (horse)
~~bridesmade~~ bridesmaid
bridesmaid
bridge, bridged, bridging
bridle, -dled, -dling (horse)
~~bridle~~ bridal (marry)
brie
brief, -ly
briefcase
briefs
brig
brigade, -gaded, -gading
~~brigadeer~~ brigadier
brigadier
brigalow
brigand
~~brige~~ bridge
bright, -ly
brighten, -ed, -ing
brightness
brilliance
brilliant, -ly
brilliantine
~~brilyanse~~ brilliance
~~brilyansy~~ brilliancy
~~brilyant~~ brilliant
brim, brimmed, brimming (edge)
~~brim~~ bream (fish)
brimstone
brindled
brine, brined, brining
~~briney~~ briny
bring, brought, bringing
brink
brinkmanship
briny, brinier, briniest
bri-nylon
briquette
~~brisel~~ bristle
brisk, -ly
brisket
~~brisle~~ bristle
bristle, -tled, -tling
bristly
Britain

~~brite~~ bright
~~briten~~ brighten
British
~~britle~~ brittle
brittle, brittler, brittlest
brittleness
broach, -ed, -ing (mention)
~~broach~~ brooch (pin)
broad, -ly
broadcast, -cast, -casting
broadcaster
broaden, -ed, -ing
broad-minded
broadsheet
brocade, -caded
broccoli
~~broch~~ broach (mention)
~~broch~~ brooch (pin)
brochure
~~brocoli~~ broccoli
~~brog~~ brogue
brogue
broil, -ed, -ing
broken, -ly
broken-hearted
broker
brokerage
~~brokeridge~~ brokerage
brolly, -lies
bromide
bromine
bronchial
bronchitis
bronco, -cos
~~bronkial~~ bronchial
~~bronkitis~~ bronchitis
bronze, bronzed, bronzing
brooch, -ches (pin)
brood (worry)
~~brood~~ brewed (beer)
broody, broodier, broodiest
brook, -ed, -ing
broom
~~broonette~~ brunette
~~broose~~ bruise
~~broot~~ brute

brootal — brutal
brootality — brutality
brootish — brutish
brorn — brawn
brort — brought
broshure — brochure
brosure — brochure
broth
brothel
brother
brotherhood
brother-in-law, brothers-in-law
brotherliness
brotherly
brow, brows (eyebrow)
browbeat, -beat, -beaten, -beating
brown
brownee — brownie
brownie
brows — browse (read)
browse, browsed, browsing
browser
bruise, bruised, bruising (hurt)
bruise — brews (beer)
bruiser
brumby, brumbies
brunch
brunet — brunette
brunette
bruse — brews (beer)
bruse — bruise (hurt)
brush, -ed, -ing
brushwood
brushwork
brusk — brusque
brusque, -ly
brusqueness
brutal, -ly
brutality, -ties
brute
brutish
bubbel — bubble
bubble, -bled, -bling
bubble-and-squeak
buble — bubble
bubly — bubbly
bubonic plague

bubul — bubble
bucaneer — buccaneer
buccaneer
buccaneering
bucher — butcher
buck, -ed, -ing
buckaneer — buccaneer
buckel — buckle
bucket, -ed, -ing
bucketful, bucketfuls
buckjump, -ed, -ing
buckjumper
buckle, -led, -ling
buckshot
buckskin
bucktooth, -teeth
buckul — buckle
bucolic
bud, budded, budding
Buddhism
Buddhist
buddy, -dies
budge, budged, budging
budgereegar — budgerigar
budgerigar
budget, -eted, -eting
budgetary
budgie
budgrigar — budgerigar
Budhism — Buddhism
Budhist — Buddhist
buf — buff
bufalo — buffalo
bufay — buffet
bufer — buffer
buff
buffalo, -loes, -los
buffay — buffet
buffer
buffet (food)
buffet, -ed, -ing (hit)
buffoon
buffoonery, -eries
bufit — buffet
bufoon — buffoon
bufoonery — buffoonery
bug, bugged, bugging

bugbare	bugbear
bugbear	
bugel	bugle
bugerigar	budgerigar
buget	budget
buggy, -gies	
bugie	buggy
bugle, -gled, -gling	
bugler	
bugy	buggy
build, built, building	
builder	
build-up	
buisness	business
bukshee	

> For **buk-** words, look under
> **buc-**.

bul	bull
bulb	
bulbar	bull-bar
bulbous	
bulbul	
buldog	bulldog
buldoze	bulldoze
bulet	bullet
buletin	bulletin
bulfight	bullfight
bulfrog	bullfrog
bul-headed	bull-headed
bulion	bullion
bulk	
bulkhead	
bulky, bulkier, bulkiest	
bull-bar	
bulldog	
bulldoze, -dozed, -dozing	
bulldozer	
bullet	
bulletin	
bullfight	
bullfrog	
bull-headed	
bullion	
bullock	
bullring	
bullroarer	

bullrush	
bullseye	
bull-terrier	
bullwark	bulwark
bully, -lies	
bully, -lied, -lying	
bulock	bullock
bulring	bullring
bulroarer	bullroarer
bulrush	
bulseye	bullseye
bulwalk	bulwark
bulwark	
buly	bully
bulyun	bullion
bum, bummed, bumming	
bumbel	bumble
bumble, bumbled, bumbling	
bumf	
bump, -ed, -ing	
bumper	
bumpey	bumpy
bumpiness	
bumpkin	
bumpshus	bumptious
bumptious, -ly	
bumptiousness	
bumpy, bumpier, bumpiest	
bumshus	bumptious
bunch, -ches	
bunch, -ed, -ing	
buncum	bunkum
bundel	bundle
bundle, -dled, -dling	
bundul	bundle
bundy	
buney	bunny
bung, -ed, -ing	
bungaloe	bungalow
bungalow	
bungel	bungle
bunger	
bunghole	
bungkum	bunkum
bungle, -gled, -gling	
bungler	
bungul	bungle

bunie   bunny
bunion
bunk, -ed, -ing
bunker, -ed, -ing
bunkum
bunny, -nies
bunnyip   bunyip
Bunsen burner
bunt
bunting
buny   bunny
bunyip
bunyon   bunion
buoy, -ed, -ing (float)
buoy   boy (child)
buoyancy
buoyansy   buoyancy
buoyant, -ly
burbel   burble
burble, -bled, -bling
burbul   burble
burch   birch
burd   bird
burden, -ed, -ing
burdensome
burdensum   burdensome
burdie   birdie
burdseye   bird's-eye
bureau, -eaus, -eaux
bureaucracy, -cies
bureaucrasy   bureaucracy
bureaucrat
bureaucratic
buret   burette
burette
burgandy   burgundy
burgel   burgle
burgeon, -ed, -ing
burger   burgher
burgess
burgher
burglar
burglary, -ries
burgle, -gled, -gling
burgler   burglar
burgul   burgle
burgundy

burial
burke, burked, burking
burl, -ed, -ing
burlap
burlesk   burlesque
burlesque, -lesqued, -lesquing
burlie   burly (large)
burly, -lier, -liest (large)
burly   berley (bait)
burn, burnt, burned, burning
burnable
burn-back
burner
burnish, -ed, -ing
buro   bureau
buro   burro
burocrasy   bureaucracy
burocrat   bureaucrat
burow   bureau
burow   burrow (hole)
burr, burred, burring
burra   borough (town)
burro, -ros (donkey)
burro   bureau
burrocracy   bureaucracy
burrocrat   bureaucrat
burrow, -ed, -ing (hole)
burrow   borough (town)
burrow   burro (donkey)
bursar
bursary, -ries
burser   bursar
bursery   bursary
burst, burst, bursting
burth   berth (ship)
burth   birth (born)
bury, buried, burying (cover)
bury   berry (fruit)
bus, buses, busses
bus, bused, busing or bussed, bussing
busbie   busby
busby, -bies
busel   bustle
bush, -ed, -ing
bushcraft
bushel
bushfire

bushie (farmer)
  bushie   bushy
bush-lawyer
bushman, -men
bushranger
bushranging
bushwalk
bushy, bushier, bushiest
busier
busily
business
businesslike
businessman, -men
businesswoman, -women
busk, -ed, -ing
busker
bust, -ed, -ing
bustard
  busted   bustard
  bustel   bustle
buster
bustle, -tled, -tling
bust-up
  busul   bustle
busy, busied, busying
busy, busier, busiest
busybody, -bodies
but (contrary)
  but   butt (end)
butane
butcher, -ed, -ing
  buteek   boutique
  buten   button
  buter   butter
  buterfly   butterfly
  butey   beauty
  butician   beautician
  butify   beautify
  butique   boutique
  butishun   beautician
butler
  butock   buttock
  buton   button
  butress   buttress
butt, -ed, -ing (end)
  butt   but (contrary)
butter, -ed, -ing

butter-fingers
butterfly, -flies
butterscotch
buttock
button
buttonhole, -holed, -holing
buttress, buttresses
buxom, -ly
buy, bought, buying (purchase)
  buy   by (near to)
  buy   bye (sport)
buyer
  buz   buzz
  buzard   buzzard
  buzer   buzzer
  buz-saw   buzz-saw
buzz, -ed, -ing
buzz, -es
buzzard
buzzer
buzz-saw
by (near to)
  by   bye (sport)
  by   buy (purchase)
bye (sport)
  bye   by (near to)
  bye   buy (purchase)
bye-bye, bye-byes
by-election
  byennial   biennial
  byer   buyer
  byer   byre (shed)
  byfocal   bifocal
bygone
  bying   buying
  byke   bike
by-law
  byle   bile
  bylore   by-law
  bymetallic   bimetallic
  bymonthly   bimonthly
  bynominal   binominal
  byopsey   biopsy
  bypartisan   bipartisan
  bypartite   bipartite
bypass
  byped   biped

byplane	biplane
by-product	
byre (shed)	
bysecshun	bisection
bysect	bisect
byseksual	bisexual
bystander	
byte (computer)	
byte	bite (chew)
byway	
byword	
Byzantine	

Cc

cab
cabal, -balled, -balling
  cabaray   cabaret
cabaret
cabbage
  cabbidge   cabbage
cabby, cabbies
  cabel   cable
  cabey   cabby
  cabie   cabby
  cabige   cabbage
cabin
cabinet
cable, -bled, -bling
caboose
  cabul   cable
cacao, -caos
  cach   cache
  cach   catch
  cachay   cachet
cache, cached, caching (hide)
  cache   cash (money)
cachet
  cachou   cashew
  cachword   catchword
  cackel   cackle
cackle, -led, -ling
  cacktus   cactus
  cackul   cackle
  cacofony   cacophony
cacophony, -nies
cactoblastis
cactus, -ti, -tuses
  cacul   cackle
cad
cadaver
cadaverous, -ly
  caddey   caddie (golf)

  caddey   caddy (tea)
caddie, -died, -dying (golf)
  caddie   caddy (tea)
caddy, -ies (tea)
  caddy   caddie (golf)
cadence
  cadense   cadence
cadenza
cadet
cadetship
cadge, cadged, cadging
  cadjole   cajole
cadmium
Caesar
caesarean section
  cafay   cafe
cafe
  cafeen   caffeine
cafeteria
caffeine
  caffeteria   cafeteria
  cafiene   caffeine
  cafitiria   cafeteria
caftan
cage, caged, caging
cagey, cagier, cagiest
  cagy   cagey
cahoots
  cain   cane
cairn
caisson
  caje   cage
cajole, -joled, -joling
cake, caked, caking
calabash
calamari
calamine
calamitous, -ly
calamity, -ties
  calarie   calorie
calcareous
  calcarious   calcareous
calcification
calcify, -fied, -fying
calcium
calculable
  calculabul   calculable

calculate, -lated, -lating	calm, -ly
calculation	calmness
calculative	calorie
calculator	calorific
calculaytor — calculator	calorimeter
calculus, -luses	calory — calorie
Caledonian	calow — callow
calendar (time)	calsify — calcify
calender (roll)	calsium — calcium
calendula	calumniate, -ated, -ating
calf, calves	calumniation
calfskin	calumnious, -ly
caliber — calibre	calumnius — calumnious
calibrate, -brated, -brating	calumny, -nies
calibration	calus — callous (cruel)
calibrator	calus — callus (skin)
calibre	Calvary
calicks — calyx	calve, calved, calving (give birth)
calico, -coes, -cos	calve — carve (cut)
calif — caliph	Calvinism
caligraphy — calligraphy	Calvinist
caling — calling	calypso, -sos
caliper	calyx, calyces, calyxes
caliph	cam
calipso — calypso	camaflage — camouflage
calisthenics	camaraderie
calix — calyx	camber
calk — caulk	cambric
call, -ed, -ing (cry out)	came
call — caul (membrane)	camel
	camelhair
callamity — calamity	camellia
calldron — cauldron	camelya — camellia
caller	camember — camembert
callgirl	camembert
calligrapher	cameo, -os
calligraphy	camera
calliper	cameraman
callistemon	camerardery — camaraderie
callisthenics	camfer — camphor
callosity, -ties	camio — cameo
callous, -ly (cruel)	camisole
callous — callus (skin)	camle — camel
callousness	camouflage, -flaged, -flaging
callow	camp, -ed, -ing
callus, calluses (skin)	campaign
callus — callous (cruel)	campain — campaign

campanology
camper
campervan
campher *camphor*
camphor
campus, -es
camshaft
camul *camel*
can, could (able to)
can, canned, canning (tinned)
canabis *cannabis*
Canadian
canal
canape
canary, -ries
canasta
cancan
cancel, -celled, -celling
cancelation *cancellation*
cancellation
cancer
cancerous
cancerus *cancerous*
candel *candle*
candelabrum
candellight *candlelight*
candelstick *candlestick*
cander *candour*
candey *candy*
candid (open)
candid *candied (sugar)*
candidate
candied (sugar)
candied *candid (open)*
candle
candlelight
candlestick
candour
candul *candle*
candulstick *candlestick*
candy, -dies
candy, candied, candying (sugar)
cane, caned, caning (hit)
caned *canned (tinned)*
canee *canny*
canery *cannery*
cane-sugar

canibal *cannibal*
canibalism *cannibalism*
canie *canny*
canine
canister
cannabis
cannary *canary*
canned (tinned)
canned *caned (hit)*
cannelloni
cannery, -ries
cannibal
cannibalism
canniness
cannon (gun)
cannon *canon (law)*
cannot
canny, -nier, -niest

> For other **cann-** words,
> look under **can-**.

canoe, -es
canoe, -noed, -noeing
canoeist
canon (law)
canon *cannon (gun)*
canonical
canonisation
canonise, -nised, -nising
canoo *canoe*
canoodle, -dled, -dling
canooist *canoeist*
canopy, -pies
cansel *cancel*
canser *cancer*
canserous *cancerous*
cant (insincere)
can't (cannot)
cantaloup
cantaloupe
cantankerous, -ly
cantankerus *cantankerous*
cantata
canteen
canter, -ed, -ing
cantilever
canto, -tos

canton

cantor

  canue   canoe

canvas, -es (tent)

  canvas   canvass
                    (gather)

canvass, -ed, -ing (gather)

  canvass   canvas (tent)

  cany   canny

canyon

cap, capped, capping

capability, -ties

capable, -bly

  capabul   capable

capacious, -ly

capacitor

capacity, -ties

  capasitor   capacitor
  capasity   capacity
  capchure   capture

cape

caper, -ed, -ing

  capilary   capillary

capillary, -laries

capital

capitalisation

capitalise, -lised, -lising

capitalism

capitalist

capitalistic

capitulate, -lated, -lating

capitulation

capon

cappuccino

For all other capp- words,
look under **cap-**.

---

caprice

capricious, -ly

capriciousness

Capricorn

  caprise   caprice
  caprishus   capricious
  capshulate   capsulate
  capshun   caption
  capshus   captious

capsicum

capsize, -sized, -sizing

capstan

capsule

captain, -ed, -ing

captaincy

  capter   captor
  captin   captain

caption

captious, -ly

captiousness

  captius   captious

captivate, -vated, -vating

captivation

captive

captivity, -ties

captor

capture, -tured, -turing

  caracter   character
  caracteristic characteristic

carafe

  caraffe   carafe

caramel

  caramul   caramel

carat (weight)

  carat   carrot (food)
  carate   karate

caravan, -vanned, -vanning

caraway

carbine

carbohydrate

carbon

carbonate, -nated, -nating

carbon dioxide

carbonise, -nised, -nising

carbon monoxide

carbuncle

  carbuncul   carbuncle

carburettor

carcase

carcass

carcinogen

carcinogenic

carcinoma, -mata, -mas

card, -ed, -ing

  cardagan   cardigan

cardboard

  cardbord   cardboard

cardiac
cardigan
cardinal, -ly
  cardiograf   cardiograph
cardiologist
cardiology
cardiovascular
cardsharp
care, cared, caring
careen
career, -ed, -ing
carefree
careful, -ly
careless, -ly
carelessness
caress, -ed, -ing
caressingly
caret (mark)
  caret   carat (weight)
caretaker
cargo, -goes
caribou, -bou
caricature, -tured, -turing
caricaturist
  caricter   character
  caricteristic   characteristic
  caridge   carriage
  carie   carry (bear)
  carier   carrier
caries (decay)
  caries   carries (bear)
  carillion   carillon
carillon
  carillyon   carillon
  carion   carrion
  carisma   charisma
  carkey   khaki
  carki   khaki
  carm   calm
carmine
carnage
carnal, -ly
carnality
carnation
  carnidge   carnage
  carnije   carnage
carnival

carnivore
carnivorous, -ly
carol, -rolled, -rolling (song)
  carol   carrel (study)
  carol   corral (yard)
caroller
  carot   carat (weight)
carousal (feast)
  carousal   carousel
                     (merry-go-
                     round)
carouse, -roused, -rousing
carousel (merry-go-round)
  carousel   carousal (feast)
carp, -ed, -ing
carpenter
carpentry
carpet, -ed, -ing
carrel (study)
  carrel   carol (song)
  carrel   corral (yard)
carriage
carriageway
carrier
carries (bears)
  carries   caries (decay)
carrion
carrot (food)
  carrot   carat (weight)
carry, -ried, -rying
  carryon   carrion
  carsinoma   carcinoma
cart, -ed, -ing
carte blanche
cartel
cartilage
  cartilege   cartilage
  cartilidge   cartilage
  cartografy   cartography
cartographer
cartographic
cartography
carton
cartoon, -ed, -ing
cartoonist
cartridge
  cartrige   cartridge

cartrije cartridge
cartwheel
carve, carved, carving (cut)
 carve calve (give birth)
 cary carry
 casava cassava
cascade, -caded, -cading
case, cased, casing
 caseen casein
casein
casement
 caserole casserole
 casette cassette
 casock cassock
 casowary cassowary
cash, -ed, -ing (money)
 cash cache (hide)
 cashay cachet
 casheer cashier
cashew
cashier
 cashmear cashmere
cashmere
 cashoo cashew
 casia cassia
casing
casino, -nos
cask
 caskade cascade
casket
 caskit casket
 casock cassock
cassava
 cassel castle
casserole, -roled, -roling
 casset cassette
cassette
cassia
cassock
cassowary, -ries
cast, cast, casting (fling)
 cast caste (class)
castanet
castaway
caste (class)
caster or castor (sugar)

caster castor (oil)
castigate, -gated, -gating
castigation
cast-iron
castle, -tled, -tling
castor (oil)
 castrait castrate
castrate, -trated, -trating
castration
 castrayte castrate
casual, -ly
 casuality casualty
casualty, -ties
casuarina
casuistic
casuistry, -tries
 casulty casualty
 catachism catechism
cataclysm
cataclysmic
catacomb
 catalise catalyse
 catalist catalyst
 catalitic catalytic
 catalog catalogue
catalogue, -logued, -loguing
cataloguer
catalyse, -lysed, -lysing
catalyst
catalytic
catamaran
 catapiler caterpillar
catapult
 catar catarrh
cataract
 catarh catarrh
catarrh
catarrhal
 catastrofic catastrophic
 catastrofy catastrophe
catastrophe
catastrophic, -ally
catcall, -ed, -ing
catch, caught, catching
catcher
catchment
catchword

catchy, catchier, catchiest
catechise, -chised, -chising
catechism
catechist
categorical, -ly
categorise, -rised, -rising
categorist
category, -ries
   catel   cattle
cater, -ed, -ing
caterer
caterpillar
   caterpiller   caterpillar
   caterwall   caterwaul
caterwaul
catfish, -fishes, -fish
catgut
catharsis
cathartic
cathedral
catheter
cathode
catholic (universal)
Catholic (religion)
Catholicism
Catholicity
   caticise   catechise
   catigoric   categoric
   catigorise   categorise
   catigory   category
   catikism   catechism
   catish   cattish
catkin
   catle   cattle
catnap, -ed, -ing
cat-o'-nine-tails
   cattel   cattle
   catterpillar   caterpillar
cattle
cattlegrid
cattle-run
cattish, -ly
catty, -ier, -iest
   catul   cattle
catwalk
Caucasian
caucus, -ed, -ing

caught (did catch)
   caught   court (law)
   cauk   caulk
caul (membrane)
   caul   call (cry)
cauldron
   cauliflour   cauliflower
cauliflower
caulk, -ed, -ing
causal, -ly
   causal   casual
causality, -ties
causation
causative, -ly
cause, caused, causing
causeway
caustic, -ally
cauterise, -rised, -rising
caution, -ed, -ing
cautionary
cautious, -ly
cavalcade, -caded, -cading
   cavaleer   cavalier
cavalier
cavalry, -ries
cavalryman, -men
cave, caved, caving
caveman, -men
cavern
cavernous
caviar
cavil, -illed, -illing
cavity, -ties
   caw   core (heart)
   caw   corps (group)
   cawcas   caucus
   Cawcasian   Caucasian
   cawcus   caucus
cay
cayenne
cease, ceased, ceasing
cease-fire
ceaseless, -ly
cedar
cede, ceded, ceding (yield)
   cede   seed (plant)
   ceder   cedar

ceeling	ceiling (roof)	censorious, -ly	
ceese	cease	censorship	
cefalic	cephalic	censurable	
ceiling (roof)		censurabul	censurable
ceiling	sealing (close)	censure, -sured, -suring	
celebrant		census	
celebrate, -brated, -brating		cent (coin)	
celebration		cent	scent (perfume)
celebrity, -ties		cent	sent (away)
celerity		centaur	
celery (food)		centenarian	
celery	salary (wage)	centenary, -ries	
celestial, -ly		centenery	centenary
celibacy, -cies		centennial, -ly	
celibasy	celibacy	center	centre
celibate		Centigrade	
celibrant	celebrant	centimeter	centimetre
celibrate	celebrate	centimetre	
cell (prison)		centipede	
cell	sell (goods)	centor	centaur
cellar (basement)		central, -ly	
cellar	seller (goods)	Centralia	
cellarman, -men		centralisation	
celler	seller (goods)	centralise, -lised, -lising	
cellist		centralism	
cello, -los		centralist	
cellofane	cellophane	centrality	
cellophane		centre, -tred, -tring	
cellular		centreboard	
celluler	cellular	centrefold	
celluloid		centrepiece	
cellulose		centrifugal, -ly	
celofane	cellophane	centrifuge	
Celsius		centripetal, -ly	
cement, -ed, -ing		centupel	centuple
cemetary	cemetery	centuple, -pled, -pling	
cemetery, -teries		centupul	centuple
cemical	chemical	centurion	
cemist	chemist	century, -ries	
cemistry	chemistry	cephalic	
cenotaf	cenotaph	ceramic	
censer (incense)		ceramicist	
censer	censor (books)	ceramics	
censership	censorship	ceramist	
censhure	censure		
censor (books)			
censor	censer (incense)		

For any cerc- words,
look under **circ-**.

cereal (grain)
  cereal   serial (part)
  cerebelum   cerebellum
cerebellum, -bella
cerebral
cerebrate, -brated, -brating
cerebration
cerebrum, -bra
ceremonial, -ly
ceremonious, -ly
  ceremonius   ceremonious
ceremony, -monies
  cerial   cereal (grain)
  cerial   serial (part)
  ceribellum   cerebellum
  ceribrum   cerebrum
cerise

> For any **cerk-** words,
> look under **circ-**.

certain, -ly
certainty, -ties
  certanty   certainty
  certen   certain
  certenty   certainty
certifiable, -fiably
  certifiabul   certifiable
certificate, -cated, -cating
certification
certifier
certify, -fied, -fying
  certinty   certainty
certitude
cervical
  cervicul   cervical
  cerviks   cervix
cervix, cervixes, cervices
  cesation   cessation
  ceshun   session (time)
  cesion   cession (yield)
  cespit   cesspit
  cespool   cesspool
cessation
cession(yield)
  cession   session (time)
cesspit
cesspool

chablis
cha-cha
  chacoal   charcoal
chafe, chafed, chafing (rub)
  chafe   chaff (straw)
chaff (straw)
chaffinch, -es
chagrin, -ed, -ing
chain
chain-drive
chain-reaction
chainsaw
chain-smoke, -smoked, -smoking
chain-stitch, -ed, -ing
chain-store
chair, -ed, -ing
chairlift
chairman, -men
chairperson
chairwoman, -women
  chaise   chase
chalet
chalice
  chalinge   challenge
  chalis   chalice
chalk, -ed, -ing
challenge, -lenged, -lenging
challenger
  chamba   chamber
chamber
chamberlain
  chamberlin   chamberlain
  chambermade   chambermaid
chambermaid
chameleon
  chamee   chamois
chamfer, -ed, -ing
  chamie   chamois
chamois
champ, -ed, -ing
champagne
  champaign   champagne
champers
champignon
champion, -ed, -ing
championship
  champiun   champion

chance, chanced, chancing
chancel
  chanceler   chancellor
  chancelery   chancellery
  chanceller   chancellor
chancellery, -ries
chancellor
chancellorship
chancery, -ceries
chancy, chancier, chanciest
  chandeleer   chandelier
chandelier
chandler
  chane   chain
  chane-drive   chain-drive
  chanel   channel
  chane-reaction   chain-reaction
  chanesaw   chainsaw
change, changed, changing
changeable, -bly
  changeabul   changeable
changeling
changeover
channel, -nelled, -nelling
  chanse   chance
  chansel   chancel
  chanseler   chancellor
  chanselery   chancellery
  chansey   chancy
chant, -ed, -ing
chaos
chaotic, -ally
chap, chapped, chapping
chapel
chaperone
  chaple   chapel
chaplain
chaplaincy
chaplet
  chaplin   chaplain
chapter
char, charred, charring
character
characterise, -rised, -rising
characteristic, -ally
charade
  charaid   charade

charcoal
  chare   chair
  chareman   chairman
  chareperson   chairperson
  charewoman   chairwoman
  charey   chary
charge, charged, charging
charger
chariot
charioteer
charisma
charismatic
charitable
charitableness
charitably
  charitabul   charitable
charity, -ties
charlady, -ladies
charlatan
charleston
charm, -ed, -ing
charmer
chart, -ed, -ing
charter, -ed, -ing
chartreuse
  chartroos   chartreuse
chary, charier, chariest
chase, chased, chasing
chased (follow)
  chased   chaste (pure)
  chasen   chasten
chaser
  chasis   chassis
chasm
  chassie   chassis
chassis, chassis
chaste (pure)
  chaste   chased (follow)
chasten, -ed, -ing
chastener
chastise, -tised, -tising
chastisement
chastiser
chastity
chat, chatted, chatting
chateau, -teaus, -teaux
  chatel   chattel

chater	chatter	cheerie	cheery
chatily	chattily	cheerily	
chatiness	chattiness	cheeriness	
chattel		cheerio, -os	
chatter, -ed, -ing		cheery, -rier, -riest	
chatterbox, -boxes		cheese	
chattily		cheesecake	
chattiness		cheesecloth	
chatty, -tier, -tiest		cheesed-off	
chaty	chatty	cheeseparing	
chauffer	chauffeur	cheesy, -sier, -siest	
chauffeur		cheet	cheat
chauvinism		cheeta	cheetah
chauvinist		cheetah	
chauvinistic, -ally		cheeter	cheetah
cheap (price)		chef	
cheap	cheep (sound)	chef-d'oeuvre, chefs-d'oeuvre	
cheapen, -ed, -ing		cheif	chief
cheapish, -ly		cheiftan	chieftain
cheapskate		chelist	cellist
chear	cheer	chelo	cello
chearful	cheerful	chemical, -ly	
chease	cheese	chemise	
cheat, -ed, -ing		chemist	
cheater		chemistrey	chemistry
check, -ed, -ing (stop)		chemistry, -tries	
check	cheque (money)	chemotherapist	
Check	Czech (person)	chemotherapy	
checkers		chenille	
checkmate, -mated, -mating		cheongsam	
checkout		cheque (money)	
checkpoint		cheque	check (stop)
checkup		Cheque	Czech (person)
chedar	cheddar	cheque-book	
cheddar		chequer	
cheder	cheddar	chequered	
cheef	chief	cherie	cherry
cheeftan	chieftain	cherio	cheerio
cheekily		cherish, -ed, -ing	
cheekiness		cheroot	
cheeky, cheekier, cheekiest		cherp	chirp
cheep, -ed, -ing (sound)		cherry, -ries	
cheep	cheap (price)	cherub, cherubim, cherubs	
cheer, cheered, cheering		cherubic, -ally	
cheerey	cheery	chery	cheery
cheerful, -ly		chery	cherry
cheerfulness		ches	chess

chesbord	chessboard	childproof	
chess		chili, -ies (fruit)	
chessboard		chili	chilly (cold)
chessnut	chestnut	chill, -ed, -ing	
chest		chilli, -ies (fruit)	
chesterfield		chilli	chilly (cold)
chestnut		chilliness	
chevalier		chilly, -ier, -iest (cold)	
chevon (goat meat)		chilly	chilli (fruit)
chevron (stripe)		chimbly	chimney
chew, -ed, -ing (eat)		chime, chimed, chiming	
chewie		chimera, -ras	
chewing gum		chimeric, -ally	
chews	choose (select)	chimnee	chimney
chewy		chimney, -neys	
chiack, -ed, -ing		chimpanzee	
chic (stylish)		chin	
chicanery, -ries		china	
chick (young bird)		chinchilla	
chickenfeed		Chinese	
chickenpox		chink, -ed, -ing	
chickpea		chintz, chintzes	
chickweed		chintzy	
chicle		chip, chipped, chipping	
chicory, -ries		chipboard	
chide, chided, chiding		chipmonk	chipmunk
chidingly		chipmunk	
chief, chiefs		chipolata	
chiefly		chiropodey	chiropody
chieftain		chiropodist	
chieftaincy		chiropody	
chiffon		chiropracter	chiropractor
chiffonier		chiropractic	
chifon	chiffon	chiropractor	
chignon		chirp, -ed, -ing	
chihuahua		chirpily	
chil	chill	chirpy, -pier, -piest	
chilblain		chisel, -elled, -elling	
chilblane	chilblain	chiseller	
child, children		chit	
childbaring	childbearing	chitchat	
childbearing		chivalrous, -ly	
childberth	childbirth	chivalrus	chivalrous
childbirth		chivalry	
childhood		chive	
childish, -ly		chivvy, -ied, -ying	
childlike		chloride	

chlorinate, -nated, -nating
chlorination
chlorine
  chlorofill   chlorophyll
chloroform, -ed, -ing
chlorophyll
chock, -ed, -ing
chock-a-block
chock-full
chocks
  choclat   chocolate
chocolate
choice, choicer, choicest
choir (singers)
  choir   quire (measure)
  choise   choice
choke, choked, choking
choker
choko
choler (anger)
  choler   collar (neck)
cholera
choleric
cholesterol
  choo   chew
chook
choose, chose, chosen, choosing
  (select)
  choose   chews (eats)
choosy
chop, chopped, chopping
chopper
choppy, -pier, -piest
  chopsooey   chop suey
chopstick
  chopy   choppy
choral, -ly (sing)
  choral   chorale (tune)
chorale (tune)
  chorale   choral (sing)
chord (music)
  chord   cord (string)
chore
  choreograf   choreograph
choreograph, -ed, -ing
choreographer
choreographic

choreography
chorister
chortle, -tled, -tling
  chortul   chortle
chorus, -ruses
chorus, -rused, -rusing
chose
chosen
chow
chowder
chow mein
  chrisalis   chrysalis
chrism
  Chrismas   Christmas
Christ
  Christain   Christian
christen, -ed, -ing
christendom
Christian
Christianity
Christmas
chromatic, -ally
chrome
chromium
chromosome
  chronalogical   chronological
chronic, -ally
  chronical   chronicle
chronicle, -cled, -cling
chronicler
chronologer
chronological, -ly
chronology, -gies
chronometer
chrysalis, chrysalises
chrysanthemum
chubbily
chubbiness
chubby, -bier, -biest
  chubier   chubbier
  chuby   chubby
chuck, -ed, -ing
  chuckel   chuckle
chuckle, chuckled, chuckling
chuckler
chuff, -ed, -ing
chug, chugged, chugging

chum, chummed, chumming
chummy, -mier, -miest
chump
chunk
chunkiness
chunky, -kier, -kiest
church, -es
churinga
churl
churlish, -ly
churn, -ed, -ing
  churp   chirp
chute (drop)
  chute   shoot (gun)
chutney, -neys
  chutny   chutney
chutzpah
  cianide   cyanide
  cibernetics   cybernetics
cicada, -dae, -das
  cicatriss   cicatrix
cicatrix, cicatrices, cicatrixes

> For all other cic- words,
> look under cyc-.

cider
  cifer   cipher
cigar
  cigaret   cigarette
cigarette
  cignet   cygnet (swan)
  cignet   signet (ring)
  cilestial   celestial
cilium, cilia
  cilinder   cylinder
  cilindrical   cylindrical
  cimbal   cymbal(music)
  cimbal   symbol (sign)
  ciment   cement
  cinamon   cinnamon
cinch, -ches
cincture
cinder
cinderella
cinema
cinemascope
cinematic, -ally

cinematograph
cineraria
  cinic   cynic
  cinical   cynical
  cinicul   cynical
  cinima   cinema
  cinimatograf   cinematograph
  cinimatograph   cinematograph
  cinimon   cinnamon
cinnamon
  cinosure   cynosure
cipher
  cipress   cypress
circa
  circel   circle
  circit   circuit
circle, -cled, -cling
circlet
circuit, -ed, -ing
circuit-breaker
circuitous, -ly
circuitry
  circul   circle
circular, -ly
circularise, -rised, -rising
circularity
circulate, -lated, -lating
circulation
circulator
circulatory
circumcise, -cised, -cising
circumcision
circumference
  circumferense   circumference
circumnavigate, -gated, -gating
circumnavigation
circumnavigator
circumscribe, -ribed, -ribing
circumscription
circumspect
circumspection
circumstance
  circumstanse   circumstance
  circumstanshul   circumstantial
circumstantial, -ly
circumvent, -ed, -ing
circumvention

circus, circuses		clamer	clamour
cirrhosis		clamerus	clamorous
cirriculum	curriculum	clammily	
cirrosis	cirrhosis	clamminess	
cirrus		clammy, -mier, -miest	
cissy, cissies		clamorous, -ly	
cist	cyst	clamour, -ed, -ing	
cistern		clamp, -ed, -ing	
cistitis	cystitis	clamy	clammy
citadel		clan	
citation		clandestine, -ly	
cite, cited, citing (quote)		clang, -ed, -ing	
cite	sight (see)	clanger (error)	
cite	site (place)	clangour (loud sound)	
citie	city	clangourous, -ly	
citizen		clank, -ed, -ing	
citric acid		clannish, -ly	
citris	citrus	clap, clapped, clapping	
citron		clapper	
citronella		clapperboard	
citros	citrus	claptrap	
citrous		claret	
citrus		clarify, -fied, -fying	
city, cities		clarification	
civet		clarifier	
civic		clarinet	
civies	civvies	clarinettist	
civik	civic	clarion	
civil, -ly		clarionet	
civilian		clarity	
civilisation		clark	clerk
civilise, -lised, -lising		claryon	clarion
civility, -ties		clash, -ed, -ing	
civit	civet	clasify	classify
civvies		clasp, -ed, -ing	
clad		clasroom	classroom
cladding		class, classes	
claim, -ed, -ing		classable	
claimable		classabul	classable
claimabul	claimable	classer	
claimant		classic	
claimer		classical, -ly	
clairvoyance		classicism	
clairvoyant		classicist	
clam, clammed, clamming		classifiable	
clamber, -ed, -ing		classifiabul	classifiable
clame	claim	classification	

classify, -fied, -fying
classroom
classy, classier, classiest
clatter, -ed, -ing
clause (grammar)
   clause   claws (animal)
   claustrofobia   claustrophobia
claustrophobia
claves
   clavicel   clavicle
clavichord
   clavicord   clavichord
clavier
claw, -ed, -ing
claws (animal)
   claws   clause
                    (grammar)
clay
clayey
   clayie   clayey
clayish
   claym   claim
clean, -ed, -ing
cleanliness
cleanse, cleansed, cleansing
cleanskin
clear, -ed, -ing
clearance
clearly
clearness
clearway
cleat
cleavage
cleave, cleaved, cleaving
cleaver
   cleavidge   cleavage
   cleek   clique
   cleeshay   cliché
   cleet   cleat
   cleeve   cleave
   cleevage   cleavage
   cleever   cleaver
   cleevidge   cleavage
clef
cleft
clematis
clemency

   clemensy   clemency
clement
clench, -ed, -ing
   clenliness   cleanliness
   clense   cleanse
cleptomania
clergy, -gies
clergyman, -men
cleric
clerical, -ly
clerk
clever, cleverer, cleverest
cleverly
cleverness
clew (ball)
   clew   clue (hint)
clianthus
   clichay   cliché
cliché, -chés
click, -ed, -ing (sound)
   click   clique (group)
clicker
   clidesdale   clydesdale
client
clientele
   clientell   clientele
cliff
cliff-hanger
climacteric (crucial)
climactic (climax)
   climaks   climax
climate (weather)
climatic, -ally
climatology
climax, -maxes
climb, -ed, -ing (upward)
clime (region)
clinch, -ed, -ing
clincher
cling, clung, clinging
clinger
clinic
clinical, -ly
clink, -ed, -ing
clinker, -ed, -ing
clip, clipped, clipping
clipper

clique (group)
clique — click (sound)
clitoris
clitris — clitoris
cloak
cloak-and-dagger
cloakroom
clobber, -ed, -ing
clock, -ed, -ing
clockwise
clockwork
clod
cloddish
clodhopper
clog, clogged, clogging
cloggy
cloister, -ed, -ing
cloistral
cloke — cloak
clone, cloned, cloning
cloride — chloride
clorinate — chlorinate
clorine — chlorine
clorofil — chlorophyll
cloroform — chloroform
clorophyll — chlorophyll
close, closed, closing
close, closer, closest
closed-circuit
closeness
closet, -ed, -ing
closure
clot, clotted, clotting
cloth, cloths (fabric)
clothe, clothed, clothing
clothes (garments)
clothier
cloud, -ed, -ing
cloudbank
cloudburst
cloudless, -ly
cloudy, cloudier, cloudiest
clout, -ed, -ing
clove
cloven
cloven-hoofed
clover

cloverleaf, -leaves
clowd — cloud
clowdless — cloudless
clowdy — cloudy
clown, -ed, -ing
clownery
clownish, -ly
clowt — clout
cloy, -ed, -ing
cloyster — cloister
club, clubbed, clubbing
clubhouse
cluch — clutch
cluck, -ed, -ing
clucky
clue, clued, cluing (hint)
clue — clew (ball)
clump, -ed, -ing
clumpish
clumpy
clumsily
clumsiness
clumsy, -sier, -siest
clung
clurgy — clergy
cluster, -ed, -ing
clutch, -ed, -ing
clutch-start
clutter, -ed, -ing
Clydesdale
coach, -ed, -ing
coachman, -men
coacksial — coaxial
coagulate, -lated, -lating
coagulation
coagulator
coaks — coax
coal
coaldust
coalesce, -lesced, -lescing
coalescence
coalescent
coaless — coalesce
coalessence — coalescence
coalessent — coalescent
coalface
coalfield

coalishun	coalition
coalition	
coalitionist	
coalmine	
coalminer	
coalmining	
coarse, coarser, coarsest (rough)	
coarse	course (path)
coarsen, -ed, -ing	
coast, -ed, -ing	
coastal	
coaster	
coastgard	coastguard
coastguard	
coastline	
coat, -ed, -ing	
coat-hanger	
coatless	
coax, -ed, -ing	
coaxial	
coaxingly	
coaxiul	coaxial
cobalt	
cobber	
cobble, -bled, -bling	
cobbler	
cobblestone	
cober	cobber
coble	cobble
cobler	cobbler
coblestone	cobblestone
cobulstone	cobblestone
cobra	
cobweb	
cocain	
cocaine	
cocane	cocaine
cocanut	coconut
cocatoo	cockatoo
coccix	coccyx
coccyx, -coccyges	
coch	coach
cochineal	
cochineel	cochineal
cock, -ed, -ing	
cockade	
cockatoo	

cockatrice	
cockatriss	cockatrice
cockcrow	
cockelshell	cockleshell
cockerel	
cocker spaniel	
cocket	coquette
cocketry	coquetry
cockeyed	
cockfight	
cockily	
cockiness	
cockle	
cockleshell	
cockney, -neys	
cockpit	
cockroach, -es	
cockroch	cockroach
cockscomb	
cockshure	cocksure
cocksure	
cocktail	
cocktale	cocktail
cockul	cockle
cocky, cockier, cockiest	
coco, -cos (palm tree)	
cocoa (drink)	
coconut	
cocoon	
coddle, -dled, -dling	
code, coded, coding	
codecks	codex
codeen	codeine
codeine	
codex, codices	
codger	
codicil	
codiene	codeine
codification	
codifier	
codify, -fied, -fying	
codisil	codicil
codle	coddle
codswallop	
codul	coddle
co-ed	
coeducashun	coeducation

coeducation			cohabit, -ed, -ing	
coeducational			cohabitation	
coefficient			cohearent	coherent
coefishent	coefficient		cohere, -hered, -hering	
coegsist	coexist		coherence	
coequal, -ly			coherense	coherence
coequality			coherent, -ly	
coerce, -erced, -ercing			coheshun	cohesion
coercible			cohesion	
coercibul	coercible		cohesive, -ly	
coercion			cohort	
coercive, -ly			coiffure	
coerse	coerce		coifur	coiffure
coershun	coercion		coil, -ed, -ing	
coersible	coercible		coin, -ed, -ing	
coersive	coercive		coinage	
coeval, -ly			coincide, -cided, -ciding	
coevil	coeval		coincidence	
coevul	coeval		coincident, -ly	
coexist, -ed, -ing			coinidge	coinage
coexistence			coinsidence	coincidence
coexistense	coexistence		coinsident	coincident
coexistent			coir	
cofee	coffee		coishun	coition
cofer	coffer		coition	
cofey	coffee		coitus	
coff	cough		coke, coked, coking	
coffee			coket	coquette
coffer			cokoon	cocoon
coffin			col	
cofin	coffin		cola	
cog			colander	
cogency			colapse	collapse
cogenital	congenital		cold, -er, -est	
cogent, -ly			cole	coal
coger	codger		colender	colander
cogitate, -tated, -tating			coler	choler (anger)
cogitation			colera	cholera
cogitative			coleric	choleric
cognac			colesterol	cholesterol
cognate			coleus	
cognisance			colic	
cognisanse	cognisance		colicky	
cognisant			colitis	
cognishun	cognition		collaborate, -rated, -rating	
cognition			collaboration	
cognitive			collaborator	

collage
collapsable
collapse, -lapsed, -lapsing
collapsible
collar, -ed, -ing (neck)
  collar — choler (anger)
collarbone
collate, -lated, -lating
collateral
collation
collator
colleague
collect, -ed, -ing
collectable
collection
collective, -ly
collectivism
collector
college
collegian
collegiate
  coller — choler (anger)
  coller — collar (neck)
collide, -lided, -liding
collie
collier
colliery, -ries
collinear, -ly
collision
collocate, -cated, -cating
collocation
  collonial — colonial
colloquial, -ally
colloquialism
colloquy, -quies
collusion
collusive, -ly
cologne
colon
  colonade — colonnade

For other **col**- words, look under **coll-**.

colonel
colonial, -ly
colonisation
colonise, -nised, -nising

coloniser
colonnade
colony, -nies
  color — colour
coloratura
  colorful — colourful
colossal, -ly
colossus, -lossuses
colour, -ed, -ing
colour-bar
colour-blindness
colourful, -fully
colt
coltish, -ly
  colum — column
columbine
column

For other **col**- words, look under **coll-**.

columnist
coma (sleep)
  coma — comma (mark)
comatose, -ly
comb, -ed, -ing
combat, -bated, -bating
combatant
combative, -ly
comber
combination
combine, -bined, -bining
combustible
combustibility
  combustibul — combustible
combustion
come, came, come, coming
comeback
comedian
comedienne
comedy, -dies
comeliness
comely, -lier, -liest
  comend — commend
comestible
  comestibul — comestible
comet
comeuppance

comfert — comfort
comfertable — comfortable
comferter — comforter
comfort, -ed, -ing
comfortable, -bly
comforter
comfortless, -ly
comfy
comic
comical, -ly
comicality

> Look under **comm-** if the word is not under **com-**.

comma (mark)
comma — coma (sleep)
command, -ed, -ing
commandant
commander
commandment
commando, -dos, -does
commemorate, -rated, -rating
commemoration
commemorative, -ly
commence, -menced, -mencing
commencement
commend, -ed, -ing
commendable, -bly
commendabul — commendable
commendation
commendatory
commense — commence
commensurable, -bly
commensurabul — commensurable
commensurate
comment, -ed, -ing
commentary, -aries
commentater — commentator
commentator
commentry — commentary
commer — comma
commerce
commercial, -ly
commercialisation
commercialise, -lised, -lising
commercialism
commershal — commercial

commershalise — commercialise
commisar — commissar
commisariat — commissariat
commisary — commissary
commiserate, -rated, -rating
commiseration
commishun — commission
commision — commission
commisionaire — commissionaire
commisioner — commissioner
commissar
commissariat
commissary, -saries
commission
commissionaire
commissioner
commit, -mitted, -mitting
commitment
committal
committee
commitul — committal
commo
commodaty — commodity
commode
commodious, -ly
commodity, -ties
commodius — commodious
commodoor — commodore
commodore
common, -ly
commonality, -ties
commoner
commonplace
Commons
commonsense
commonsensical
Commonwealth
Commonwelth — Commonwealth
commoshun — commotion
commotion
communal, -ly
commune, -muned, -muning
communicable
communicabul — communicable
communicate, -cated, -cating
communication
communicative

communicator
communikay   communique
communion
communique
communism
communist
communistic
community, -ties
commutation
commute, -muted, -muting
commuter

> Look under **comm-** if the
> word is not under **com-**.

compact
compair   compare (liken)
compair   compere (stage)
companion
companionable, -bly
companionship
company, -nies
companyun   companion
comparable, -bly
comparabul   comparable
comparative, -ly
compare, -pared, -paring (liken)
compare   compere (stage)
comparison
compartment
compartmentalise, -ised, -ising
compas   compass
compashun   compassion
compashunate   compassionate
compass, -es
compass, -ed, -ing
compassion
compassionate, -nated, -nating
compatibility
compatible, -bly
compatibul   compatible
compatition   competition
compatriot
compel, -pelled, -pelling
compendium, -diums, -dia
compensate, -sated, -sating
compensation
compensator

compensatory
compensatry   compensatory
compeny   company
compere, -pered, -pering (stage)
compere   compare (liken)
competant   competent
competative   competitive
compete, -peted, -peting
competency
competense   competence
competent, -ly
competishun   competition
competition
competitive, -ly
competitor
compilation
compile, -piled, -piling
compiler
compinsation   compensation
complacency, -cies
complacent, -ly (smug)
complain, -ed, -ing
complainant
complaint
complaisant (obliging)
complanant   complainant
complane   complain
complant   complaint
complasense   complacence
complasent   complacent
complement, -ed, -ing (complete)
complement   compliment
                    (praise)
complementary (completing)
complementary   complimentary
                    (free)
complete, -pleted, -pleting
completion
complex, -ly
complexion
complexity, -ties
compliable
compliabul   compliable
compliance
compliant, -ly
complicate, -cated, -cating
complication

complicity
complient   compliant
compliment, -ed, -ing (praise)
compliment   complement
                    (completely)
complimentary (free)
complimentary   complementary
complissity   complicity
comply, -plied, -plying
compo
component
comport
comportment
compose, -posed, -posing
composedly
composhure   composure
composishun   composition
composite, -ly
composition
compositor
compost
composure
compot   compote
compote
compound, -ed, -ing
compoundable
compoundabul   compoundable
comprehend, -ed, -ing
comprehendingly
comprehenshun   comprehension
comprehensible, -bly
comprehension
comprehensive, -ly
comprehensiveness
compress, -ed, -ing
compressibility
compressible
compressibul   compressible
compression
compressor
comprisal
comprise, -prised, -prising
compromise, -mised, -mising
comptroller
compulsery   compulsory
compulshun   compulsion
compulsion

compulsive, -ly
compulsorily
compulsory
compulsrey   compulsory
compunction
computability
computation
compute, -puted, -puting
computer
computerisation
computer program
computer terminal
comrad   comrade
comrade
comradeship

> Look under **comm-** if the
> word is not under **com-**.

con, conned, conning
conbine   combine
concave, -ly
concavity, -ties
conceal, -ed, -ing
concealable
concealabul   concealable
concealment
concede, -ceded, -ceding
conceit
conceited, -ly
conceivable
conceivably
conceivabul   conceivable
conceive, -ceived, -ceiving
concensus   consensus
concentrate, -trated, -trating
concentration
concentric
concentricity
concepshun   conception
concept
conception
conceptual, -ly
conceptualise, -lised, -lising
concern, -ed, -ing
concert, -ed, -ing
concertina
concertmaster

concerto, -tos, -ti
concession
conch, conchs, conches
   concherto   concerto
   conciet   conceit
   concieted   conceited
   concievable   conceivable
   concieve   conceive
conciliate, -ated, -ating
conciliation
conciliator
conciliatory
concise, -ly

> Look under **cons-** if the
> word is not under **conc-**.

conciseness
conclave
conclude, -cluded, -cluding
   conclushun   conclusion
conclusion
conclusive, -ly
concoct, -ed, -ing
concoction
concomitance
concomitancy
concomitant, -ly
concord
concordance
   concordanse   concordance
concordant
   concorse   concourse
concourse
   concreet   concrete
concrete, -creted, -creting
concretely
concreteness
concubinage
concubine
concupiscence
concupiscent
   concupissense   concupiscence
   concupissent   concupiscent
concur, -curred, -curring
   concurence   concurrence
   concurent   concurrent
concurrence

concurrent, -ly
   concus   concuss
   concushun   concussion
concuss, -ed, -ing
concussion
concussive
   condament   condiment
   condaminium   condominium
   condansation   condensation
   condem   condemn
condemn, -ed, -ing
condemnation
condemnatory
   condence   condense
   condencer   condenser
condensation
condense, -densed, -densing
condenser
   condensor   condenser
condescend, -ed, -ing
condescension
condiment
   condisend   condescend
   condisension   condescension
   condishun   condition
   condishunal   conditional
condition, -ed, -ing
conditional, -ly
condolatory
condole, -doled, -doling
condolence
   condolense   condolence
condolingly
condominium
condonation
condone, -doned, -doning
condor
conducive
   conducshun   conduction
conduct, -ed, -ing
   conducter   conductor
conductible
conductibility
   conductibul   conductible
conduction
conductivity, -ties
conductor

conductress
conduit
  condusive   conducive
cone
  conecshun   connection
  conect   connect
  conective   connective
confection
confectionary, -aries (factory)
confectionery, -eries (sweets)
  confedence   confidence
confederacy, -cies
  confederasy   confederacy
confederate, -rated, -rating
confederation
confer, -ferred, -ferring
conference
  conferm   confirm
confess, -ed, -ing
confesser
confession
confessional
confessor
confetti
confidant (trusted man)
  confidant   confident (sure)
confidante (trusted woman)
confide, -fided, -fiding
confidence
  confidenshul   confidential
confident (sure)
  confident   confidant
                    (trusted man)
confidential, -ly
confidentiality
  configeration   configuration
configuration
confine, -fined, -fining
confinement
confirm, -ed, -ing
confirmable
confirmation
confiscate, -cated, -cating
confiscation
conflagration
conflict, -ed, -ing
confluence

confluent
conform, -ed, -ing
conformable, -bly
  conformabul   conformable
conformist
conformity, -ties
confound, -ed, -ing
  confownd   confound
  confrence   conference
confront, -ed, -ing
confrontation
  confurm   confirm
confuse, -fused, -fusing
confusion
confutation
confute, -futed, -futing
conga (dance)
  conga   conger (eel)
congeal, -ed, -ing
  congeel   congeal
  congeneal   congenial
congenial, -ly
congeniality
congenital, -ly
conger (eel)
  conger   conga (dance)
congest, -ed, -ing
congestion
congestive
conglomerate, -rated, -rating
conglomeration
  congradulation   congratulation
  congragation   congregation
congratulate, -lated, -lating
congratulation
congratulatory
congregate, -gated, -gating
congregation
congregational
congress
congressional
  congrewent   congruent
  congrewus   congruous
congruence
congruent
congruity, -ties
congruous, -ly

conic
conical, -ly
conifer
coniferous
  conjeckture   conjecture
conjecturable, -bly
conjecture, -tured, -turing
  conjenial   congenial
  conjestion   congestion
conjoin, -ed, -ing
conjoint, -ly
  conjuce   conduce
conjugal, -ly
conjugality
conjugate, -gated, -gating
conjugation
  conjugel   conjugal
  conjuice   conduce
  conjuncshun   conjunction
conjunct, -ly
conjunction
conjunctional, -ly
conjunctive, -ly
conjunctivitis
conjuncture
conjuration
conjure, -jured, -juring
conjurer
conjuror
conk, -ed, -ing
conker (nut)
  conker   conquer (win)
  conkwest   conquest
con man, -men
connect, -ed, -ing
connectedly
connecter
connection
connective, -ly
connector
  connesser   connoisseur
  connewbial   connubial
conning tower
connivance
  connivanse   connivance
connive, -nived, -niving
connoisseur

connotation
connote, -noted, -noting
connubial, -ly
  connubiul   connubial
  conosseur   connoisseur
  conote   connote
conquer, -ed, -ing
conquerable
  conquerabul   conquerable
  conquerer   conqueror
conqueror
conquest
conquistador
consanguine
consanguineous, -ly
consanguinity
  consceintious   conscientious
conscience
  conscienshus   conscientious
conscientious, -ly
conscious, -ly
consciousness
  conscripshun   conscription
conscript, -ed, -ing
conscription
  conseal   conceal
  conseat   conceit
consecrate, -crated, -crating
consecration
consecutive
  consede   concede
  consekwence   consequence
consensus
consent, -ed, -ing
consequence
consequent
consequential, -ly
  conservatery   conservatory
conservation
conservational
conservationist
conservative, -ly
conservatism
conservatoire
conservatorium
conservatory, -tries
  conservatry   conservatory

conserve, -served, -serving
conserver
  consession   concession
  consicrate   consecrate
consider, -ed, -ing
considerable, -ably
  considerabul   considerable
considerate, -ly
consideration
consign, -ed, -ing
consignable
  consignabul   consignable
consignee
consigner
  consignible   consignable
consignment
consignor
  consiliate   conciliate
  consine   consign
  consinee   consignee
  consinement   consignment
  consinor   consignor
  consise   concise
consist, -ed, -ing
consistence
consistency, -cies
  consistense   consistence
  consistensy   consistency
consistent, -ly
consolable
  consolabul   consolable
consolation
console, -soled, -soling
consoler
consolingly
consolidate, -dated, -dating
consolidated revenue
consolidation
consolidator
consommé
consonance
consonant, -ly
consort, -ed, -ing
consortium, -tia
conspicuous, -ly
conspicuousness
conspiracy, -cies

  conspirasy   conspiracy
  conspirater   conspirator
conspirator
conspiratory
  conspiratry   conspiratory
conspire, -spired, -spiring
constable
  constabul   constable
constabulary, -ries
constancy
  constansy   constancy
constant, -ly
  constapation   constipation
constellation
consternation
constipate, -pated, -pating
constipation
constituency, -cies
  constituensy   constituency
constituent
constitute, -tuted, -tuting
constitution
constitutional, -ly
constrain, -ed, -ing
constraint
  constrickshun   constriction
constrict, -ed, -ing
constriction
construct, -ed, -ing
construction
constructive, -ly
constructor
construe, -strued, -struing
consul
consular
consulate
  consuler   consular
consult, -ed, -ing
consultant
consultation
consultative
  consultent   consultant
consulter
consumable
  consumabul   consumable
consume, -sumed, -suming
consumer

consumerism
consummate, -mated, -mating
consummation
consummative
  consummé   consommé
  consumpshun   consumption
consumption
consumptive, -ly
contact, -ed, -ing
contact lenses
  contageous   contagious
contagion
contagious, -ly
  contagus   contagious
  contajus   contagious
contain, -ed, -ing
container
containment
contaminate, -nated, -nating
contamination
  contane   contain
  contanement   containment
  contaner   container
contemplate, -plated, -plating
contemplation
contemplative, -ly
contemporaneous, -ly
contemporary, -raries
contempt
  contemptable   contemptible
contemptible, -bly
  contemptibul   contemptible
contemptuous, -ly
contend, -ed, -ing
contender
  contenshun   contention
  contenshus   contentious
content
contented, -ly
contention
contentious, -ly
contentment
contest, -ed, -ing
contestant
  contestent   contestant
context
contextual, -ly

contiguity
contiguous, -ly
continence
  continense   continence
continent
continental
contingency, -cies
  contingensy   contingency
contingent, -ly
  continnuation   continuation
continual, -ly
continuance
  continuanse   continuance
continuation
continue, -ued, -uing
continuity, -ties
continuous, -ly
continuum, -tinuums, -tinua
  contorshun   contortion
contort, -ed, -ing
contortion
contortionist
contour
contraband
contraception
contraceptive, -ly
  contrackshun   contraction
contract, -ed, -ing
contraction
contractor
contractual
  contradickshun   contradiction
contradict, -ed, -ing
contradiction
contradictory, -ries
contralto, -ti
  contrapshun   contraption
contraption
contrarily
contrariness
contrariwise
contrary, -ries
  contrasepshun   contraception
  contraseptive   contraceptive
contrast, -ed, -ing
contravene, -vened, -vening
  contravenshun   contravention

contribushun contribution
contribute, -buted, -buting
contribution
contributor
contributory
contributry contributory
contrishun contrition
contrite, -ly
contrition
contrivance
contrivanse contrivance
contrive, -trived, -triving
control, -trolled, -trolling
controllable
controllabul controllable
controller
controvershal controversial
controversial, -ly
controversy, -sies
contumely, -lies
contuse, -tused, -tusing
contushun contusion
contusion
contusive
conurbation
convalesce, -lesced, -lescing
convalescence
convalescense convalescent
convalescent
convaless convalesce
convalessence convalescence
convection
convective, -ly
convector
convene, -vened, -vening
convenience
conveniense convenience
convenient, -ly
convenor
convenshun convention
convenshunal conventional
convent
convention
conventional, -ly
conventionalism
converge, -verged, -verging
conversant, -ly

conversation
conversational, -ly
conversationalist
converse, -versed, -versing
conversely
conversent conversant
convershun conversion
conversion
convert, -ed, -ing
convertabul convertible
converter
convertible, -ly
convertibul convertible
convex, -ly
convexity, -ties
convey, -ed, -ing
conveyance
conveyancer
conveyancing
conveyanse conveyance
conveyor belt
convickshun conviction
convict, -ed, -ing
conviction
convienence convenience
convince, -vinced, -vincing
convincible
convincibul convincible
convincingly
convivial, -ly
convivialty
convocation
convoke, -voked, -voking
convolushun convolution
convolute, -luted, -luting
convolution
convoy, -ed, -ing
convulse, -vulsed, -vulsing
convulshun convulsion
convulsion
convulsive, -ly
conyac cognac
coo, cooed, cooing
cooee, cooeed, cooeeing
cooger cougar
cook, -ed, -ing
cookery, -eries

cookhouse
cookie, cookies
  cookoo   cuckoo
cool, -ed, -ing
coolabah
  coolabar   coolabah
coolamon
coolant
coolie (labourer)
coolly (calmly)
coop, -ed, -ing
co-op
cooper
cooperage
cooperate, -rated, -rating
cooperation
cooperative, -ly
  coopon   coupon
co-opt, -ed, -ing
coordinate, -nated, -nating
coordination
coordinator
cop, copped, copping (accept)
  coparison   comparison
cope, coped, coping (put up with)
  coper   copper
copha
copier
co-pilot
copious, -ly
cop-out
copper
copperhead
copperplate
  coppy   copy
copra
  cops   copse
copse
cop shop
copula, -lae
copulate, -lated, -lating
copulation
copulative, -ly
copy, copies
copy, copied, copying
copybook
copycat, -catted, -catting

  copyer   copier
copyist
copyright, -ed, -ing (licence)
  copyrite   copyright
copywriter
coquet, -quetted, -quetting
coquetry
coquette
coquettish, -ly
coral (reef)
  coral   choral (sing)
  coral   corral (yard)
coralfish
  corcus   caucus
cord (rope)
  cord   chord (music)
cordage
corded
cordial, -ly
cordiality
  cordige   cordage
cordon, -ed, -ing
cordon bleu
cords (trousers)
corduroy
core, cored, coring (centre)
  core   caw (cry)
  core   corps (group)
  corecshun   correction
  corect   correct
  corection   correction
  corective   corrective
  corelate   correlate
corella
  coreografy   choreography
  corespond   correspond
  corespondence   correspondence
  corespondense   correspondence
co-respondent (divorce)
  corespondent   correspondent
coriander
  coridoor   corridor
  coridor   corridor
Corinthian
  coriografy   choreography
  corispond   correspond
  corispondence   correspondence

corispondent	correspondent	corpse (body)	
corister	chorister	corpse	corps (group)
cork, -ed, -ing		corpulence	
corkage		corpulense	corpulence
corker		corpulent, -ly	
corkscrew, -ed, -ing		corpus, -pora	
corm		corpuscle	
cormorant		corpuscular	
corn		corpusle	corpuscle
corncob		corpussel	corpuscle
cornea, -neas, -neae		corral, -ralled, -ralling (yard)	
corneal		corral	choral (sing)
corned beef		correckshun	correction
corneel	corneal	correct, -ed, -ing	
corner, -ed, -ing		correction	
cornerstone		correctional	
cornet		corrective, -ly	
cornflour		correlate, -lated, -lating	
cornia	cornea	correlation	
cornice, -niced, -nicing		correlative, -ly	
cornstalk		correlativity	
cornucopia		correspond, -ed, -ing	
corny, -nier, -niest		correspondence	
coroborate	corroborate	correspondent	
coroborator	corroborator	corridor	
coroboree	corroboree	Corriedale	
corode	corrode	corroborate, -rated, -rating	
corola	corolla	corroboration	
corolary	corollary	corroborative, -ly	
corolla		corroborator	
corollary, -ries		corroboree	
corona, -nas, -nae		corrode, -roded, -roding	
coronary		corrodible	
coronary thrombosis		corrodibul	corrodible
coronation		corrollary	corollary
coroner		corroshun	corrosion
coronet		corrosion	
coroshun	corrosion	corrosive, -ly	
corosive	corrosive	corrugate, -gated, -gating	
corparation	corporation	corrugated iron	
corperal	corporal	corrugation	
corporal, -ly		corrupshun	corruption
corporate, -ly		corrupt, -ed, -ing	
corporation		corruptabul	corruptible
corporeal, -ly		corruptible, -bly	
corps (group)		corruptibility	
corps	corpse (body)	corruptibul	corruptible

corruption		cost, cost, costed, costing	
corsage		cost	coast
corsair		co-star, -starred, -starring	
corsashun	causation	coster	
corse	coarse (rough)	costguard	coastguard
corse	course (path)	costliness	
corsen	coarsen	costly, -lier, -liest	
corset		costume, -tumed, -tuming	
corsetry		costume jewellery	
corshun	caution	cosy, -sies	
corshus	cautious	cosy, -sier, -siest	
corsit	corset	cot	
cort	caught (held)	cotage	cottage
cort	court (law)	cotchineal	cochineal
cort marshal	court martial	cote (shelter)	
cortage	cortege	cote	coat (garment)
cortege		coterie	
corterise	cauterise	cotige	cottage
cortex, -tices		coton	cotton
cortier	courtier	cotoneaster	
cortion	caution	cotonwool	cottonwool
cortious	cautious	cottage	
cortisan	courtesan	cotter pin	
cortisone		cotton	
cortly	courtly	cottonbush	
cortroom	courtroom	cottonwood	
cortship	courtship	cottonwool	
cortyard	courtyard	cottony	
corugate	corrugate	cou daytar	coup d'état
corupt	corrupt	couch	
coruptible	corruptible	cougar	
coruption	corruption	cough, -ed, -ing	
corus	chorus	could	
corvet	corvette	couldn't (could not)	
corvette		couldnt	couldn't
cos		coulter	
cosh		councel	council (meeting)
cosmetic			
cosmetically		councel	counsel (advice)
cosmografy	cosmography		
cosmography, -phies		council (meeting)	
cosmology		council	counsel (advice)
cosmonaut			
cosmonort	cosmonaut	counciller	councillor
cosmopolitan		councillor (member)	
cosmos		councillor	counsellor (adviser)
Cossack			

counsel, -selled, -selling (advice)
| counsel | council (meeting) |
| counseller | counsellor |

counsellor (adviser)
| counsellor | councillor (member) |

count, -ed, -ing
countdown
countenance, -nanced, -nancing
| countenanse | countenance |

counter
counteract, -ed, -ing
counteraction
counteractive, -ly
counterattack, -ed, -ing
counterbalance, -anced, -ancing
counter culture
counterespionage
| counterfeet | counterfeit |

counterfeit, -ed, -ing
counterfeiter
counterintelligence
countermand, -ed, -ing
counterpane
counterpart
counterpoint
counterproductive
counter-revolution
counter-revolutionary, -aries
countersign, -ed, -ing
countersignature
| countersine | countersign |
| counterwait | counterweight |

counterweight
countess
| countie | county |

countless
country, -tries
countryman, -men
countryside
county, -ties
coup, -coups
| coupay | coupé |

coup de grace
coup d'état
coupé

couple, -led, -ling
couplet
coupon
courage
courageous, -ly
courier
course (path)
| course | coarse (rough) |
| coursen | coarsen |

court, -ed, -ing (law)
| court | caught (held) |

courtesan
courtesy, -sies
courthouse
courtier
courtly, -lier, -liest
| court marshal | court martial |

court martial
courtroom
courtyard
cousin
couture
couturier
covenant
cover, -ed, -ing
coverage
covert, -ly
cover-up
covet, -ed, -ing
covetous, -ly
covey, -eys
coward (scared)
| coward | cowered (cringed) |

cowardice
| cowardiss | cowardice |

cowardly
cowboy
cower, -ed, -ing (cringe)
| cowerd | coward |
| cowered | coward (scared) |

cowl, -ed, -ing
cowlick
cowling

For **cown-** words,
look under **coun-**.

cowslip
cox
coxcomb
   coxe   coax
coxswain
coy, -ly
   coyn   coin
coyote
crab, crabbed, crabbing
crab-apple
crabby, -bier, -biest
crablouse
crack, -ed, -ing
crackdown
cracker
crackle, -led, -ling
crackpot
   crackul   crackle
cradle, -dled, -dling
cradle-snatcher
   cradul   cradle
craft
craftily
craftiness
craftsman, -men
craftsmanship
crafty, -tier, -tiest
crag
cragged
craggy, -gier, -giest
   crain   crane
crake
cram, crammed, cramming
cramp, -ed, -ing
cranberry, -ries
crane, craned, craning
cranial, -ly
cranium, -nia
crank, -ed, -ing
crankcase
crankiness
crankshaft
cranky, -kier, -kiest
cranny, -nies
craps
crapulous
crash, -ed, -ing

crasher
crass
crate, crated, crating
crater
cravat
crave, craved, craving
craven, -ly
craw
crawl, -ed, -ing
crawler
crayfish, -fishes, -fish
crayon, -ed, -ing
   craype   crepe
craypot
   craysh   crèche
craze, crazed, crazing
crazily
craziness
crazy, -zier, -ziest
   creacher   creature
creak, -ed, -ing (squeak)
   creak   creek (stream)
cream, -ed, -ing
creaminess
creamy, -mier, -miest
   creap   creep
crease, creased, creasing
create, -ated, -ating
   creater   creator
creation
creative, -ly
creativeness
creativity
creator
creature
crèche
   creecher   creature
credence
   credense   credence
   credenshul   credential
credential
credibility
credible
credibly
   credibul   credible
credit, -ed, -ing
creditable, -bly

creditabul — creditable
credit card
crediter — creditor
creditor
credo, -dos
credulity
credulous, -ly
credulousness
creed
creek (stream)
creek — creak (squeak)
creel
creem — cream
creep, crept, creeping
creeper
creepiness
creeps
creepy, -pier, -piest
cremate, -mated, -mating
cremation
crematorium
creme
crenellate, -lated, -lating
creole
creosote, -soted, -soting
crepe, creped, creping
crept
crepuscular
crescendo, -dos
crescent
cresh — crèche
creshendo — crescendo
cress
cressent — crescent
crest, -ed, -ing
crestfallen, -ly
cretin
cretinism
cretinous
creture — creature
crevase — crevasse
crevase — crevice
crevasse, -vassed, -vassing
crevice
creviss — crevice
crew, -ed, -ing
crewel (yarn)

crewel — cruel (harsh)
crewl — cruel
crew neck
crews (sailors)
crews — cruise (ship)
crib, cribbed, cribbing
cribage — cribbage
cribbage
cribbidge — cribbage
crick
cricket
cricketer
crier
crime
criminal, -ly
criminality, -ties
criminologist
criminology
crimp, -ed, -ing
crimpy, -pier, -piest
crimson
cringe, cringed, cringing
crinkle, -kled, -kling
crinkul — crinkle
crinkly
crinoline
cripple, -pled, -pling
cript — crypt
criptic — cryptic
criptograf — cryptograph
criptogram — cryptogram
criptograph — cryptograph
cripul — cripple
crisalis — chrysalis
crisalus — chrysalis
criscros — crisscross
crisen — christen
Crisendom — Christendom
crisis, -ses
crisp, -ed, -ing
crispness
crispy
crisscross
Crist — Christ
cristal — crystal
cristaline — crystalline
cristalise — crystallise

Cristian	Christian
Cristianity	Christianity
criteek	critique
criterion, -teria	
critic	
critical, -ly	
criticise, -cised, -cising	
criticism	
critique	
critisise	criticise
croak, -ed, -ing	
croaky	
crochet, -ed, -ing	
crock	
crockadile	crocodile
crockery	
crocodile	
crocus, crocuses	
croft	
crofter	
croissant	
crokay	croquet
cromatic	chromatic
crome	chrome
cromosome	chromosome
crone	
crony, -nies	
crood	crude
crook	
crooked, -ly	
crookedness	
croon, -ed, -ing	
crooner	
crop, cropped, cropping	
crop-dust, -ed, -ing	
crop-duster	
cropper	
croquet (sport)	
croquette (food)	
crosier	
cross, -ed, -ing	
crossbar	
crossbench	
crossbencher	
crossbones	
crossbow	
crossbreed, -bred, -breeding	

crosscheck	
cross-country	
crosscut, -cut, -cutting	
cross-examination	
cross-examine, -ined, -ining	
cross-examiner	
cross-eyed	
cross-fertilisation	
cross-fertilise, -lised, -lising	
crossover	
cross-pollinate, -nated, -nating	
cross-purpose	
cross-reference, -renced, -rencing	
crossroad	
cross-section	
cross-stitch, -ed, -ing	
crosswise	
crossword puzzle	
crotch	
crotchet	
crotchetiness	
crotchety	
crouch, -ed, -ing	
croup	
croupier	
crouton	
crow, crowed, crowing	
crowbar	
crowd, -ed, -ing	
croweater	
crown, -ed, -ing	
crown-of-thorns	
crow's-foot, -feet	
crow's-nest	
crucial, -ly	
crucibel	crucible
crucible	
crucibul	crucible
crucifix	
crucifixion	
cruciform, -ly	
crucify, -fied, -fying	
crude, cruder, crudest	
crudeness	
crudity, -ties	
cruel, cruelled, cruelling	
cruelty, -ties	

cruet
cruise, cruised, cruising (ship)
   cruise   crews (sailors)
cruiser
   crum   crumb
crumb, -ed, -ing
crumble, -bled, -bling
crumbly, -blier, -bliest
   crumbul   crumble
crummy, -mier, -miest
crumpet
crumple, -pled, -pling
   crumpul   crumple
   crumy   crummy
crunch, -ed, -ing
crunchy, -chier, -chiest
crusade, -saded, -sading
crusader
crush, -ed, -ing
   crushal   crucial
crusher
   crusibul   crucible
crust
crustacean
   crustashun   crustacean
crustiness
crusty, crustier, crustiest
crutch, -ed, -ing
crux, cruxes, cruces
   cruze   cruise
cry, cries
cry, cried, crying
crypt
cryptic, -ally
cryptogram
cryptograph
cryptographer
cryptographic
cryptography
   crysalis   chrysalis
crystal
crystalline
crystallisation
crystallise, -lised, -lising
cub
cubby, -bies
cubbyhole

cubbyhouse
cube, cubed, cubing
cubic
cubical, -ly (cube-shaped)
cubicle (room)
cubism
cubist
cubmaster
   cuboard   cupboard
   cuby   cubby
   cubyhole   cubbyhole
   cubyhouse   cubbyhouse
cuckold, -ed, -ing
cuckoldry
cuckoo
cucumber
cud
   cuddel   cuddle
cuddle, -dled, -dling
cuddlesome
cuddly
cuddy, -dies
cudgel, -elled, -elling
cudgerie
   cudly   cuddly
   cudos   kudos
cue, cued, cuing (billiards)
   cue   queue (line)
cuff, -ed, -ing
cuisine
   culcher   culture
cul-de-sac
   culer   colour
culinary
cull, -ed, -ing
culminate, -nated, -nating
culmination
   culots   culottes
culottes
culpability
culpable, -bly
   culpabul   culpable
culprit
cult
cultism
cultist
cultivate, -vated, -vating

cultivater — cultivator
cultivation
cultivator
cultural, -ly
culture, -tured, -turing
cultured pearl
culture shock
culvert
cumbasome — cumbersome
cumbersome, -ly
cumbersum — cumbersome
cumfurt — comfort
cumin
cummerbund
cumpass — compass
cumquat
cumulative, -ly
cumulus
cuning — cunning
cunning, -ly
cuntry — country
cup, cupped, cupping
cupboard
cupbord — cupboard
cupful, cupfuls
cupid
cupidity
cupola
cuppa
cur
curable, -bly
curacao
curacy, -cies
curage — courage
curant — currant (fruit)
curare
curate
curater — curator
curative, -ly
curator
curatorial
curb, -ed, -ing (control)
curb — kerb (gutter)
curcuit — circuit
curd
curdle, -dled, -dling
curdul — curdle

cure, cured, curing
curency — currency
curent — current (flow)
curette, -retted, -retting
curfew
curiculum — curriculum
curio, curios
curiosity, -ties
curious, -ly
curiousness
curius — curious
curl, -ed, -ing
curler
curlew
curly, -lier, -liest
curnel — colonel
currage — courage
curragus — courageous
currajong
currant (fruit)
currant — current (flow)
currawong
currency, -cies
currensy — currency
current (flow)
current — currant (fruit)
current account
currently
curriculum, -lums, -la
curriculum vitae
curry, -ries
curry, -ried, -rying
curse, cursed, cursing
cursive, -ly
cursor
curt, -ly
curtail, -ed, -ing
curtailment
curtain, -ed, -ing
curtale — curtail
curtsy, -sies
curtsy, -sied, -sying
curvaceous
curvachure — curvature
curvashus — curvaceous
curvature
curve, curved, curving

curvilinear
cushion, -ed, -ing
   cushon   cushion
cushy, cushier, cushiest
cusp
cuspid
cuss
cussed, -ly
custard
custard-apple
custodial
custodian
   custodiul   custodial
   custodiun   custodian
custom
customarily
customary, -aries
custom-built
customer
custom-made
cut, cut, cutting
cutback
cute, cuter, cutest
cuteness
   cutical   cuticle
cuticle
   cuticul   cuticle
cutlass
cutlery
cutlet
cut-off
cut-out
cut-price
cutter
cutthroat
cuttlebone
cuttlefish, -fishes, -fish
   cuttulbone   cuttlebone
cutworm
   cuvenant   covenant
   cuver   cover
   cuvet   covet
   cuvey   covey
cyanide
cybernetics
cyclamate
cyclamen

cycle, cycled, cycling
cyclic
cyclist
cycloid
cyclone
cyclonic
cyclostyle, -led, -ling
cyder
cygnet (swan)
   cygnet   signet (ring)
cylinder
cymbal (instrument)
   cymbal   symbol (sign)
cymbalist
cymbidium
cynic
cynical, -ly
cynicism
   cynoshure   cynosure
cynosure
cypher
cypress
cyst
cystitis
cytology
czar
czarina
czarist
Czech
Czechoslovak
Czechoslovakia

Dd

dab, dabbed, dabbing
dabble, -bled, -bling

dabed	dabbed
dabing	dabbing
dable	dabble
dabul	dabble

dachshund

dacks	daks
dacor	decor

dad
daddy-long-legs
daemon
daffodil

daffodill	daffodil

daffy, daffier, daffiest

dafny	daphne
dafodil	daffodil

daft

dager	dagger

dagger
dahlia

dail	dale

daily

daim	dame
daintie	dainty

daintily
dainty, -tier, -tiest

dair	dare

dairy, -ries (milk)

dairy	diary (book)

dais

daisie	daisy

daisy
daks

dalee	dally
dalia	dahlia

dally,-lied, -lying
Dalmatian

daly	daily

dam, dammed, damming (water)

dam	damn (swear)

damage, -aged, -aging
damageable
damask
dame

damedge	damage
damestic	domestic

damn, -ed, -ing (swear)

damn	dam (water)

damnable, -bly

damnabul	damnable

damnation
damp
dampcourse
dampen, -ed, -ing
damper
damsel

damsil	damsel
damsul	damsel

dance, danced, dancing
dancer
dandelion

dandilion	dandelion

dandle, -dled, -dling
dandruff

dane	deign
dangel	dangle

danger
dangerous, -ly

dangerus	dangerous

dangle, -gled, -gling

dangul	dangle
danjer	danger
danjerus	dangerous
daper	dapper
dappel	dapple

dapper, -ly
dapple, -pled, -pling

darby	derby

dare, dared, daring
daredevil

darey	dairy

dark, -ly
darken, -ed, -ing

darkin	darken

darkness

darkroom

  darlin — darling

darling

darn, -ed, -ing

dart, -ed, -ing

  darta — data

  dartabase — database

darter

dash, -ed, -ing

dashboard

  dashbord — dashboard

  dashound — dachshund

dastard, -ly

  dastid — dastard

  dastud — dastard

data

database

date, dated, dating

  dater — data

  datim — datum

datum

daub

  daufin — dauphin

daughter

daunt, -ed, -ing

dauphin

  dauter — daughter

  dawb — daub

dawdle, -dled, -dling

  dawdul — dawdle

dawn, -ed, -ing

  dawnt — daunt

  dawter — daughter

day

  daybrake — daybreak

daybreak

daydream

  daycor — decor

  dayify — deify

  dayis — dais

  dayity — deity

  daylia — dahlia

daylight

  daylite — daylight

  dayly — daily

  dayn — deign

  daysy — daisy

daze, dazed, dazing (stun)

  daze — days (time)

dazzle, -zled, -zling

dazzler

deacon

deactivate, -ated, -ating

dead, -ly

dead centre

deaden, -ed, -ing

dead heart

dead heat

deadline

deadlock

deadly, -lier, -liest

deadpan

dead reckoning

dead weight

deadwood

deaf

deafen, -ed, -ing

  deaft — deft

deal, dealt, dealing

dealer

  deam — deem

dean

deanery

dear, -ly (loved)

  dear — deer (animal)

dearth

death

death adder

deathly

death-wish

> Look under **di-** if the
> word is not under **de-**.

debacle

  debacul — debacle

debar, -barred, -barring

debase, -based, -basing

debasement

debatable, -bly

  debatabul — debatable

debate, -bated, -bating

  debatible — debatable

debauch, -ed, -ing

debauchery, -ries
debbit   debit
debensher   debenture
debenshure   debenture
debenture
debilitate, -tated, -tating
debilitation
debility, -ties
debit, -ed, -ing
debonair
deboo   debut
debree   debris
debrief, -ed, -ing
debris
debt
debter   debtor
debtor
debug, -bugged, -bugging
debunk, -ed, -ing
debut
debutante
decade
decadence
decadense   decadence
decadent, -ly
decamp, -ed, -ing
decant, -ed, -ing
decanter
decapitate, -tated, -tating
decapitation
decathalon   decathlon
decathlon
decay, -ed, -ing
decease, -ceased, -ceasing
deceit
deceitful, -ly
deceive, deceived, deceiving
decelerate, -rated, -rating
December
decency, -cies
decent, -ly
decentralisation
decentralise, -lised, -lising
decepshun   deception
deception
deceptive, -ly
decibel

decibell   decibel
decide, -cided, -ciding
decidedly
deciduous
decieve   deceive
decifer   decipher
decimal
decimate, -mated, -mating
decipher, -ed, -ing
decishun   decision
decision
decisive, -ly
deck, -ed, -ing
deckade   decade
deckchair
deckchare   deckchair
deckerate   decorate
deckhand
deckle
deckul   deckle
declaim, -ed, -ing
declamation
declarable
declarabul   declarable
declaratory
declaratry   declaratory
declare, -clared, -claring
declassify, -fied, -fying
decline, -clined, -clining
decode, -coded, -coding
decompose, -posed, -posing
decomposishun   decomposition
decomposition
decompreshun   decompression
decompress, -ed, -ing
decompression
decongestant
decor
decorate, -rated, -rating
decoration
decorative, -ly
decorous, -ly
decorum
decorus   decorous
decoy, -ed, -ing
decrease, -creased, -creasing
decree, -creed, -creeing

decreese   decrease
decrepit
decrepitude
decrese   decrease
decry, -cried, -crying
ded   dead
deden   deaden

> Look under **di-** if the word
> is not under **de-**.

dedicate, -cated, -cating
dedication
dedly   deadly
deduce, -duced, -ducing
deduct, -ed, -ing
deductible
deductibul   deductible
deduction
deed
deel   deal
deem, -ed, -ing
deen   dean
deep, -ly
deepen, -ed, -ing
deep freeze, -frozen, -freezing
deepwater
deer (animal)
deer   dear (loved)
de-escalate, -lated, -lating
def   deaf
deface, -faced, -facing
defacit   deficit
de facto
defamation
defamatory
defamatry   defamatory
defame, -famed, -faming
default, -ed, -ing
defaulter
defeat, -ed, -ing
defeatism
defeatist
defecate, -cated, -cating
defeckshun   defection
defect, -ed, -ing
defection
defective, -ly

defector
defeet   defeat
defen   deafen
defence
defend, -ed, -ing
defendant
defendent   defendant
defensable   defensible
defensible
defensibul   defensible
defensive, -ly
defer, -ferred, -ferring
deferance   deference
deference
deferense   deference
deferenshul   deferential
deferential, -ly

> For **deff**-words,
> look under **def-**.

defiance
defianse   defiance
defiant, -ly
deficiency, -cies
deficit
defience   defiance
defile, -filed, -filing
definate   definite
define, -fined, -fining
definishun   definition
definit   definite
definite, -ly
definition
definitive, -ly
defishency   deficiency
defishent   deficient
defisit   deficit
deflate, -flated, -flating
deflation
deflationary
defleckshun   deflection
deflect, -ed, -ing
deflection
defnite   definite
defoliant
defoliate, -ated, -ating
defoliation

deform, -ed, -ing
deformity, -ies
defraud, -ed, -ing
defrauder
defray, -ed, -ing
defreeze, -frozen, -freezing
defrord   defraud
defrost, -ed, -ing
deft, -ly
deftness
defunct
defuse, -fused, -fusing
defy, -fied, -fying
defyance   defiance
defyant   defiant

> Look under **di-** if the word is
> not under **de-**.

degeneracy
degenerasy   degeneracy
degenerate, -rated, -rating
degeneration
degradation
degrade, -graded, -grading
degree
degridation   degradation
dehidrate   dehydrate
dehydrate, -drated, -drating
dehydration
deifie   deify
deify, -fied, -fying
deign
deisel   diesel
deitee   deity
deity, -ties
dejeckshun   dejection
dejection
dekay   decay
delay, -ed, -ing
delecate   delicate
delectable, -bly
delectabul   delectable
delegate, -gated, -gating
delegation
delerious   delirious
deleshun   deletion
delete, -leted, -leting

deleterious, -ly
deletion
delfinium   delphinium
deli
deliberate, -rated, -rating
deliberately
deliberation
deliberative, -ly
delicacy, -cies
delicate, -ly
delicatessen
delicious, -ly
delicous   delicious
deligate   delegate
delight, -ed, -ing
delightful, -ly
delineate, -ed, -ing
delineation
deliniate   delineate
delinkwency   delinquency
delinkwent   delinquent
delinquancy   delinquency
delinquency
delinquent
delirious, -ly
delirium
delirius   delirious
delishus   delicious
delite   delight
deliteful   delightful
deliver, -ed, -ing
deliverance
deliverence   deliverance
delivery, -eries
dell
dellie

> For other **dell-** words, look
> under **del-**.

delood   delude
delphinium
delt   dealt
delta
delude, -luded, -luding
deluge, -uged, -uging
deluks   de luxe
delushun   delusion

delusion
delusive, -ly
delusory
delve, delved, delving
demagogue
demagogy
demand, -ed, -ing
demarcate, -cated, -cating
demarcation
demean, -ed, -ing
  demeaner   demeanour
demeanour
  demensha   dementia
demented, -ly
dementia
demerara
demerit
demigod
demilitarised zone
demise
demister
demo
demob
demobilisation
demobilise, -lised, -lising
democracy, -cies
  democrasy   democracy
democrat
democratic, -ally
democratisation
  demografy   demography
demographic, -ally
demography
demolish, -ed, -ing
  demolishun   demolition
demolition
demolitionist
demon
demonic
demonology
demonstrable, -bly
  demonstrabul   demonstrable
demonstrate, -strated, -strating
  demonstrater   demonstrator
demonstration
demonstrator
demoralise, -lised, -lising

demote, -moted, -moting
demur, -murred, -murring (object)
  demur   demure (coy)
demure, -murer, -murest (coy)
  demure   demur (object)
den
  dence   dense
  dencher   denture
  dencity   density
  denem   denim
dengue
  deni   deny
denial
denigrate, -grated, -grating
denigration
denim
denizen

> For **denn-** words, look under
> **den-**.

denominate, -nated, -nating
denomination
denominational, -ly
denominator
denotable
  denotabul   denotable
denote, -noted, -noting
denounce, -nounced, -nouncing
denouncement
  denownse   denounce
dense, denser, densest
densely
  densitee   density
density
dent, -ed, -ing
dental
dentist
dentistry
denture
denude, -nuded, -nuding
denunciate, -ated, -ating
deny, denied, denying
  deoderant   deodorant
  deoderise   deodorise
deodorant
deodorise, -rised, -rising
  deparcher   departure

depart, -ed, -ing
department
departmental, -ly
departure
   depen   deepen
depend, -ed, -ing
dependable, -bly
   dependabul   dependable
dependant (noun)
dependence
dependency, -cies
   dependensy   dependency
dependent, -ly (adjective)
   dependible   dependable
   depickshun   depiction
depict, -ed, -ing
depiction
   depilatery   depilatory
depilatory, -ries
   depilatry   depilatory
   depleshun   depletion
deplete, -pleted, -pleting
depletion
   deploi   deploy
deplorable, -bly
   deplorabul   deplorable
deplore, -plored, -ploring
deploy, -ed, -ing
deployment
   depo   depot
deport, -ed, -ing
deportation
deportee
depose, -posed, -posing
deposit, -ed, -ing
   deposishun   deposition
   depositer   depositor
deposition
depositor
depository, -ries
   depositry   depository
depot

> For **depp-**words, look under **dep-**.

depraved
depravity, -ties

deprecate, -cated, -cating
deprecation
depreciate, -ated, -ating
depreciation
depredation
   depresherise   depressurise
   depreshiate   depreciate
   depreshun   depression
   depresive   depressive
   depresor   depressor
depress, -ed, -ing
depressant
   depressent   depressant
   depresshun   depression
depression
depressive, -ly
depressor
depressurise, -ised, -ising
   depricate   deprecate
deprive, -prived, -priving
depth
deputation
depute, -puted, -puting
   deputey   deputy
deputise, -tised, -tising
deputy, -ties

> Look under **di-** if the word is
> not under **de-**.

derail, -ed, -ing
derailment
   derale   derail
derange, -ranged, -ranging
derby, -bies
deregister, -ed, -ing
   derelickshun   dereliction
derelict
dereliction
   derick   derrick
deride, -rided, -riding
   derigible   dirigible
   derishun   derision
derision
derisive, -ly
derivation
derivative
derive, -rived, -riving

dermatitis
dermatologist
dermatology
derogatery — derogatory
derogatory
derogatry — derogatory
derrick

> For other **derr-** words, look
> under **der-**.

dert — dirt
derth — dearth
derty — dirty
dervish
desalination
desastrous — disastrous
descant
descend, -ed, -ing
descendant (noun)
descendent (adjective)
descent (down)
descent — dissent (differ)
desciple — disciple
describe, -scribed, -scribing
descripshun — description
description
descriptive, -ly
descry, -cried, -crying
desease — disease
deseat — deceit
deseave — deceive
desecrate, -crated, -crating
desecration
desegregate, -gated, -gating
desegregation
desel — diesel
deselerate — decelerate
Desember — December
desency — decency
desend — descend
desensitise, -tised, -tising
desent — decent
desent — descent
desentralise — decentralise
desershun — desertion
desert, deserts
desert, -ed, -ing (leave)

desert — dessert (food)
deserter
desertion
deserve, -served, -serving
desese — disease
desibel — decibel
de-sex, -sexed, -sexing
desicate — desiccate
desication — desiccation
desiccate, -cated, -cating
desiccation
deside — decide
desiduous — deciduous
design, -ed, -ing
designate, -nated, -nating
designation
desimal — decimal
desimate — decimate
desimul — decimal
desine — design
desipher — decipher
desirability
desirable, -bly
desirabul — desirable
desire, -sired, -siring
desirous
desirus — desirous
desist, -ed, -ing
desk
deskant — descant

> Look under **di-** if the word is
> not under **de-**.

desolate, -lated, -lating
desolation
despach — despatch
despair, -ed, -ing
despare — despair
despatch, -ed, -ing
despensable — dispensable
desperado, -does, -dos
desperate, -ly
desperation
despicable, -bly
despicabul — despicable
despise, -spised, -spising
despite

despoil, -ed, -ing
despoliation
despondency
   despondensy   despondency
despondent, -ly
despot
despotic
despotism
   desprate   desperate
dessert (food)
   dessert   desert (leave)
dessertspoon
destination
destine, -tined, -tining
destiny, -nies
   destitushen   destitution
destitute
destitution
destroy, -ed, -ing
destroyer
   destruckshun   destruction
destruct, -ed, -ing
destructible
   destructibul   destructible
destruction
destructive, -ly
desultory
   det   debt
detach, -ed, -ing
detachable
   detachabul   detachable
detail, -ed, -ing
detain, -ed, -ing
detainee
detainment
   detale   detail
   detane   detain
   deteckshun   detection
detect, -ed, -ing
detectable
   detectabul   detectable
detection
detective
detector
   detektive   detective
   detenshun   detention
detention

deter, -terred, -terring
   deter   debtor
   deterent   deterrent
detergent
   deterjent   detergent
deteriorate, -rated, -rating
deterioration
determinant
determination
determine, -mined, -mining
determinism
deterrence
deterrent
detest, -ed, -ing
detestable, -bly
   detestabul   detestable
detestation
   deth   death
detonate, -nated, -nating
detonation
detonator
detour, -ed, -ing
   detrackshun   detraction
detract, -ed, -ing
detraction
detractor
   detramental   detrimental
detriment
detrimental, -ly
   detterent   deterrent
   dettor   debtor
deuce
deutschmark
devaluation
devalue, -valued, -valuing
devastate, -tated, -tating
devastation
   devel   devil
develop, -ed, -ing
   develope   develop
   developement   development
developer
development
developmental, -ly
deviance
deviancy
   devianse   deviance

deviansy — deviancy
deviant, -ly
deviate, -ated, -ating
deviation
device (thing)
  device — devise (plan)
  devide — divide
devil
devilish, -ly
devilment
devilry
devil's advocate
devious, -ly
devise, -vised, -vising (plan)
  devise — device (thing)
  devius — devious
devoid
  devolushun — devolution
devolution
devolutionary
devolve, -volved, -volving
Devonshire tea
  devoshun — devotion
devote, -voted, -voting
devotee
devotion
devour, -ed, -ing
devout, -ly
dew (water)
  dew — due (payable)
dewdrop
  dewey — dewy
dewy, dewier, dewiest
dexterity
dexterous, -ly
  dexterus — dexterous

> Look under **de-** if the word is
> not under **di-**.

  diabeetes — diabetes
diabetes
diabetic
diabolic
diabolical, -ly
diadem
  diafanus — diaphanous
  diafram — diaphragm

diagnose, -nosed, -nosing
diagnosis, -ses
diagnostic
diagnostician
  diagnostishun — diagnostician
diagonal, -ly
diagram
diagrammatic, -ally
dial, dialled, dialling
dialect
dialectic
dialectician
  dialectishun — dialectician
  dialise — dialyse
  dialisis — dialysis
  dialog — dialogue
dialogue
dialyse, -lysed, -lysing
dialysis, -ses
diamante
diameter
diametrical, -ly
diamond
diaper
diaphanous, -ly
  diaphanus — diaphanous
diaphragm
  diarea — diarrhoea
diarist
diarrhoea
diary, -ries (book)
  diary — dairy (milk)
diatonic, -ally
diatribe
  dibase — debase
  dibate — debate
dibs
dice, diced, dicing
dicey
dichotomy, -mies
  dicipul — disciple
dick
dickens
dicky
  dicotomy — dichotomy
  dicshun — diction
  dicshunry — dictionary

dictate, -tated, -tating
dictation
dictator
dictatorial, -ly
   dictatoriul   dictatorial
   dictayshun   dictation
diction
dictionary, -aries
dictum, -ta, -tums
did
didactic, -ally
   diddel   diddle
diddle, -dled, -dling
diddler
   didel   diddle
didgeridoo
   didgit   digit
   didgitalis   digitalis
didn't (did not)
   didnt   didn't
   didul   diddle
die (singular of dice)
die, dies (tool)
die, died, dying (death)
   die   dye (colour)
dieback
die-casting
diehard
   dieing   dying (death)
   dieing   dyeing (colour)
   diernal   diurnal
diesel
diet, dieted, dieting
dietary
dietician
   dietishen   dietician

> For **dif-** words, look under
> **diff-**.

differ, -ed, -ing
difference
   differense   difference
   differenshul   differential
different, -ly
differential, -ly
differentiate, -ated, -ating
differentiation

difficult
difficulty, -ties
diffidence
diffident, -ly
diffuse, -fused, -fusing
   diffushun   diffusion
diffusion
   diflect   deflect
dig, dug, digging
   diger   digger
digest, -ed, -ing
digestible
   digestibul   digestible
digestion
digger
diggings
digit
digital
digital computer
digitalis
dignify, -fied, -fying
dignitary, -taries
   dignitry   dignitary
dignity, -ties
digress, -ed, -ing
   digresshun   digression
digression
digs
dike
   dil   dill
dilapidated
dilapidation
dilate, -lated, -lating
dilation
dilatory
   dilatry   dilatory
   dilema   dilemma
dilemma
   dilatent   dilettante
dilettante, -ti
   dilibag   dillybag
   dilidali   dilly dally
diligence
   diligense   diligence
diligent, -ly
dill
dillybag

dilly dally
dilushen   dilution
dilution
diluvial
diluvian

> Look under **de-** if the word is
> not under **di-**.

dim, dimmed, dimming
dim, dimmer, dimmest
dime
dimenshun   dimension
dimension
dimensional,-ly
dimer   dimmer
diminish, -ed, -ing
diminishing returns
diminushen   diminution
diminution
diminutive, -ly
dimmer
dimple, -pled, -pling
dimpul   dimple
dim sim
dimwit
dimwitted, -ly
dinamic   dynamic
dinamite   dynamite
dinamo   dynamo
dinasty   dynasty
dine, dined, dining (eat)
dine   dyne (unit)
diner (eating)
diner   dinner (food)
ding
dingbats
ding-dong
dinghy, -ghies (boat)
dingie   dinghy
dingo, -goes, -gos
dingy, -gier, -giest (dull)
dingy   dinghy (boat)
dink, -ed, -ing
dinkum
dinky, dinkier, dinkiest
dinky-di
dinner (food)

dinner   diner (eating)
dinosaur
dinosoar   dinosaur
dinosore   dinosaur
dint, -ed, -ing
diocese
diode
diokside   dioxide
dioxide
dip, dipped, dipping
diper   diaper
diper   dipper
diphtheria
diphthong
diploma
diplomacy, -cies
diplomasy   diplomacy
diplomat
diplomatic, -ally
dipper
dipsomania
dipsomaniac
diptych
dire, direr, direst
direckshun   direction
direct, -ed, -ing
direct current
directer   director
direct evidence
direction
directional
direction-finder
directive
directly
director
directory, -ries
directry   directory
direct tax
dirge
dirigible
dirigibul   dirigible
dirk
dirt
dirtily
dirty, dirtied, dirtying
dirty, dirtier, dirtiest
disable, -bled, -bling

disabul | disable
disabuse, -bused, -busing
disadvantage, -taged, -taging
disadvantageous, -ly
disadvantige | disadvantage
disadvantij | disadvantage
disafect | disaffect
disaffect, -ed, -ing
disaffection
disagree, -greed, -greeing
disagreeable, -bly
disagreeableness
disagreeabul | disagreeable
disagreement
disallow,-ed, -ing
disalow | disallow
disapear | disappear
disapoint | disappoint
disappear, -ed, -ing
disappearance
disappearanse | disappearance
disappoint, -ed, -ing
disappointment
disapproval
disapprove, -proved, -proving
disaprove | disapprove
disaray | disarray
disarray
disasociate | disassociate
disassociate, -ated, -ating
disassociation
disaster
disastrous, -ly
disastrus | disastrous
disatisfy | dissatisfy
disavow, -ed, -ing
disavowal
disband, -ed, -ing
disbandment
disbeleif | disbelief
disbeleive | disbelieve
disbelief
disbelieve, -lieved, -lieving
disc
discard, -ed, -ing
disc brake
discern, -ed, -ing

discernible, -bly
discernibul | discernible
discernment
discharge, -charged, -charging
disciple
disciplinarian
disciplinary
discipline, -plined, -plining
discipul | disciple
disc jockey
disclaim, -ed, -ing
disclaimer
disclaym | disclaim
disclose, -closed, -closing
disclosure
disco
discolor | discolour
discolour, -ed, -ing
discolouration
discomfert | discomfort
discomfit, -ed, -ing (thwart)
discomfit | discomfort
discomfort, -ed, -ing (pain)

> Look under **de-** if the word is
> not under **di-**.

discompose, -posed, -posing
discomposhur | discomposure
discomposure
disconcert, -ed, -ing
disconneckshun | disconnection
disconnection
disconsert | disconcert
disconsolate, -ly
discontent
discontinue, -tinued, -tinuing
discontinuity
discontinuous, -ly
discord
discordance
discordanse | discordance
discordant, -ly
discotheque
discount, -ed, -ing
discourage, -raged, -raging
discouragement
discourse, -coursed, -coursing

discourteous, -ly
discourtesy
discourtius   discourteous
discover, -ed, -ing
discoverer
discovery, -eries
discownt   discount
discredit, -ed, -ing
discreditable, -bly
discreditabul   discreditable
discreet (prudent)
discreet   discrete (apart)
discrepancy
discrepansy   discrepancy
discreshun   discretion
discreshunry   discretionary
discrete (apart)
discretion
discretionary
discribe   describe
discriminate, -nated, -nating
discrimination
discriminator
discriminatory
discriminatry   discriminatory
discripshun   description
discriptive   descriptive
discuridge   discourage
discursive, -ly
discurtious   discourteous
discus (sport)
discushun   discussion
discuss, -ed, -ing (talk)
discussion
disdain, -ed, -ing
disdainful, -ly
dise   dice
disease
diseased
diseave   deceive
diseckshun   dissection
disect   dissect
disembark, -ed, -ing
disembarkation
disemble   disembowel
disembodied
disembowel, -elled, -elling

diseminate   disseminate
disenchant, -ed, -ing
disenchantment
disenshun   dissension
disentangle, -gled, -gling
disentanglement
disentry   dysentery
disern   discern
disernibul   discernible
disertation   dissertation
diservise   disservice
disesed   diseased
disfaver   disfavour
disfavour, -ed, -ing
disfiger   disfigure
disfigure, -ed, -ing
disfranchise, -chised, -chising
disfranchisement
disgise   disguise
disgorge, -gorged, -gorging
disgrace, -graced, -gracing
disgraceful, -ly
disgracefull   disgraceful
disgruntled
disguise, -guised, -guising
disgust, -ed, -ing
disgustedly
dish, -ed, -ing
disharmoney   disharmony
disharmony
disharten   dishearten
dishcloth
dishearten, -ed, -ing
dishevelled
dishonest, -ly
dishonesty
dishonor   dishonour
dishonour, -ed, -ing
dishonourabel   dishonourable
dishonourable, -bly
dishonourabul   dishonourable
disidence   dissidence
disident   dissident
disign   design
disillusion, -ed, -ing
disillusionment
disilushun   disillusion

disimilar — dissimilar
disimulate — dissimulate
disinclination
disincline, -clined, -clining
disinfect, -ed, -ing
disinfectant
disinfectent — disinfectant
disinherit, -ed, -ing
disinheritance
disintegrate, -grated, -grating
disintegration
disinter, -terred, -terring
disinterment
disinterested, -ly
disintigrate — disintegrate
disipate — dissipate
disipation — dissipation
disiple — disciple
disiplinary — disciplinary
disipline — discipline
disjoint, -ed, -ing
disk
diskwalify — disqualify
diskwiet — disquiet
diskwolify — disqualify
dislexia — dyslexia
dislike, -liked, -liking
dislocate, -cated, -cating
dislocation
dislodge, -lodged, -lodging
disloge — dislodge
disloyal, -ly
disloyalty, -ties
dismal, -ly
dismantel — dismantle
dismantle, -tled, -tling
dismantul — dismantle
dismay, -ed, -ing
dismember, -ed, -ing
dismemberment
dismisal — dismissal
dismiss, -ed, -ing
dismissal
dismount, -ed, -ing
dismownt — dismount
disobay — disobey
disobedience

disobediense — disobedience
disobedient, -ly
disobey, -ed, -ing
disoblige, -bliged, -bliging
disoloot — dissolute
disoluble — dissoluble
disolute — dissolute
disolution — dissolution
disolve — dissolve
disonance — dissonance
disonanse — dissonance
disonant — dissonant
disone — disown
disoner — dishonour
disonerable — dishonourable
disonest — dishonest

Look under **de-** if the word is
not under **di-**.

disorder
disorderliness
disorderly
disorganisation
disorganise, -nised, -nising
disorientate, -tated, -tating
disown, -ed, -ing
dispair — despair
disparage, -raged, -raging
disparagement
disparagingly
disparate, -ly
disparidge — disparage
disparige — disparage
disparity, -ties
dispashonate — dispassionate
dispashunate — dispassionate
dispassionate, -ly
dispatch, -ed, -ing
dispel, -pelled, -pelling
dispencable — dispensable
dispencary — dispensary
dispence — dispense
dispensable
dispensabul — dispensable
dispensary, -saries
dispensry — dispensary
dispensation

dispenser
   dispepsia   dyspepsia
dispersal
disperse, -persed, -persing
   dispershun   dispersion
dispersion
   dispicable   despicable
dispirit, -ed, -ing
   dispite   despite
displace, -placed, -placing
displaceable
   displaceabul   displaceable
displacement
   displacment   displacement
   displase   displace
display, -ed, -ing
displease, -pleased, -pleasing
displeasure
   displese   displease
   displeshur   displeasure
   displesure   displeasure
disport, -ed, -ing
disposable
disposable income
   disposabul   disposable
dispose, -posed, -posing
   disposeshun   dispossession
   disposess   dispossess
   disposishun   disposition
disposition
dispossess, -ed, -ing
dispossession
disprin
   disproporshun   disproportion
disproportion
disproportionate, -ly
disprove, -proved, -proving
   dispursal   dispersal
   dispurse   disperse
   dispurshun   dispersion
disputable, -bly
   disputabul   disputable
disputation
disputatious
dispute, -puted, -puting
disqualification
disqualify, -fied, -fying

disquiet, -ed, -ing
disquietude
   disquite   disquiet
disregard, -ed, -ing
   disreguard   disregard
disrepair
   disrepare   disrepair
disreputable, -bly
   disreputible   disreputable
disrespect
disrespectful, -ly
   disrespectfull   disrespectful
   disrigard   disregard
   disrispect   disrespect
disrobe, -robed, -robing
   disrupshun   disruption
disrupt, -ed, -ing
disruption
disruptive, -ly
   dissapate   dissipate
   dissapear   disappear
   dissapoint   disappoint
   dissaprove   disapprove
dissatisfaction
dissatisfy, -fied, -fying
   disscord   discord
dissect, -ed, -ing
dissemble, -bled, -bling
disseminate, -nated, -nating
dissemination
   dissenshun   dissension
dissension
dissent, -ed, -ing
dissenter
dissertation
   disservicabul   disserviceable
disservice
disserviceable
dissidence
   dissidense   dissidence
dissident, -ly
dissimilar, -ly
dissimilarity
dissimulate, -lated, -lating
dissimulation
dissipate, -pated, -pating
dissipation

dissociate, -ated, -ating	
dissociation	
disoloot	dissolute
dissoluble	
dissolubul	dissoluble
dissolushun	dissolution
dissolute, -ly	
dissolution	
dissolvable	
dissolvabul	dissolvable
dissolve, -solved, -solving	
dissonance	
dissonanse	dissonance
dissonant, -ly	
disstil	distil
dissuade, -suaded, -suading	
distaff	
distance, distanced, distancing	
distanse	distance
distant, -ly	
distaste	
distasteful, -ly	
distastefull	distasteful
distemper, -ed, -ing	
distend, -ed, -ing	
distenshun	distention
distent	distant
distention	
disterb	disturb
disterbance	disturbance
distil, -tilled, -tilling	
distillate	
distillation	
distillery, -eries	
distillry	distillery
distincshun	distinction
distinct, -ly	
distinction	
distinctive, -ly	
distinguish, -ed, -ing	
distinguishable, -bly	
distingwish	distinguish
distink	distinct
distorshun	distortion
distort, -ed, -ing	
distortion	
distrackshun	distraction

distract, -ed, -ing	
distraction	
distraught, -ly	
distrawt	distraught
distress, -ed, -ing	
distressful, -ly	
distressfull	distressful
distressingly	
distress signal	
distribushun	distribution
distribution	
distributive, -ly	
distributor	
district	
distrust, -ed, -ing	
disturb, -ed, -ing	
disturbance	
disturbanse	disturbance
disunion	
disunite, -nited, -niting	
disunity, -ties	
disurn	discern
disurnible	discernible
disuse, -used, -using	
diswade	dissuade
diswashun	dissuasion
diswasive	dissuasive
ditch, -ed, -ing	
ditch, -ditches	
dither	
dithering	
dithery	
dito	ditto
ditto	
ditty, -ties	
dity	ditty
divan	
dive, dived, diving	
dive-bomb	
diver	
diverge, -verged, -verging	
divergence	
divergense	divergence
divergent, -ly	
diverse, -ly	
divershun	diversion
diversification	

diversify, -fied, -fying

> Look under **de-** if the word is
> not under **di-**.

diversion
diversionary
  diversionry   diversionary
diversity, -ties
divert, -ed, -ing
divest, -ed, -ing
divestible
divide, -vided, -viding
dividend
divider
divination
divinatory
divine, -vined, -vining
divinely
diviner
  divinitey   divinity
divinity, -ties
  diviser   divisor
  divishun   division
divisible, -bly
  divisibul   divisible
  divisif   divisive
division
divisional, -ly
divisive, -ly
divisor
divorce, -vorced, -vorcing
divorcee
  divorse   divorce
  divorsee   divorcee
divulge, -vulged, -vulging
divulgence
  divulgense   divulgence
divvy, -vies
divvy, -vied, -vying
dixie
  dizier   dizzier
  diziest   dizziest
  dizmal   dismal
  dizolve   dissolve
  dizy   dizzy
dizzily
dizziness

dizzy, dizzied, dizzying
dizzy, dizzier, dizziest
do, did, done, doing
  do   doe (animal)
dob, dobbed, dobbing
dobbin
docile, -ly
docility
dock, -ed, -ing
docker
docket
  dockit   docket
dockyard
  docter   doctor
doctor, -ed, -ing
doctoral
doctorate
  doctrin   doctrine
  doctrinair   doctrinaire
doctrinaire
doctrinal, -ly
doctrine
  doctrinul   doctrinal
  doctrut   doctorate
document, -ed, -ing
documentary, -ries
documentation
  documentry   documentary
dodder, -ed, -ing
doddery
doddle
  doder   dodder
dodge, dodged, dodging
dodgem
dodger
dodgy, dodgier, dodgiest
  dodje   dodge
  dodjy   dodgy
dodo, -does, -dos
doe (animal)
  doe   dough (bread)
doer
does
doesn't (does not)
  doesnt   doesn't
  dof   doff
doff, -ed, -ing

doffin	dauphin
dog, dogged, dogging	
dogbox	
dogerul	doggerel
dogfight	
dogfish	
dogfite	dogfight
doggerel	
doggo	
doghouse	
dogleg	
doglegged	
dogma, -mas, -mata	
dogmatic	
dogmatical, -ly	
dogmatism	
dogmatist	
dog paddle	
dog paddul	dog paddle
dog watch	
doilie	doily
doily, -lies	
doings	
dol	dole (pay)
dol	doll (toy)
dolar	dollar
Dolby system	
doldrums	
dole, doled, doling (pay)	
dole	doll (toy)
doler	dollar
dolerus	dolorous
dolfin	dolphin
doll, -ed, -ing (toy)	
doll	dole (pay)
dollar	
doller	dollar
dollop	
dolly, dollies	
dolomite	
dolorous, -ly	
dolorus	dolorous
dolour	
dolphin	
dolt	
doltish, -ly	
domain	

domane	domain
dome	
domed	
domestic, -ally	
domesticate, -cated, -cating	
domestication	
domesticity	
domestisity	domesticity
domicile, -ciled, -ciling	
domiciliary	
dominance	
dominanse	dominance
dominant, -ly	
dominate, -nated, -nating	
dominater	dominator
domination	
dominative	
dominator	
dominear	domineer
domineer, -ed, -ing	
dominent	dominant
dominion	
domino, -noes	
domino theory	
dominyun	dominion
domisile	domicile
domminate	dominate
don, donned, donning	
donate, -nated, -nating	
donater	donator
donation	
donator	
done	
doner	donor
dong, -ed, -ing	
donkey, -keys	
donkey vote	
donkey's years	
donky	donkey
donnybrook	
donor	
don't (do not)	
dont	don't
donut	
dooch	douche
doodad	
doodah	

doodle, -dled, -dling
  doodul — doodle
doom, -ed, -ing
doomsday
door
  door — dour
doorjamb
doorknock, -ed, -ing
  doornock — doorknock
  doosh — douche
dope, doped, doping
dopey, dopier, dopiest
  dophin — dauphin
  dore — door
dormancy
  dormansy — dormancy
dormant
  dormitery — dormitory
  dormitry — dormitory
  dorn — dawn
dorsal
  dorsul — dorsal
  dorter — daughter
dory, -ries
dosage
dose, dosed, dosing
  dosier — dossier
  dosige — dosage
  dosije — dosage
  dosile — docile
  dosility — docility
doss, -ed, -ing
dossier
dot, dotted, dotting
dotage
dote, doted, doting
  dotidge — dotage
  dotije — dotage
dotterel
dottle
dotty, dottier, dottiest
  doubel — double
double, -led, -ling
double agent
double-barrelled
double bass
double-breasted

doublecross, -ed, -ing
double-dealing
double dissolution
double-dutch
double exposure
double-jointed
double standard
doublet
doublethink
double time
doubloon
doubt, -ed, -ing
doubtful, -ly
  doubtfull — doubtful
doubtingly
doubtless, -ly
douche, douched, douching
  douel — dowel
dough
doughnut
doughty, -tier, -tiest
dour, -ly
dourness
douse, doused, dousing
  dout — doubt
  doutful — doubtful
  doutless — doubtless
  douty — doughty
dove
dover
dovetail
  dovetale — dovetail
  dow — dhow (boat)
  dow — doe (animal)
  dow — dough (bread)
dowager
  dowdie — dowdy
dowdily
dowdiness
dowdy, -dier, -diest
  dowery — dowry
  dowey — doughy
down, -ed, -ing
down-and-out
downcast
  downey — downy
downfall

downfallen
downgrade, -graded, -grading
downhearted, -ly
downhill
down payment
downpipe
  downpore   downpour
downpour
downright, -ly
  downrite   downright
downstairs
downstream
down-to-earth
downtown
downtrodden
down-under
downward, -ly
downwards
  downwerds   downwards
downwind
downy, downier, downiest
  dowrie   dowry
dowry, -ries
dowse, dowsed, dowsing
  dowt   doubt
  dowtey   doughty
  dowtful   doubtful
  dowtless   doubtless
doxology, -gies
doyen
doze, dozed, dozing (sleep)
  doze   does
dozen, dozen, dozens
dozily
doziness
drab, drabber, drabbest
  draconean   draconian
draconian
draft, -ed, -ing (plan)
  draft   draught (air)
draft dodger
  draftey   draughty
  draftiness   draughtiness
  drafts   draughts
draftsman, -men
  drafty   draughty
drag, dragged, dragging

dragnet
dragonfly, -flies
dragoon, -ed, -ing
drag race
dragster
drain, -ed, -ing
drainage
  drainige   drainage
drainpipe
drake
dram
drama
dramatic, -ally
dramatics
dramatisation
dramatise, -tised, -tising
dramatist
drank
drape, draped, draping
draper
drapery, -eries
drastic, -ally
draught (air)
  draught   draft (plan)
draughtboard
draughthorse
draughts
draughtsman, -men
draughty, -tier, -tiest
draw, drew, drawn, drawing
drawback
drawbridge
  drawbrije   drawbridge
drawcard
drawer
drawing-pin
drawl, -ed, -ing
drawn
dray
dread, -ed, -ing
dreadful, -ly
  dreadfull   dreadful
  dreadnort   dreadnought
dreadnought
dream, dreamed, dreamt, dreaming
dreamer
dreamily

dreamless, -ly
dreamy, dreamier, dreamiest
drearily
dreariness
dreary, drearier, dreariest
dred   dread
dredful   dreadful
dredger
drednort   dreadnought
dreem   dream
drege   dredge
dregs
dreje   dredge
dremt   dreamt
drench, -ed, -ing
drerie   dreary
drery   dreary
dres   dress
dresie   dressy
dresige   dressage
dresmaker   dressmaker
dress, -ed, -ing
dressage
dress circle
dress down
dresser
dressmaker
dressmaking
dressy
drew
dri   dry
dribble, -bled, -bling
dribbler
dribbul   dribble
dribs and drabs
dribul   dribble
dried
drier
driest
drift, -ed, -ing
drifter
driftwood
drill, -ed, -ing
drily
drink, drunk, drinking
drinkable
drinkabul   drinkable

drink-driving
drive-in
drivel, -elled, -elling
driver
driveway
drizzle, -zled, -zling
drizzly
drizzul   drizzle
droll
drollery, -eries
drolly
dromedary, -daries
drone, droned, droning
drongo, -gos
drool, -ed, -ing
droop, -ed, -ing
droopy, -ier, -iest
drop, dropped, dropping
droplet
drop-out
dropper
dropsey   dropsy
dropsy
dross
drought
drousy   drowsy
drout   drought
drove, droved, droving
drover
drown, -ed, -ing
drowse, drowsed, drowsing
drowsey   drowsy
drowsily
drowsy, drowsier, drowsiest
drowt   drought
drub, drubbed, drubbing
drudge, drudged, drudging
drudgery, -eries
drug, drugged, drugging
druge   drudge
drugery   drudgery
drugstore
drum, drummed, drumming
drummer
drumstick
drunk
drunkard

drunken, -ly
drunkenness
dry, dried, drying
dry, drier, driest
dry cell
dry-clean
dryer
dryly
dryness
dual, -ly (two)
   dual   duel (fight)
dualism
duality
dub, dubbed, dubbing
   dubel   double
dubious, -ly
   dubius   dubious
   duble   double
   dubly   doubly
ducal, -ly
   duce   deuce
duck, -ed, -ing
duckbill
duckling
   ducktile   ductile
duco
duct
ductile
dud
dudgeon
due (owing)
   due   dew (water)
   duedrop   dewdrop
duel, -ed, -ing (fight)
   duel   dual (two)
   duelist   duellist
duellist
duet
duettist
   dufel   duffle
duffer
duffle
   dufful   duffle
dugong
dugout
duke
   dul   dull

dulcet
   duler   duller
   dulie   duly
dull
dullard
dullness
dully
   dulset   dulcet
duly
   dum   dumb
dumb, -ly
dumbbell
   dumbell   dumbbell
dumbfound, -ed, -ing
dumbness
   dumfound   dumbfound
dummy, -mies
dummy, -mied, -mying
   dumness   dumbness
dump, -ed, -ing
dumper
dumpling
   dumy   dummy
dun, dunned, dunning (demand)
   dun   done
dunce
dunderhead
dune
dung
dungaree
   dungen   dungeon
dungeon
   dunjun   dungeon
dunk, -ed, -ing
dunny
   dunse   dunce
duodenal
duodenum
dupe, duped, duping
   duplacate   duplicate
   duplecks   duplex
duplex
duplicate, -cated, -cating
duplication
duplicity, -ties
   duplisity   duplicity
durable, -bly

durability
  durabul   durable
duration
duress
  durge   dirge
  durible   durable
during
  durt   dirt
  durtie   dirty
  durty   dirty
dusk
duskiness
dusky, duskier, duskiest
dust, -ed, -ing
dustbin
duster
dustman, -men
dustpan
dust-up
dusty, dustier, dustiest
Dutch courage
  Dutch curije   Dutch courage
duteous, -ly
dutiable
  dutiabul   dutiable
  dutifree   duty-free
dutiful, -ly
duty, -ties
duty-free
  duv   dove
duvet
  duvtail   dovetail
  duvtale   dovetail
dux
  duzen   dozen
dwarf, dwarfs, dwarves
dwarf, -ed, -ing
dwarfish, -ly
dwell, dwelt, dwelled, dwelling
dwindle, -dled, -dling
  dworf   dwarf
  dworves   dwarfs
dye, dyed, dyeing (colour)
  dye   die (dead)
  dyed   died (dead)
  dyehard   diehard
  dyeing   dying (death)

dyer
dyke, dyked, dyking
dynamic, -ally
dynamics
dynamism
dynamite, -mited, -miting
dynamo, -mos
dynasty, -ties
dyne (unit)
  dyne   dine (eat)
dysentery
  dysentry   dysentery
dysfunction
dyslectic
dyslexia
dyslexic
dyspepsia
dyspeptic
dystrophy

Ee

each
eagel — eagle
eager
eagle
eaglehawk
eaglet
eal — eel
ear
earache
eardrum
earfone — earphone
earie — eerie (weird)
earie — eyrie (nest)
earing — earring
early, -lier, -liest
earmark, -ed, -ing
earmuf — earmuff
earmuff
earn, -ed, -ing
earner
earnest, -ly
earnestness
earnings
earphone
earring
earshot
earth, -ed, -ing
earthbound
earthen
earthenware
earthiness
earthling
earthly, -lier, -liest
earthquake
earthworm
earthy, earthier, earthiest
earwig
ease, eased, easing

easel
easement
easily
east
easten — eastern
East End
Easter
easterly
eastern
eastward, -ly
eastwards
easiness
easy, easier, easiest
eat, ate, eaten, eating
eatable
eatabul — eatable
eater
eau-de-Cologne
eaves
eavesdrop, -dropped, -dropping
eavesdropper
ebb, -ed, -ing
ebbony — ebony
ebonie — ebony
ebony, -onies
ebuliense — ebullience
ebulient — ebullient
ebullience
ebullient, -ly
eccentric, -ally
eccentricity, -ties
ecclesiastic
ecclesiastical, -ly
ecentric — eccentric
ech — each
echelon
echidna
echo, echoes
echo, echoed, echoing
eclair
eclare — eclair
eclectic, -ally
eclesiastic — ecclesiastic
eclipse, eclipsed, eclipsing
ecliptical, -ly
ecologey — ecology
ecological, -ly

ecologist
ecology
economic
economical, -ly
economics
economise, -mised, -mising
economist
economy, -mies
ecosphere
ecosystem

ecsema	eczema
ecsentric	eccentric

ecstasy, -sies
ecstatic, -ally
ecumenical, -ly
ecumenism
eczema
edam

edem	edam

eddy, eddies
eddy, eddied, eddying
edelweiss
edge, edged, edging
edger
edgeways

edgey	edgy

edginess
edgy, -ier, -iest
edible
edibility

edibul	edible

edict

edie	eddy

edify, -fied, -fying
edit, -ed, -ing

editer	editor

edition (book)

edition	addition (add)

editor
editorial, -ly
educable

educabul	educable

educate, -cated, -cating
education
educational, -ly
educationalist
educative

educator
Edwardian

edy	eddy
eeger	eager
eegle	eagle

eel

eenin	oenin
eer	ear

eerie, eerier, eeriest (weird)

eerie	eyrie (nest)

eerily
eeriness

eermark	earmark

> For **ef-** words,
> look under **eff-**.

efface, -faced, -facing
effect, -ed, -ing
effective, -ly
effectual, -ly
effeminacy

effeminasy	effeminacy

effeminate, -ly
effervesce, -vesced, -vescing
effervescence
effervescent, -ly

effervesent	effervescent
effervess	effervesce
effervessence	effervescence

efficacious, -ly
efficacy, -cies

efficayshus	efficacious

efficiency, -cies

efficiensy	efficiency

efficient, -ly
effigy, -gies
effloresce, -resced, -rescing
efflorescence
efflorescent
effluent
effluvium, -via, -viums
effort
effortless, -ly
effrontery, -teries

effrontrey	effrontery
effushun	effusion

effusion

effusive, -ly
   efigy   effigy
   eg   egg
egalitarian
egalitarianism
egg, -ed, -ing
eggcup
egghead
eggplant
eggshell
eggwhite
   eggwite   eggwhite
   Egipshun   Egyptian
   Egipt   Egypt
   egis   aegis
ego, egos
egocentric
egocentricity
egoism
egoist
egoistical, -ly
   egosentric   egocentric
egotism
egotist
egotistical, -ly
egress
egret

For **egs-** words,
look under **ex-**.

Egypt
Egyptian
eiderdown
eight
eighteen
eighth
eightieth
eighty, eighties
eisteddfod
either
ejaculate, -lated, -lating
ejaculation
   ejeckshun   ejection
eject, -ed, -ing
ejection
ejector
eke, eked, eking

   eklipse   eclipse
   eko   echo

For **eks-** words,
look under **ex-**.

   ekumenical   ecumenical

For **ekw-** words,
look under **eq-**.

elaborate, -rated, -rating
elaborately
elaboration
elan
eland
elapse, elapsed, elapsing
elastic, -ally
elasticity
   elastisitey   elasticity
elate, elated, elating
elbow, -ed, -ing
elbowroom
elder, -ly
elderberry, -ries
eldest
   elecshun   election
elect, -ed, -ing
election
electioneer, -ed, -ing
elective
elector
electoral, -ly
electorate
electric
electrical, -ly
electrician
electricity
electrification
   electrishun   electrician
   electrisity   electricity
electrocardiogram
electrocardiograph
   electrocushun   electrocution
electrocute, -cuted, -cuting
electrode
electrolysis
electromagnet
electromagnetic

electromotive
electron
electronic
electronic data processing
electronics
electroplate, -plated, -plating
electrostatic
elegance

eleganse	elegance

elegant, -ly

elegey	elegy

elegy, -gies
element
elemental, -ly
elementary

elementery	elementary
elementul	elemental

elephant
elephantine

elevan	eleven

elevate, -vated, -vating

elevater	elevator

elevation
elevator
eleven
eleventh
elf, elves
elfin
elfish

elfs	elves

elicit, -ed, -ing (draw)

elicit	illicit (wrong)
elifant	elephant
eliganse	elegance
eligant	elegant

eligible, -bly
eligibility

eligibul	eligible
elikser	elixir
eliment	element
elimentry	elementary

eliminate, -nated, -nating
eliminator

elipse	ellipse
elipsis	ellipsis
elishun	elision

elision

elite
elitism
elitist

elivate	elevate

elixir
Elizabethan
elk
ellipse
ellipsis, -ses
elliptical, -ly

ellite	elite

elm

elocushun	elocution

elocution
elocutionist

elokwence	eloquence

elongate, -gated, -gating
elongation
elope, eloped, eloping
elopement
eloper

eloquant	eloquent

eloquence

eloquense	eloquence

eloquent, -ly
else

elsewere	elsewhere

elsewhere

elswhere	elsewhere

elucidate, -dated, -dating
elucidation
elucidatory
elude, eluded, eluding (evade)

elude	allude (say)
elusidate	elucidate

elusive, -ly
elves
emaciate, -ated, -ating
emaciation
emanate, -nated, -nating
emanation
emancipate, -pated, -pating
emancipation
emancipator
emancipist

emanent	eminent
emansipate	emancipate

emasculate, -lated, -lating
emasculation
  emasiate   emaciate
embalm, -ed, -ing
embankment
  embarass   embarrass
embargo, -goes
embargo, -goed, -going
embark, -ed, -ing
embarkation
embarrass, -ed, -ing
embarrassment
embassy, -sies
embed, -bedded, -bedding
embellish, -ed, -ing
embellishment
ember
  embezel   embezzle
embezzle, -zled, -zling
embezzlement
embitter, -ed, -ing
emblazon, -ed, -ing
emblem
emblematic, -ally
  embodie   embody
embodiment
embody, -bodied, -bodying
embolism
  embos   emboss
emboss, -ed, -ing
embrace, -braced, -bracing
embraceable
  embrase   embrace
  embrio   embryo
embroider, -ed, -ing
embroidery, -deries
embroil, -ed, -ing
embryo, -os
embryonic
emend, -ed, -ing
emerald
  emerey   emery
emerge, emerged, emerging
emergence
emergency
  emergense   emergence
  emergensy   emergency

emergent
  emerie   emery
emeritus
emery
emetic
  emfasema   emphysema
  emfasise   emphasise
  emfatic   emphatic
emigrant
emigrate, -grated, -grating
eminence (high)
  eminense   eminence
eminent, -ly (known)
  eminent   imminent
               (near)
  emisary   emissary
  emishun   emission
emissary, -saries
emission
emit, emitted, emitting
emitter
emollient
emolument
  emoshun   emotion
emotion
emotional, -ly
emotionalism
emotionless, -ly
emotive, -ly
empanel, -elled, -elling
empathy
  emperer   emperor
emperor
emphasis, -ses
emphasise, -sised, -sising
emphatic, -ally
emphysema
empire
empirical, -ly
empiricism
empiricist
  empirisism   empiricism
employ,-ed, -ing
employable
  employabul   employable
employee
employer

employment

emporium, -poriums, -poria

empower, -ed, -ing

empress

emptie   empty

emptiness

empty, -tied, -tying

empty, -tier, -tiest

emrald   emerald

emu

emulate, -lated, -lating

emulation

emulshun   emulsion

emulsion

enable, -bled, -bling

enabul   enable

enact, -ed, -ing

enactment

enamel, -elled, -elling

enameller

enamer   enamour

enamour, -ed, -ing

encapsulate, -lated, -lating

encephalitis

encephalogram

enchant, -ed, -ing

enchantment

enciclical   encyclical

enciclopedia   encyclopaedia

encircle, -cled, -cling

encirclement

encircul   encircle

enclave

enclose, -closed, -closing

encloshur   enclosure

enclosure

encode, -coded, -coding

encompass, -ed, -ing

encore, -cored, -coring

encounter

encownter   encounter

encourage, -raged, -raging

encouragement

encroach, -ed, -ing

encumber, -ed, -ing

encumbrance

encumbranse   encumbrance

encyclical

encyclopaedia

encyclopaedic

end, -ed, -ing

endanger, -ed, -ing

endear, -ed, -ing

endearment

endeavour, -ed, -ing

endeer   endear

endemic, -ally

endever   endeavour

endive

endless, -ly

endorse, -dorsed, -dorsing

endorsement

endow, -ed, -ing

endowment

endurable, -bly

endurance

enduranse   endurance

endure, -dured, -during

endurible   endurable

endways

enema

enemy, -mies

energetic, -ally

energy, -gies

enervate, -vated, -vating

enervative

enfeeble, -bled, -bling

enfeebul   enfeeble

enfold, -ed, -ing

enforce, -forced, -forcing

enforceable

enforceabul   enforceable

enforcement

enforcer

enforse   enforce

enforsibul   enforceable

enfranchise, -chised, -chising

engage, -gaged, -gaging

engagement

engajment   engagement

engender, -ed, -ing

engine

enginear   engineer

engineer, -ed, -ing

English
engrave, -graved, -graving
engraver
engross, -ed, -ing
engulf, -ed, -ing
enhance, -hanced, -hancing
enhancement
   enhanse   enhance
enigma
enigmatic, -ally
   enima   enema
   enimy   enemy
   enithing   anything
   eniwhere   anywhere
   enjender   engender
   enjin   engine
   enjineer   engineer
   enjoi   enjoy
   enjoiabul   enjoyable
   enjoiment   enjoyment
enjoin, -ed, -ing
enjoy, -ed, -ing
enjoyable, -bly
   enjoyabul   enjoyable
enjoyment
enlarge, -larged, -larging
enlargement
enlarger
enlighten, -ed, -ing
enlightenment
enlist, -ed, -ing
enlistment
   enliten   enlighten
enliven, -ed, -ing
en masse
enmity, -ties
ennoble, -bled, -bling
enoblement
ennui
   enobul   ennoble
enormity, -ties
enormous, -ly
   enormus   enormous
enough
enquire, -quired, -quiring
enquirer
enquiry, -ries

enrage, -raged, -raging
   enrap   enwrap
   enrapcher   enrapture
enrich, -ed, -ing
enrichment
enrol, -rolled, -rolling
enrolment
en route
ensconce, -ed, -ing
   ensconse   ensconce
ensemble
   ensembul   ensemble
   ensercul   encircle
   enshure   ensure
ensign
   ensine   ensign
ensue, -sued, -suing
en suite
ensure, -sured, -suring
   ensweet   en suite
entail, -ed, -ing
   entale   entail
entangle, -gled, -gling
entanglement
   entangul   entangle
entente
enter, -ed, -ing
enteritis
enterprise
enterprising, -ly
entertain, -ed, -ing
entertainer
entertainment
   entertane   entertain
enthral, -led, -ling
enthuse, -thused, -thusing
enthusiasm
enthusiast
enthusiastic, -ally
entice, -ticed, -ticing
entire, -ly
entirety
   entise   entice
   entitel   entitle
   entitey   entity
entitle, -tled, -tling
entitlement

entity, -ties
entourage
  entouraje   entourage
entrails
entrance
  entranse   entrance
entrant
  entre   entree
entreat, -ed, -ing
entreaty, -treaties
entree
  entreet   entreat
  entreprener   entrepreneur
entrepreneur
entrepreneurial
entrust, -ed, -ing
entry, -tries
  enuff   enough
enumerable
  enumerabul   enumerable
enumerate, -rated, -rating
enumeration
enunciate, -ated, -ating
enunciation
  enunsiate   enunciate
enuresis
envelop, -ed, -ing (wrap up)
envelope (letter)
enviable, -bly
  enviabul   enviable
  envie   envy
envious, -ly
  envirament   environment
environment
environmental, -ly
environmentalism
environmentalist
environs
envisage, -aged, -aging
  envisidge   envisage
  envius   envious
  envoi   envoy
envoy
envy, -vies
envy, envied, envying
enwrap, enwrapped, enwrapping
  enzime   enzyme

enzyme
epaulet
  epawlet   epaulet
ephemeral, -ly
epic
epical, -ly
  epicenter   epicentre
epicentre
epicure
epicurean
epidemic
epidemical, -ly
epidermal
epidermis
  epigraf   epigraph
epigram
epigrammatic, -ally
epigraph
epilepsy
epileptic
  epilog   epilogue
epilogue
episcopacy, -cies
episcopal
Episcopalian
episode
episodic, -ally
  epissel   epistle
epitaph
  epitarf   epitaph
epithet
epitome
epitomise, -mised, -mising
epoch
epochal
  epok   epoch
  eppigram   epigram
equable, -bly
equal, equalled, equalling
equalise, -lised, -lising
equality, -ties
equanimity, -ties
equate, equated, equating
  equater   equator
equation
equator
equatorial

equestrian		erl	earl
equidistant, -ly		erly	early
equilateral		ermine	
equilibrium		ern	earn (money)
equine		ern	urn (vessel)
equinocks	equinox	ernest	earnest
equinoctial		erode, eroded, eroding	
equinox		erogenous	
equip, equipped, equipping		eroneous	erroneous
equipment		eror	error
equitable, -bly		Eros	
equitabul	equitable	eroshun	erosion
equity, -ties		erosion	
equivalence		erotic, -ally	
equivalense	equivalence	erotica	
equivocal, -ly		eroticism	
equivocate, -cated, -cating		erotisism	eroticism
equivocation		err, -ed, -ing	
era		errand	
eradicable, -bly		erratic, -ally	
eradicate, -cated, -cating		erratum, -ta	
eradication		erroneous, -ly	
erand	errand	erronius	erroneous
erant	errant	error	
erase, erased, erasing		errupt	erupt
eraser		ersatz	
erasion		erstwhile	
erata	errata	erth	earth
eratic	erratic	erthen	earthen
erayshure	erasure	erthly	earthly
erban	urban	erudishun	erudition
erbane	urbane	erudition	
erbanise	urbanise	erupt, -ed, -ing	
erbanity	urbanity	eruption	
erchun	urchin	erwig	earwig
erecshun	erection	esay	essay
erect, -ed, -ing		escalate, -lated, -lating	
erection		escalater	escalator
erer	error	escalation	
erge	urge	escalator	
ergent	urgent	escapade	
ergonomics		escape, -caped, -caping	
erie	eerie (weird)	escapee	
erie	eyrie (nest)	escaper	
erk (rank)		escapement	
erk	irk (bore)	escapism	
erksome	irksome	escapist	

escarpment
eschew, -ed, -ing
  eschue   eschew
escort, -ed, -ing
escutcheon
  escutshun   escutcheon
  esel   easel
  esence   essence
  esenshul   essential
Eskimo, -mos
  eskwire   esquire
esky
  esophagus   oesophagus
esoteric, -ally
especial, -ly
  espeshul   especial
espionage
esplanade
  esplanaid   esplanade
espousal
espouse, -poused, -pousing
  espowse   espouse
espresso
esprit
espy, -pied, -pying
esquire
essay, -ed, -ing (try)
  essay   assay (analyse)
essayist
essence
  essense   essence
  essenshul   essential
essential, -ly
establish, -ed, -ing
establishment
estate
esteem, -ed, -ing
  Ester   Easter
  estern   eastern
estimable, -bly
  estimabul   estimable
estimate, -mated, -mating
estimation
estimator
estrange, estranged, estranging
  estrogen   oestrogen
estuary, -aries

et cetera
etch, -ed, -ing
etcher
eternal, -ly
eternity, -ties
ether
  ether   either
ethereal, -ly
ethic
ethical, -ly
ethics
ethnic, -ally
ethnology
ethos
  etiket   etiquette
  etimology   etymology
  etiquet   etiquette
etymology, -gies
eucalyptus, -tuses, -ti
euchre, -chred, -chring
Euclid

> For **euf-** words, look under
> **euph-**.

eugenics
  Euklid   Euclid
eulogise, -gised, -gising
eulogy, -gies
eunuch
euphemism
euphemistic, -ally
euphony, -nies
euphoria
euphoric
  Eurapean   European
  Eurashun   Eurasian
Eurasian
eureka flag
eurhythmics
  eurithmics   eurhythmics
European
euthanasia
evacuate, -uated, -uating
evacuation
evacuee
evade, evaded, evading
evaluate, -ated, -ating

evaluation

evangalist   evangelist

evangelical, -ly

envangelicul   evangelical

evangelism

evangelist

evaperate   evaporate

evaporate, -rated, -rating

evaporation

evasion

evasive, -ly

eve

evedence   evidence

even, -ed, -ing

evenly

evenness

event

eventual, -ly

eventuality, -ties

eventuate, -ated, -ating

ever

evergreen

everlasting, -ly

every

everybody

everyday

everyone

everything

everywhere

eves   eaves

evict, -ed, -ing

eviction

evictor

evictshun   eviction

evidence, -denced, -dencing

evident, -ly

evil, -ly

evince, evinced, evincing

evinse   evince

eviscerate, -rated, -rating

evocative

evoke, evoked, evoking

evolushun   evolution

evolution

evolve, evolved, evolving

evolvement

evry   every

ewe (sheep)

ewe   yew (tree)

exacerbate, -bated, -bating

exacerbation

exackly   exactly

exact, -ed, -ing

exactitude

exactly

exactness

exagerate   exaggerate

exaggerate, -rated, -rating

exaggeration

exalt, -ed, -ing

exaltation

examination

examine, -ined, -ining

examiner

example

exampul   example

exaserbate   exacerbate

exasperate, -rated, -rating

exasperation

excavate, -vated, -vating

excavation

excavator

exceed, -ed, -ing (surpass)

exceed   accede (agree)

exceedingly

excel, -celled, -celling

excell   excel

excellence

excellency, -cies

excellense   excellence

excellent, -ly

excepshun   exception

except, -ed, -ing

exception

exceptional, -ly

excerpt

excess

excessive, -ly

exchange, -changed, -changing

exchangeable

exchequer

excise, -cised, -cising

excishun   excision

excision

excitable, -bly
  excitabul   excitable
excite, -cited, -citing
excitement
exclaim, -ed, -ing
exclamation
exclamatory
  exclamatry   exclamatory
exclude, -luded, -luding
  exclushun   exclusion
exclusion
exclusive, -ly
excommunicate, -cated, -cating
excommunication
excrement
excrescence
  excreshun   excretion
  excressense   excrescence
excreta
excrete, -creted, -creting
excretion
excretory
excruciating, -ly
excursion
excusable, -bly
excuse, -cused, -cusing
execrable, -bly
execrate, -crated, -crating
  execushun   execution
execute, -cuted, -cuting
execution
executioner
executive
executor
exemplary
exemplify, -fied, -fying
  exempshun   exemption
exempt
exemptible
  exemptibul   exemptible
exemption
exercise, -cised, -cising
  exershun   exertion
exert, -ed, -ing
exertion
ex gratia
exhalation

exhale, -haled, -haling
exhaust, -ed, -ing
exhaustion
exhaustive, -ly
  exhibishun   exhibition
exhibit, -ed, -ing
exhibition
exhibitionism
exhibitionist
exhibitor
exhilarate, -rated, -rating
exhilaration
exhort, -ed, -ing
exhortation
exhume, -humed, -huming
exhumation
  exibit   exhibit
exigency, -cies
  exigensy   exigency
exile, -iled, -iling
exist, -ed, -ing
existence
  existense   existence
  existenshul   existential
existent
existential, -ly
existentialism
existentialist
exit
exodus
exonerate, -rated, -rating
exorbitant, -ly
exorcise, -cised, -cising
exorcism
exorcist
  exorsism   exorcism
  exorst   exhaust
  exort   exhort
  exortashun   exhortation
exoteric, -ally
exotic, -ally
expand, -ed, -ing
expanse
  expanshun   expansion
expansion
expansive, -ly
expansiveness

expatiate, -ated, -ating
expatriate, -ated, -ating
expatriation
expect, -ed, -ing
expectancy, -cies
expectant, -ly
expectation
expectorant
expectorate, -rated, -rating
expediency
   expediensy   expediency
expedient, -ly
   expedishun   expedition
expedite, -dited, -diting
expedition
expeditionary
expeditious, -ly
expeditiousness
expel, -pelled, -pelling
expend, -ed, -ing
expendable
   expendicher   expenditure
expenditure
expense
expensive, -ly
experience, -enced, -encing
experiment, -ed, -ing
experimental, -ly
experimentation
expert, -ly
expertise
expiate, -ated, -ating
expiation
expiration
expire, -pired, -piring
expiry, -ries
explain, -ed, -ing
explanation
explanatory
   explane   explain
   explanetry   explanatory
expletive
explicable, -bly
   explicabul   explicable
explicate, -cated, -cating
explicit, -ly
   explisit   explicit

explode, -ploded, -ploding
exploit, -ed, -ing
exploitation
exploration
exploratory
explore, -plored, -ploring
explorer
explosion
explosive, -ly
exponent
exponential, -ly
export, -ed, -ing
exporter
   exposay   exposé
expose, -posed, -posing
exposé
   exposhur   exposure
expostulate, -lated, -lating
exposure
expound, -ed, -ing
   expreshun   expression
   expresive   expressive
express, -ly
express, -ed, -ing
expression
expressionism
expressionist
expressive, -ly
   expresso   espresso
expressway
expropriate, -ated, -ating
expropriation
expulsion
expunction
expunge, -punged, -punging
expurgate, -gated, -gating
expurgation
exquisite, -ly
exquisiteness
   exseed   exceed
   exsel   excel
   exselence   excellence
   exserpt   excerpt
ex-serviceman, -men
extant
   extasy   ecstasy
   extatic   ecstatic

extemporaneous, -ly
extempore
extend, -ed, -ing
extendible
  extendibul   extendible
  extenshun   extension
extension
extensive, -ly
extent
extenuate, -ated, -ating
extenuation
  exterier   exterior
exterior
exterminate, -nated, -nating
extermination
exterminator
external, -ly
extinct
extinction
  extingshun   extinction
extinguish, -ed, -ing
extinguisher
extol, -tolled, -tolling
  extorshun   extortion
extort, -ed, -ing
extortion
extortionate, -ly
extortioner
extortionist
extra
  extracshun   extraction
extract, -ed, -ing
extractable
extraction
extracurricular
  extradishun   extradition
extradite, -dited, -diting
extradition
extramarital
extraneous, -ly
extraordinary
extrapolate, -ated, -ating
extrapolation
extrasensory
extraterrestrial
extravagance
extravagancy

extravagant, -ly
extravaganza
  extravert   extrovert
  extremast   extremist
extreme, -tremer, -tremest
extremely
extremism
extremist
extremity, -ties
extricate, -cated, -cating
extrication
extrovert
extrude, -truded, -truding
extrusion
exuberance
  exuberanse   exuberance
exuberant, -ly
exude, -uded, -uding
exult, -ed, -ing
exultant, -ly
exultation
  exume   exhume
eye, eyed, eyeing
eyeball
eyebrow
eyelash
eyelet
eyelid
eyesight
eyesore
eyetooth, -teeth
eyewash
eyewitness, -nesses
eyrie (nest)
  eyrie   eerie (weird)
  eze   ease
  ezel   easel
  ezy   easy

Ff

fable, -bled, -bling
fabric
fabricate, -cated -cating
fabrication
fabulous, -ly
fabulus   fabulous
facade
face, faced, facing
faceless
facelift
faceshus   facetious
facet, -eted, -eting
facetious, -ly
facia (panel)
facia   fascia (band)
facial, -ly
facile, -ly
facilitate, -tated, -tating
facility, -ties
facist   fascist
facsimile, -led, -leing
fact
faction
factionalism
factor
factory, -ries
factotum
factual, -ly
faculty, -ties
fad
faddish, -ly
fade, faded, fading
faeces
fag, fagged, fagging
faggot
fagot   faggot
Fahrenheit
fail, -ed, -ing

fail-safe
failure
   failyer   failure
   faim   fame
   faimus   famous
fain (gladly)
   fain   feign (pretend)
faint, -ed, -ing (weak)
   faint   feint (pretend)
fair, -ly (honest)
   fair   fare (price)
fair game
fairway
fair-weather
   fairwell   farewell
fairy, -ries
fairytale
   fait   fate
   faitful   fateful
fait accompli
faith
faithful, -ly
faith-healing
fake, faked, faking
faker (fraud)
fakir (holy)
   falacy   fallacy
   falanx   phalanx
   falasius   fallacious
   falasy   fallacy
falcon
falconry
   fale   fail
   falesy   fallacy
   falible   fallible
   falic   phallic
fall, fell, fallen, falling
fallacious, -ly
fallacy, -cies
fallible, -bly
   fallibul   fallible
fallout
fallow
   fallus   phallus
   falow   fallow
false, falser, falsest
falsehood

falsetto, -tos
falsification
falsify, -fied, -fying
falt   fault
falter, -ed, -ing
falteringly
falure   failure
falus   phallus
fame, famed, faming
familial
familiar, -ly
familiarisation
familiarise, -rised, -rising
familiarity, -ties
familier   familiar
family, -lies
famine
famished
famous, -ly
famus   famous
fan, fanned, fanning
fanatic
fanatical, -ly
fanaticism
fancier
fanciful, -ly
fancy, -cies
fancy, -cied, -cying
fancy, -cier, -ciest
fane   fain (glad)
fane   feign (pretend)
fanfair   fanfare
fanfare
fang
fanlight
fansie   fancy
fansiful   fanciful
fansy   fancy
fantam   phantom
fantasey   fantasy
fantasia
fantasise, -sised, -sising
fantastic, -ally
fantasy, -ies
fantom   phantom
far, farther, farthest
far, further, furthest

faranyx   pharynx
faraway
farce
fare, fared, faring (get on)
fare   fair (honest)
farenhite   Fahrenheit
farewell
far-fetched
farm, -ed, -ing
farmacist   pharmacist
farmacy   pharmacy
farmasist   pharmacist
farmer
farmstead
farrago, -goes
farrier
farrow, -ed, -ing
far-sighted
farther (away)
farther   father (parent)
farthing
faryngitis   pharyngitis
farytale   fairytale
fascia, fasciae (band)
fascia   facia (panel)
fascinate, -nated, -nating
fascination
fascism
fascist
fase   face
fase   phase
fasen   fasten
faset   facet
fasetious   facetious
fasha   facia (panel)
fasha   fascia (band)
fashal   facial
fashion, -ed, -ing
fashionable, -bly
fashism   fascism
fashist   fascist
fashon   fashion
fashonabul   fashionable
fasilitate   facilitate
fasility   facility
fasinate   fascinate
fasination   fascination

fast, -ed, -ing
fasten, -ed, -ing
fastener
fastidious, -ly
fastidiousness
   fastidius   fastidious
fat, fatted, fatting
fat, fatter, fattest
fatal, -ly
fatalism
fatalist
fatalistic, -ally
fatality, -ties
fate (destiny)
   fate   fete (fair)
fated
fateful, -ly
   faten   fatten
father, -ed, -ing (parent)
   father   farther (away)
Father Christmas
fatherhood
father-in-law, fathers-in-law
fatherland
fatherly
fathom, -ed, -ing
fathomable
fatigue, -tigued, -tiguing
fatten, -ed, -ing
fattener
fatty, -tier, -tiest
fatuous, -ly
faucet
fault, -ed, -ing
faultless, -ly
faulty, faultier, faultiest
faun (god)
   faun   fawn (deer)
fauna
faux pas
   faver   favour
   faverite   favourite
   faveritism   favouritism
   favorite   favourite
favour, -ed, -ing
favourable, -bly
favourite

favouritism
fawn, -ed, -ing (deer)
   fawn   faun (god)
   fawna   fauna
   faysha   facia (panel)
   faysha   fascia (band)
   fayshal   facial
faze, fazed, fazing
   feacher   feature
fealty, -ties
fear, -ed, -ing
fearful, -ly
   fearfull   fearful
fearless, -ly
fearsome, -ly
feasible, -bly
feasibility
   feasibul   feasible
feast, -ed, -ing
feat (act)
   feat   feet (body)
feather, -ed, -ing
featherbed, -bedded, -bedding
featherweight
feathery
feature, -tured, -turing
febrile
February
   Febuary   February
   feces   faeces
   fech   fetch
feckless, -ly
fecund
fecundity
   fedaration   federation
federal, -ly
federalism
federalist
federate, -rated, -rating
federation
fee
feeble, -bler, -blest
   feebul   feeble
feebleness
feebly
feed, fed, feeding
feedback

feeder
feel, felt, feeling
feeld   field
feeler
feend   fiend
feest   feast
feet (body)
feet   feat (act)
feetul   foetal
feetus   foetus
feign, -ed, -ing (pretend)
feign   fain (glad)
feild   field
feind   fiend
feint, -ed, -ing (pretend)
feint   faint (weak)
fekund   fecund
fekundity   fecundity
felicitate, -tated, -tating
felicitation
felicitous, -ly
felicity, -ties
feline, -ly
felisitous   felicitous
felisity   felicity
fell
fellow
fellowship
felon
felonious, -ly
felony, -nies
felow   fellow
felt
female
feminine, -ly
femininity
feminism
femme fatale
femur
fence, fenced, fencing
fend, -ed, -ing
fender
fenix   phoenix
fennel
fenomenon   phenomenon
fenominal   phenomenal
fense   fence

fer   fir (tree)
fer   fur (pelt)
feral
feret   ferret
ferie   ferry
ferl   furl
ferlong   furlong
ferment, -ed, -ing
fermentation
fern
fernery, -ries
ferny
fernice   furnace
fernish   furnish
ferniture   furniture
ferocious, -ly
ferocity
feroshus   ferocious
ferret, -ed, -ing
ferrous
ferrule , -ruled, -ruling (tip)
ferrule   ferule (rod)
ferry, -ries
ferry, -ried, -rying
ferryboat
ferther   further
ferthest   furthest
fertile, -ly
fertilisation
fertilise, -lised, -lising
fertiliser
fertility
ferule, -ruled, -ruling (rod)
ferule   ferrule (tip)
fervency
fervent, -ly
ferver   fervour
fervid, -ly
fervour
fery   ferry
fesant   pheasant
fesible   feasible
festal, -ly
fester, -ed, -ing
festival
festive, -ly
festivity, -ties

festoon, -ed, -ing

  feta   fetta (cheese)

fetch, -ed, -ing

fete, feted, feting (fair)

  fete   fate (destiny)

  feter   fetter (chain)

  fether   feather

fetid, -ly

fetish

fetishism

fetlock

fetta (cheese)

fetter, -ed, -ing (chain)

fettle

fettler

feud, -ed, -ing

feudal, -ly

feudalism

fever

fevered

feverish, -ly

few

  fewd   feud

  fewdal   feudal

fey, -ly

fez, fezzes

  fezant   pheasant

  fial   file (papers)

  fial   phial (tube)

fiance (man)

fiancee (woman)

  fiansey   fiancee

fiasco, -cos

fib, fibbed, fibbing

fibber

  fiber   fibber

  fiber   fibre

fibre

fibreglass

fibro

fibrositis

fibrous, -ly

  fibrus   fibrous

fibula

fickle, -kly

fickleness

  ficshun   fiction

fiction

fictional, -ly

  fictishus   fictitious

fictitious, -ly

fiddle, -dled, -dling

fiddler

fiddlesticks

fiddly

fidelity, -ties

fidget, -ed, -ing

fidgety

  fidle   fiddle

field, -ed, -ing

fielder

fieldsman, -men

fiend

fiendish, -ly

fierce, fiercer, fiercest

fiercely

fierceness

  fierey   fiery

  fierse   fierce

fiery, fierier, fieriest

fiesta

fife

fifteen

fifteenth

fifth

fiftieth

fifty

fifty-fifty

fig

  figer   figure

  figerative   figurative

  figet   fidget

fight, fought, fighting

fighter

figment

figuration

figurative, -ly

figure, -ured, -uring

figurehead

figurine

Fiji

Fijian

  fiksation   fixation

  fiksative   fixative

fikscher   fixture

> For other fila- words,
> look under **phila-**.

filch, -ed, -ing
filcher
file, filed, filing (paper)
file   phial (tube)
filet   fillet
filial, -ly
filibuster
filie   filly
filigree
filip   fillip
Filipino
Filippines   Philippines
filistine   philistine
fill, -ed, -ing
filler
fillet
fillip
filly, -lies
film, -ed, -ing
filmy, filmier, filmiest

> For filo- words,
> look under **philo-**.

filter, -ed, -ing
filth
filthily
filthiness
filthy, filthier, filthiest
filtrate, -trated, -trating
filtration
fily   filly
fin, finned, finning
final, -ly (end)
finale (last part)
finalisation
finalise, -lised, -lising
finalist
finality, -ties
finance, -nanced, -nancing
financial, -ly
financier
finanse   finance
finch, -ches

find, found, finding
finder
fine, fined, fining
fine, finer, finest
finely
fineness
finery, -ries
finesse, -nessed, -nessing
finetuner
finger
fingernail
fingerprint
fingertip
finical, -ly
finicky
finis (conclusion)
finish, -ed, -ing
finisher
finite, -ly
fiord
fir (tree)
fir   fur (pelt)
fire, fired, firing
firearm
firebreak
fire-escape
fire-extinguisher
firefly, -flies
fireman, -men
fireplace
fireproof
firescreen
fireworks
firm,-ed, -ing
firmament
first, -ly
first-hand
first-past-the-post
fiscal, -ly
fish, fishes, fish
fisherman, -men
fishery, -ries
fish-eye lens
fishmonger
fish-net
fishplate
fishun   fission

fishy, fishier, fishiest
  fisile   fissile
  fision   fission

> For other **fisi-** words,
> look under **physi-**.

  fiskle   fiscal
fissile
fission
fissure, -sured, -suring
fist
fisticuff
fistula, -las, -lae
fit, fitted, fitting
fit, fitter, fittest
  fite   fight
fitful, -ly
  fitfull   fitful
fitness
fitter
five
fiver
fix, fixed, fixing
fixated
fixation
fixative
  fixcher   fixture
fixity, -ties
fixture
fizz, -ed, -ing
fizzer
fizzle, -zled, -zling
  fizzul   fizzle
fizzy, -zier, -ziest
fjord
flabbergast, -ed, -ing
flabbily
flabbiness
flabby, -bier, -biest
  flabergast   flabbergast
  flaby   flabby
flaccid, -ly
flaccidity
flag, flagged, flagging
flagellate, -lated, -lating
flagon
flagrant, -ly

flagship
flagstone
flail, -ed, -ing
flair (talent)
  flair   flare (blaze)
flak
flake, flaked, flaking
flakily
flaky, flakier, flakiest
flamboyance
flamboyancy
flamboyant, -ly
flame, flamed, flaming
flamenco, -cos
flamethrower
flame-tree
flamingo, -gos, -goes
flammable
  flammabul   flammable
flan
  flanel   flannel
flange, flanged, flanging
  flanje   flange
flank, -ed, -ing
flannel, -elled, -elling
flannelette
  flanul   flannel
flap, flapped, flapping
flapjack
flapper
flare, flared, flaring (blaze)
  flare   flair (talent)
flash, -ed, -ing
flashback
flashbulb
flashgun
flashlight
flashpoint
flashy, flashier, flashiest
flask
flat, flatted, flatting
flat, flatter, flattest
  flaten   flatten
  flater   flatter
flatette
flatfoot, -feet
flat-footed, -ly

flathead
flatten, -ed, -ing
flatter, -ed, -ing
flatterer
flattery, -teries
flatulence
flatulense   flatulence
flatulent, -ly
flaunt, -ed, -ing
flautist
flaver   flavour
flavour, -ed, -ing
flaw, -ed, -ing (fault)
flaw   floor (room)
flax
flaxen
flay, -ed, -ing
flea (insect)
flea   flee (escape)
flea-bitten
fleat   fleet
fleck, -ed, -ing
flecks (spots)
flecks   flex (bend)
fledge, fledged, fledging
flee, fled, fleeing (escape)
flee   flea (insect)
fleece, fleeced, fleecing
fleeciness
fleecy, fleecier, fleeciest
fleese   fleece
fleet, -ly
fleeting, -ly
fleetness
flegling   fledgling
flegmatic   phlegmatic
fleks   flecks (spots)
fleksible   flexible
flem   phlegm
flert   flirt
flesh
fleshy, fleshier, fleshiest
fleur-de-lis, fleurs-de-lis
flew (fly)
flew   flu (ill)
flew   flue (passage)
flex, -ed, -ing (bend)

flex   flecks (spots)
flexible, -bly
flexitime
fli   fly
flibbertigibbet
flick, -ed, -ing
flicker, -ed, -ing
flick-knife, flick-knives
flier
flight
flightiness
flighty, -tier, -tiest
flimsily
flimsiness
flimsy, -sies
flimsy, -sier, -siest
flinch, -ed, -ing
flinchingly
fling, flung, flinging
flint
flinty, flintier, flintiest
flip, flipped, flipping
flipansy   flippancy
flipant   flippant
fliper   flipper
flippancy
flippant, -ly
flipper
flirt, -ed, -ing
flirtation
flirtatious, -ly
flit, flitted, flitting
flite   flight
flo   floe (ice)
flo   flow (pour)
float, -ed, -ing
floatation
floater
flock, -ed, -ing
flocks (groups)
flocks   phlox (plant)
floe (ice)
floe   flow (pour)
flog, flogged, flogging
flood, -ed, -ing
floodgate
floodlight, -lit, -lighting

floor, -ed, -ing (room)
floor   flaw (fault)
floorboard
flooride   fluoride
floot   flute
flop, flopped, flopping
floppily
floppy, -pier, -piest
floppy disc
flora, floras, florae
floral, -ly
florescence (flowering)
florescence   fluorescence
                  (giving light)
florescent
florescent   fluorescent
florid, -ly
floridate   fluoridate
florin
florish   flourish
florist
floss
flossy, flossier, flossiest
flotation
flote   float
flotilla
flotsam and jetsam
flounce, flounced, flouncing
flounder, -ed, -ing
flounse   flounce
flour (grain)
flour   flower (plant)
flourish, -ed, -ing
floury
flout, -ed, -ing
flow, -ed, -ing
flower, -ed, -ing (plant)
flower   flour (grain)
flowerbed
flowery, -rier, -riest
flown
flownder   flounder
flownse   flounce
flow-on
flowt   flout
flox   phlox
flu (ill)

flu   flew (fly)
flu   flue (passage)
fluctuate, -ated, -ating
fluctuation
flue (passage)
flue   flew (fly)
flue   flu (ill)
fluency
fluensy   fluency
fluent, -ly
fluff, -ed, -ing
fluffily
fluffiness
fluffy, fluffier, fluffiest
fluid, -ly
fluidity
fluke, fluked, fluking
fluks   flux
fluky, flukier, flukiest
flunk, -ed, -ing
fluoresce, -resced, -rescing
fluorescence (giving light)
fluoridate, -dated, -dating
fluoridation
flurish   flourish
flurry, -ries
flurry, -ried, -rying
flurt   flirt
flurtation   flirtation
flury   flurry
flush, -ed, -ing
fluster, -ed, -ing
flute, fluted, fluting
flutter, -ed, -ing
fluvial
flux
fly, flies
fly, flew, flown, flying
flyblown
flycatcher
flyleaf, -leaves
flyover
flytrap
flyweight
flywheel
foal, -ed, -ing
foam, -ed, -ing

fob, fobbed, fobbing

  fobia   phobia

focal, -ly

focus, -ci or -cuses

focus, -cused, -cusing or -cussed,
  -cussing

focuser

fodder

foe

  foe pas   faux pas

foetal

foetus

fog, fogged, fogging

fogey, fogeys

fogginess

foggy, -gier, -giest

foghorn

fogy, -gies

foible

  foier   foyer

foil, -ed, -ing

foist, -ed, -ing

  foks   fox

fold, -ed, -ing

folder

  fole   foal

foliage

foliaged

  foliaje   foliage

foliation

  folie   folly

folio, -lios

folk

folk dance

  folklaw   folklore

folklore

follicle

  follicul   follicle

follow, -ed, -ing

follower

folly, -lies

  folow   follow

  foly   folly

  fome   foam

foment, -ed, -ing

fond, -ly

fondant

fondle, -dled, -dling

fondness

fondue

  fondul   fondle

  fone   phone

  fonetic   phonetic

  fonograf   phonograph

font

  fony   phony

food

foodstuff

fool, -ed, -ing

foolery, -eries

foolhardiness

foolhardy, -dier, -diest

foolish, -ly

foolishness

foolproof

foolscap

foot, feet

football

footballer

foothill

foothold

footie

footing

footlights

footloose

footman, -men

footnote

footpath

footprint

footsore

footstep

footwork

fop

foppish, -ly

for (with the purpose of)

  for   fore (front)

  for   four (number)

forage, -raged, -raging

foray

  forbarance   forbearance

forbear, -bore, -borne, -bearing

forbearance

forbid, -bad, -bidden, -bidding

  forbode   forebode

forcasle   forecastle
forcast   forecast
forcastle   forecastle
force, forced, forcing
forceful, -ly
forceps, -ceps, -cipes
forcible, -bly
     forcibul   forcible
     forclose   foreclose
ford, -ed, -ing
fordable
fore (front)
     fore   four (number)
forearm
forebear
forebode, -boded, -boding
forecast, -ed, -ing
forecaster
forecastle
foreclose, -closed, -closing
forefather
forefinger
forego, -gone, -going (go before)
     forego   forgo (give up)
foreground
forehand
forehead
foreign
foreigner
foreknow, -knew, -knowing
foreknowledge
foreman, -men
     foren   foreign
     forener   foreigner
forerunner
foresee, -saw, -seeing
foreshadow, -ed, -ing
foreshore
foresight
foreskin
forest, -ed, -ing
forestall, -ed, -ing
forester
forestry
foretaste, -tasted, -tasting
foretell, -told, -telling
forethought

forever
forewarn, -ed, -ing
foreword (book)
     foreword   forward
                       (ahead)
forfeit, -ed, -ing
forfeiture
     forfit   forfeit
     forfiture   forfeiture
     forgary   forgery
forge, forged, forging
forgery, -eries
forget, -got, -gotten, -getting
forgetful, -ly
forget-me-not
forgettable
forgive, -gave, -given, -giving
forgiveness
forgo, -went, -gone, -going (give up)
     forgo   forego (go
                       before)

For **for-** words, also
look under **fore-**.

---

     forige   forage
     forin   foreign
fork, -ed, -ing
fork-lift
forlorn, -ly
form, -ed, -ing
formal, -ly
formalise, -lised, -lising
formality, -ties
format
formation
formative, -ly
former, -ly
formica
formidable, -bly
     formidabul   formidable
formula, -las, -lae
formulate, -lated, -lating
formulation
formulator
     forn   faun (god)
     forn   fawn (deer)
fornicate, -cated, -cating

fornication
  forsable   forcible
forsake, -sook, -saken, -saking
  forse   force
  forseps   forceps
  forsful   forceful
  forsible   forcible
  forsight   foresight
fort (soldiers)
  fort   fought (fight)
forte (strong)
forth (away)
  forth   fourth (number)
forthcoming
forthright
forthwith
fortieth
fortification
fortify, -fied, -fying
fortitude
fortnight
fortnightly
  fortnite   fortnight
fortress
fortuitous, -ly
  fortuitus   fortuitous
fortunate, -ly
fortune
fortune-teller
forty, -ties
forum, forums, fora
forward (ahead)
  forward   foreword (book)
forwards
  fosfate   phosphate
  fosforesent   phosphorescent
  fosforus   phosphorus
  fosil   fossil
fossick, -ed, -ing
fossil
foster, -ed, -ing

> For *foto-* words,
> look under **photo-**.

foul, -ed, -ing (dirt)

  foul   fowl (bird)
found, -ed, -ing
foundation
founder, -ed, -ing
foundling
foundry, -dries
fount
fountain
four (number)
  four   fore (ahead)
four-stroke
  fourt   fort (soldiers)
  fourt   fought (fight)
fourteen
fourteenth
fourth, -ly
  fourty   forty
fowl (bird)
  fowl   foul (dirt)
  fownd   found
  fowndation   foundation
  fowndry   foundry
  fownt   fount
  fowntain   fountain
fox, foxes
foxhole
fox-hunting
foxtrot
foxy, foxier, foxiest
  foyble   foible
foyer
fracas
  fracshun   fraction
  fracshus   fractious
fraction
fractional, -ly
fractious, -ly
fracture, -tured, -turing
fragile, -ly
fragility, -ties
fragment, -ed, -ing
fragmentary
fragmentation
fragmented
  fragmentry   fragmentary
fragrance
  fragranse   fragrance

fragrant, -ly
frail, -ly
frailty, -ties
frame, framed, framing
frame-up
framework
franc (money)
   franc   frank (mark)
franchise
frangipanni, -nies
frank, -ed, -ing (mark)
   frank   franc (money)
frankfurt
frankincense
frantic, -ally
   frase   phrase
   frate   freight
fraternal, -ly
fraternisation
fraternise, -nised, -nising
fraternity, -ties
fraud
fraudulence
   fraudulense   fraudulence
fraudulent, -ly
fraught
   fraut   fraught
   frawd   fraud
   frawdulence   fraudulence
   frawdulent   fraudulent
   frawt   fraught
fray, -ed, -ing
frazzle, -zled, -zling
   frazzul   frazzle
freak
freakish, -ly
freckle, -led, -ling
free, freed, freeing
free, freer, freest
freeborn
freedom
freehand
freehold
freelance, -lanced, -lancing
freelancer
freeload, -ed, -ing
freeloader

freely
freeman, -men
Freemason
Freemasonry
free-range
freesia
freestanding
freestyle
freeway
freewheel, -ed, -ing
freeze, froze, frozen, freezing (cold)
   freeze   frieze (band)
freezer
freight, -ed, -ing
freighter
   freind   friend
   frekwency   frequency
   frekwent   frequent
French
   frend   friend
   frendly   friendly
   frendship   friendship
frenetic, -ally
   frenzie   frenzy
frenzied
frenzy, -zies
frenzy, -zied, -zying
frequency, -cies
   frequensy   frequency
frequent, -ly
fresco, -coes
fresco, -coed, -coing
fresh, -ly
freshen, -ed, -ing
freshener
fresher
freshness
freshwater
   fresko   fresco
fret, fretted, fretting
fretful, -ly
fretwork
Freudian
   fri   fry
friable
   friabul   friable
friar

fricassee, -seed, -seeing
   fricshun   friction
friction
frictional, -ly
Friday
fridge
friend
friendliness
friendly, -lier, -liest
friendship
   frier   friar
Friesian
frieze (band)
   frieze   freeze (cold)
frigate
fright
frighten, -ed, -ing
frightener
frightful, -ly
   frightfull   frightful
frigid, -ly
frigidity, -ties
frigidness
frill, -ed, -ing
frill-necked lizard
fringe, fringed, fringing
frippery, -ries
frisk, -ed, -ing
friskily
frisky, friskier, friskiest
   frite   fright
   friteful   frightful
   friten   frighten
   friter   fritter
fritter, -ed, -ing
frivolity, -ties
frivolous, -ly
   frivolus   frivolous
frizz, frizzes
frizz, frizzed, frizzing
frizzle, -zled, -zling
frizzy
   frizzul   frizzle
fro
frock, -ed, -ing
frog
frogman, -men

frogmarch, -ed, -ing
frogmouth
   Froidian   Freudian
frolic, -icked, -icking
frolicsome, -ly
frond
front, -ed, -ing
frontage
frontal, -ly
frontbencher
frontier
   frontige   frontage
   froogal   frugal
   frooishun   fruition
   froot   fruit
   frootful   fruitful
frost, -ed, -ing
frostbite, -bit, -bitten, -biting
frostily
frosty, -tier, -tiest
froth, -ed, -ing
frothiness
frothy, frothier, frothiest
frown, -ed, -ing
frowzy, -zier, -ziest
froze
frozen, -ly
fructose
frugal, -ly
frugality, -ties
   fruishun   fruition
fruit, -ed, -ing
fruiterer
fruit-fly
fruitful, -ly
fruition
fruitless, -ly
fruity, -tier, -tiest
frump
frumpish, -ly
   frunt   front
   fruntal   frontal
   fruntier   frontier
frustrate, -trated, -trating
frustration
   frut   fruit
   fruterer   fruiterer

frutful fruitful
frutie fruity
fry, fried, frying
fry, fries
fucher future
fucheristic futuristic
fuchsia
fudal feudal
fudalism feudalism
fuddle, -dled, -dling
fuddul fuddle
fude feud
fudge, fudged, fudging
fuel, fuelled, fuelling
fuel-injection
fuel-injector
fugitive
fugue
ful full
fulcrum, -crums, -cra
fulfil, -filled, -filling
fulfilment
full
full-back
full-blooded
fullfil fulfil
fully
fully-fledged
fulminate, -ated, -ating
fulscap foolscap
fulsome, -ly
fulsomeness
fumble, -bled, -bling
fumbler
fumbul fumble
fume, fumed, fuming
fumigant
fumigate, -gated, -gating
fumigation
fumigator
fun
funcshun function
function
functional, -ly
functionalism
functionary, -ries
fund, -ed, -ing

fundamental, -ly
funel funnel
funeral
funereal, -ly
funfair
fungicide
fungus, fungi
funicular
funily funnily
funk, -ed, -ing
funnel, -nelled, -nelling
funnel-web
funnily
funny, -nier, -niest
fur, furred, furring (pelt)
fur fir (tree)
furbish, -ed, -ing
furie furry (fur)
furie fury (anger)
furier furrier
furious, -ly
furius furious
furl, -ed, -ing
furlong
furlough
furm firm
furmament firmament
furment ferment
furmentation fermentation
furn fern
furnace
furnish, -ed, -ing
furnisher
furnishings
furniture
furore
furphy,-phies
furrier
furrow, -ed, -ing
furry, -rier, -riest (fur)
furst first
further
furtherance
furthest
furtive, -ly
fury, -ries (anger)
fus fuss

fuse, fused, fusing
fuselage
 fusha   fuchsia
 fusier   fussier
 fusiest   fussiest
 fusilade   fusillade
 fusilage   fuselage
fusilier
fusillade
fusion
fuss, -ed, -ing
fusspot
fussy, -sier, -siest
futile, -ly
futility, -ties
future
futurism
futuristic
futurology
fuzz
fuzzily
fuzziness
fuzzy, -zier, -ziest
 fyord   fiord
 fyord   fjord

> For **fysi-** words, look
> under **physi-**.

Gg

gab, gabbed, gabbing
gabardine
gabble, -bled, -bling (talk)
gable (roof)
  gabul   gabble (talk)
  gabul   gable (roof)
gadget
Gaelic
  gaf   gaff (hook)
  gaf   gaffe (mistake)
gaff (hook)
gaffe (mistake)
gag, gagged, gagging
gaga
  gage   gauge
  gaget   gadget
gaggle
  gagit   gadget
  gagul   gaggle
gaiety, -ties
  gail   gale
gaily
gain, -ed, -ing
gainful, -ly
gainsay, -said, -saying
gait (walk)
  gait   gate (opening)
gaiter
  gaitey   gaiety
gala (festival)
  gala   galah (bird)
galah (bird)
  galaksey   galaxy
  galant   gallant
  galantry   gallantry
  galaw   galore
galaxy, -axies
gale

  galery   gallery
  galey   galley
  galivant   gallivant
gall, -ed, -ing
gallant, -ly
gallantry, -tries
galleon
gallery, -leries
galley, -leys
gallivant, -vanted, -vanting
gallon
gallop, galloped, galloping (pace)
gallows
gallstone
gallup poll (survey)
  galon   gallon
  galop   gallop (pace)
galore
galoshes
  galows   gallows
  galup poll   gallup poll
galvanise, -nised, -nising
galvanised iron
  galy   galley
gambit
gamble, -bled, -bling (chance)
gambol, -bolled, -bolling (frolic)
game, gamed, gaming
gamesmanship
gamin (urchin)
gamma
gammon (bacon)
gammy, -mier, -miest
gamut
gander
gang
gangling
ganglion, -glia, -glions
gangplank
  gangreen   gangrene
gangrene
gangrenous
  gangrenus   gangrenous
gangster
gangway
gannet
gantry, -tries

gaol (prison)
    gaol   goal (aim)
gaolbird
gaoler
gap
gape, -ed, -ing
garage, -raged, -raging
    garantee   guarantee
    garantee   guaranty
    garantor   guarantor
garb, -ed, -ing
garbage
    garbige   garbage
garble, -bled, -bling
    garbul   garble
    gard   guard
garden, -ed, -ing
gardener
gardenia
    gardian   guardian
garfish, -fish, -fishes
gargle, -gled, -gling
    gargoil   gargoyle
gargoyle
    gargul   gargle
garish, -ly
    garison   garrison
garland, -landed, -landing
garlic
garment
garner, -ed, -ing
garnet
garnish, -ed, -ing
garnishee, -sheed, -sheeing
    garnit   garnet
garrison, -ed, -ing
    garrot   garrotte
garrotte, -rotted, -rotting
garrulity
garrulous, -ly
garter
    garulus   garrulous
gas, gases
gas, gassed, gassing
gasbag, -bagged, -bagging
    gasebo   gazebo
    gaselene   gasoline

gaseous
gash, gashed, gashing
    gasious   gaseous
gasket
gasmask
gasolene
gasoline
gasometer
gasp, -ed, -ing
    gassey   gassy
gassy, -sier, -siest
    gastley   ghastly
gastric
gastritis
gastroenteritis
gastronome
gastronomy
gate (opening)
    gate   gait (walk)
gateau, -teaux
gatecrash, -crashed, -crashing
    gater   gaiter
gateway
gather, -ed, -ing
gauche
    gaudie   gaudy
gauge, gauged, gauging
gaunt, -ly
gauntlet
gauze
gave
gavel
    gavot   gavotte
gavotte
    gawdie   gaudy
gawk, -ed, -ing
gawky, -kier, -kiest
    gawl   gall
    gawnt   gaunt
    gawntlet   gauntlet
    gawse   gauze
gay, gayer, gayest
    Gaylic   Gaelic
    gayn   gain
    gaysha   geisha
gaze, -ed, -ing
gazebo, -bos, -boes

gazel — gazelle
gazelle
gazette, -etted, -etting
gazump, -ed, -ing
gear, -ed, -ing
gearbox, -boxes
gear-ratio
gearstick
gearwheel
gecko, -os, -oes
geebung
geek
gees — geese
geese
geezer
Geiger counter
geisha, -shas
gel, gelled, gelling
gelatin — gelatine
gelatine
gelatinous, -ly
gelatinus — gelatinous
gelato
geld, gelded, gelding
gelignite
gem, gemmed, gemming
gemfish, -fish, -fishes
Gemini
gen, genned, genning
gendarme, -darmes
gender
gene
genealogist
genealogy, -gies
genee — genie
general, -ly
generalise, -ised, -ising
generality, -ties
generate, -ed, -ing
generation
generation-gap
generator
generic
generical, -ly
generosity, -ties
generous, -ly
generus — generous

genesis, -ses
genetic
genetical, -ly
genetics
geney — genie
genial, -ly
genie
geniology — genealogy
genital
genius, geniuses
genocide
genoside — genocide
genre
gent
genteel, -ly (proper)
genteel — gentle
gentile (Christian)
gentility, -ties
gentle, -tler, -tlest
gentleman, -men
gentlewoman, -women
gentrey — gentry
gentrification
gentry
gentul — gentle
gentulman — gentleman
genuflect, -ed, -ing
genuin — genuine
genuine, -ly
genuineness
genus, genera
geny — genie
geofysics — geophysics
geografey — geography
geography, -phies
geologist
geology, -gies
geometrey — geometry
geometric
geometrical, -ly
geometry, -tries
geophysicist
geophysics
georgette
geranium
gerd — gird
gerder — girder

gerdle	girdle
gerdul	girdle
geriatric	
gerilla	gorilla
gerilla	guerilla
gerkin	gherkin
gerl	girl
germ	
German	
germane	
germinal	
germinate, -nated, -nating	
gerontology	
gerth	girth
gerund	
gerymander	gerrymander
gescha	gesture
geser	geyser
gess	guess
gest	guest
gestate, -tated, -tating	
gestation	
gesticulate, -lated, -lating	
gesture, -tured, -turing	
get, got, getting	
getaway	
getto	ghetto
geyser	
ghastly, -lier, -liest	
gherkin	
ghetto, ghettos, ghettoes	
ghost, -ly	
ghoul	
ghoulish, -ly	
ghoulishness	
giant	
gibber	
gibberish	
gibbet, -beted, -beting	
gibe, gibed, gibing (mock)	
gibe	jibe (sail)
giber	gibber
giberish	gibberish
gibet	gibbet
giblet	
gidance	guidance
gidanse	guidance

giddy, -dier, -diest	
gide	guide
gidgee	
gidgie	gidgee
gidie	giddy
gidy	giddy
gift	
gig, gigged, gigging	
gigantic, -ally	
giggle, -gled, -gling	
gigolo, -los	
gigul	giggle
gil	gill
gild, gilded, gilding (gold)	
gild	guild (union)
gile	guile
gilgai	
gilgy	gilgai
gill	
giloteen	guillotine
gilotine	guillotine
gilt (gold)	
gilt	guilt
giltey	guilty
gilty	guilty
gim	gym
gimick	gimmick
gimkana	gymkhana
gimlet	
gimmick	
gimnasium	gymnasium
gimnastics	gymnastics
gin, ginned, ginning	
ginecology	gynaecology
giney	guinea
gineypig	guineapig
gingam	gingham
ginger	
gingerley	gingerly
gingerly	
gingham	
gingivitis	
ginie	guinea
giniepig	guineapig
ginjer	ginger
ginjivitis	gingivitis
ginseng	

gip	gyp
gipsey	gipsy
gipsie	gipsy
gipsum	gypsum
gipsy, -sies	
giraf	giraffe
gird, -ed, -ing	
girder	
girdle, -dled, -dling	
girdul	girdle
girl	
girocompass	gyrocompass
giroscope	gyroscope
girth	
gise	guise
gismo	
gist	
gitar	guitar
give, gave, given, giving	
giy	guy
gizerd	gizzard
gizzard	
glacial, -ly	
glacier	
glad, gladded, gladding	
glad, gladder, gladdest	
glade	
gladen	gladden
gladiater	gladiator
gladiator	
glamer	glamour
glamorous, -ly	
glamour	
glance, -ed, -ing	
gland	
glandular	
glanduler	glandular
glanse	glance
glare, glared, glaring	
glas	glass
glashal	glacial
glasier	glacier
glass, glasses	
glasshouse	
glassy, -sier, -siest	
glaucoma	
glawcoma	glaucoma

glaze, glazed, glazing	
glazier	
glea	glee
gleam, -ed, -ing	
glean, -ed, -ing	
glee	
gleem	gleam
gleen	glean
glib, glibber, glibbest	
glicerine	glycerine
glide, glided, gliding	
glider	
glimmer, -ered, -ering	
glimpse, glimpsed, glimpsing	
glimse	glimpse
glint, -ed, -ing	
glisen	glisten
gliserin	glycerine
glisten, -ed, -ing	
glitter, -ed, -ing	
glo	glow
gloat, -ed, -ing	
glob	
global, -ly	
globe, globed, globing	
globule	
gloo	glue
gloocose	glucose
gloom	
gloomily	
gloomy, -mier, -miest	
glooten	gluten
glorie	glory
glorify, -fied, -fying	
glorious, -ly	
glorius	glorious
glory, glories	
glory, gloried, glorying	
glos	gloss
glosary	glossary
gloss, glossed, glossing	
glossary, -ries	
glossie	glossy
glossy, glossier, glossiest	
glote	gloat
glove	
glow, -ed, -ing	

glower, -ered, -ering
glucose
glue, glued, gluing
glum, -ly
glut, glutted, glutting
gluten (glue)
glutten   glutton
glutton (eat)
gluv   glove
glycerine
gnarled
gnash, -ed, -ing
gnat
gnaw, gnawed, gnawing
gnome
gnu, gnus
go, gone, going
goad, -ed, -ing
goal (aim)
goal   gaol (prison)
goalkeeper
goanna
goat
goatee
gob
gobbel   gobble
gobble, -bled, -bling
gobbledegook
gobbler
go-between
goblet
goblin
gobul   gobble
go-cart
God
godchild, -children
goddess
godforsaken
godly, -lier, -liest
godparent
godsend, -sent, -sending
godspeed
goer
goes
goggle, -gled, -gling
gogul   goggle
goiter   goitre

goitre
go-kart
gold
golden, -ly
goldfield
goldfish
goldmine
gole   goal (aim)
golf (game)
golf   gulf (bay)
golliwog
gollywog
gon   gone
gondola
gondolier
gone
goner
gong
goo
good, better, best
gooda   gouda
goodbye, -byes
goodnight
goodwill
gooey, gooier, gooiest
goof, goofed, goofing
googly
gool   ghoul
goolash   goulash
goormand   gourmand
goormay   gourmet
goose, geese
gooseberie   gooseberry
gooseberry, -ries
goosestep, -stepped, -stepping
gopher
gore, gored, goring
gorge, gorged, gorging
gorgeous, -ly
gorgus   gorgeous
gorilla (ape)
gorilla   guerilla (soldier)
gormandise, -dised, -dising
gorse
gory, gorier, goriest
gosamer   gossamer

goshawk
  gosip   gossip
gosling
go-slow
gospel
gospeller
gossamer
gossip, -ed, -ing
  gost   ghost
  gote   goat
Gothic
gouda
gouge, gouged, gouging
  goul   ghoul
goulash
gourd
gourmand
gourmet
gout
  goven   govern
govern, -ed, -ing
  governer   governor
governess
government
governmental, -ly
governor
governor-general, governors-general
  govner   governor
  gowge   gouge
  gowt   gout
grab, grabbed, grabbing
grace, graced, gracing
graceful, -ly
gracious, -ly
gradation
grade, graded, grading
grader
gradient
gradual, -ly
graduate, -ated, -ating
graduation
  graf   graph
graffiti
  grafic   graphic
  grafics   graphics
  grafite   graphite
  grafiti   graffiti

graft, grafted, grafting
grail
grain
  graling   grayling
gram
  gramar   grammar
  gramarian   grammarian
  gramatical   grammatical
  gramer   grammar
  gramerfone   gramophone
grammar
grammarian
grammatical, -ly
gramophone
grampus
gran
granary, -ries
grand
grandeur
grandiloquent, -ly
grandiose, -ly
grandiosity
grandparent
grandstand
  grane   grain
grange
  granie   granny
  granit   granite
granite
granny, grannies
grant, -ed, -ing
granular
granulate, -lated, -lating
granule
  grany   granny
grape
grapefruit, grapefruit
grapevine
graph, -ed, -ing
graphic
graphical, -ly
graphics
graphite
  graple   grapple
grapnel
grapple, -pled, -pling
  grappul   grapple

gras — grass
grase — grace
grashoper — grasshopper
grashus — gracious
grasp, -ed, -ing
grass
grasshopper
glassland
grassroots
grassy, -sier, -siest
grate (fireplace)
grate, grated, grating (rub)
grate — great (large)
grateful, -ly
gratification
gratify, -fied, -fying
gratingly
gratis
gratitude
gratuitey — gratuity
gratuitous, -ly
gratuitousness
gratuitus — gratuitous
gratuity
grave
gravel, gravelled, gravelling
gravelly
gravie — gravy
gravitashun — gravitation
gravitate, -tated, -tating
gravitation
gravity, -ties
gravure
gravvity — gravity
gravy, -vies
grayhownd — greyhound
grayl — grail
grayling
grayn — grain
graze, grazed, grazing
grazier
grease, greased, greasing
greasepaint
great (large)
great — grate (rub)
greatful — grateful
grede — greed

greed
greedily
greedy, greedier, greediest
greef — grief
green
greenery, -eries
greengrocer
greenhorn
greenhouse
greese — grease
greet, -ed, -ing
gregarious, -ly
gregarius — gregarious
greif — grief
greive — grieve
greivus — grievous
gremlin
grenade
grenadier
grene — green
grenery — greenery
grengroser — greengrocer
grenhorn — greenhorn
grenhous — greenhouse
grese — grease
grete — greet
grevance — grievance
grevanse — grievance
greve — grieve
grevillea
grevus — grievous
grew
grey
greyhound
greyness
grid
griddle, -dled, -dling
griddul — griddle
gridiron
grief
grief-stricken
grievance
grievanse — grievance
grieve, -ed, -ing
griever
grievous, -ly
griffin

grill, -ed, -ing (cook)
grille (screen)
griller (barbeque)
  griller   gorilla
  griller   guerilla
grim, grimmer, grimmest
grimace, -maced, -macing
  grimase   grimace
grime, grimed, griming
grimy, grimier, grimiest
grin, grinned, grinning
grind, ground, grinding
grinder
grindstone
  grined   grind
grip, gripped, gripping (hold)
gripe, griped, griping (pain)
grippe (flu)
  grisel   gristle (fibre)
  grisel   grizzle (whine)
grisly, -lier, -liest
  grissle   gristle (fibre)
  grissle   grizzle (whine)
grist
gristle (fibre)
grit, gritted, gritting
grizzle, -zled, -zling (whine)
  grizzle   gristle (fibre)
grizzleguts
  gro   grow
groan, groaned, groaning (moan)
  groan   grown (mature)
grocer
grocery, -ceries
grog
groggy, -gier, -giest
groin (body)
  groin   groyne (jetty)
  grone   groan
  grone   grown
  groo   grew
  grool   gruel
  groop   group
  groosum   gruesome
groove, grooved, grooving
  groovey   groovy
groovy, -vier, -viest

  grooyere   gruyere
grope, groped, groping
groper
  gros   gross
  groser   grocer
gross, grosses
  grotesk   grotesque
grotesque, -ly
  groto   grotto
grotto, -toes, -tos
grotty, -tier, -tiest
  groty   grotty
grouch, -ed, -ing
  groun   grown
ground, -ed, -ing
  groundsheat   groundsheet
groundsheet
groundsman, -men
group, -ed, -ing
grouse, groused, grousing
grout, -ed, -ing
grove
grovel, -elled, -elling
  grovle   grovel
grow, grew, grown, growing
grower
growl, -ed, -ing
grown (mature)
  grown   groan (moan)
  grownd   ground
  growse   grouse
growth
groyne (jetty)
  groyne   groin (body)
grub, grubbed, grubbing
grubber
grubby, -bier, -biest
grudge, -ed, -ing
gruel, gruelled, gruelling
gruesome, -ly
gruesomeness
  gruf   gruff
gruff, -ly
  gruge   grudge
grumble, -led, -ling
  grumbul   grumble
grummet

grumpie grumpy
grumpy, -pier, -piest
grunt, -ed, -ing
grunter
grusome gruesome
grusum gruesome
gruyaire gruyère
gruyare gruyère
gruyère
G-string
guano, -nos
guarantee, -teed, -teeing
guarantor
guaranty, -tied, -tying
guaranty, -ties
guard, -ed, -ing
guardian
guava
gudgeon
guerilla (soldier)
guerilla gorilla (ape)
guernsey, -seys
guess, -ed, -ing
guest
guesthouse, -houses
gufaw guffaw
guffaw, -awed, -awing
guidance
guide, guided, guiding
guideline
guild (union)
guild gild (gold)
guile
guileless, -ly
guillotine, -tined, -tining
guiloteen guillotine
guilotine guillotine
guilt
guiltily
guilty, -tier, -tiest
guinea
guineapig
guise, guised, guising
guitar
gul gull
gulash goulash
gulch

gulet gullet
guley gully
gulf (bay)
gulf golf (game)
gulible gullible
gulie gully
gull, -ed, -ing
gullet
gullible, -bly
gullibility
gullibul gullible
gully, gullies
gulp, -ed, -ing
guly gully
gum, gummed, gumming
gumboil
gumboot
gummy, -mier, -miest
gumnut
gumption
gumshun gumption
gun, gunned, gunning
gung ho
gunk
gunl gunwale
gunman, -men
gunmetal
gunnel gunwale
gunner
gunnery, -eries
gunny, -nies
gunnysack
gunpowder
gunsmith
gunwale
guppy, -pies
gurdle girdle
gurgle, -gled, -gling
gurgul gurgle
gurnard, -nards
gurnerd gurnard
gurth girth
guru, gurus
gush, gushed, gushing
gusset
gussit gusset
gust, -ed, -ing

gusto
gut, gutted, gutting

guter	gutter
guteral	guttural
gutersnipe	guttersnipe

gutless, -ly

gutsa	gutser

gutser

gutsie	gutsy

gutsy
gutter
guttersnipe
guttural, -ly

guvern	govern
guverness	governess
guvernment	government
guvner	governor

guy

guzul	guzzle

guzzle, guzzled, guzzling

gwano	guano
gwava	guava
gybe	gibe

gym

gymkana	gymkhana

gymkhana
gymnasium, -nasiums, -nasia
gymnastics
gynaecological
gynaecologist
gynaecology
gyp, gypped, gypping
gypsum
gypsy, -sies
gyrate, -ed, -ing
gyrocompass
gyroscope

Hh

habeas corpus
haberdasher
haberdashery, -ries
  habet — habit
  habias corpus — habeas corpus
  habichual — habitual
  habichuate — habituate
habit
habitable, -bly
  habitabul — habitable
habitat
habitation
habitual, -ly
habituate, -ated, -ating
  hach — hatch
  hachery — hatchery
  hachett — hatchet
hacienda
hack, -ed, -ing
hackle, -led, -ling
hackney, -neyed, -neying
hacksaw
  hackul — hackle
hackwork
haddock
hades
hadn't (had not)
  hadnt — hadn't
haematology
  haemefilia — haemophilia
haemoglobin
haemophilia
  haemorage — haemorrhage
haemorrhage, -haged, -haging
haemorrhoid
  haemorroid — haemorrhoid
haft, -ed, -ing
hag

  hagard — haggard
  hagerd — haggard
haggard, -ly
haggis
haggle, -gled, -gling
hagiography, -phies
  hagis — haggis
  hagul — haggle
haiku
hail (ice)
  hail — hale (robust)
hailstone
hailstorm
hair (head)
  hair — hare (animal)
  hair — heir (inherit)
hairdo, -dos
hairdresser
hairline
hairpiece
hairpin
hairspring
hair-trigger
hairy, -rier, -riest
haka
hake, hake, hakes
hakea
  halcion — halcyon
halcyon
hale, haler, halest (robust)
  hale — hail (ice)
  haleluya — hallelujah
  halestone — hailstone
  halestorm — hailstorm
half
half-back
half-baked
half-blood
half-breed
half-brother
half-caste
half-cock
half-forward
half-hearted, -ly
half-life
half-mast
half-measure

half-mesure	half-measure
half-moon	
half-sister	
half-time	
half-truth	
halfway	
halfway house	
halfwit	
halibut, -buts	
halilooya	hallelujah
halitosis	
hall (room)	
hall	haul (carry)
hallelujah	
halleluyah	hallelujah
hallmark	
hallo (greet)	
hallow, -ed, -ing (holy)	
Halloween	
hallucinate, -nated, -nating	
hallucination	
hallucinogen	
halmark	hallmark
halo, -loes, -los (light)	
halo	hallo (greet)
halo	hallow (holy)
halogen	
Haloween	Halloween
halsiun	halcyon
halt, -ed, -ing	
halter	
halusinate	hallucinate
halusinogen	hallucinogen
halve, -ed, -ing	
halyard	
halyerd	halyard
ham, hammed, hamming	
hamburger	
hamer	hammer
ham-fisted	
hamlet	
hammer, -ed, -ing	
hammerhead	
hammock	
hamper, -ered, -ering	
hamster	
hamstring, -strung, -stringing	

hand, handed, handing	
handbag	
handball	
handbill	
handbook	
handbrake	
handclap, -clapped, -clapping	
handcuff, -cuffed, -cuffing	
handey	handy
handeywork	handiwork
handicap, -capped, -capping	
handicraft	
handie	handy
handiwork	
handkerchief, -chiefs, -chieves	
handle, -dled, -dling	
handlebar	
handler	
handmade (article)	
handmaid (servant)	
hand-me-down	
handout	
hand-pick, -picked, -picking	
handpiece	
handrail	
handriting	handwriting
handset	
handshake	
handsome, -somer, -somest (fine)	
handspring	
handstand	
hand-to-mouth	
handul	handle
handwriting	
handy, -dier, -diest	
handyman	
hang, hung or hanged, hanging	
hangar (shed)	
hangar	hanger (clothes)
hangdog	
hanger (clothes)	
hanger	hangar (shed)
hanger-on, hangers-on	
hang-glider	
hangi	
hangkerchief	handkerchief

hangman
hangover
hang-up
hank
hanker, -ed, -ing
   hankerchief   handkerchief
hankie
   hankuff   handcuff
hanky, hankies
hanky-panky
Hansard
hansom (cab)
   hansom   handsome
                  (fine)
   hansum   handsome
   hapen   happen
haphazard, -ly
   hapie   happy
hapless, -ly
happen, -ened, -ening
happily
happy, happier, happiest
happy-go-lucky
   hapy   happy
   harang   harangue
harangue, -rangued, -ranguing
   haras   harass
harass, -ed, -ing
harassment
   harber   harbour
harbinger
harbour, -ed, -ing
hard, -ly
hardback
hard-bitten
hardboard
hard-core
hard-court
harden, -ed, -ing
hard-hearted, -ly
   hardie   hardy
hard-hit
hardihood
hardiness
   hardlie   hardly
hardline
hardness

hardnose
hard-pressed
hardship
hardtop
hardware
   hardwear   hardware
hardwood
hardy, hardier, hardiest
hare (animal)
   hare   hair (head)
   hare   heir (inherit)
harebrained
harelip
harem
   harico   haricot
haricot
hark, -ed, -ing
harlot
harm, -ed, -ing
harmonic
harmonica
harmonious, -ly
harmonise, -nised, -nising
harmonium
   harmonius   harmonious
harmony, -nies
harness, -ed, -ing
   harow   harrow
harp, -ed, -ing
harpoon
harpsichord
   harpsicord   harpsichord
harpy
harrier
harrow, -ed, -ing
harry, -ried, -rying
harsh, -ly
hart (deer)
   hart   heart (body)

> For all other **hart-** words,
> look under **heart-**.

harum-scarum
   harve   halve
harvest, -ed, -ing
harvester
   harvist   harvest

hary	hairy	hawlidge	haulage
has-been		hawlige	haulage
hasen	hasten	hawlier	haulier
hash, -ed, -ing		hawnch	haunch
hashish		hawnet	hornet
hasn't (has not)		hawnt	haunt
hasnt	hasn't	hawse (ship)	
hasock	hassock	hawse	horse (animal)
hasp		hawser	
hassel	hassle	hawthorn	
hassle, -led, -ling		hawticulcher	horticulture
hassock		hawticulture	horticulture
haste, -tily		hawtie	haughty
hasten, -ed, -ing		hawty	haughty
hasty, hastier, hastiest		hay (grass)	
hatch, -ed, -ing		hay	hey (cry)
hatchback		hayday	heyday
hatcherey	hatchery	hayfever	
hatchery, -eries		haystack	
hatchet		haywire	
hatchway		hazard	
hate, -ed, -ing		hazardous, -ly	
hateful, -ly		haze, hazed, hazing	
hatred		hazel	
hatrid	hatred	hazerd	hazard
hatstand		head, -ed, -ing	
hatter		headache	
hat-trick		headcount, -ed, -ing	
haughty, -tier, -tiest		headdress	
haul, -ed, -ing (carry)		header	
haul	hall (room)	headfirst	
haulage		headfone	headphone
haulier		head-hunting	
haulige	haulage	headlamp	
haunch		headland	
haunt, -ed, -ing		headlight	
haute cuisine		headline, -lined, -lining	
hav	have	headlite	headlight
have		headlong	
haven		headman	
haven't (have not)		headmaster	
havent	haven't	headmistress	
haversack		head-on	
havoc, -ocked, -ocking		headphone	
hawk, -ed, -ing		headquarters	
hawker		headset	
hawl	haul	headshrinker	

headspring
headstand
head start
headstone
headstream
headstrong
headwaters
headway
headwind
headword
heady, -dier, -diest
heal (health)
   heal   heel (shoe)
health
healthy, -thier, -thiest
heap, -ed, -ing
hear, heard, hearing (listen)
   hear   here (place)
heard (listen)
   heard   herd (animals)
hearer
hearing aid
hearsay
hearse
heart (body)
heartache
heart attack
heartbeat
heartbreak
heartbroken, -ly
heartburn
hearten, -ed, -ing
heartfelt
hearth
heartless, -ly
heart-rending, -ly
heartstring
heart-throb
hearty, -tily
heat, -ed, -ing
heater
heath
heathen, -then, -thens
heather
heatwave
heave, -ed, -ing
heave-ho

heaven, -ly
heavy, -ily
heavy-duty
heavy-handed, -ly
heavy-hearted, -ly
heavy-laden
heavyweight
Hebrew
   Hebroo   Hebrew
heck
heckle, -led, -ling
hectare
hectic, -ally
hector, -ed, -ing
he'd (he would)
   hed   head (body)
   hed   he'd (he would)
hedge, hedged, hedging
hedgehog
hedonism
heed, -ed, -ing
heedless, -ly
heehaw
heel (shoe)
   heel   heal (health)
heeler
   heematology   haematology
   heemoglobin   haemoglobin
   heemophilia   haemophilia
   heep   heap
   heer   hear (listen)
   heer   here (place)
   heet   heat
   heeth   heath
   hefer   heifer
   heftie   hefty
heft, -ed, -ing
hefty, -tier, -tiest
   hege   hedge
hegemony, -nies
heifer
height
heighten, -ed, -ing
   heighth   height
heinous, -ly
   heinus   heinous
heir (inherit)

heir	hair (head)	hena	henna
heir	here (place)	hence	
heir apparent, heirs apparent		henchman, -men	
heiress		henge	
heirloom		henna	
heist, -ed, -ing		henpeck, -pecked, -pecking	
heith	height	hens	hence
hel	hell	henus	heinous
held		hepatic	
helicopter		hepatitis	
heliograf	heliograph	heptagon	
heliograph		herald, -ed, -ing	
heliotrope		heraldic, -ally	
helipad		heraldrey	heraldry
heliport		heraldry, -dries	
helium		herb	
hell		herbaceous	
he'll (he will)		herbage	
hell	he'll	herbalist	
hell-bent		herbashus	herbaceous
hellcat		herbicide	
Hellenic		herbiside	herbicide
hellfire		herbivore	
hello, -los		herbivorous	
hello, -loed, -loing		herbivorus	herbivorous
hell's angel		herculean	
helm		herd (animals)	
helmet		herd	heard (listen)
helmsman, -men		herdsman, -men	
helo	hello	here (place)	
helot		here	hear (listen)
help, -ed, -ing		hereafter	
helpless, -ly		hereby	
helpmate		hereditary	
helter-skelter		hereditey	heredity
helth	health	hereditrey	hereditary
helthy	healthy	heredity, -ties	
hemerige	haemorrhage	Hereford	
hemeroid	haemorrhoid	herein	
hem, hemmed, hemming		hereof	
hemisfare	hemisphere	heresay	hearsay
hemisfear	hemisphere	heresie	heresy
hemisphere		heresy, -sies	
hemlock		heretic	
hemp		hereto	
hemstitch, -stitched, -stitching		hereunder	
hen		hereupon	

herewith

hering   herring

heritable, -ly

heritage

heritige   heritage

herl   hurl

hermafrodite   hermaphrodite

hermaphrodite

hermaphroditism

hermatage   hermitage

hermetic

hermetical, -ly

hermit

hermitage

hermitige   hermitage

hernia, -nias

hero, -roes

heroic

heroical, -ly

heroicle   heroical

heroin (drug)

heroine (female hero)

heroism

heron

hero-worship, -shipped, -shipping

herpeas   herpes

herpes

herring, -rings, -ring

herringbone

hers

herse   hearse

herself

hert   hurt

hertle   hurtle

hertul   hurtle

hertz

he's (he is, or he has)

hes   he's

hesian   hessian

hesitancy

hesitansey   hesitancy

hesitant, -ly

hesitate, -tated, -tating

hesitation

hessian

heterogeneity

heterogeneous, -ly

heterogenius   heterogeneous

heterosexual,-ly

hethen   heathen

hether   heather

het-up

heuristic, -ally

heve   heave

heven   heaven

hevenly   heavenly

hevie   heavy

hevily   heavily

heviwait   heavyweight

hevy   heavy

hew, hewed, hewn, hewing (cut)

hew   hue (colour)

hex

hexagon

hexagonal,- -ly

hexameter

hey (cry)

hey   hay (grass)

heyday

> For other **hi-** words, look
> under **hy-**.

hi (cry)

hi   high (up)

hiasinth   hyacinth

hiatus, -tuses

hiatus hernia

hibernate, -nated, -nating

hibiscus

hibrid   hybrid

hiccup, -ed, -ing

hich   hitch

hichhike   hitchhike

hick

hickory, -ries

hicup   hiccup

hidden

hide, hid, hiding

hideaway

hidebound

hideous, -ly

hide-out

hidius   hideous

hidy-hole

hier	hire
hierarchy, -chies	
hierarkey	hierarchy
hieroglific	hieroglyphic
hieroglyphic, -ally	
hi-fi	
high, -ly	
highborn	
highbrow	
high-class	
higher (up)	
higher	hire (rent)
highfalutin	
high-fidelity	
high-grade	
high-handed, -ly	
highland	
highlight	
highly-wrought	
high-minded, -ly	
highness	
high-pitched	
high-powered	
high-pressure	
high-rise	
high-speed	
high-spirited	
hight	height
high-tension	
highway	
highwayman, -men	
hijack, -ed, -ing	
hike, -ed, -ing	
hil	hill
hiland	highland
hilarious, -ly	
hilarius	hilarious
hilight	highlight
hilite	highlight
hill	
hillbilly, -lies	
hillock	
hilly, hillier, hilliest	
hilt	
him (he)	
him	hymn (song)
himself	

hind	
hinder, -ed, -ing	
hinderanse	hindrance
Hindoo, -doos	
Hindooism	
hindquarter	
hindrance	
hindranse	hindrance
hindsight	
hindsite	hindsight
Hindu	
Hinduism	
hiness	highness
hinge, -ed, -ing	
hint, -ed, -ing	
hinterland	
hip, hipped, hipping	
hipbath	
hipie	hippie
hipopotamus	hippopotamus
hippie, -ies	
Hippocratic oath	
hippopotamus, -muses, -mi	
hipster	
hipy	hippie
hire, hired, hiring (rent)	
hire	higher (up)
hireling	
hire-purchase	
hiroglific	hieroglyphic
hiss, -ed, -ing	
histerey	history
histeria	hysteria
histogram	
historian	
historic	
historiography	
history, -ries	
histrey	history
histrionic, -ally	
hit, hit, hitting	
hitch, -ed, -ing	
hitchhike, -hiked, -hiking	
hite	height
hither	
hitherto	
hive, -ed, -ing	

hiway	highway

> For other **hi-** words,
> look under **hy-**.

ho	hoe
hoaks	hoax

hoard, -ed, -ing (gather)

hoard	horde (mob)

hoarding

hoare	whore

hoarse, hoarser, hoarsest (voice)

hoarse	hawse (ship)
hoarse	horse (animal)

hoary, hoarier, hoariest (old)
hoax, -ed, -ing
hob

hobbel	hobble

hobble, -bled, -bling
hobby, -bies
hobbyhorse

hobie	hobby

hobnail
hobnob, -nobbed, -nobbing
hobo, -bos, -boes

hochpoch	hotchpotch

hock, -ed, -ing
hockey

hockie	hockey

hocus-pocus, -cussed, -cussing
hod
hoe, hoed, hoeing (tool)

hoes	hose (water)

hog, hogged, hogging
hogget
hogshead

hogshed	hogshead

hogwash
hoi polloi
hoist, -ed, -ing

hokem	hokum

hokey pokey
hokum
hold, held, holding
holdfast
hold-up
hole, holed, holing (opening)

hole	whole (all)

holey	wholly

holiday

holie	holly (plant)
holie	holy (saint)
holie	wholly (all)
holihock	hollyhock

holiness
holland
holler, -ed, -ing (shout)
hollow, -ly (hole)
holly, -lies (plant)

holly	holy (saint)
holly	wholly (all)

hollyhock
holocaust

holocost	holocaust
holow	hollow

holster
holus-bolus
holy, -lier, -liest (saint)

holy	holly (plant)
holy	wholly (all)

homage
homburg
home, -ed, -ing
home-brew
homeland
homely, -lier, -liest
homeopathy
homesick
homespun
homestead
homeward
homework
homicide

homige	homage
homiley	homily

homily, -lies

homiopathy	homeopathy
homiside	homicide

homogeneous, -ly
homogenise, -nised, -nising

homogenius	homogeneous
homonim	homonym

homonym
homophone
Homo sapiens

homoseksual homosexual
homoseksuality homosexuality
homosexual
homosexuality
hone, honed, honing
honest, -ly
honesty
honey, honeys
honeybee
honeycomb
honeydew
honeyeater
honeymoon
honeysuckle
hongi
　honie honey
honk,-ed, -ing
honky-tonk
honorarium, -rariums, -raria
honorary
honorific, -ally
honour, -ed, -ing
honourable, -bly
　hony honey
hood, -ed, -ing
hoodlum
hoodwink, -ed, -ing
hoof, hoofs, hooves
hook, -ed, -ing
hookah
hooker
　hookie hooky
hook-up
hookworm
hooky
　hoola-hoola hula-hula
hooligan
hoop
　hooping coff whooping
　 cough
hoopla
hooray
hooroo
hoot, -ed, -ing
hooter
hoover
hop, hopped, hopping

hope, hoped, hoping
hopeful
　hopefull hopeful
hopeless, -ly
hopper
hopping-mouse
hopsack
hopscotch
horde, horded, hording (animals)
　horde hoard (gather)
　hore whore
　horendus horrendous
　horer horror
　horible horrible
　horid horrid
　horific horrific
　horify horrify
horizon
horizontal, -ly
hormone
horn, -ed, -ing
hornbill
hornpipe
horn-rimmed
horny, -nier, -niest
horology
　horor horror
horoscope
horrendous, -ly
horrible, -bly
　horribul horrible
horrid, -ly
horrific
horrify, -fied, -fying
horror
hors d'oeuvre
horse, horses (animal)
horse, horsed, horsing
　horse hawse (ship)
　horse hoarse (voice)
horseflesh
horseplay
horsepower
horserace
horseradish
horseshoe, -shoed, -shoeing
horsy, -sier, -siest

hortative, -ly
hortatory
   horthorn   hawthorn
   horticulcher   horticulture
horticulture
   hortie   haughty
hose, hosed, hosing (water)
   hose   hoes (tools)
hosiery
hospice
hospitable, -bly
   hospitabul   hospitable
hospital
hospitality, -ties
host, -ed, -ing
hostage
   hostaple   hospital
hostel
hostess
   hostige   hostage
hostile, -ly
hostility, -ties
hot, hotted, hotting
hot, hotter, hottest
hot-blooded
hotchpotch
hotel
hotelier
   hoter   hotter
   hotest   hottest
hotfoot
hothead
hot-headed, -ly
   hothed   hothead
   hotheded   hotheaded
hothouse
hotplate
hotpot
hot rod
hot seat
hot-shot
hot-water bottle
hound, -ed, -ing
hound's-tooth
hour (time)
   hour   our
hourglass

houri, -ris
hourly
house, houses
house, housed, housing
houseboat
housebreaker
housebroken
housecoat
housefly, -flies
household
housekeeper
housemaid
House of Commons
houseproud
house-train
house-warming
housewife, -wives
housey-housey
housie-housie
housing
hovel, -elled, -elling
hover, -ed, -ing
hovercraft
how
however
howl, -ed, -ing
howler
   hownd   hound
   howse   house
howsoever
hoy
hoyden
   hu   hew (cut)
   hu   hue (colour)
hubbub
   huch   hutch
huckster
huddle, -dled, -dling
hue (colour)
   hue   hew (cut)
   huf   huff
huff, -ed, -ing
hug, hugged, hugging
huge, huger, hugest
   hul   hull
hula-hula
   hulabaloo   hullabaloo

hulk
hull,-ed, -ing
hullabaloo
hullo
hum, hummed, humming
human
humane, -ly
humanism
humanist
humanitarian
humanity, -ties
humanly
humanoid
humble, -bled, -bling
humble, -bler, -blest
humble pie
humbug, -bugged, -bugging
humbul — humble
humdinger
humdrum
humer — humour
humerist — humorist
humerus, -meri (bone)
humerus — humorous
(funny)
humid, -ly
humidifier
humidity
humiliate, -ated, -ating
humiliation
humility, -ties
hummingbird
hummock
humock — hummock
humorist
humorous, -ly (funny)
humorous — humerus (bone)
humour, -ed, -ing
hump, -ed, -ing
humpback
humpy, -pier, -piest
humus
hunch, -ed, -ing
hunchback
hundred, -dreds
hundredfold
hundredth

huney — honey
hunger
hungrie — hungry
hungry, -grier, -griest
hunie — honey
hunk
hunt, -ed, -ing
hunter
huntress
huntsman, -men
Huon pine
huray — hurray
hurd — heard (listen)
hurd — herd (animals)
hurdiegurdie — hurdy-gurdy
hurdle, -dled, -dling
hurdul — hurdle
hurdy-gurdy, -dies
huricane — hurricane
hurie — hurry
hurl, -ed, -ing
hurlie-burlie — hurly-burly
hurly-burly, -burlies
hurmit — hermit
hurnia — hernia
hurray
hurricane
hurry, -ried, -rying
hurse — hearse
hurt, hurt, hurting
hurtel — hurtle
hurtle, -tled, -tling
hurtul — hurtle
hurtz — hertz
hury — hurry
husband
husbandry
hush, -ed, -ing
husie — hussy
husk
huskie — husky
husky, -kier, -kiest (hoarse)
husky, -kies (dog)
hussar
hussel — hustle
hussey — hussy
hussul — hustle

hussy, -sies
hustings
hustle, -tled, -tling
hut, hutted, hutting
hutch
hutkeeper
hyacinth
hybrid
hydatids
hydra, -dras, -drae
hydrangea
   hydranja   hydrangea
hydrant
hydrate, -drated, -drating
hydration
hydraulic, -ally
hydrocarbon
hydrochloric acid
hydro-electric
   hydrofobia   hydrophobia
hydrofoil
hydrogen
hydrologist
hydrology
   hydrolic   hydraulic
hydrolysis, -ses
hydrometer
hydroplane, -planed, -planing
hydroponics
hydrous
hydroxide
hyena
   hygene   hygiene
hygiene
hygienic, -ally
hygroscopic
   hym   hymn
hymen
hymn (song)
hymnal
hype, hyped, hyping
hyperactive
hyperbola, -las (curve)
hyperbole (overstatement)
hypersensitive
hypertension
hyphen

hyphenate, -nated, -nating
hypnosis, -ses
hypnotherapy
hypnotise, -tised, -tising
hypnotism
hypo
hypochondria
hypocrisy, -sies
hypocrite
hypodermic
hypodermic syringe
hypotenuse
hypothesis, -ses
hypothesise, -sised, -sising
hypothetical, -ly
hysterectomy, -mies
hysteria
hysteric
hysterical, -ly

Ii

ibis
ice, iced, icing
iceberg
icebound
icebox
icebreaker
ice-cream
icepack
icepick
ich — itch
icicle
iclesiastic — ecclesiastic
iclipse — eclipse
icon, icons
iconoclast
iconomey — economy
iconomist — economist
icy, icier, iciest
idea
ideal, -ly
idealise, -ised, -ising
idealism
idem
identical, -ly
identicul — identical
identification
identify, -fied, -fying
identikit
identity, -ties
ideology, -gies
iderdown — eiderdown
ides
idilic — idyllic
idill — idyll
idiocy, -cies
idiologey — ideology
idiom
idiomatic, -ally

idiosincrasy — idiosyncrasy
idiosyncrasy, -sies
idiot
idium — idiom
idle, idled, idling (not busy)
idle — idol (statue)
idler
idol (statue)
idol — idle (not busy)
idolatry, -tries
idolise, -lised, -lising
idyl — idyll
idyll
idyllic, -ally
iface — efface
ifect — effect
ifel — Eiffel
ifeminite — effeminate
ificiency — efficiency
igalitarian — egalitarian
igloo, -loos
igneous
ignishun — ignition
ignite, -nited, -niting
ignition
ignition coil
ignius — igneous
ignoble, -bly
ignominy, -minies
ignor — ignore
ignoramus, -muses
ignorant, -ly
ignore, -nored, -noring
iguana
iguarna — iguana
ijaculation — ejaculation
ijection — ejection
ikon, ikons
ikuip — equip
ikwivocal — equivocal
ikwivocate — equivocate
il — I'll (I will)
il — ill (sick)
ilaberate — elaborate
iland — island
ilapse — elapse
ilation — elation

ilastic	elastic
ilate	elate
ile	aisle (passage)
Ile	I'll (I will)
ile	isle (island)
ilect	elect
ilection	election
ilectorate	electorate
ilectrocute	electrocute
ilectronic	electronic
ilegal	illegal
ilegibul	illegible
ilegitimate	illegitimate
ileven	eleven
ilicit	elicit
ilicit	illicit
ilikser	elixir
iliminate	eliminate
ilimination	elimination
ilipse	ellipse
iliptic	elliptic
ilisit	elicit
ilisit	illicit
iliteracy	illiteracy
iliterate	illiterate
ilixir	elixir

ilk
I'll (I will)
ill, worse, worst (sick)
ill-advised, -ly
ill-assorted
ill-bred
ill-defined
illegal, -ly
illegible, -bly

illegibul	illegible

illegitimate, -ly
ill-fated
ill-gotten
ill health
illiberal, -ly
illicit, -ly (unlawful)

illicit	elicit (evoke)

illiteracy
illiterate
ill-mannered, -ly
ill-natured, -ly

illness
illogical, -ly
ill-treat, -ed, -ing
illuminate, -nated, -nating
illumination
illumine, -mined, -mining
ill-use, -used, -using
illusion (deception)

illusion	allusion (brief reference)
illusion	elusion (evade)

illusive (deceptive)

illusive	allusive
illusive	elusive

illusory
illustrate, -strated, -strating
illustration
illustrative, -ly
illustrator
illustrious, -ly
ill will

ilogical	illogical
ilope	elope
ilucidate	elucidate
ilude	elude
iluminate	illuminate
ilumination	illumination
ilusidate	elucidate
ilusion	allusion
ilusion	elusion
ilusion	illusion
ilusive	allusive
ilusive	elusive
ilusive	illusive
ilustrate	illustrate
ilustration	illustration
ilustrator	illustrator
ilustrius	illustrious

I'm (I am)

Im	I'm
imaciate	emaciate
imaculate	immaculate

image, -aged, -aging
imagery, -ries

imagin	imagine

imaginary, -ries
imagination

imaginative
imagine, -ined, -ining

imancipate	emancipate
imansipation	emancipation
imashiate	emaciate
imaterial	immaterial
imature	immature
imaturity	immaturity

imbalance

imbalanse	imbalance
imbarrass	embarrass

imbecile, -ly

imbeseal	imbecile

imbibe, -bibed, -bibing
imbroglio, -os
imbue, -bued, -buing

imerge	emerge
imergence	emergence
imergency	emergency
imergent	emergent
imetic	emetic
imission	emission
imit	emit

> For other **im**- words, look
> under **imm**-.

imitate, -tated, -tating
imitation
immaculate, -ly
immanent (inherent)

immanent	eminent
	(known)
immanent	imminent
	(near)

immaterial, -ly
immature, -ly
immeasurable, -bly
immediate, -ly
immemorial, -ly
immense, -ly
immerse, -mersed, -mersing

immershun	immersion

immersion

immesurable	immeasurable

immigrant
immigrate, -grated, -grating
imminent (near)

imminent	eminent
	(known)
imminent	immanent
	(inherent)

immobile
immobility
immoderate, -ly
immodest, -ly
immolate, -lated, -lating
immoral, -ly
immortal, -ly
immortalise, -lised, -lising
immortality, -ties
immovable, -bly
immune, -ly
immunise, -nised, -nising
immunology
immure, -mured, -muring
immutable, -bly

imolient	emollient
imolument	emolument
imoshen	emotion
imoshun	emotion
imoshunal	emotional
imotion	emotion
imotive	emotive

imp
impact, -ed, -ing
impair, -ed, -ing
impale, -paled, -paling
impalpable, -bly

impare	impair
imparshal	impartial

impart, -ed, -ing
impartial, -ly

impasable	impassable
impashent	impatient
impasioned	impassioned
impasive	impassive

impassable, -bly
impasse
impassioned, -ly
impassive, -ly
impatient, -ly
impeach, -ed, -ing

impecabul	impeccable

impeccable, -bly

impecunious, -ly
   impecunius   impecunious
impede, -peded, -peding
impediment, -ary
   impeech   impeach
impel, -pelled, -pelling
impenetrable, -bly
   impenge   impinge
imperative, -ly
   imperceptibel   imperceptible
imperceptible, -bly
imperfect, -ly
imperial, -ly
imperialism
imperil, -rilled, -rilling
imperious, -ly
   imperius   imperious
impermeable, -bly
   impermeabul   impermeable
   imperseptibul   imperceptible
impersonal, -ly
impersonate, -nated, -nating
impertinence
   impertinense   impertinence
imperturbable, -bly
impervious, -ly
   impervius   impervious
impetuous, -ly
impetus, -tuses
impiety, -ties
impinge, -pinged, -pinging
impious, -ly
impish, -ly
   impius   impious
implacable, -bly
   implacabul   implacable
implant, -ed, -ing
implausible, -bly
   implausibul   implausible
implement, -ed, -ing
implicate, -cated, -cating
implication
implicit, -ly
   implie   imply
implied
   implisit   implicit
implode, -ploded, -ploding

implore, -plored, -ploring
imply, -plied, -plying
impolite, -ly
impolitic, -ly
import, -ed, -ing
importance
   importanse   importance
important, -ly
importunate, -ly
importune, -tuned, -tuning
   imposcher   imposture
impose, -posed, -posing
   imposibul   impossible
   imposishun   imposition
imposition
impossible, -bly
   imposter   impostor
impostor
imposture
impotence
impotent, -ly
impound, -ed, -ing
impoverish, -ed, -ing
impracticability
impracticable, -bly
   impracticabul   impracticable
impractical, -ly
imprecate, -cated, -cating
imprecise, -ly
impregnable, -bly
   impregnabul   impregnable
impregnate, -nated, -nating
   impres   impress
impresario, -os
   impreshun   impression
   impreshunable   impressionable
   impreshunism   impressionism
   impresise   imprecise
   impresive   impressive
impress, -pressed, -pressing
impression
impressionable, -bly
impressionism
impressive, -ly
imprimatur
imprint, -ed, -ing
imprison, -ed, -ing

improbable, -bly
impromptu
improper, -ly
impropriety, -ties
improve, -proved, -proving
improvement
improvident, -ly
improvise, -vised, -vising
imprudent, -ly

| impruve | improve |

impudent, -ly
impugn, -ed, -ing
impulse

| impune | impugn |

impunity
impure, impurer, impurist
impute, -puted, -puting

imulshun	emulsion
imune	immune
imunologey	immunology
imurge	emerge

in

| in | inn (hotel) |

inability

| in absenshia | in absentia |

in absentia

| inaccessabul | inaccessible |

inaccessible, -bly
inaccuracy, -cies
inactive, -ly

inacuracy	inaccuracy
inacurasey	inaccuracy
inadekwat	inadequate

inadequate, -ly
inadvertent, -ly
inalienable, -bly

| inalienabul | inalienable |

inane, -ly
inanimate, -ly
inappreciable, -bly

| inappreciabul | inappreciable |

inappropriate, -ly

| inapropriate | inappropriate |

inapt, -ly
inaptitude
inarticulate, -ly
inasmuch as

| inate | innate |
| inatentive | inattentive |

inattentive, -ly
inaugural
inaugurate, -rated, -rating
inauspicious, -ly

| inawmus | enormous |
| inawspishus | inauspicious |

inborn
inbreed, -bred, -breeding
incalculable, -bly
in camera
incandescence
incandescent, -ly

| incandesence | incandescence |

incantation
incapable, -bly

| incapabul | incapable |

incapacitate, -tated, -tating
incapacity, -ties

| incapasitate | incapacitate |
| incapasitey | incapacity |

incarcerate, -rated, -rating
incarnate, -nated, -nating

| incarserate | incarcerate |

incendiary, -aries
incense (perfume)
incense, -censed, -censing (angry)
incentive
inception
incessant, -ly

| incessent | incessant |

incest
incestuous, -ly
inch, -ed, -ing
incidence
incident
incidental, -ly
incinerate, -rated, -rating
incinerator
incipient, -ly
incise, -cised, -cising
incision
incisive, -ly
incisor
incite, -cited, -citing (urge)

| incite | insight (see) |

incivility, -ties
inclement, -ly
inclination
incline, -clined, -clining
inclose   enclose
include, -cluded, -cluding
inclusion
inclusive, -ly
incognito, -tos
incoherent, -ly
income
incommensurable, -bly
incommensurate, -ly
incommode, -moded, -moding
incommodity, -ties
incommunicability
incommunicable, -bly
incommunicado
incommunicative, -ly
incomparable, -bly
incompatible, -bly
incompatibul   incompatible
incompetent, -ly
incomplete, -ly
incomprehensible, -bly
incomprehension
incomunicado   incommunicado
inconceivable, -bly
inconcievable   inconceivable
inconclusive, -ly
incongruous, -ly
incongruus   incongruous
inconseavable   inconceivable
inconsequent, -ly
inconsequential, -ly
inconsiderate, -ly
inconsistant   inconsistent
inconsistent,-ly
inconsolable, -bly
inconsolabul   inconsolable
inconspicuous, -ly
inconstant, -ly
incontestable, -bly
incontestabul   incontestable
incontinent, -ly
incontrovertible, -bly
inconvenience, -ienced, -iencing

inconvenient, -ly
incorect   incorrect
incorigibul   incorrigible
incorporate, -rated, -rating
incorporation
incorrect, -ly
incorrigible, -bly
incorrupt, -ly
incorruptible, -bly
increase, -creased, -creasing
incredible, -bly
incredibul   incredible
incredulity
incredulous, -ly
incredulus   incredulous
increment
incremental
increse   increase
incriminate, -nated, -nating
incubate, -bated, -bating
incubator
inculcate, -cated, -cating
incum   income
incumbent, -ly
incumbrance
incur, -curred, -curring
incurable, -bly
incurabul   incurable
incurshun   incursion
incursion
indebted
indecent, -ly
indecipherable
indecishun   indecision
indecision
indecisive, -ly
indeclinable
indeclinabul   indeclinable
indecorous, -ly
indecorus   indecorous
indeed
indefatigable, -bly
indefatigabul   indefatigable
indefeasible, -bly
indefeasibul   indefeasible
indefensible, -bly
indefensibul   indefensible

indefinable, -bly
  indefinabul   indefinable
indefinite, -ly
  indeks   index
indelible, -bly
  indelibul   indelible
indelicate, -ly
  indemnifie   indemnify
indemnify, -fied, -fying
indemnity, -ties
  indencher   indenture
indent, -ed, -ing
indenture, -tured, -turing
independent, -ly
in-depth
indescribable, -bly
  indescribabul   indescribable
  indesent   indecent
  indesiferable   indecipherable
  indespensable   indispensable
indestructible, -bly
  indestructibul   indestructible
  indeted   indebted
indeterminate, -ly
index, -dexes, -dices
indexation
Indian
indiarubber
indicate, -cated, -cating
indicative, -ly
indicator
indices
indict, -ed, -ing
indictment
  indiferent   indifferent
indifferent, -ly
indigenous, -ly
indigent, -ly
indigestible, -bly
  indigestibul   indigestible
indigestion
indignant, -ly
indignation
indignity, -ties
indigo, -gos
  indipendent   independent
indirect, -ly

indiscreet, -ly
  indiscreshun   indiscretion
  indiscrete   indiscreet
indiscretion
indiscriminate, -ly
  indisishun   indecision
  indisisive   indecisive
  indisoluble   indissoluble
indispensable, -bly
  indispensabul   indispensable
indisposed
indisposition
indisputable, -bly
  indisputabul   indisputable
indissoluble, -bly
indistinct, -ly
indistinguishable, -bly
indite, -dited, -diting (write)
  indite   indict (accuse)
individual, -ly
individualism
individualist
individuality, -ties
indivisible, -bly
  indivisibul   indivisible
indoctrinate, -nated, -nating
indolent, -ly
indomitable, -bly
  indomitabul   indomitable
indoor
indubitable, -bly
  indubitabul   indubitable
induce, -duced, -ducing
  inducshion   induction
  inducshun   induction
induct, -ed, -ing
induction
inductive, -ly
inductor
indulge, -dulged, -dulging
indulgence
  indulgense   indulgence
indulgent, -ly
  industrey   industry
industrial, -ly
industrialise, -lised, -lising
industrialism

industrialist
industrious, -ly
   industrius — industrious
industry, -tries
inebriate, -ated, -ating
inebriation
inedible
   inedibul — inedible
   inefable — ineffable
   inefective — ineffective
   inefectual — ineffectual
ineffable, -bly
ineffective, -ly
ineffectual, -ly
inefficient, -ly

> For **ineks-** words, look
> under **inex-**.

inelegant, -ly
ineligible, -bly
   ineligibul — ineligible
inept, -ly
inequality, -ties
inequitable, -bly
   inequitabul — inequitable
inequity, -ties
ineradicable, -bly
   ineradicabul — ineradicable
   inersha — inertia
inert, -ly
inertia
inescapable, -bly
   inescapabul — inescapable
   inesenshul — inessential
inessential, -ly
inestimable, -bly
   inestimabul — inestimable
inevitable, -bly
   inevitabul — inevitable
inexact, -ly
inexcusable, -bly
inexhaustible, -bly
inexorable, -bly
   inexorabul — inexorable
inexpedient, -ly
inexpensive, -ly
inexperienced

   inexperiense — inexperience
inexpert, -ly
inexplicable, -bly
inexplicit, -ly
inexpressible, -bly
in extremis
inextricable, -bly
   infalible — infallible
   infalibul — infallible
infallible, -bly
   infamey — infamy
infamous, -ly
   infamus — infamous
infamy, -mies
infancy, -cies
   infansey — infancy
infant
infanticide
   infantiside — infanticide
infantile
   infantrey — infantry
infantry
infatuate, -ated, -ating
infatuation
   infecshun — infection
infect, -ed, -ing
infection
infectious, -ly
infelicity, -ties
infer, -ferred, -ferring
inference
   inferense — inference
   inferier — inferior
inferior
inferiority complex
   inferm — infirm
   infermarey — infirmary
infernal, -ly
inferno, -nos
infertile
infest, -ed, -ing
infidel
infidelity, -ties
infighting
infiltrate, -trated, -trating
infinite, -ly
infinitesimal, -ly

infinitey   infinity
infinitive, -ly
infinity, -ties
infirior   inferior
infirm, -ly
infirmary, -ries
inflamabul   inflammable
inflamatry   inflammatory
inflame, -flamed, -flaming
inflammable, -bly
inflammation
inflammatory
inflatable
inflate, -flated, -flating
inflation
inflect, -ed, -ing
inflection
inflexible, -bly
inflict, -ed, -ing
infliction
inflow
influence, -enced, -encing
influense   influence
influenshul   influential
influential, -ly
influenza
influks   influx
inform, -ed, -ing
informal, -ly
informant
information
informer
infracshun   infraction
infraction
infra-red
infrastructure
infrekwency   infrequency
infrekwent   infrequent
infrequency
infrequent, -ly
infringe, -fringed, -fringing
infuriate, -ated, -ating
infurnal   infernal
infuse, -fused, -fusing
infusion
infusun   infusion
ingenious, -ly (clever)

ingenius   ingenious
ingenue
ingenuity, -ties
ingenuous, -ly (innocent)
ingenuus   ingenuous
ingest, -ed, -ing
ingestion
Inglish   English
ingot
ingrain, -ed, -ing
ingrashiate   ingratiate
ingrate
ingratiate, -ated, -ating
ingratitude
ingrave   engrave
ingredient
ingress
in-groop   in-group
in-group
ingrown
inhabit, -ed, -ing
inhalant
inhalation
inhale, -haled, -haling
inhear   inhere
inhere, -hered, -hering
inherent, -ly
inherit, -ed, -ing
inheritance
inheritanse   inheritance
inhibishun   inhibition
inhibit, -ed, -ing
inhospitable, -bly
inhospitabul   inhospitable
inhospitality
inhuman, -ly
inhumane, -ly
inhumanity, -ties
inikwality   inequality
inikwity   iniquity
inikwitus   iniquitous
inimical, -ly
inimitable, -bly
inimitability
inimitabul   inimitable
inings   innings
iniquitey   iniquity

iniquitous, -ly
   iniquitus — iniquitous
iniquity, -ties (sin)
   iniquity — inequity (unfair)
   inishal — initial
   inishative — initiative
   inishiate — initiate
initial, -ialled, -ialling
initiate, -ated, -ating
initiation
initiative
inject, -ed, -ing
injection
   injenue — ingenue
   injere — injure
in-joke
injudicious, -ly
   injudishus — injudicious
injunction
   injunkshun — injunction
injure, -jured, -juring
   injurey — injury
   injurius — injurious
injury, -ries
injustice
   injustise — injustice
ink
   inkeeper — innkeeper
inkling
   inkwest — inquest
   inkwire — enquire
   inkwisitive — inquisitive
   inkwisitor — inquisitor

> For other ink- words,
> look under inc-.

   inlade — inlaid
inland
in-law
inlay, -laid, -laying
inlet
in loco parentis
inmate
in memoriam
inmost
inn (hotel)

innards
innate, -ly
inner
   innerject — interject
innermost
innings
innkeeper
innocence
innocent, -ly
innocuous, -ly
innovate, -vated, -vating
innovation
innovative, -ly
innovatory
innuendo, -dos
innumerable, -bly
innumerate
   inocent — innocent
inoculate, -lated, -lating
inoculation
   inocuus — innocuous
   inofensive — inoffensive
inoffensive, -ly
inoperable, -bly
inoperative, -ly
   inoportune — inopportune
inopportune, -ly
   inordible — inaudible
   inordibul — inaudible
inordinate, -ly
inorganic, -ally
   inorgural — inaugural
   inorgurate — inaugurate
   inormity — enormity
   inormous — enormous
   inorspishus — inauspicious
   inosence — innocence
   inosent — innocent
   inough — enough
   inovate — innovate
in-patient
   in-payshent — in-patient
input
inquest
inquietude
inquire, -quired, -quiring
inquiry, -ries

inquisitive, -ly
   inrage — enrage
inroad
   inrode — inroad
insalubrious, -ly
   insalubrius — insalubrious
   insaine — insane
insane, -ly
insanitary
   insanitey — insanity
   insanitry — insanitary
insanity, -ties
insatiable, -bly
   insayshabul — insatiable
inscribe, -scribed, -scribing
inscription
inscrutable, -bly
inscrutability
insect
insecticide
   insectiside — insecticide
insecure, -ly
insecurity, -ties
inseminate, -nated, -nating
insemination
   insendiary — incendiary
insensate, -ly
   insense — incense
insensible, -bly
insensibility, -ties
   insensibul — insensible
insensitive, -ly
insensitivity
   insentive — incentive
inseparable, -bly
   inseperabul — inseparable
   inseprabul — inseparable
   insepshun — inception
insert, -ed, -ing
insertion
   insertitude — incertitude
in-service
   insesent — incessant
   insest — incest
   insestuous — incestuous
inset, -set, -setting
   inshoranse — insurance

   inshore — ensure (certain)
   inshore — insure (protect)
   inshorense — insurance
inside
   insidense — incidence
   insident — incident
   insidentul — incidental
insidious, -ly
   insidius — insidious
insight, (see)
   insight — incite (urge)
insignia
insignificance
insignificant, -ly
insincere, -ly
insincerity, -ties
   insinerate — incinerate
   insinerater — incinerator
   insinsere — insincere
   insinserity — insincerity
insinuate, -ated, -ating
insipid, -ly
   insipient — incipient
   insiser — inciser
   insision — incision
   insisive — incisive
insist, -ed, -ing
insistence
insistent, -ly
   insite — incite (urge)
   insite — insight (see)
   insivility — incivility
insobriety
insofar
insolence
   insolense — insolence
insolent, -ly
insolubility
insoluble, -bly
   insolubul — insoluble
insolvency
   insolvensy — insolvency
insolvent
insomnia
   inspechun — inspection
inspect, -ed, -ing
   inspecter — inspector

inspection

inspector

inspiration

inspire, -spired, -spiring

instability

instagate	instigate
instal	install

install, -ed, -ing

installment	instalment

instalment

instance, -stanced, -stancing

instanse	instance

instant, -ly

instantaneous, -ly

instantanius	instantaneous
instatution	institution

instead

insted	instead

instep

instigate, -gated, -gating

instigater	instigator

instigation

instigator

instil	instill
instilashun	instillation

instill, -stilled, -stilling

instillation

instinct

instinctive, -ly

institushen	institution

institute, -tuted, -tuting

institution

institutional, -ly

institutionalise, -lised, -lising

instremunt	instrument

instruct, -ed, -ing

instruction

instructive, -ly

instrument

instrumental, -ly

instrumentalist

instrumentation

instrument panel

insubordinate, -ly

insubordination

insubstanshul	insubstantial

insubstantial, -ly

insue	ensue

insufferable, -bly

insufficiency

insufficient, -ly

insuffishency	insufficiency
insufrabul	insufferable

insular, -ly

insularity

insulate, -lated, -lating

insulation

insulin

insult, -ed, -ing

insuperable, -bly

insuperabul	insuperable

insurance

insuranse	insurance

insure, -sured, -suring

insurecshun	insurrection

insurgence

insurgency

insurgense	insurgence

insurgent

insurmountable, -bly

insurrection

insurshun	insertion
insurt	insert

intact

intaglio, intaglios, intagli

intail	entail

intake

intangible, -bly

intangibul	intangible

integer

integral, -ly

integrate, -grated, -grating

integrated circuit

integration

integrity

intelect	intellect
intelectual	intellectual
inteligense	intelligence
inteligensia	intelligentsia
inteligent	intelligent
inteligibul	intelligible

intellect

intellectual, -ly

intelligence

intelligent, -ly
intelligentsia
intemperance
  intemperanse   intemperance
intemperate, -ly
intend, -ed, -ing
intense, -ly
  intenshun   intention
intensify, -fied, -fying
intensive, -ly
intent, -ly
intention
intentional, -ly
inter, -terred, -terring
interact, -ed, -ing
interaction
inter alia
intercede, -ceded, -ceding
intercept, -ed, -ing
interception
interceptor
  interceshun   intercession
intercession
intercessor
interchange, -changed, -changing
interchangeable, -bly
intercom
intercontinental
  intercorse   intercourse
intercourse
interdependence
interdependency
interdependent, -ly
interdict
interdisciplinary
  interelate   interrelate
interest, -ed, -ing
interface, -faced, -facing
  interfear   interfere
interfere, -fered, -fering
interference
interfuse, -fused, -fusing
intergalactic
  interier   interior
interim
interior
interject, -ed, -ing

interjection
injector
interlace, -laced, -lacing
interline, -lined, -lining
interlock, -ed, -ing
  interloap   interlope
  interlood   interlude
interlope, -loped, -loping
interloper
interlude
  intermarie   intermarry
intermarry, -ried, -rying
intermediary, -aries
intermediate, -ly
interment
intermesh, -ed, -ing
intermezzo, -zos, -zi
interminable, -bly
  interminabul   interminable
  intermishun   intermission
intermission
intermittent, -ly
intern
internal, -ly
internal-combustion engine
internalise, -lised, -lising
  internashunal   international
international, -ly
internationale
internationalism
internecine
internee
  internisine   internecine
  interogate   interrogate
interpersonal, -ly
interplay, -ed, -ing
interpolate, -lated, -lating
interpose, -posed, -posing
interpret, -ed, -ing
interpretation
interpreter
interracial, -ly
interregnum, -nums
interrelate, -lated, -lating
interrogate, -gated, -gating
interrogation
interrogative, -ly

interrogator
interrupt, -ed, -ing
interruption
intersect, -ed, -ing
intersection
  intersede   intercede
  intersepshun   interception
  intersept   intercept
  interseshun   intercession
intersperse, -spersed, -spersing
  interspurse   intersperse
interstate
interstice, -tices
intertwine, -twined, -twining
  interupshun   interruption
interurban
interval
  interveiw   interview
intervene, -vened, -vening
intervener
  intervenor   intervener
  intervenshun   intervention
intervention
interview, -ed, -ing
interviewer
  intervue   interview
interweave, -woven, -weaving
interweaver
intestate
intestine
  intice   entice
  intiger   integer
  intigral   integral
  intigrate   integrate
intimacy, -cies
  intimasy   intimacy
intimate, -ly
intimate, -mated, -mating
intimation
intimidate, -dated, -dating
intimidation
intimidator
  intoksicate   intoxicate
intolerable, -bly
  intolerabul   intolerable
intolerance
  intoleranse   intolerance

intolerant, -ly
intonation
intone, -toned, -toning
in toto
intoxicant
intoxicate, -cated, -cating
intoxication
intractable, -bly
  intractabul   intractable
intransigence
intransigency
  intransigense   intransigence
  intransigensy   intransigency
intransigent, -ly
intransitive, -ly
intrastate
intra-uterine device
intravenous, -ly
  intravenus   intravenous
in-tray
  intreege   intrigue
intrepid, -ly
intricacy, -cies
  intricasey   intricacy
intricate, -ly
intrigue, -trigued, -triguing
intriguer
intrinsic, -ally
introduce, -duced, -ducing
  introducshun   introduction
introduction
introductory
  introduse   introduce
  introode   intrude
  introosive   intrusive
introspection
introvert, -ly
intrude, -truded, -truding
intruder
  intrushun   intrusion
intrusion
intrusive, -ly
  intrust   entrust
  intuishun   intuition
intuition
intuitive, -ly
  inturn   intern

inturnal	internal
inuendo	innuendo
inumerabul	innumerable
inumerate	enumerate
inumeration	enumeration
inunciate	enunciate

inundate, -dated, -dating
inundation

inunsiate	enunciate

inure, inured, inuring

inursha	inertia
inurt	inert

invade, -vaded, -vading
invalid, -ly
invalidate, -dated, -dating
invalidation
invaluable, -bly

invaluabul	invaluable
invaluble	invaluable

invariability
invariable, -bly

invariabul	invariable

invasion

invatation	invitation
invay	inveigh
invaygul	inveigle

invective, -ly
inveigh, -ed, -ing
inveigle, -gled, -gling

inveigul	inveigle
invenshun	invention

invent, -ed, -ing
invention
inventive, -ly
inventor
inventory, -tories

inventry	inventory

inverse, -ly

invershun	inversion

inversion
invert, -ed, -ing
invertebrate
invest, -ed, -ing

investagation	investigation
investichure	investiture

investigate, -gated, -gating
investigation

investigator
investiture
investment
inveterate

invidios	invidious

invidious, -ly
invidiousness

inviegh	inveigh
inviegle	inveigle

invigorate, -rated, -rating
invincible, -bly

invinsibul	invincible

inviolable, -bly

inviolabul	inviolable

inviolate, -ly
invisibility
invisible, -bly

invisibul	invisible

invitation
invite, -vited, -viting
in vitro
invocation
invoice, -voiced, -voicing

invoise	invoice

invoke, -voked, -voking
involuntary, -tarily

involuntrey	involuntary
involushun	involution

involution
involve, -volved, -volving
involvement
invulnerable, -bly

invulnerabul	invulnerable
inverce	inverse
invirt	invert

inward, -ly
inwardness
inwards

inwood	inward
inyure	inure
iodene	iodine

iodine
ion (atom)

ion	iron (metal)
ionesfere	ionosphere

ionise, -nised, -nising
ionosphere

iony	irony
iota	
IOU	
iradiate	irradiate
iradicate	eradicate
irascibility	
irascible, -bly	
irascibleness	
irascibul	irascible
irase	erase
irate, -ly	
irational	irrational
ire	

> For other ir- words,
> look under **irr-**.

iridesense	iridescence
iridesent	iridescent
iridescence	
iris, irises	
Irish	
irk (bore)	
irk	erk (rank)
irksome, -ly	
irksum	irksome
iron, -ed, -ing (metal)	
iron	ion (atom)
ironbark	
ironeus	erroneous
ironic, -ally	
ironmonger	
ironmongery	
ironware	
irony, -nies	
iroshun	erosion
irosion	erosion
irotic	erotic
irradiashun	irradiation
irradiate, -ated, -ating	
irradiation	
irrashionul	irrational
irrational, -ly	
irreconcilable, -bly	
irrecoverable, -bly	
irrecoverabul	irrecoverable
irredeemable, -bly	
irredeemabul	irredeemable

irreducibility	
irreducible, -bly	
irreducibul	irreducible
irrefutable, -bly	
irrefutabul	irrefutable
irregardless	
irregular, -ly	
irregularity, -ties	
irrelevance	
irrelevancy	
irrelevansey	irrelevancy
irrelevant, -ly	
irreligious, -ly	
irreligus	irreligious
irreparable, -bly	
irreparabul	irreparable
irreplacabul	irreplaceable
irreplaceable, -bly	
irrepresibul	irrepressible
irrepressible, -bly	
irreproachable, -bly	
irreprochabul	irreproachable
irresistabul	irresistible
irresistible, -bly	
irresolute, -ly	
irrespective, -ly	
irresponsibility	
irresponsible, -bly	
irresponsibul	irresponsible
irretraceable, -bly	
irretraseabul	irretraceable
irretrievable, -bly	
irretrievabul	irretrievable
irreverant	irreverent
irreverence	
irreverent, -ly	
irreverint	irreverent
irreversibility	
irreversible, -bly	
irreversibul	irreversible
irrevocable, -bly	
irrevocabul	irrevocable
irridescent	iridescent
irrigate, -gated, -gating	
irrigation	
irrisistabel	irresistible
irrisistabul	irresistible

irritability

irritable, -bly

  irritabul — irritable

irritancy

  irritansey — irritancy

irritant

irritate, -tated, -tating

irritation

  irrupshun — irruption

irrupt, -ed, -ing

irruption

irruptive, -ly

  isalate — isolate

  isatope — isotope

  ise — ice

  ishue — issue

  isicul — icicle

  isight — eyesight

Islam

Islamic

island

islander

isle (island)

  isle — aisle (passage)

isn't (is not)

  isnt — isn't

isobar

isolate, -lated, -lating

isolation

isolationism

isolationist

isosceles

  isosilese — isosceles

isotope

Israeli

  Isralie — Israeli

issue, issued, issuing

isthmus, -muses

  istmus — isthmus

italic

itch, -ed, -ing

item

itemise, -mised, -mising

iterate, -rated, -rating

iteration

  iternal — eternal

  iternally — eternally

  iternity — eternity

itinerant, -ly

itinerary, -ries

it'll (it will)

  itll — it'll

it's (it is)

its (possessive)

  its — it's (it is)

itself

  ivacuate — evacuate

  ivacuation — evacuation

  ivade — evade

  ivaluate — evaluate

  ivaluation — evaluation

  ivaporate — evaporate

  ivaporation — evaporation

  ivasion — evasion

  ivasive — evasive

I've (I have)

  Ive — I've

  ivent — event

  iventual — eventual

  ivery — ivory

  ivey — ivy

  ivict — evict

  iviction — eviction

  ivoke — evoke

  ivolve — evolve

ivory, -ries

ivory tower

  ivry — ivory

ivy, ivies

Ivy League

Jj

jab, jabbed, jabbing
jabber
jabiru
jacana
jacaranda
jack
jackal
jackass
jackdaw
jackdoor   jackdaw
jackeroo
jacket
jackhammer
jack-in-the-box
jackknife, -knives
jack-of-all-trades
jackpot, -potted, -potting
Jacobean
jade, jaded, jading
jaffle
jafful   jaffle
jag, jagged, jagging
jaguar
jail
jake
jalopy, -lopies
jam, jammed, jamming
jam (food)
jam   jamb (door)
jamb (door)
jamboree
jamborie   jamboree
jangle, -gled, -gling
jangul   jangle
janiter   janitor
janitor
January
Janurey   January

Japanese, -nese
japonica
jar, jarred, jarring
jargon
jarrah
jarrar   jarrah
jasmin   jasmine
jasper
jaundice, -diced, -dicing
jaundise   jaundice
jaunt, -ed, -ing
jauntie   jaunty
jaunty, -tier, -tiest
javelin
javlin   javelin
jaw
jawndise   jaundice
jawnt   jaunt
jay
jaywalk, -ed, -ing
jaywalker
jaz   jazz
jazz
jazzy, -zier, -ziest
jealous, -ly
jealousy, -ousies
jealus   jealous
jeans
jeep
jeer, -ed, -ing
Jehovah
Jehovah's Witness
jejune
jelie   jelly
jelly, -lies
jelly, -lied, -lying
jellyfish, -fish, -fishes
jelous   jealous
jelus   jealous
jely   jelly
jemey   jemmy
jemie   jemmy
jemmy, -mies
jemmy, -mied, -mying
jemy   jemmy
jeopardise, -dised, -dising
jeopardy

jepardise   jeopardise
jepardy   jeopardy
jerboa
   jeribilt   jerry-built
jerk, -ed, -ing
jerkin
jerky, -kily
jerry, -ries
jerry-build, -built, -building
jerry can
jersey
   jersie   jersey
jest, -ed, -ing
jester
Jesuit
Jesus
jet, jetted, jetting
   jetie   jetty
   jetison   jettison
jet lag
jettison, -ed, -ing
jetty, -ties
   jety   jetty
Jew
Jewish
jewel, -elled, -elling (cut gem)
   jewel   dual (two)
   jewel   duel (fight)
   jewel   joule (unit)
   jeweler   jeweller
jeweller
jewellery
   jewelrey   jewellery
jewfish
Jewry (Jewish people)
   jewry   jury (court)
jew's harp
jib, jibbed, jibbing
jibe, jibed, jibing (sail)
   jibe   gibe (scoff)
jiffy, -fies
   jifie   jiffy
   jify   jiffy
jig, jigged, jigging
jigger
jiggle, -gled, -gling
   jiggul   jiggle

jigsaw
jillaroo
jilt, -ed, -ing
   jim   gym
   jimkana   gymkhana
   jin   gin
   jingel   jingle
jingle, -gled, -gling
jingoism
   jingul   jingle
   jinks   jinx
jinx, -es
   jirashun   gyration
   jiration   gyration
   jiro   gyro
   jiroscope   gyroscope
   jist   gist
   jiter   jitter
jitter, -ed, -ing
jittery
jive, jived, jiving
job, jobbed, jobbing
jobber
jockey, -eys
jockey, -eyed, -eying
   jockie   jockey
jockstrap
   jocky   jockey
jocose, -ly
jocosity, -ties
jocular, -ly
jocularity, -ties
jocund, -ly
jocundity, -ties
jodhpurs
   jodpurs   jodhpurs
joey, -eys
jog, jogged, jogging
jogger
jogtrot, -trotted, -trotting
johnnycake
   joi   joy
join, joined, joining
joiner
joinery
joint, -ly
joist

joke, joked, joking

joker

   jollitey   jollity

jollity, -ties

jolly, -lier, -liest

jolt, -ed, -ing

   joly   jolly

jonah

jonathan

jonquil

   Joo   Jew

   Jooish   Jewish

   jool   joule (unit)

   Joone   June

   joopiter   Jupiter

   joose   deuce (two)

   joose   juice (liquid)

   joote   jute

jostle, -tled, -tling

   josul   jostle

jot, jotted, jotting

jotter

joule (unit)

   joule   dual (two)

   joule   duel (fight)

   joule   jewel (gem)

journal

journalese

journalism

journalist

   journel   journal

journey, -neys

journey, -neyed, -neying

joust, -ed, -ing

Jove

jovial, -ly

joviality

jowl

joy

joyful, -ly

joyous, -ly

joy-ride, -rode, -riding

joystick

   joyus   joyous

   ju   Jew

jube

jubilant, -ly

jubilate, -lated, -lating

jubilation

jubilee

   jubilie   jubilee

   juce   deuce (two)

   juce   juice (liquid)

Judaism

judas

judge, judged, judging

judgement

judgment

   judicacher   judicature

   judicachur   judicature

judicature

judicial, -ly

judiciary, -aries

judicious, -ly

   judishul   judicial

   judisharey   judiciary

   judishous   judicious

   judishus   judicious

judo

   juel   dual (two)

   juel   duel (fight)

   juel   jewel (gem)

   juel   joule (unit)

jug, jugged, jugging

   juge   judge

   juggement   judgement

juggernaut

juggle, -gled, -gling

juggler

   jugul   juggle

jugular

juice (liquid)

   juice   deuce (two)

juiciness

juicy, -cier, -ciest

   Juish   Jewish

jujitsu

jukebox

   jukstapose   juxtapose

julep

   Juli   July

July

jumble, -bled, -bling

jumbo, -bos

jumbuck
   jumbul   jumble
jump, -ed, -ing
jumper
jump-start
jump suit
jumpy, jumpier, jumpiest
junction
juncture
June
jungle
   jungul   jungle
   junier   junior
junior
juniper
junk
   junkcher   juncture
junket
junkie
   junkshere   juncture
   junkshun   junction
   junkshure   juncture
junta
Jupiter
   jurer   juror
   juri   jury
juridical, -ly
   jurisdickshion   jurisdiction
   jurisdickshun   jurisdiction
jurisdiction
jurisprudence
   jurisprudense   jurisprudence
   jurisprudunse   jurisprudence
jurist
   jurnal   journal
   jurney   journey
juror
jury, -ries
   juse   juice
   jusie   juicy
jussive
just, -ly
justice
justice of the peace
   justifiabel   justifiable
justifiable, -bly
justification

justify, -fied, -fying
   justise   justice
jut, jutted, jutting
jute
juvenile, -ly
   juwel   dual (two)
   juwel   duel (fight)
   juwel   jewel (gem)
   juwel   joule (unit)
   juxapose   juxtapose
   juxaposition   juxtaposition
juxtapose, -posed, -posing
juxtaposition
   jym   gym
   jyroscope   gyroscope

> Look under **c** if
> the word is not under **k**

kadaicha man
kaleidoscope
kalidascope — kaleidoscope
kalidescope — kaleidoscope
kalsomine, -mined, -mining
kamikaze
kampong
kanaka
kangaroo
kaolin
ka pai
kapok
kaput
karate
karkey — khaki
karki — khaki
karma
karri, -ris (tree)
karri — carry (bring)
kauri, -ris
kayak
kebab
kedgeree
keel, -ed, -ing
keen, -ly
keenness
keep, kept, keeping
keeper
keg
kelp
kelpey — kelpie
kelpie
kelt — Celt
keltic — Celtic
ken, kenned, kenning

kenel — kennel
kennel, -nelled, -nelling
kept
keratin
kerb (gutter)
kerb — curb (check)
kerchief
kerfuffle
kernel (core)
kernel — colonel (army)
kero
keropody — chiropody
keroseen — kerosene
kerosene
kerosine
kestrel
ketch
ketchup
ketle — kettle
kettle
kettledrum
kettul — kettle
kew — cue
kew — queue (line)
kewpie
key, keys (lock)
key, keyed, keying
key — quay (wharf)
keyboard
keystone
khaki, -kis
kibble, -bled, -bling
kibbul — kibble
kiak — kayak
kibbutz
kick, kicked, kicking
kick-off
kid, kidded, kidding
kidnap, -napped, -napping
kidney, -neys
kikuyu
kill, killed, killing
killer
killjoy
kiln
kilo
kilogram

kilojoule
  kilometer   kilometre
kilometre
kilowatt
kilowatt-hour
kilt
kilter
kimono, -nos
kin
kina
kind, -ly
kindness
kindergarten
kindle, -dled, -dling
kindly, -lier, -liest
kindred
  kindrid   kindred
  kindrud   kindred
  kindul   kindle
kinetics
king
kingdom
kingly
kingfish
kingfisher
kingpin
kink, kinked, kinking
kinkiness
kinky, -kier, -kiest
kinsfolk
kinship
kinsman, -men
kiosk
kip, kipped, kipping
kipper
kirk
  kiropody   chiropody
kismet
kiss, kissed, kissing
kissable
kit, kitted, kitting
kitbag
kitchen
kite
  kiten   kitten
kith
  kitie   kitty

kitsch
kitten
kittenish, -ly
kitty, -ties
  kity   kitty
kiwi
  kiyak   kayak
klaxon
kleptomania
knack
knacker
knapsack
knave (rogue)
  knave   nave (church)
knead, -ed, -ing, (dough)
  knead   need (want)
knee, kneed, kneeing
kneecap
kneel, knelt, kneeling
knell, -ed, -ing
knew
  knew   gnu (animal)
  knew   new
knickerbockers
knick-knack
knife, knives
knife, knifed, knifing
knight (lord)
  knight   night (time)
knighthood
knit, knitted, knitting
knitwear
knob, knobbed, knobbing (handle)
knobbly
knobby, -bier, -biest
knock, -ed, -ing
knockabout
knock-back
knockdown
knocker
knock-knee
knockout
knoll
knot, knotted, knotting (tie)
  knot   not (denial)
knothole
knotty, -tier, -tiest

know, knew, known, knowing
know-all
know how
knowledge
knowledgeable, -bly
knuckle, -led, -ling
knuckle-duster
koala
kola   koala
kookaburra
koori
korodji
Koran
korowai
koroway   korowai
kosher
kowtow, -ed, -ing
Kremlin
kris
Krishna
kudos
kumquat
kung-fu
kurrajong

> For kw- words, look under
> **qu-**.

kylie

LI

label, -belled, -belling
  laber   labour
labial, -ly
labiate
  labirinth   labyrinth
labium, -bia
  lable   label
  labor   labour
laboratory, -ries
  laboratrey   laboratory
laborious, -ly
  laborius   laborious
labour, -ed, -ing
labourer
labour-intensive
Labrador
  labratory   laboratory
  labrinth   labyrinth
  laburnem   laburnum
laburnum
labyrinth
labyrinthine
lace, laced, lacing
lacebark
lacerate, -rated, -rating
laceration
  lach   latch
lack, -ed, -ing
lackadaisical, -ly
  lacker   lacquer
lackey, -eys
lackey, -eyed, -eying
  lacky   lackey
laconic, -ally
lacquer, -ed, -ing
  lacross   lacrosse
lacrosse
lactate, -tated, -tating

lactation
lacteal, -ly
lactic
lactose
lad
ladder
lade, laded, laden, lading (load)
  lade   laid (placed)
  ladel   ladle
  lader   ladder
  ladie   lady
ladle, -dled, -dling
  ladul   ladle
lady, -dies
ladybird
lag, lagged, lagging
  lagard   laggard
lager
laggard, -ly
  laghable   laughable
lagoon
laid (placed)
  laid   lade (load)
laid-back
  laim   lame
lain (did lie)
  lain   lane (passage)
lair (den)
  lair   layer
  laissay fair   laissez faire
laissez faire
  laitie   laity
laity
lake
  lakross   lacrosse
  laks   lax
  laksative   laxative
lam, lammed, lamming (spike)
  lam   lamb (sheep)
lama
lamb (sheep)
  lamb   lam (spike)
lambaste, -basted, -basting
lame, lamed, laming
lame, lamer, lamest
lament, -ed, -ing
lamentable, -bly

lamentation
laminate, -nated, -nating
lamington
lamp
lampoon, -ed, -ing
lampoonist
lamp-post
   lampray   lamprey
lamprey, -reys
lance, lanced, lancing
lancet
land, -ed, -ing
landfall
landform
landlady, -dies
landlocked
landlord
landlubber
landmark
landmass
landmine
land rights
landscape, -scaped, -scaping
landslide
lane (passage)
   lane   lain (did lie)
language
languid, -ly
languish, -ed, -ing
   languer   languor
languorous, -ly
   langwid   languid
   langwidge   language
   langwish   languish
lank, -ly
   landladie   landlady
   lanladie   landlady
   lanlady   landlady
   lanlord   landlord
lanolin
lanoline
   lanse   lance
   lanser   lancer
   lanset   lancet
lantana
lantern
lanyard

lap, lapped, lapping
lapel
lapelled
lapidary, -ries
lapis lazuli
lap-lap
lapse, lapsed, lapsing
larceny, -nies
larcenous, -ly
   larconic   laconic
lard
larder
large, -ly
largess
lariat
   laringitis   laryngitis
   larinx   larynx
lark
larrikin
   larseny   larceny
larva, -vae (insect)
   larva   lava (rock)
laryngitis
larynx, larynxes
lascivious, -ly
   lase   lace
laser
   laserate   lacerate
lash, -ed, -ing
   lasitude   lassitude
   lasivious   lascivious
   lasivius   lascivious
   lasoo   lasso
   lasor   laser
lass
lassitude
lasso, -sos, -soes
lasso, -soed, -soing
last, lasted, lasting
last-ditch
lastly
latch, -ed, -ing
latchkey
late, later, latest
lately
latency
   latensey   latency

latent, -ly
lateral, -ly
latex, latexes
lath (strip)
lathe (machine)
lather, -ed, -ing
lathery
Latin
   latise — lattice
latitude
latrine
latter
lattice
laud, lauded, lauding (praise)
   laud — lord (ruler)
laudable, -bly
laudanum
laudation
laudatory
laugh, laughed, laughing
laughable, -bly
laughter
   laun — lawn
launch, launched, launching
launder, -ed, -ing
   laundrey — laundry
laundromat
laundry, -dries
laureate
laurel, -relled, -relling
   lauyer — lawyer
lava (rock)
   lava — larva (insect)
lavatory, -ries
   lavatree — lavatory
   lavatrey — lavatory
lave, laved, laving
lavender
lavish, lavished, lavishing
law (rule)
   law — lore (learn)
   lawd — laud (praise)
   lawd — lord (ruler)
   lawdabul — laudable
lawful, -ly
lawless, -ly
lawn

   lawnch — launch
   lawnder — launder
   lawndrey — laundry
   lawndromat — laundromat
   lawndry — laundry
lawsuit
   lawsute — lawsuit
lawyer
lax, -ly
   lax — lacks
   laxadasical — lackadaisical
laxative
laxity
lay, laid, laying (rest)
   lay — lei (flowers)
   laybie — lay-by
lay-by
layer
layette
layman, -men
layout
laze, lazed, lazing
lazily
lazy, -zier, -ziest
lea (meadow)
   lea — lee (shelter)
leach, -ed, -ing (filter)
   leach — leech (worm)
lead, led, leading (show)
lead (metal)
   lead — led (shown)
leaden, -ly
leader
leadership
leaf, leaves
leaflet
league
leak (hole)
   leak — leek (food)
leakage
lean, leant or leaned, leaning (bend)
   leant — Lent (season)
   leant — lent (did lend)
lean-to
leap, leapt or leaped, leaping
leapfrog, -frogged, -frogging
learn, learnt or learned, learning

learner
lease, leased, leasing
leasehold
leash, -ed, -ing
  leashur — leisure
  leason — liaison
least
  leasure — leisure
  leasurely — leisurely
leather
leatherjacket
leave, left, leaving
leaven, -ed, -ing
  leaver — lever
lecher (man)
  lecher — lecture (talk)
lecherous, -ly   ·
  lecherus — lecherous
lechery
lectern
lector
lecture, -tured, -turing
lecturer
led (shown)
  led — lead (metal)
ledge
ledger (book)
  ledger — leger (stand)
lee (shelter)
  lee — lea (meadow)
  leeason — liaison
leech (worm)
  leech — leach (filter)
  leed — lead
  leef — leaf
  leeflet — leaflet
  leege — liege
  leegue — league
leek (food)
  leek — leak (hole)
  leen — lean
  leep — leap
leer, -ed, -ing
lees
  leese — lease
  leesh — leash
  leesion — lesion

  leesiun — lesion
leeward
leeway
  leewood — leeward
left
  leftenant — lieutenant
  leftenent — lieutenant
left-footer
left-handed
leftist
leftward
left-winger
leg, legged, legging
legacy, -cies
legal, -ly
legalese (language)
legalisation
legalise, -lised, -lising (authorise)
legalism
legality, -ties
  legand — legend
  legasey — legacy
  legashen — legation
legate
legation
legend
legendary, -ries
  legendrey — legendary
leger (stand)
  leger — ledger (book)
leghorn
  legibel — legible
legibility
legible, -bly
legion
legionary, -ries
legionnaire
  legislachur — legislature
legislate, -lated, -lating
legislation
legislative, -ly
legislator
legislature
legitimacy
  legitimasey — legitimacy
legitimate, -mated, -mating
legume

lei, leis (flowers)	
lei	lay (rest)
leisure	
leisurely	
lejun	legion
lejunry	legionary
leksicografer	lexicographer
leksicografey	lexicography
leksicographer	lexicographer
leksicon	lexicon
leming	lemming
lemming	
lemon	
lemonade	
lemur	
lend, lent, lending	
lender	
length	
lengthen, -ed, -ing	
lengthily	
lengthways	
lengthwise	
lengthy, -thier, -thiest	
lenience	
leniency	
leniense	lenience
leniensy	leniency
lenient, -ly	
lenity, -ties	
lens, lenses	
lense	lens
Lent (season)	
lent	leant (bent)
lenth	length
lentil (pea)	
lentil	lintel (beam)
Leo	
leonine	
leopard	
leotard	
lepard	leopard
leper	
leperd	leopard
leprechaun	
leprechorn	leprechaun
leprosy	
lept	leapt
lerch	lurch
lerk	lurk
lern	learn
lesen	lessen (reduce)
lesen	lesson (study)
lesbian	
lesbianism	
leishur	leisure
lesion	
leson	lessen (reduce)
leson	lesson (study)
less	
lessee	
lessen (reduce)	
lesson (study)	
lessor	
lest	
lesure	leisure
let, let, letting	
letdown	
leter	letter
leter	litre
lethal, -ly	
lethargey	lethargy
lethargic, -ally	
lethargy, -gies	
lether	leather
letice	lettuce
letise	lettuce
letre	litre
letter	
lettered	
letterhead	
letterpress	
lettuce	
let-up	
letuse	lettuce
leucosis	
leukaemia	
leve	leave
levee (bank)	
levee	levy (tax)
level, -elled, -elling	
leveller	
level-headed	
levelheded	level-headed
leven	leaven

lever, -ed, -ing
leverage
leviathan
    levie   levee (bank)
    levie   levy (tax)
levitate, -tated, -tating
levitation
levity, -ties
    levrage   leverage
levy, levies (tax)
levy, levied, levying (tax)
    levy   levee (bank)
lewd, -ly
    lexicografer   lexicographer
    lexicografey   lexicography
lexicographer
lexicography
lexicon
    lezbian   lesbian
    li   lie
liability, -ties
liable (legal)
    liabul   libel (crime)
    liabul   liable (legal)
liaise, -aised, -aising
liaison
liana
liar (tell lies)
    liar   lyre (music)
    liason   liaison
    libarian   librarian
    libary   library
libel, -belled, -belling (crime)
    libel   liable (legal)
    libelus   libellous
    libul   liable
libellous, -ly
liberal, -ly
liberalism
liberate, -rated, -rating
liberation
liberator
    libertey   liberty
libertine
liberty, -ties
libidinal
libidinous, -ly

libido
Libra
    libralism   liberalism
librarian
library, -ries
libretto, -tos, -ti
    librian   librarian
lice
    licee   lychee
licence (noun)
license, -censed, -censing
licensee
    licenshiate   licentiate
    licenshius   licentious
    licenshus   licentious
licentiate
licentious, -ly
    lichee   lychee
lichen
    lichenis   lichenous
lichenous
    lichenus   lichenous
lick, -ed, -ing
    licker   liqueur
    licker   liquor
licorice
    licorish   licorice
    licoriss   licorice
    lickrish   licorice
lid
lie, lied, lying (untruth)
lie, lay, lain, lying (recline)
    lie   lye (solution)
liege
lien
    liesure   leisure
lieu (instead)
    lieu   loo (toilet)
lieutenant
life, lives
lifebelt
lifeboat
    lifeboy   lifebuoy
lifebuoy
lifeguard
lifeless, -ly
lifelike

lifelong
lifesaver
lifestyle
lifetime
lift, -ed, -ing
lift-off
ligacher   ligature
ligachur   ligature
ligament
light, lighted, lighting
lighten, -ed, -ing
light-fingered
light-headed
light-hearted, -ly
lighthouse
lightly
lightning
lightweight
ligneous
lignite
like, liked, liking
likeable
likelihood
likely, -lier, -liest
likelyhood   likelihood
liken, likened, likening
likeness
likewise
likorish   licorice
likoriss   licorice
likrish   licorice

For likw- words, look
under **liqu-**.

---

lilac
lilak   lilac
lile   lisle
lilie   lily
Lilliputian
lilly pilly
lilt, -ed, -ing
lily, -ies
lily-livered
limb
limber, limbered, limbering
limbo, -bos
lime, limed, liming

limelight
limelite   limelight
limerick
limersene   limousine
limestone
limey, -meys
limf   lymph
limfatic   lymphatic
limit, -ed, -ing
limitation
limousine
limp, -ed, -ing
limpet
limph   lymph
limphatic   lymphatic
limpid, -ly
linchpin
linch   lynch
linctus
line, lined, lining (mark)
line   lion (cat)
lineage
lineal, -ly
lineament (detail)
linear, -ly
lineige   lineage
linen
liner
linesman, -men
line-up
ling, lings
linger, -ed, -ing
lingerie
lingo, -goes
lingual, -ly
linguist
linguistic, -ally
lingwal   lingual
lingwist   linguist
linier   linear
liniment (oil)
liniment   lineament
                       (detail)
link, linked, linking
linkage
linnet
linocut

linoleum
  linolium — linoleum
linotype, -typed, -typing
linseed
lint
lintel (beam)
  lintel — lentil (pea)
  linx — lynx
lion (cat)
  lion — line (mark)
lioness
lion-hearted, -ly
lionisation
lionise, -nised, -nising
  liotard — leotard
lip
lip-read, -read, -reading
lip-salve
lip-service
lipstick
liquefier
liquefy, -fied, -fying
  liquer — liqueur
  liquer — liquor
liqueur (drink)
  liqueur — liquor (spirits)
liquid
liquidambar
liquidate, -dated, -dating
liquidation
liquidator
liquidity
liquor (spirits)
  liquor — liqueur (drink)
liquorice
  liquoris — liquorice
  liquorish — liquorice
  lire — lyre
  lirebird — lyrebird
  liric — lyric
  lirical — lyrical
  lise — lice
  lisen — listen
  lisence — licence (noun)
  lisence — license (verb)
  lisen — listen
  lisensee — licensee

  lisentiate — licentiate
  lisentius — licentious
lisle
lisp, -ed, -ing
lissom
  lissum — lissom
list, -ed, -ing
listen, -ed, -ing
listless, -ly
lit
litany, -nies
  lite — light
  litel — little
  liter — litre
  liter — litter
  literacher — literature
  literachur — literature
literacy
literal, -ly
literary, -ily
  literasy — literacy
  literat — literate
literate
literati
literature
  litergy — liturgy
  litewait — light-weight
lithe, -ly
lithesome
lithium
  lithograf — lithograph
lithograph
lithographic, -ally
lithography
litigant
litigation
litigator
  litle — little
litmus
  litening — lightning
  litracher — literature
  litrachur — literature
litre
litter, -ed, -ing
litterbug
little, less, least
  litul — little

liturgey | liturgy
liturgical, -ly
liturgy, -gies
liv | live
livary | livery
live, lived, living
livelihood
lively, -lier, -liest
livelyhood | livelihood
liven, -ed, -ing
liver
liverish
liverwurst
livery, -ries
livestock
livewire
livid, -ly
livlie | lively
livrey | livery
liying | lying
lizard
lizerd | lizard
llama
lo | low
load, -ed, -ing (burden)
load | lode (ore)
loaf, loaves
loam, -ed, -ing
loan (lend)
loan | lone (alone)
loath (unwilling)
loathe, loathed, loathing (hate)
loathsome, -ly
lob, lobbed, lobbing
lobby, -bies
lobby, -bied, -bying
lobe
lobie | lobby
lobotomy
lobster
loby | lobby
local, -ly
locale
localise, -lised, -lising
locality, -ties
locate, -cated, -cating
location

loch (lake)
lock (door)
locker
locket
lockjaw
locksmith
lockup
locomoshun | locomotion
locomotion
locomotive
locum
locust
lode (ore)
lode | load (burden)
lodestar
lodestone
lodge, lodged, lodging
lodger
lofe | loaf
loft, lofted, lofting
loftily
lofty, -tier, -tiest
log, logged, logging
loganberie | loganberry
loganberry, -ries
logarithm
logbook
loge | lodge
loger | logger
logerithm | logarithm
loggerhead
logic
logical, -ly
logicality
logistics
loier | lawyer
loin
loincloth
loiter, -ed, -ing
loiterer
lol | loll
lolipop | lollipop
loll, -ed, -ing
lollipop
lolly, -lies
lome | loam
lone (alone)

lone   loan (lend)
loneliness
lonely, -lier, -liest
loner
lonesome, -ly
lonesum   lonesome
long, -ed, -ing
longevity
longhand
longing, -ly
longitude
longitudinal, -ly
long-playing
long-sighted
longstanding
long-suffering
long-term
longwinded, -ly
loo (toilet)
loo   lieu (instead)
loobricant   lubricant
loobricate   lubricate
loocid   lucid
loocrative   lucrative
loodicrous   ludicrous
loodicrus   ludicrous
loofah
look, -ed, -ing
lookemia   leukaemia
looker   lucre
lookout
lookwarm   lukewarm
loom, -ed, -ing
loominus   luminous
loon
loona   luna
loonatic   lunatic
loony, loonier, looniest
loop, -ed, -ing
loophole
loose, loosed, loosing (free)
loose, looser, loosest
loose   lose (fail)
loose-leaf
loosen, -ed, -ing
loosing   losing
loot (booty)

loot   lute (music)
lop, lopped, lopping (cut)
lope, loped, loping (run)
lopsided, -ly
loquacious, -ly
loquacity
loquashius   loquacious
loquashus   loquacious
loquat
lord (ruler)
lord   laud (praise)
lordly, -lier, -liest
lord mayor
lore (learn)
lore   law (rule)
lorel   laurel
lorgnette
loriat   laureate
lorie   lorry
lorikeet
lornch   launch
lornyet   lorgnette
lorry, lorries (truck)
lory, lories (bird)
los   loss
lose, lost, losing (fail)
lose   loose (free)
loser
loshion   lotion
loshun   lotion
loss
lot, lotted, lotting
lotery   lottery
lothe   loathe
lothsum   loathsome
lotion
lotry   lottery
lots
lottery, -teries
lotto
lotus
loud, -ly
loudhailer
loudspeaker
lounge, lounged, lounging
louse, lice
louse, loused, lousing

lousy, lousier, lousiest		ludicrous, -ly	
lout		ludo	
louver	louvre	luff, -ed, -ing	
louvre		lug, lugged, lugging	
love, loved, loving		lugage	luggage
loveliness		luggage	
lovelorn		lugger	
lovely, -lier, -liest		lugige	luggage
lover		lugsuriant	luxuriant
loves	loaves	lugubrious, -ly	
low, lower, lowest		lukemia	leukaemia
lowboy		lukewarm	
lowbrow		luksuriant	luxuriant
lowd	loud	luksuriate	luxuriate
low-down (mean)		luksurius	luxurious
lowdown (truth)		luksury	luxury
lower, -ed, -ing		lul	lull
low-key		lulabie	lullaby
lowland		lull, -ed, -ing	
lowly, -lier, -liest		lullaby, -bies	
lownge	lounge	lullaby, -bied, -bying	
low-pressure		lumbago	
lowse	louse	lumbar (back)	
lowt	lout	lumber (timber)	
low-voltage		lumberjack	
loyal, -ly		luminance	
loyalty, -ties		luminary, -naries	
loyle	loyal	luminescence	
lozenge		luminescent	
lozinge	lozenge	luminessence	luminescence
lu	lieu (instead)	luminessent	luminescent
lu	loo (toilet)	luminosity, -ties	
lubber, -ly		luminous, -ly	
luber	lubber	luminus	luminous
lubricant		lump, -ed, -ing	
lubricate, -cated, -cating		lunacy, -cies	
lubrication		lunar	
lucer	lucre	lunasey	lunacy
lucerne		lunatic	
lucid, -ly		lunch, -ed, -ing	
Lucifer		luncheon	
luck, -ily		lung	
lucky, -ier, -iest		lunge, lunged, lunging	
lucky dip		lungfish	
lucrative, -ly		lupin	
lucre		lupus	
lude	lewd	lurch, lurched, lurching	

lure, lured, luring
lurex
lurid, -ly
lurk, lurked, lurking
  lurn   learn
luscious, -ly
lush, -ly
  lushes   luscious
  lushious   luscious
  lushus   luscious
  lused   lucid
  lusid   lucid
lust, lusted, lusting
  luster   lustre
lustful, -ly
  lustie   lusty
lustre
lustrous, -ly
lusty, -tier, -tiest
lute, luted, luting (music)
  lute   loot (booty)
Lutheran
  luv   love
  luve   love
  luver   lover
  luvley   lovely
  luvlier   lovelier
lux
  luxery   luxury
luxuriance
luxuriant, -ly
luxuriate, -ated, -ating
luxurious, -ly
luxury, -ries
lyceum
lychee
lye (solution)
  lye   lie (untruth)
  lye   lie (recline)
lying-in
lymph
lymphatic
lynch, -ed, -ing
lynx, lynxes (wildcat)
  lynx   links
lyre (musical instrument)
  lyre   liar (tell lies)

lyrebird
lyric
lyrical, -ly
lyricist

Mm

macabre
macadam
macadamia nut
macaroni, -nis, -nies
macaw
mace
   mach   match
machete
machinate, -nated, -nating
machination
machine, -chined, -chining
machinery, -ries
mackerel
mackintosh, mackintoshes
macramé
mad, madder, maddest
mad, madded, madding
madam
madcap
made (produced)
   made   maid (girl)
madeira
mademoiselle
   maden   madden
   madera   madeira
madness
madonna
madrigal
maelstrom
maestro
mafia
magazine
maggot
magic
magical, -ly
magician
   magishion   magician
   magishun   magician

magisterial, -ly
magistrate
   magizine   magazine
   magnanimis   magnanimous
magnanimity
magnanimous, -ly
   magnanimus magnanimous
   magnat   magnate
   magnat   magnet
magnate (wealth)
magnesium
magnet (attract)
magnetic, -ally
magnetisation
magnetise, -tised, -tising
magnetism
magnetite
magneto, -tos
magnification
magnificence
magnificent, -ly
magnifier
   magnifisense magnificence
   magnifisent   magnificent
   magnifisunt   magnificent
magnify, -fied, -fying
magnitude
magnolia
magnum, -nums
   magot   maggot
magpie
   mahem   mayhem
mah-jong
mahogany, -nies
maid (girl)
   maid   made
maiden
mail (letters)
   mail   male (man)
mailbox, mailboxes
maim, -ed, -ing
main (chief)
   main   mane (hair)
mainland
mainline, -lined, -lining
mainliner
mainstay

mainstream	
maintain, -ed, -ing	
maintenance	
maintenanse	maintenance
maisonette	
maize (corn)	
maize	maze (puzzle)
majer	major
majestey	majesty
majestic, -ally	
majesty, -ties	
majong	mah-jong
major	
majority, -ties	
makaber	macabre
makadam	macadam
make, made, making	
makeshift	
make-up	
mako	
maladey	malady
maladjusted	
maladjustment	
malady, -dies	
malaise	
malapropism	
malard	mallard
malaria	
malase	malaise
male (man)	
male	mail (letters)
maleable	malleable
malefacshun	malefaction
malefaction	
malefactor	
malet	mallet
malevolence	
malevolense	malevolence
malevolent, -ly	
malformation	
malformed	
malfuncshion	malfunction
malfuncshun	malfunction
malfunction, -ed, -ing	
maliable	malleable
malice	
malicious, -ly	

malign, -ed, -ing	
malignance	
malignancy	
malignansey	malignancy
malignant, -ly	
maline	malign
malinger, -ed, -ing	
malingerer	
malise	malice
malishus	malicious
mall	
mallard, -lards, -lard	
malleability	
malleable	
malleabul	malleable
mallee	
mallet	
mallow	mellow
malnutrishun	malnutrition
malnutrition	
malpractice	
malpractise	malpractice
malstrom	maelstrom
malt (liquor)	
malt	moult (lose)
Malthusian	
maltreat, -ed, -ing	
maltreet	maltreat
maluka	
mamal	mammal
mamarey	mammary
mame	maim
mamilla, -millae	
mamma, mammae	
mammal	
mammary	
mammon	
mammoth	
mamon	mammon
mamoth	mammoth
man, men	
man, manned, manning	
manacle, -cled, -cling	
manacul	manacle
manage, -aged, -aging	
manageability	
manageable, -bly	

management
manager
manageress
managerial, -ly
manana
manchester
mandarin (bureaucrat)
mandarine (fruit)
mandate, -dated, -dating
mandatory, -ries
   mandatry   mandatory
mandolin
mandrax
mane (hair)
   mane   main (chief)
   maner   manner (way)
   maner   manor (house)
mange
   mangel   mangle
manger
mangle, -gled, -gling
mango, -goes, -gos
mangrove
   mangul   mangle
mangy, -gier, -giest
   manhandel   manhandle
manhandle, -dled, -dling
   manhandul   manhandle
manhole
manhood
mania
maniacal, -ly
manic
manic-depression
manic-depressive
manicure, -cured, -curing
   manidge   manage
manifest, -ed, -ing
manifestation
manifesto, -tos
manifold
   manige   manage
manikin (dwarf)
   manikin   mannequin
                 (model)
manila
   manipulashun   manipulation

manipulate, -lated, -lating
manipulation
manipulative
manipulator
manipulatory
   manje   mange
   manjer   manger
   manjy   mangy
mankind
manly, -lier, -liest
manna (food)
   manna   manner (way)
   manna   manor (house)
mannequin
manner (way)
   manner   manna (food)
   manner   manor (house)
mannered
mannerism
manoeuvrability
manoeuvrable
manoeuvre, -vred, -vring
   manoover   manoeuvre
   manoovrabul   manoeuvrable
manor (house)
   manor   manna (food)
   manor   manner (way)
manpower
manse
   manshun   mansion
mansion
manslaughter
   manslorter   manslaughter
mantel (shelf)
   mantel   mantle (cloak)
mantelpiece
mantilla
mantis, -tises
mantissa
mantle (cloak)
   mantle   mantel (shelf)
   mantul   mantel (shelf)
   mantul   mantle (cloak)
manual, -ly
   manufacsher   manufacture
manufacture, -tured, -turing
manure, -nured, -nuring

manuscript
many, more, most
maonaise   mayonnaise
Maori, -ris
map, mapped, mapping
mapel   maple
maple
mar, marred, marring
marathon
maraud, -ed, -ing
marawed   maraud
marble, -bled, -bling
marbul   marble
marcasite
March
march, -ed, -ing
marcher
marchioness
mare (horse)
mare   mayor (chief)
mareene   marine
margarine
margin
marginal, -ly
mariage   marriage
marie   marry
marijuana
marina
marinade, -naded, -nading
marinate, -nated, -nating
marine
mariner
marionet   marionette
marionette
marital, -ly
maritime
maritul   marital
mariwana   marijuana
marjoram
mark, marked, marking
marker
market, -ed, -ing
marketeer
markey   marquee
markey   marquis
marksman, -men
marksmanship

markuis   marquis
marlin
marlock
marmalade
marone   maroon
maroon
marow   marrow
marquee (tent)
marquis (nobleman)
marri (tree)
marri   marry (unite)
marriage
marrow
marry, -ried, -rying (unite)
marry   marri (tree)
Mars
marsh
marshal, -shalled, -shalling (officer)
marshal   martial (brave)
marshland
marshmallow
marshul   marshal
marshul   martial
marshy, -shier, -shiest
marsupial
mart
marter   martyr
martial (brave)
martial   marshal
                    (officer)
martinet
martini
martyr
martyrdom
marvel, -velled, -velling
marvellous, -ly
Marxism
Marxist
mary   marry
marzipan
mas   mass
masacer   massacre
masacre   massacre
masage   massage
mascara
mascot
masculine, -ly

masculinity
  mase — mace
mash, -ed, -ing
  mashene — machine
  mashine — machine
  mashinry — machinery
  masive — massive
mask, -ed, -ing
  maskerade — masquerade
masochism
masochist
  masocism — masochism
mason
masonic
masonite
masonry, -ries
masquerade, -raded, -rading
mass, -ed, -ing
  massacer — massacre
massacre, -cred, -cring
massage, -saged, -saging
masseur
massif (mountain)
massive, -ly (large)
mass media
mass-produce, -duced, -ducing
  massur — masseur
mast
mastectomy, -mies
master
  masterbate — masturbate
masterful, -ly
mastermind
  masterpeace — masterpiece
masterpiece
masthead
mastiff
masturbate, -bated, -bating
masturbation
mat, matted, matting (rug)
  mat — matt (dull)
matador
match, -ed, -ing
matchmaker
mate, mated, mating
  mater — matter
material, -ly

materialisation
materialise, -lised, -lising
materialism
materialist
maternal, -ly
maternity
mateship
matey
mathematical, -ly
mathematician
mathematics
  mathematisian — mathematician
maths
matilda
  matinay — matinee
matinee
  mating — matting
  matress — mattress
matriarch
matriarchal
matriarchic
matriarchy, -chies
matriculant
matriculate, -lated, -lating
matriculation
matrimony, -nies
matrix, matrices
matron, -ly
matt (dull)
matter
matting
mattock
mattress
maturation
mature, -tured, -turing
maturity
maudlin, -ly
maul, -ed, -ing
mausoleum, -leums, -lea
mauve
maverick
  mawgage — mortgage
mawkish, -ly
  mawl — maul
  mawsoleum — mausoleum
maxi
maxim

maximisation
maximise, -mised, -mising
maximum, -ma, -mums
maybe
May Day
mayhem
mayonnaise
mayor (chief)
   mayor   mare (horse)
mayoralty, -ties
mayoress
maypole
maze (puzzle)
   maze   maize (corn)
mazurka
mead
meadow
   meager   meagre
meagre, -ly
   meak   meek
meal
mean, meant, meaning (intend)
   mean   mien (show)
meander, -ed, -ing
meantime
meanwhile
   measels   measles
measles
measure, -ured, -uring
measurement
meat (flesh)
   meat   meet (contact)
   meat   mete (measure)
   mecanic   mechanic
   mecanise   mechanise
   mecanism   mechanism
mechanic
mechanical, -ly
mechanisation
mechanise, -nised, -nising
mechanism
medal, -alled, -alling (award)
medallion
   medcine   medicine
meddle, -dled, -dling (interfere)
meddler
   medeval   mediaeval

media
mediaeval
median
   mediashun   mediation
mediate, -ated, -ating
mediation
meditator
medic
medical, -ly
medicate, -cated, -cating
medication
medicinal, -ly
medicine
medieval, -ly
   mediocer   mediocre
mediocre
mediocrity, -ties
   medisinal   medicinal
   medisine   medicine
meditate, -tated, -tating
meditation
meditator
medium, -dia, -diums
   medle   meddle
   medler   meddler
medley, -leys
   medly   medley
   medow   meadow
   medsine   medicine
   medul   meddle
   meed   mead
meek, -ly
   meel   meal
   meen   mean (intend)
   meen   mien (show)
   meening   meaning
meerschaum
   meershum   meerschaum
   meesels   measles
meet, met, meeting (contact)
   meet   meat (flesh)
   meet   mete (measure)
   megafone   megaphone
megalomania
megalomaniac
megaphone
   meger   meagre

mekanic	mechanic
mekanical	mechanical
mekanise	mechanise
mekanism	mechanism
melaleuca	
melancholia	
melancholic, -ally	
melancholy, -cholies	
Melanesian	
melee	
meliflous	mellifluous
meliorate, -rated, -rating	
melioration	
meliorator	
mellifluous, -ly	
melodey	melody
melodic, -ally	
melodious, -ly	
melodius	melodious
melodrama	
melodramatic, -ally	
melody, -dies	
melon	
melow	mellow
melt, melted, melting	
member	
membership	
membrain	membrane
memento, -tos	
memo, memos	
memoir	
memorabel	memorable
memorabilia	
memorable,-bly	
memorabul	memorable
memorandum, -dums	
memorey	memory
memorial, -ly	
memorise, -rised, -rising	
memory, -ries	
memrable	memorable
menace, -aced, -acing	
menagerie	
menajery	menagerie
menase	menace
mend, -ed, -ing	

mendacious, -ly	
mendacity, -ties	
mendashus	mendacious
mendasity	mendacity
mendicant	
menial, -ly	
meningitis	
meninjitis	meningitis
meniscus, -nisci	
menopause	
menopaws	menopause
menshion	mention
menshun	mention
menstruate, -ated, -ating	
menstruation	
mensuration	
ment	meant
mental, -ly	
mentalitey	mentality
mentality, -ties	
menthol	
mentholated	
mention, -ed, -ing	
mentor	
menu	
merang	meringue
mercantile	
mercenary, -naries	
mercenrey	mercenary
mercer	
mercerise, -rised, -rising	
mercery, -ries	
merchandise, -dised, -dising	
merchant	
merchantman, -men	
merciful, -ly	
merciless, -ly	
mercurial, -ly	
mercury, -ries	
mercy, -cies	
mere, -ly	
meretricious, -ly	
meretrishious	meretricious
meretrishus	meretricious
merge, merged, merging	
merger	
meridian	

merie	merry	metalurgey	metallurgy
meringue		metamorfic	metamorphic
merino, -nos		metamorfosus	metamorphosis
merit, -ed, -ing		metamorphic	
meritories	meritorious	metamorphosis, -ses	
meritorious, -ly		metaphor	
meritorius	meritorious	metaphoric	
mermade	mermaid	metamorphical, -ly	
mermaid		metaphrase, -phrased, -phrasing	
merriment		metaphysical, -ly	
merry, -rier, -riest		metaphysics	
merry-go-round		metastasise, -sised, -sising	
merrymaker		mete, meted, meting (measure)	
mersenry	mercenary	mete	meat (flesh)
mersy	mercy	mete	meet (contact)
mery	merry	meteor (streak)	
mesa		meteor	metier (trade)
mescalin		meteoric, -ally	
mesenger	messenger	meteorite	
mesh, -ed, -ing		meteorological, -ly	
mesige	message	meteorology	
mesmerise, -rised, -rising		meter (measure)	
mesmerism		meter	metre (distance)
mess, -ed, -ing			
message		methadone	
messenger		methane	
Messiah		methed	method
Messianic		methedrine	
messmate		methilate	methylate
Messrs		metho	
mesure	measure	method	
metabolic		methodical, -ly	
metabolise, -lised, -lising		Methodist	
metabolism		methodology, -gies	
metafisicul	metaphysical	methylate, -lated, -lating	
metafisics	metaphysics	meticulous, -ly	
metafor	metaphor	meticulus	meticulous
metaforic	metaphoric	metier (trade)	
metaforicul	metaphorical	metier	meteor (streak)
metal, -alled, -alling (element)		metiorology	meteorology
metal	mettle (energy)	metre (distance)	
metalic	metallic	metre	meter (measure)
metallic			
metallurgic		metric	
metallurgical, -ly		metricate, -cated, -cating	
metallurgist		metrication	
metallurgy		metric system	

metronome
metropolis, -lises
metropolitan
mettle (energy)
| mettle | metal (element) |
| metul | mettle (energy) |
mew, -ed, -ing
mews (stables)
| mews | muse (think) |
| mezanine | mezzanine |
mezzanine
| mi | my |
mia-mia
| miander | meander |
miaow, -ed, -ing
miasma, -mas, -mata
miasmatical
miasmic
mica
mice
microbe
microbial
microbic
microbiological
microbiologist
microbiology
micro-economics
microfiche
microfilm
| microfone | microphone |
micrometer
micron
microphone
microprocessor
| microprosessor | microprocessor |
microscope
microscopic, -ally
microwave
midair
midday
| middel | middle |
middle, -led, -ling
middleman, -men
middle-of-the-road
| middlewait | middleweight |
middleweight
middling

| middul | middle |
middy, -dies (beer)
| middy | midi (skirt) |
| midel | middle |
midge
midget
midi (skirt)
midi	middy (beer)
midil	middle
midling	middling
midnight
midnite	midnight
mid-off
mid-on
midriff
midshipman, -men
midst
midul	middle
mid wicket
midwife, -wives
mien (show)
mien	mean (intend)
miff
mige	midge
might (power)
might	mite (small)
mighty, -tier, -tiest
migit	midget
migraine
migrane	migraine
migrant
migrate, -grated, -grating
migration
migratory
migreat	migrate
mika	mica
mikado, -dos
miksamotosis	myxomatosis
mikscher	mixture
mikschur	mixture
mikser	mixer
miksture	mixture
mil (millilitre)
mil	mill (grind)
mild, -ly
mildew, -ed, -ing
mildu	mildew

mile
mileage
milestone

mileniem	millennium
milenium	millennium
milet	millet
milibar	millibar

milieu

mililiter	millilitre
milimeter	millimetre
miliner	milliner
miling	milling
milinry	millinery
milion	million
milionair	millionaire
milipeed	millipede
milisha	militia

militancy

militansy	militancy

militant, -ly
militarism
militarist
militaristic, -ally
military
militia
milk, -ed, -ing
milksop
milky, -kier, -kiest
Milky Way
mill, milled, milling (grind)
millennial, -ly
millennium, -niums, -nia
miller
millet
millibar
millligram
millilitre
millimetre
milliner
millinery
million
millionaire
millipede
millpond
millstone
millwheel

milyou	milieu

mime, mimed, miming
mimic, -icked, -icking
mimicry, -ries
mimosa
minaret
mince, minced, mincing
mincemeat
mincer
mind, minded, minding
mindful, -ly
mine, mined, mining
minefield
miner (worker)

miner	minor (less)
miner	myna (bird)

mineral
mineralogical, -ly
mineralogist
mineralogy
minestrone

minestroney	minestrone
minestrony	minestrone

minesweeper

mingel	mingle

mingle, -led, -ling

mingul	mingle

mingy, -gier, -giest
mini
miniature
minibus

minicher	miniature
minichur	miniature

minim
minimal, -ly
minimise, -mised, -mising
minimiser
minimum, -mums, -ma
minion

miniscule	minuscule

miniskirt
minister
ministerial, -ly
ministration
ministrative, -ly

ministrey	ministry

ministry, -tries

minit	minute

mink, minks (animal)
 minks   minx (girl)
minnow, -nows
minor (lesser)
 minor   miner (worker)
 minor   myna (bird)
minority, -ties
 minow   minnow
 minse   mince
minstrel
mint, -ed, -ing
minuet
minus
minuscule
minute, -uted, -uting
minx (girl)
 minx   minks
      (animals)
 minyouet minuet
 miopia   myopia
 miow   miaow
 miracel   miracle
miracle
 miracul   miracle
miraculous, -ly
 miraculus miraculous
mirage
mire, mired, miring
 mirer   mirror
 miriad   myriad
mirrnyong
mirror, -ed, -ing
mirth
mirthful, -ly
 mis   miss
 misadvencher misadventure
 misadvenchur misadventure
misadventure
 misal   missal
misanthrope
misanthropic, -ally
misanthropist
misanthropy
misapprehension
misappropriate, -ated, -ating
misappropriation
 misapropriate misappropriate

misbehave, -haved, -having
miscarriage
miscarry, -ried, -rying
 miscariage miscarriage
 miscarie   miscarry
 miscarige miscarriage
miscast, -cast, -casting
miscellaneous, -ly
miscellany, -nies
mischance
 mischanse mischance
mischief
 mischievious mischievous
mischievous, -ly
 mischif   mischief
 mischivus mischievous
misconceive, -ceived, -ceiving
misconceiver
 misconcepshun misconception
misconception
 misconcieve misconceive
misconduct
 misconsepshun misconception
misconstrue, -strued, -struing
miscreant
misdeed
misdemeanour
 misdemener misdemeanour
misdo, -did, -done, -doing
 mise   mice
 miselanius miscellaneous
 miselany miscellany
 miself   myself
 miseltoe mistletoe
miser
miserable, -ly
 miserabul miserable
misere
miserly
misery, -ries
misfit, -fitted, -fitting
misfortune
misgiving
mishap
 mishapen misshapen
 mishion   mission
mishmash

misile	missile
misiltoe	mistletoe
misis	misses
misive	missive
misus	missus
mislay, -laid, -laying	
misle	missal (book)
misle	missile
	(weapon)
mislead, -led, -leading	
misleader	
misleed	mislead
misnoma	misnomer
misnomer	
misogynist	
misogynous	
misogyny	
misojonist	misogynist
misojonous	misogynous
misojony	misogyny
mispell	misspell
misplace, -placed, -placing	
misplacement	
misplase	misplace
misprint, -ed, -ing	
misrabul	miserable
misrepresent, -ed, -ing	
miss, misses	
miss, missed, missing	
missal (book)	
missal	missile
	(weapon)
misselaney	miscellany
misselanius	miscellaneous
misselany	miscellany
misses (fail)	
misses	missus (wife)
misshape, -shaped, -shaping	
missile (weapon)	
missile	missal (book)
mission	
missionary, -ries	
missive	
misspell, misspelt, misspelling	
missus (wife)	
mist (cloud)	
mist	missed

mistake, -took, -taking	
mistaken	
misteltoe	mistletoe
mister	
misterey	mystery
misterius	mysterious
mistery	mystery
mistic	mystic
mistic	mystique
mistify	mystify
mistletoe	
mistreat, -ed, -ing	
mistress	
mistrial	
mistrust, -ed, -ing	
misty, -tier, -tiest	
misul	missal
misul	missile
misultoe	mistletoe
misunderstand, -stood, -standing	
misuse, -used, -using	
mite (small)	
mite	might (power)
miten	mitten
miter	mitre
mith	myth
mithical	mythical
mithology	mythology
mitie	mighty
mitigate, -gated, -gating	
mitre, -tred, -tring	
mitt	
mitten	
mix, mixed, mixing	
mixamotosis	myxomatosis
mixcher	mixture
mixchur	mixture
mixer	
mixture	
mix-up	
mizzenmast	
mnemonics	
mo	mow
moa (bird)	
moa	mower (lawn)
moan, moaned, moaning	
moaner	

moat
mob, mobbed, mobbing
mobile, -ly
   mobiliety   mobility
mobilisation
mobilise, -lised, -lising
mobility
moccasin
mock, mocked, mocking
mocker
mockery, -ries
mockingbird
   mockry   mockery
mock-up
modal (manner)
   modal   model
                 (example)
   moddul   modal
   moddul   model
mode
model, -elled, -elling (example)
modeller
   moden   modern
moderate, -rated, -rating
moderation
moderator
modern, -ly
modernity, -ties
modest, -ly
modesty, -ties
modicum
   modifi   modify
modifiable
   modifiabul   modifiable
modification
modifier
modify, -fied, -fying
   modlin   maudlin
   modul   model
modular
modulate, -lated, -lating
modulation
modulator
module
   moduler   modular
   modulur   modular
mogo

mogul
mohair
Mohammedan
   mohare   mohair
moiety, -ties
   moischer   moisture
   moischur   moisture
   moisen   moisten
   moisun   moisten
moist, -ly
moisten, -ed, -ing
moisture
   mokasin   moccasin
moke
molar
   molases   molasses
molasses
   molasus   molasses
   mold   mould
mole
molecular, -ly
molecule
molest, -ed, -ing
molestation
   molicodle   mollycoddle
   molicodul   mollycoddle
moll
mollify, -fied, -fying
mollusc
mollycoddle, -dled, -dling
moloch
Molotov cocktail
   molt   malt (liquor)
   molt   moult (lose)
molten
   molusk   mollusc
molybdenum
moment
momentarily
momentary
momentous, -ly
momentum, -ta
   monakey   monarchy
monarch
monarchal, -ly
monarchic, -ally
monarchist

monarchy, -chies
monastery, -teries
monastic, -ally
monasticism
monastry   monastery
Monday
mone   moan
monetary, -rily
money, monies
moneychanger
money-grubber
money-grubbing
moneylender
money market
money order
monga   monger
mong
monger
Mongol
Mongolian
Mongolism
Mongoloid
mongoose, -gooses
mongrel
mongrul   mongrel
moniter   monitor
monitor, -ed, -ing
monk
monkey, -keys
monkey, -keyed, -keying
monkey-wrench
monochromatic, -ally
monochrome
monochromic
monocle
monocled
monocul   monocle
monogamist
monogamous
monogamus   monogamous
monogamy
monograf   monograph
monogram
monograph
monokrome   monochrome
monokside   monoxide
monolith

monolithic
monolog   monologue
monologue
monoplain   monoplane
monoplane
monopoley   monopoly
monopolisation
monopolise, -lised, -lising
monopoly, -lies
monorail
monosilabic   monosyllabic
monosilabul   monosyllable
monosyllabic, -ally
monosyllable
monotone
monotonous, -ly
monotonus   monotonous
monotony
monoxide
monsoon
monsoonal
monster
monstera deliciosa
monstrosity, -ties
monstrous, -ly
monstrus   monstrous
montage
month
monument
monumental, -ly
mooch, -ed, -ing
mood
moody, -dier, -diest
moon
moonlight
moonshine
moonstone
moony, -nier, -niest
moor, -ed, -ing (land)
moor   more (further)
Moor (Muslim)
moorhen
moose, moose (animal)
moose   mouse (rodent)
moose   mousse (food)
moosli   muesli
moot

moovabul   moveable
moove   move
mop, mopped, mopping
mope, moped, moping
moped
mopoke
moral, -ly
moralise, -lised, -lising
moralist
moralistic
moralitey   morality
morality, -ties
morass
moratorium, -toria, -toriums
moray, -rays (eel)
morays   mores (custom)
morbid, -ly
morbidity
mordant, -ly
mordern   modern
more, most (further)
more   moor (tie up)
moreover
mores (custom)
morfine   morphine
morg   morgue
morgage   mortgage
morganatic, -ally
morgige   mortgage
morgue
moribund, -ly
moribundity
Mormon
Mormonism
morn (morning)
morn   mourn (sorrow)
mornay
mornful   mournful
morning (day)
morning   mourning
                   (sorrowing)
moron
moronic
morose, -ly
morover   moreover
morow   morrow
morphine

morrow
morse code
morsel
mortafy   mortify
mortal, -ly
mortality, -ties
mortar
mortarboard
mortgage, -gaged, -gaging
mortgagee
mortgagor
mortice, -ticed, -ticing
mortifi   mortify
mortification
mortify, -fied, -fying
mortiss   mortice
mortuary, -ries
mos   moss
mosaic
moselle
moshun   motion
mosk   mosque
moskito   mosquito
mosque
mosquito, -toes
moss
most, -ly
mot
mote (dust)
mote   moat (ditch)
motel
moter   motor
motervate   motivate
motet
moth, moths
mothballs
mother
mother-in-law, mothers-in-law
motherland
mother-of-pearl
motif (figure)
motif   motive (reason)
motion, -ed, -ing
motivate, -vated, -vating
motivation
motivational
motive (reason)

motive — motif (figure)
motle — mottle
motley, -leys
motly — motley
moto — motto
motor, -ed, -ing
motorbike
motorcycle
motorcyclist
motorist
mottle, -tled, -tling
motto, -tos
mould, moulded, moulding
moulder, -ed, -ing
mouldy, -dier, -diest
moult, -ed, -ing (lose)
moult — malt (liquor)
mound
mount, mounted, mounting
mountain
mountaineer
mountainous, -ly
mountenus — mountainous
mountun — mountain
mourn, -ed, -ing (sorrow)
mourn — morn
(morning)
mourner
mournful, -ly
mourning (sorrowing)
mourning — morning (day)
mouse, mice (rodent)
mouse, moused, mousing
mouse — moose (animal)
mouse — mousse (food)
moussaka
mousse (food)
moustache
mousy, -sier, -siest
mouth, mouths
mouthful, -fuls
mouthpeace — mouthpiece
mouthpiece
mouth-to-mouth
movabel — moveable
movabul — moveable
move, moved, moving

moveable, -ly
movement
movie
mow, mowed, mowing
mower
mownd — mound
mownt — mount
mowntain — mountain
mowntenus — mountainous
mowntun — mountain
mowse — mouse
mowth — mouth
mozzarella
Mr., Messrs.
Mrs.
Ms.
much, more, most
muchooal — mutual
mucilage
mucilaginous
muck, mucked, mucking
muckrake, -raked, -raking
muck-up
mucky, -ier, -iest
mucous (of mucus)
mucus
mud, mudded, mudding
muddie (crab)
muddie — muddy (dirty)
muddle, -dled, -dling
muddler
muddy, -died, -dying (dirty)
muddy, -dier, -diest (dirty)
muddy — muddie (crab)
mudel — muddle
mudflat
mudflow
mudguard
mudhopper
mudlark
mudle — muddle
mudrunner
mudskipper
mudslinger
muesli
muezzin
muff, -ed, -ing

muffin
muffle, -fled, -fling
muffler
   mufful   muffle
   mufin   muffin
mufti, -tis
mug, mugged, mugging
mugga
mugger
muggins
muggy, -gier, -giest
   mukus   mucous
   mukus   mucus
mulatto, -tos, -toes
   mulberie   mulberry
mulberry, -ries
mulch, -ed, -ing
mule
muleteer
mulga
mulgara
mulish, -ly
mull, -ed, -ing
mullet, -lets, -let
mulligatawny
mullion
mullock
mulloway
   multaple   multiple
   multch   mulch
multicultural
multifaceted
multifarious, -ly
   multifarius   multifarious
   multifaseted   multifaceted
multigrade
multilateral, -ly
multimillionaire
   multinashionul multinational
multinational
multipartite
multiple
multiple sclerosis
   multipli   multiply
multiplication
multiplicative, -ly
multiplicity, -ties

multiplier
   multiplisity   multiplicity
multiply, -plied, -plying
   multipul   multiple
multitude
multitudinous, -ly
   multitudinus   multitudinous
   mulyun   mullion
mum
mumble, -bled, -bling
mumbo jumbo
   mumbul   mumble
   mumie   mummy
   mumifi   mummify
mummer
mummification
mummify, -fied, -fying
mummy, -mies
mummy, -mied, -mying
mumps
   mumy   mummy
munch, munched, munching
munchies
   mundain   mundane
mundane, -ly
   Munday   Monday
   munetry   monetary
   mungrel   mongrel
municipal, -ly
municipality, -ties
   munie   money
   munishun   munition
   munisipality   municipality
   munk   monk
   munky   monkey
   munth   month
   muny   money
   mur   myrrh
mural
murder, -ed, -ing
murderer
murderess
murderous, -ly
murk, -ily
murky, -kier, -kiest
   murmer   murmur
murmur, -ed, -ing

murrain
  murth — mirth
  murtle — myrtle
  mus — mews (stables)
  mus — muse(think)
muscat
muscatel
muscle, -cled, -cling (body)
  muscle — mussel (fish)
muscle-bound
Muscovy duck
muscular, -ly
muscularity
muse, mused, musing (think)
  muse — mews (stables)
  musel — muscle (body)
  musel — mussel (fish)
museum
mush, -ed, -ing
mushroom, -ed, -ing
mushy, -ier, -iest
music
musical, -ly
musician
  musishun — musician
musk
  muskatel — muscatel
musket
musketeer
musketry
muskrat, -rats
Muslim, -lims
muslin
mussel (fish)
  mussel — muscle (body)
must
  mustache — moustache
  mustash — moustache
mustang
mustard
muster, -ed, -ing
  musterd — mustard
  mustie — musty
mutant, -ly
mutate, -tated, -tating
mutation
mute, muted, muting

  muter — mutter
mutilate, -lated, -lating
mutilation
mutilator
  mutinear — mutineer
mutineer
mutinous, -ly
  mutinus — mutinous
mutiny, -nies
mutiny, -nied, -nying
  muton — mutton
mutt
mutter, -ed, -ing
mutton
mutton-bird
mutton-chops
mutual, -ly
mutuality
muu-muu
muzak
  muzul — muzzle
muzzle, -zled, -zling
myall
myna (bird)
  myna — miner (worker)
  myna — minor (less)
myopia
myopic
myriad
myrrh
myrtle
myself
mysterious, -ly
  mysterius — mysterious
mystery, -ries
mystic (symbol)
mystical, -ly
mysticism
mystification
mystify, -fied, -fying
mystique (secret)
  mystisism — mysticism
  mystry — mystery
myth
mythical, -ly
mythology, -gies
myxomatosis

Nn

nab, nabbed, nabbing
nabor	neighbour
nachur	nature
nachurul	natural
nack	knack
nacker	knacker
nacker	nacre

nacre (pearl)
nacreous
nadir
nag, nagged, nagging
nagger
nail, nailed, nailing
naive, -ly
naivety
naked, -ly
nakedness

nakid	naked
nale	nail

namby-pamby, -bies
name, named, naming
namely
namesake

nanie	nanny

nankeen kestrel
nanny, -ies
nannygai
nanny-goat

nany	nanny

nap, napped, napping
napalm

naparm	napalm

nape
napery
naphtha
naphthalene

napie	nappy

napkin

nappe (rock)
nappy, -pies (cloth)
napsack	knapsack
naptha	naphtha
narate	narrate
narative	narrative

narcissism
narcissistic
narcissus, -cissuses, -cissi
narcosis
narcotic
nark, -ed, -ing
narl	gnarl
narow	narrow

narrate, -rated, -rating
narration
narrative, -ly
narrator
narrow, -ly
narsissism	narcissism
narsissistic	narcissistic
narsisus	narcissus

nasal, -ly
nasalisation
nasalise, -lised, -lising
nasality
nascence
nascency
nascent, -ly
nasel	nasal
nash	gnash
nashun	nation
nashunal	national
nastie	nasty

nasty, -tier, -tiest
nat	gnat

natal
natch
natel	natal
nater	natter
nateral	natural
naty	natty

nation
national, -ly
nationalism
nationalist
nationalistic, -ally

nationality, -ties
nation-state
native
Nativity
  Natsi   Nazi
natter, -ed, -ing
natty, -tier, -tiest
  natul   natal
  natur   nature
natural, -ly
naturalisation
naturalise, -lised, -lising
naturalism
naturalist
naturalistic
nature
naturopathy
  naty   natty
naught
naughty, -tier, -tiest
nausea
nauseate, -ated, -ating
nauseation
nauseous, -ly
nautical, -ly
nautilus, -luses
naval (ship)
  naval   navel (body)
nave (church)
  nave   knave (rogue)
navel (body)
navel orange
  navie   navvy
  navie   navy
  navigabel   navigable
navigable, -bly
navigate, -gated, -gating
navigation
navigator
  navul   naval (ship)
  navul   navel (body)
navvy, -vies (worker)
navy, -vies (warships)
  naw   gnaw
nay (no)
  nay   neigh (horse)
  naybour   neighbour

  nayl   nail
Nazi, -zis
Nazism
  nead   knead
  nead   need
  neadel   needle
  neadil   needle
  neadle   needle
  neadless   needless
neap
near, -ed, -ing
nearby
nearly
nearside
neat, -ly
nebula, -lae, -las
nebulous, -ly
  nebulus   nebulous
  necesarey   necessary
  necesitate necessitate
  necesitey   necessity
necessarily
necessary, -saries
necessitate, -tated, -tating
necessity, -ties
neck
neckerchief
  neckliss   necklace
necklace
  necksus   nexus
necktie
necromancer
necromancy
  necromanser necromancer
  necromansey necromancy
  necrofilia   necrophilia
  necrofiliac necrophiliac
  necrofilism necrophilism
necrophilia
necrophiliac
necrophilism
necropolis, -lises
nectar
nectarine
nee (name)
  nee   knee (limb)
need, -ed, -ing (necessary)

need	knead (dough)	neither (nor)	
need	kneed (use knee)	neither	nether (below)
needful, -ly		nek	neck
needle, -dled, -dling		neklace	necklace
needless, -ly		neklis	necklace
needlework		nekrofilia	necrophilia
needul	needle	nekropolis	necropolis
neel	kneel	nell	knell
neer	near	nemesis, -ses	
ne'er-do-well		nemisis	nemesis
neet	neat	nemonics	mnemonics
nefarious, -ly		neofite	neophyte
nefarius	nefarious	Neolithic	
nefew	nephew	neologise, -gised, -gising	
negate, -gated, -gating		neon	
negation		neophyte	
negative, -tived, -tiving		nephew	
negativity		nephrism	
negatory		nephritic	
neglect, -ed, -ing		nephritis	
neglectful, -ly		nepotism	
negligee		Neptune	
negligence		nerd	
negligense	negligence	nerve, nerved, nerving	
negligent, -ly		nerve centre	
negligibility		nerve-racking	
negligible, -bly		nerveous	nervous
negligibul	negligible	nerveus	nervous
neglijay	negligee	nervous, -ly	
negoshabul	negotiable	nervy, -vier, -viest	
negoshiate	negotiate	nesessary	necessary
negotiability		nesessitate	necessitate
negotiable, -bly		nesessitey	necessity
negotiant		nesessity	necessity
negotiate, -ated, -ating		nesle	nestle
negotiation		nest, -ed, -ing	
Negro, -groes		nestle, -tled, -tling	
Negroid		nesul	nestle
neice	niece	net, netted, netting	
neigh (horse)		netball	
neigh	nay (no)	netha	neither (nor)
neighbor	neighbour	netha	nether (below)
neighbour		nether (below)	
neighbourhood		nether	neither (nor)
neighbouring		nettle, -tled, -tling	
neighbourly		nettul	nettle
		network	

neumatic	pneumatic
neural, -ly	
neuralgia	
neuralgic	
neuritic	
neuritis	
neurological, -ly	
neurologist	
neurology	
neurone	
neurosis, -ses	
neurotic, -ally	
neuter	
neutral, -ly	
neutralisation	
neutralise, -lised, -lising	
neutrality	
neutron	
neva	never
never-never	
nevertheless	
new (novel)	
new	gnu (animal)
new	knew
newclear	nuclear
newcleus	nucleus
newcomer	
newfangled	
Newfoundland	
newmatic	pneumatic
newmonia	pneumonia
newral	neural
newrologist	neurologist
newrone	neurone
newrosis	neurosis
newrotic	neurotic
news	
newsagency	
newsagent	
newscast, -cast, -casting	
newscaster	
newsletter	
newsman, -men	
newspaper	
newspeak	
newsprint	
news reader	

newsreel	
newt	
newter	neuter
newtralise	neutralise
newtron	neutron
New Zealander	
next	
next of kin	
nexus, nexus	
ni	nigh
nib	
nibbel	nibble
nibble, -bled, -bling	
nibbler	
nibul	nibble
nice, nicer, nicest	
nicety, -ties	
niche	
nick, -ed, -ing	
nickel, -elled, -elling	
nickerbockers	knickerbockers
nickers	knickers
nickle	nickel
nicknack	knick-knack
nickname, -named, -naming	
nicks	nix
nicotine	
niece	
niether	neither
nifarius	nefarious
nife	knife
niftie	nifty
nifty, -tier, -tiest	
nigel	niggle
nigerd	niggard
niggard	
niggle, -gled, -gling	
nigh	
night, -ly (time)	
night	knight (lord)
nightcap	
nightclub	
nightdress	
nightingale	
nightjar	
nightmare	
nightmarish	

nightsoil
nightwatchman
  nigle — niggle
  niglect — neglect
  nigul — niggle
nihilism
nil
  nilon — nylon
nimble, -bler, -blest
  nimbul — nimble
nimbus, -bi, -buses
  nimf — nymph
  nimph — nymph
nine
ninepins
nineteen
nineteenth
ninety, -ties
  ninie — ninny
ninny, -nies
ninth, -ly
  nion — neon
nip, nipped, nipping
  nipie — nippy
  niple — nipple
nipper
nipple
nippy, -pier, -piest
  nipul — nipple
  nipy — nippy
nirvana
  nise — nice
  nisitey — nicety
nit (insect)
  nit — knit (stitch)
  nite — knight (lord)
  nite — night (time)
  niter — nitre
  nither — neither
nitpick, -ed, -ing
nitpicker
nitrate, -trated, -trating
nitration
nitre
nitric
  nitrifi — nitrify
nitrification

nitrify, -fied, -fying
nitrite
nitrogen
nitrogenous
  nitrogliserine . — nitroglycerine
nitroglycerine
  nitrojen — nitrogen
  nitting — knitting
nitty-gritty
nitwit
  nives — knives
nix
no (denial)
  no — know
nob (person)
  nob — knob (handle)
no-ball
nobble, -bled, -bling
  nobie — knobby
nobility, -ties
noble, nobler, noblest
nobleman, -men
nobody, -bodies
  nobul — noble
  nock — knock
  nocker — knocker
  nockneed — knock-kneed
nocturnal, -ly
nocturne
nod, nodded, nodding
nodal
noddy, -dies
node
nodular
nodule
Noel
noes (denials)
  noes — knows
  noes — nose (on face)
noggin (cup, head)
nogging (timber)
no-go
no-hoper
noise, noised, noising
noisily
noisiness
noisome, -ly

noisy, noisier, noisiest
noisy miner
noledge · · · · · · · · · · · knowledge
noll · · · · · · · · · · · · · · · knoll
nomad
nomadic, -ally
nomadism
no-man's-land
nom de plume
nome · · · · · · · · · · · · · gnome
nomenclature
nominal, -ly
nominate, -nated, -nating
nomination
nominative
nominator
nominee
non · · · · · · · · · · · · · · · none
nonaggression
nonagressiun · · · · · · nonaggression
nonagon
nonce
nonchalance
non-combatant
non-commissioned
non-committal, -ly
non compos
non compus · · · · · · · · non compos
non-conducting
non-conformance
non-conformity
nondescript
none
nonentity, -ties
nonetheless
non-fiction
non-fictional
nonflammable
nong
no-nonsence · · · · · · · no-nonsense
no-nonsense
nonpareil
nonplus, -plussed, -plussing
non-productive, -ly
non-proliferation
non-representational
non-sectarian

nonsence · · · · · · · · · · nonsense
nonsense
nonsensical, -ly
non-U
non-violence
non-violent, -ly
noodle
noogar · · · · · · · · · · · · nougat
nook
noon
noose, noosed, noosing
nope
nor
nor · · · · · · · · · · · · · · · gnaw
Nordic
norm
normal, -ly
normalcy
normalisation
normalise, -lised, -lising
Norman
normative, -ly
norsia · · · · · · · · · · · · · nausea
norsiate · · · · · · · · · · · nauseate
nort · · · · · · · · · · · · · · · naught (ruin)
nort · · · · · · · · · · · · · · · nought (nil)
nortey · · · · · · · · · · · · naughty
north
northerly
northern
northerner
northward, -ly
nortickel · · · · · · · · · · nautical
nortie · · · · · · · · · · · · · naughty
nose, nosed, nosing (on face)
nose · · · · · · · · · · · · · · knows
nose · · · · · · · · · · · · · · noes (denial)
nosebag
nosedive, -dived, -diving
nosegay
nosey, -sier, -siest
nosily
nosiness
nostalgia
nostalgic, -ally
nostrem · · · · · · · · · · · nostrum
nostril

nostrim	nostrum
nostrum	
nosy, -sier, -siest	
not (denial)	
not	knot (tie)
nota bene	
notability	
notable, -bly	
notarial, -ly	
notary, -ries	
notation	
notch, -ed, -ing	
note, noted, noting	
notefy	notify
nothing	
notice, -ticed, -ticing	
noticeable, -bly	
noticeabul	noticeable
notifiable	
notification	
notifier	
notify, -fied, -fying	
notion	
notional, -ly	
not negotiable	
notories	notorious
notoriety, -ties	
notorious, -ly	
notorius	notorious
notwithstanding	
nougar	nougat
nougat	
nought	
noughts-and-crosses	
noun	
nourish, -ed, -ing	
nourishingly	
nourishment	
nous	
nouveau riche, nouveaux riches	
novel	
novelette	
novelist	
novella, novellas, novelle	
novelty, -ties	
November	
novice	

novitiate	
now	
nowadays	
nowhere	
nowing	knowing
nowledge	knowledge
noxious, -ly	
noxius	noxious
nozzle	
nozzul	nozzle
nu	gnu (animal)
nu	knew
nu	new (novel)
nuance	
nuanse	nuance
nub	
nubile	
nuckle	knuckle
nuclear	
nuclear bomb	
nuclear energy	
nuclear family	
nuclear fishun	nuclear fission
nuclear fission	
nuclear fusion	
nuclear power	
nuclear reaction	
nuclear reactor	
nucleus, -clei, -cleuses	
nude, -ly	
nudge, nudged, nudging	
nudism	
nudist	
nudity	
nuge	nudge
nugget	
nuisance	
nulifi	nullify
null	
nulla-nulla	
nullification	
nullify, -fied, -fying	
num	numb
numatic	pneumatic
numb, numbed, numbing	
number, -ed, -ing	
numberless	

numberplate
numbness
numbskull
numeracy
numeral
   numerasy   numeracy
numerate, -rated, -rating
numeration
numerator
numerical, -ly
   numericul   numerical
numerological
numerology
numerous, -ly
   numerus   numerous
numismatics
numismatist
   numonia   pneumonia
nun (woman)
   nun   none (no one)
nunnery, -neries
   nupshal   nuptial
nuptial
   nural   neural
   nuralgia   neuralgia
   nurcher   nurture
   nuritis   neuritis
   nurologist   neurologist
   nurone   neurone
   nurosis   neurosis
   nurotic   neurotic
nurse, nursed, nursing
nursery, -eries
   nursrey   nursery
nurture, -tured, -turing
   nurve   nerve
   nusance   nuisance
   nuse   news
   nuspaper   newspaper
nut, nutted, nutting
   nuter   neuter
nutcracker
nutmeg
   nutral   neutral
nutrient
nutriment
   nutrishun   nutrition

   nutrishus   nutritious
nutrition
nutritional, -ly
nutritionist
nutritious, -ly
   nutron   neutron
nuts
nutshell
nutty, -tier, -tiest
   nuty   nutty
   nuzul   nuzzle
nuzzle, -zled, -zling
nylon
   nymf   nymph
nymph
nymphomania
nymphomaniac

Oo

oaf	
oak	
oar (boat)	
oar	awe (dread)
oar	or
oar	ore (rock)
oasis, oases	
oat	
oath, oaths	
oatmeal	
obay	obey
obbese	obese
obduracy	
obdurasey	obduracy
obdurate, -ly	
obedience	
obediense	obedience
obedient, -ly	
obeisance	
obeisanse	obeisance
obelisk	
obese, -ly	
obesity	
obessence	obeisance
obey, -ed, -ing	
obituary, -aries	
objecshun	objection
objay dart	objet d'art
object, -ed, -ing	
objection	
objectionable, -bly	
objectionabul	objectionable
objective, -ly	
objectivity	
objector	
objet d'art, objets d'art	
oblation	
obleek	oblique

obligate,-gated, -gating	
obligation	
obligatory	
oblige, obliged, obliging	
oblik	oblique
oblique, obliqued, obliquing	
obliquity, -ties	
obliterate, -rated, -rating	
oblivion	
oblivious, -ly	
oblivius	oblivious
oblong	
obloquy, -quies	
obnokshus	obnoxious
obnoxious, -ly	
obo	oboe
oboe	
oboist	
obscene, -ly	
obscenity, -ties	
obscure, -scured, -scuring	
obscure, -scurer, -scurest	
obscurity, -ties	
obsecrate, -crated, -crating	
obseen	obscene
obsekwies	obsequious
obsekwius	obsequious
obsequious, -ly	
observance	
observant, -ly	
observation	
observatory, -tories	
observatry	observatory
observe, -served, -serving	
obseshun	obsession
obsess, -ed, -ing	
obsession	
obsessive, -ly	
obsolescence	
obsolescent, -ly	
obsolesense	obsolescence
obsolesent	obsolescent
obsolete, -ly	
obstacle	
obstacul	obstacle
obstatrician	obstetrician
obstetric, -ally	

obstetrician
obstetrics
  obstetrishen   obstetrician
  obstetrishun   obstetrician
obstinacy, -cies
  obstinasey   obstinacy
obstinate, -ly
obstreperous, -ly
  obstreperus   obstreperous
  obstrucshun   obstruction
obstruct, -ed, -ing
obstruction
obstructive, -ly
obtain, -ed, -ing
  obtane   obtain
  obtroode   obtrude
  obtroosive   obtrusive
obtrude, -truded, -truding
obtrusive, -ly
obtuse, -ly
obverse, -ly
obviate, -ated, -ating
obviation
obvious, -ly
  obvius   obvious
  ocasion   occasion
  occashun   occasion
occasion, -ed, -ing
occasional, -ly
Occident
occidental
occlude, -cluded, -cluding
  occlushun   occlusion
occlusion
  occular   ocular
occult
occultism
occupancy
occupant
occupation
occupational
  occupent   occupant
  occupi   occupy
occupy, -pied, -pying
occur, -curred, -curring
  occurense   occurrence
occurrence

ocean
Oceania
oceanic
  oceanografey   oceanography
oceanographer
oceanography
ocelot
  ocher   ochre
ochre, ochred, ochring
ochrous
ocker
  Ocktober   October
o'clock
  oclood   occlude
  ocloosion   occlusion
  ocsident   Occident
octagon
octagonal, -ly
octane
octave
octavo
octet
October
octogenarian
octopus, -puses, -pi
ocular, -ly
  ocult   occult
  ocupancy   occupancy
  ocupant   occupant
  ocupi   occupy
  ocur   occur
  ocurence   occurrence
  ocurents   occurrence
  od   odd
odd, -ly
oddball
oddbod
oddity, ties
oddment
odds
odds-on
  odeclone   eau-de-Cologne
  oderus   odorous
  odiferus   odoriferous
odious, -ly
  odissey   odyssey
odium

odius	odious
odontology	
odor	odour
odoriferous, -ly	
odorous, -ly	
odour	
odyssey	
Oedipus complex	
oenin	
oesofagus	oesophagus
oesophagus, -gi	
oestrogen	
of	
of	off (away)
ofal	offal
ofence	offence
ofend	offend
ofen	often
ofense	offence
ofensive	offensive
ofer	offer
off (away)	
off	of
offal	
off-beat	
off-colour	
offcourse	
off-cut	
offence	
offend, -ed, -ing	
offender	
offense	offence
offensive, -ly	
offer, -ed, -ing	
offering	
offertory, -ries	
offhand	
offhanded, -ly	
office	
officer	
official, -ly	
officialdom	
officiate, -ated, -ating	
officiation	
officious, -ly	
offing	
offise	office

offishul	official
offishus	officious
off-limits	
off-load, -loaded, -loading	
off-peak	
off-putting	
off-season	
offset, -set, -setting	
offshoot	
offshore	
off side (cricket)	
offside (rugby)	
offsider	
offspring	
oficial	official
oficiate	officiate
oficious	officious
ofis	office
ofiser	officer
ofishal	official
ofishiate	officiate
ofishus	officious
ofset	offset
ofshoot	offshoot
ofside	offside
ofspring	offspring
oft	
often	
ogel	ogle
oger	ogre
ogle, ogled, ogling	
ogre	
oh	
ohm	
oil, oiled, oiling	
oilcloth	
oilfield	
oilly	oily
oil rig	
oilskin	
oily, oilier, oiliest	
ointment	
oister	oyster
ok	oak
okay	
oks	ox
oksalic acid	oxalic acid

oksidate	oxidate	on	own
okside	oxide	once	
oksident	Occident	oncore	encore
oksidise	oxidise	oncourse	
oksyacetylene	oxyacetylene	one (number)	
oksygen	oxygen	one	won (win)
oksymoron	oxymoron	one-eyed	
old, older, oldest		one-off	
olden		oner	owner
oldish		oneres	onerous
old-timer		onerous, -ly	
oleaginous		onership	ownership
oleaginus	oleaginous	oneself	
oleander		one-sided, -ly	
olearia		onest	honest
olfachun	olfaction	one-upmanship	
olfaction		oniks	onyx
olfactory, -ries		onion	
olfactry	olfactory	onist	honest
oligarch		onor	honour
oligarchic		onistey	honesty
oligarchy, -chies		onley	only
oligarkey	oligarchy	only	
Olimpic	Olympic	onorarey	honorary
oliv	olive	onorarium	honorarium
olive		onrabul	honourable
omelette		onrush	
omen		onset	
ominous, -ly		on side (cricket)	
ominus	ominous	onside (rugby)	
omishun	omission	onslaught	
omission		onslawt	onslaught
omit, omitted, omitting		onslort	onslaught
omlet	omelette	onto	
omnibus, -buses		ontological	
omnipotence		ontology	
omnipotense	omnipotence	ontray	entree
omnipotent, -ly		ontreprener	entrepreneur
omnipresence		onus	
omnipresent		onward	
omniscience		onwards	
omniscient, -ly		onyx	
omnisiense	omniscience	oomph	
omnisient	omniscient	ooze, oozed, oozing	
omnivorous, -ly		opacity, -ties	
omnivorus	omnivorous	opake	opaque
on		opal	

opaline
opaque, opaqued, opaquing
  opasity   opacity
  opeate   opiate
open, -ed, -ing
openly
open-minded
open-range
open-verdict
opera
operable, -bly
  operabul   operable
operate, -rated, -rating
  operater   operator
operatic, -ally
operation
operational, -ly
operative, -ly
operator
operetta
ophthalmic
ophthalmologist
ophthalmology
opiate, -ated, -ating
opine, opined, opining
opinion
opinionated
  opinyun   opinion
opium
  oponent   opponent
  oportune   opportune
  oportunitey   opportunity
  opose   oppose
  oposishun   opposition
  oposite   opposite
  oposition   opposition
opossum
  oposum   opossum
opponency
opponent
opportune, -ly
opportunism
opportunist
opportunity, -ties
oppose, -posed, -posing
opposite
opposition

oppress, -ed, -ing
oppression
oppressive, -ly
oppressor
opprobrious, -ly
opprobrium
  oprabul   operable
  oprate   operate
  opreshun   oppression
  opresive   oppressive
  opress   oppress
  opshun   option
  opshunul   optional
opt, -ed, -ing
  opthalmic   ophthalmic
  opthalmology   ophthalmology
optic
optical, -ly
optician
optics
optimism
optimist
optimistic, -ally
optimum, -ma, -mums
option
optional, -ly
  optishun   optician
optometrist
optometry
opulence
  opulense   opulence
opulent, -ly
opus, opuses, opera
or
  or   awe (dread)
  or   oar (boat)
  or   ore (rock)
  ora   aura
oracle
  oracul   oracle
oracular, -ly
oral, -ly (spoken)
  oral   aural (hear)
  orangatang   orang-outang
orange
orang-outang
  orashun   oration

orater	orator	orfanaje	orphanage
oration		orful	awful
orator		orfun	orphan
oratorical, -ly		organ	
oratorio, -rios		organdie, -dies	
oratory, -ries		organic, -ally	
oratrey	oratory	organisation	
orb		organise, -nised, -nising	
orbit, -ed, -ing		organism	
orbital		organist	
orcestra	orchestra	organza	
orcestral	orchestral	orgasm	
orcestrate	orchestrate	orgenism	organism
orchard		orger	auger (tool)
orchardist		orger	augur (omen)
orchestra		orgey	orgy
orchestral, -ly		orgiastic	
orchestrate, -trated, -trating		orgy, -gies	
orchestration		orical	auricle (ear)
orchid		orical	oracle (seer)
orcid	orchid	oriel	
ordain, -ed, -ing		orient	
ordanal	ordinal	oriental	
ordane	ordain	orientate, -tated, -tating	
ordeal		orientation	
ordenrey	ordinary	orienteering	
order, -ed, -ing		orifice	
orderly, -lies		orifise	orifice
orderliness		origami	
ordinal		origin	
ordinance (law)		original, -ly	
ordinariness		originality, -ties	
ordinary, -ries		originate, -nated, -nating	
ordination		oringe	orange
ordinry	ordinary	oriole	
orditer	auditor	orjy	orgy
orditrey	auditory	orkestra	orchestra
ordnance (weapons)		orkestral	orchestral
ordnance	ordinance (law)	orkestrate	orchestrate
ordure		orkestration	orchestration
ore (rock)		orkid	orchid
ore	oar (boat)	ornament	
ore	or (either)	ornamental, -ly	
ore	awe (dread)	ornamentation	
oregano		ornate, -ly	
orfan	orphan	ornimant	ornament
orfanage	orphanage	orning	awning

ornithologist
ornithology
orotund
orphan
orphanage
Orphism
orris

orspishus	auspicious
orstruck	awestruck
orsum	awesome
ort	aught
ort	ought
orthedoks	orthodox

orthodontic
orthodontics
orthodontist
orthodox
orthodoxy, -doxies

orthografey	orthography

orthography, -phies
orthopaedic
orthopaedics
orthopaedist
orthopaedy

orthopeadic	orthopaedic
orthority	authority
oscilation	oscillation

oscillate, -lated, -lating (move)

oscillate	osculate (kiss)

oscillation
oscillator
oscilloscope
osculate, -lated, -lating (kiss)

osculate	oscillate (move)
oseanic	oceanic
oselot	ocelot
oshun	ocean

osier

osifi	ossify
osler	ostler

osmosis

ospray	osprey

osprey, -preys

ossifi	ossify

ossification
ossify, -fied, -fying

ossilate	oscillate
ossilation	oscillation
ossiloscope	oscilloscope
osteapath	osteopath

ostensible, -bly

ostensibul	ostensible

ostentation
ostentatious, -ly
osteoarthritis
osteomyelitis
osteopath
osteopathic
osteopathy
ostler
ostracise, -cised, -cising
ostracism

ostrasise	ostracise
ostrasism	ostracism

ostrich

ote	oat
oter	otter
oth	oath

other
otherwise
otherworldly
otic
otiose, -ly
otiosity

otoman	ottoman

otter
ottoman, -mans
ouch
ought (should)

ought	aught (any part)

ouija

oul	owl

ounce

ounse	ounce

our (us)

our	hour
ourly	hourly

ours
ourself, -selves
oust, ousted, ousting
ouster
out, -ed, -ing
outback

outbilding   outbuilding
outboard
outbrake   outbreak
outbreak
outbuilding
outburst
outcast
outcome
outcri   outcry
outcrop, -cropped, -cropping
outcry, -cries
outdate, -dated, -dating
outdo, -done, -doing
outdoor
outdoors
outer
outfall
outfield
outfit, -fitted, -fitting
outflank, -ed, -ing
outfox, -ed, -ing
outgoing
outgrow, -grew, -grown, -growing
outgrowth
outhouse
outhowse   outhouse
outlandish, -ly
outlast, -ed, -ing
outlaw
outlawry
outlay, -laid, -laying
outlet
outline, -lined, -lining
outlive, -lived, -living
outlook
outlying
outmode, -moded, -moding
out-of-date
out-of-doors
out-of-pocket
out-of-the-way
outpatient
outpayshent   outpatient
outperform, -ed, -ing
outplay, -ed, -ing
outpoint, -ed, -ing
outpooring   outpouring

outpost
outpouring
output
outrage, -raged, -raging
outrageous, -ly
outraygus   outrageous
outrider
outrigger
outright
outrite   outright
outset
outside
outsider
outsize
outskirts
outspoken, -ly
outstanding, -ly
outstretch, -ed, -ing
outstrip, -stripped, -stripping
outward, -ly
outwards
outweigh
outwit, -witted, -witting
ouze   ooze
ov   of
oval, -ly
ovarey   ovary
ovary, -ries
ovate
ovation
oven
ovenproof
ovenware
ovenwear   ovenware
over, -ly
overall
overarm
overawe, -awed, -awing
overawl   overall
overbalance, -anced, -ancing
overbalanse   overbalance
overbare   overbear
overbear, -bore, -borne, -bearing
overbid, -bid, -bidding
overboard
overbord   overboard
overbridge

overcast, -cast, -casting
overcharge, -charged, -charging
overcoat
overcome, -came, -come, -coming
overdew   overdue
overdo, -did, -done, -doing
overdose, -dosed, -dosing
overdraft
overdraw, -drew, -drawn, -drawing
overdress, -ed, -ing
overdrive, -drove, -driven, -driving
overdu   overdue
overdue
overestimate, -mated, -mating
overestimation
overflow, -flowed, -flowing
overgrown
overhang, -hung, -hanging
overhaul, -ed, -ing
overhawl   overhaul
overhead
overhear, -heard, -hearing
overhearer
overhed   overhead
overherd   overheard
overhere   overhear
overjoid   overjoyed
overjoyed
overkill
overland
overlander
overlap, -lapped, -lapping
overlay, -laid, -laying
overleaf
overleef   overleaf
overlie, -lay, -lain, -lying (lie over)
overlie   overly
overlook
overly (excessively)
overly   overlie
overnight
overnite   overnight
overore   overawe
overought   overwrought
overpass
overpower, -ed, -ing
overeach   overreach

overeech   overreach
overiding   overriding
overreach, -ed, -ing
override, -rode, -ridden, -riding
overrool   overrule
overrule, -ruled, -ruling
overrun, -ran, -run, -running
overule   overrule
overun   overrun
overseas (abroad)
oversee, -saw, -seen, -seeing
overseer
overshadow, -ed, -ing
overshoot, -shot, -shooting
oversight
oversite   oversight
overstate, -stated, -stating
overstatement
overstay, -ed, -ing
overstep, -stepped, -stepping
overstock, -ed, -ing
oversubscribed
overt, -ly
overtake, -taken, -taking
overtaks   overtax
overtax
overthrow, -thrown, -throwing
overtime, -timed, -timing
overtone
overture, -tured, -turing
overturn, -ed, -ing
overview
overwait   overweight
overwate   overweight
overweight
overwelm   overwhelm
overwerk   overwork
overwhelm, -ed, -ing
overwork, -worked, -working
overwrought
ovine
ovipares   oviparous
oviparis   oviparous
oviparous, -ly
oviparus   oviparous
ovoid (egg)
ovoid   avoid (evade)

ovulate, -lated, -lating
ovulation
ovule
ovum, ova
  owa   hour
  owa   our
owe, owed, owing (debt)
  owe   oh (cry)
owl
own, -ed, -ing
  ownce   ounce
owner
ownership
  ownly   only
  owst   oust
  owt   out
ox, oxen
oxalis
oxidate, -dated, -dating
oxidation
oxide
oxidisable
  oxidisabul   oxidisable
oxidisation
oxidise, -dised, -dising
oxidiser
  oxigenate   oxygenate
oxyacetylene
oxygen
oxygenate, -nated, -nating
oxygenation
oxygenise, -nised, -nising
oxymoron, -mora
oyster
Oz
ozone
ozonize, -ized, -izing
ozonosphere

Pp

pace, paced, pacing
pacemaker
pacer
　　pach　　　　　　　patch
　　pachwork　　　　　patchwork
pacific, -ally
pacification
pacifier
pacifism
pacifist
pacify, -fied, -fying
pack, -ed, -ing
package
packer
packet
packhorse
　　packije　　　　　　package
pact
pad, padded, padding
paddle, -dled, -dling
paddler
paddle-steamer
paddock
　　paddul　　　　　　paddle
paddy, -dies
paddy-wagon
　　pade　　　　　　　paddy
　　padie　　　　　　　paddy
padlock, -ed, -ing
padre
　　padrey　　　　　　padre
　　pady　　　　　　　paddy
paediatrician
paediatrics
pagan
paganism
page, paged, paging
pageant

pageantry, -ries
　　pagentry　　　　　pageantry
pageboy
pager
pagoda
pail (bucket)
　　pail　　　　　　　pale (white)
pain (ache)
　　pain　　　　　　　pane (glass)
painful, -ly
pain-killer
painstaking, -ly
paint, -ed, -ing
painter
pair, -ed, -ing (two)
　　pair　　　　　　　pare (trim)
　　pair　　　　　　　pear (fruit)
pakeha
pal, palled, palling (friend)
palace
　　palase　　　　　　palace
palatable, -bly
palatal, -ly (taste)
palate (mouth)
　　palate　　　　　　palette (board)
　　palate　　　　　　pallet (bed)
　　palate　　　　　　pellet (ball)
palatial, -ly (palace)
pale, paled, paling (white)
pale, paler, palest
　　pale　　　　　　　pail (bucket)
palette (board)
　　palette　　　　　　pallet (bed)
　　paliate　　　　　　palliate
　　palid　　　　　　　pallid
palindrome
paling
palisade, -saded, -sading
pall, palled, palling (satiate)
pallbearer
pallet (bed)
　　pallet　　　　　　palette (paint)
　　pallet　　　　　　pellet (ball)
palliate, -ated, -ating
palliation
palliative, -ly
pallid, -ly

pall-mall (game)
pall-mall   pell-mell
               (haste)
pallor
palm, -ed, -ing
palmist
palmistry
palmy, -mier, -miest
palomino, -nos
palor   pallor
palpable, -bly
palpabul   palpable
palpitate, -tated, -tating
palpitation
palsie   palsy
palsied
palsy, -sies
paltrie   paltry
paltriness
paltry, -trier, -triest
pamplet   pamphlet
pampas
pamper, -ed, -ing
pamphlet
pamphleteer
pan, panned, panning
panacea
panache
Panama hat
panash   panache
pancake, -caked, -caking
pancreas
pancreatic
panda (animal)
pandemonium
pander, -ed, -ing (indulge)
pane (glass)
pane   pain (ache)
paneful   painful
panegyric, -ally
panel, -elled, -elling
panellist
panestaking   painstaking
pang
panic, -icked, -icking
paniced   panicked
panicky

panic-stricken
panigiric   panegyric
panik   panic
pannier
pannikin
panorama
panoramic, -ally
pansie   pansy
pansy, -sies
pant, -ed, -ing
pantaloon
pantechnicon
pantheism
pantheist
pantheistic, -ally
pantheon
panther
panthion   pantheon
panties
pantihose
pantingly
pantograf   pantograph
pantograph
pantomime
pantomine   pantomime
pantrey   pantry
pantry, -ries
pants
panza   panzer
panzer
pap
papa
papacy, -cies
papal
papasy   papacy
paper
paperback
paperbark
paperboy
paperclip
paper-mache   papier-mâché
paperwait   paperweight
paperweight
papier-mâché
papirus   papyrus
papism
papoose

papouse	papoose	parameter	
pappa	papa	paramiter	parameter
pappoose	papoose	paramoor	paramour
papprika	paprika	paramount	
pappyrus	papyrus	paramour	
paprica	paprika	paramownt	paramount
paprika		paranoia	
papul	papal	paranoiac	
papyrus, -ri		paranoid	
parable		parapet	
parabola		paraphernalia	
parabul	parable	paraphrase, -phrased, -phrasing	
parachute		paraplegic	
paracide	parricide	paraplijic	paraplegic
paracleet	paraclete	parashoot	parachute
paraclete		parashute	parachute
parade, -raded, -rading		parasite	
paradice	paradise	parasitic, -ally	
paradigm		parasitism	
paradime	paradigm	parasol	
paradise		parasoll	parasol
paradoks	paradox	paratrooper	
paradox		parboil, -ed, -ing	
parady	parody	parboyle	parboil
parafernalia	paraphernalia	parcel, -celled, -celling	
paraffin		parch, -ed, -ing	
parafin	paraffin	parchment	
parafrase	paraphrase	pardon, -ed, -ing	
paragon		pardonable	
paragraf	paragraph	pardonabul	pardonable
paragraph		pardoner	
parakeet		pare (trim)	
parakete	parakeet	pare	pair (two
paralax	parallax	pare	pear (fruit)
paralel	parallel	parent	
paralelagram	parallelogram	parentage	
paralise	paralyse	parental, -ly	
paralisis	paralysis	parenthesis, -ses	
paralitic	paralytic	parentige	parentage
parallax		parfait	
parallel, -leled, -leling or -lelled,		parfay	parfait
-lelling		pariah	
parallelogram		parie	parry
paralyse, -lysed, -lysing		parish, parishes	
paralysis		parishioner	
paralytic		parishoner	parishioner
paramedical		pariside	parricide

parisidul	parricidal	parsimony	
parity		parsley	
park, -ed, -ing		parslie	parsley
parka		parsly	parsley
parket	parquet	parsnip	
parking-meter		parson	
Parkinson's disease		parsonage	
parlament	parliament	parsonige	parsonage
parlance		parsul	parcel
parlans	parlance	part, -ed, -ing	
parlay	parley	partake, -took, -taken, -taking	
parlement	parliament	partial, -ly	
parlementarey	parliamentary	partiality, -ties	
parlementry	parliamentary	participant	
parler	parlour	participate, -pated, -pating	
parlermade	parlour-maid	participle	
parley, -leyed, -leying		participul	participle
parliament		particle	
parliamentarian		particul	particle
parliamentary		particular, -ly	
parlour		partie	party
parlour-maid		partime	part-time
parm	palm	partisan	
parmist	palmist	partishun	partition
parochial, -ly		partisipant	participant
parochialism		partisipate	participate
parody, -dies		partisipul	participle
parody, -died, -dying		partition, -ed, -ing	
parograf	paragraph	partly	
parograph	paragraph	partner, -ed, -ing	
parokial	parochial	partridge	
paroksism	paroxysm	partrige	partridge
parole, -roled, -roling		part-time	
paroll	parole	party, -ties	
parot	parrot	pars	pass
paroxysm		pary	parry
parquet, -queted, -queting		pasabul	passable
parranoia	paranoia	pascal	paschal
parricide		paschal	
parrot		pascher	pasture
parry, parried, parrying		pase	pace
parse, parsed, parsing		pasemaker	pacemaker
parsel	parcel	paserby	passer-by
parshal	partial	pashonate	passionate
parshialitey	partiality	pashun	passion
parsimonious, -ly		pasific	pacific
parsimonius	parsimonious	pasify	pacify

pasige — passage
pasinger — passenger
pasive — passive
pasivitey — passivity
Pasover — Passover
paspalum
pasport — passport
pass, passed, passing
passable, -bly
passabul — passable
passage, -saged, -saging
passbook
passé
passenger
passer-by, passers-by
passige — passage
passion
passionate, -ly
passionfruit
passive, -ly
passivity
Passover
passport
password
past
pasta (dough)
pasta — pastor (priest)
paste, pasted, pasting
pasteboard
pastel
pasterise — pasteurise
pasteurise, -ed, -ing
pastiche
pastie — pasty
pastime
pastor (priest)
pastoral, -ly
pastoralist
pastrami
pastry, -tries
pasture, -ed, -ing
pasty, -ties
password — password
pat, patter, patting
patay — pâté
patch, -ed, -ing
patchwork

patchy, patchier, patchiest
pâté
patella, -tellae
paten — pattern
patent, -ed, -ing
patent-leather
pater — patter
patern — pattern
paternal, -ly
paternalism
paternity
path
pathetic, -ally
pathological, -ly
pathology, -gies
pathos
patie — patty
patience (calm)
patient, patients (ill)
patient, -ly
patina
patio, patios
patiserey — patisserie
patisserie
patois, patois
patriarch
patriarchal, -ly
patriarchy, -archies
patriark — patriarch
patrician
patricide
patrimony, -monies
patriot
patriotic, -ally
patriotism
patrishun — patrician
patriside — patricide
patrol, patrolled, patrolling
patron
patronage
patroness
patronige — patronage
patronise, -ed, -ing
patter, -ed, -ing
pattern, -ed, -ing
patty, -ies
paturnal — paternal

paturnitey	paternity	payshent	patient
patwa	patois	paytent	patent
paucity		pea	
paun	pawn	peace (calm)	
paunch, paunches		peace	piece (part)
paunchy		peaceable, -bly	
pauper		peaceabul	peaceable
pause, paused, pausing (stop)		peaceful, -ly	
pause	paws (feet)	peach, peaches	
pave, paved, paving		peacock	
pavement		peak, -ed, -ing (top)	
pavilion		peak	peek (look)
pavlova		peak	pique (anger)
paw (foot)		peal, -ed, -ing (ring)	
paw	poor (needy)	peal	peel (skin)
paw	pore (skin)	peanut	
paw	pour (flow)	peap	peep
pawcelain	porcelain	pear (fruit)	
pawch	porch	pear	pair (two)
pawk	pork	pear	pare (trim)
pawkupine	porcupine	pearage	peerage
pawl	pall	pearce	pierce
pawlbarer	pall-bearer	pearl (gem)	
pawlsied	palsied	pearl	purl (knit)
pawlsy	palsy	pearly, -lies	
pawltrey	paltry	peasant	
pawn, -ed, -ing		peasantry	
pawnbroker		peashooter	
pawnbroking		peashuter	peashooter
pawnch	paunch	peat	
pawnografey	pornography	pebble	
pawpaw		pecadillo, -loes, -los	
pawper	pauper	pecan	
pawpus	porpoise	peck, -ed, -ing	
pawse	pause (stop)	peckish, -ly	
pawselin	porcelain	pecock	peacock
pawshun	portion	pectin	
pawsitey	paucity	pectoral	
pay, paid, paying		peculiar, -ly	
payable		peculiarity, -ties	
payabul	payable	pecuniary	
payload		pedagog	pedagogue
payment		pedagogic, -ally	
paynt	paint	pedagogue	
payola		pedagogy	
payroll		pedal, -alled, -alling (bike)	
payshence	patience	pedant	

pedantic, -ally
pedantry, -ries
peddle, -dled, -dling (sell)
   peddle   pedal (bike)
pederast
pederastic, -ally
pederasty
pedestal, -stalled, -stalling
pedestrian
pedicure
pedigree
pedlar
peek, -ed, -ing (look)
   peek   peak (top)
   peek   pique (anger)
peel, -ed, -ing (skin)
   peel   peal (ring)
peep, -ed, -ing
peepshow
peer, -ed, -ing (look)
   peer   pier (wharf)
peerage
peeress
   peerige   peerage
peerless, -ly
peevish
peewee
peewit
peg, pegged, pegging
   peice   piece
pejorative, -ly
   pek   peck
   pekant   piquant
Pekinese
Pekingese
   pekish   peckish
pelargonium
pelican
pellet (ball)
   pellet   palate (mouth)
   pellet   palette (board)
   pellet   pallet (bed)
pell-mell (haste)
   pell-mell   pall-mall
                  (game)
pellucid, -ly
pelmet

pelt, -ed, -ing
   pelusid   pellucid
pelvis, -ves
pen, penned, penning
penal
penalisation
penalise, -lised, -lising
penalty, -ties
penance
   penanse   penance
   penant   pennant
pence
penchant
pencil, -cilled, -cilling
pendant
pendent
pending
pendulous, -ly
pendulum
   pendulus   pendulous
penetrable, -bly
   pentrabul   penetrable
penetrate, -trated, -trating
penetration
penfriend
penguin
   pengwin   penguin
penicillin
   peniless   penniless
peninsula
penis, -nes, -nises
   penisilin   penicillin
   penitenshary   penitentiary
   penitenshul   penitential
penitent, -ly
penitential, -ly
penitentiary, -ries
penknife, -knives
pen-name
pennant
penniless
pennon
penny, pennies, pence
penny-farthing
penny-pinching
penological
penologist

penology
pen-pusher
  pense   pence
  penshun   pension
  penshuner   pensioner
  pensil   pencil
pension
pensionable
  pensionabul   pensionable
pensioner
pensive, -ly
pentagon
  pentathalon   pentathlon
pentathlon
penthouse
  penthowse   penthouse
pent-up
penultimate, -ly
penumbra, -brae, -bras
penurious, -ly
penury
  penut   peanut
peon
peony, -nies
people, -pled, -pling
pep, pepped, pepping
  peper   pepper
  pepermint   peppermint
  pepery   peppery
pepper
peppercorn
peppermint
peppery
pep pill
pep talk
peptic
perambulate, -lated, -lating
perambulation
perambulator
perambulatory
per annum
per capita
perceivable, -bly
perceive, -ceived, -ceiving
per cent
percentage
  percentige   percentage

percentile
  percepshun   perception
  perceptabul   perceptible
perceptible, -bly
perception
perceptive, -ly
perceptual, -ly
  percession   procession
perch, perches
perch, -ed, -ing
  perchase   purchase
percipience
percipient
percolate, -lated, -lating
  percolater   percolator
percolation
percolator
  percushun   percussion
percussion
percussionist
percussive
  perdishun   perdition
perdition
peregrinate, -nated, -nating
peremptoriness
peremptory, -torily
perennial, -ly
  perfeckshun   perfection
perfect, -ed, -ing
perfectible
  perfectibul   perfectible
perfection
perfectionism
perfectionist
perfidious, -ly
  perfidius   perfidious
perfidy, -dies
perforate, -rated, -rating
perforation
perforce
perform, -ed, -ing
performance
  performanse   performance
perfume, -fumed, -fuming
perfumery, -ries
perfunctory, -torily
  perfunctry   perfunctory

pergarey — perjury
pergative — purgative
pergatry — purgatory
perge — purge
pergola
perhaps
perhibit — prohibit
periferal — peripheral
perifery — periphery
peril, -rilled, -rilling
perilous, -ly
perilus — perilous
perimeter
period
periodic
periodical, -ly
peripatetic
peripheral, -ly
periphery, -ries
periscope
perish, -ed, -ing
perishable
perishabul — perishable
perisher
peritonitis
periwinkle
perjure, -jured, -juring
perjurer
perjury, -ries
perk, -ed, -ing
perkushun — percussion
perky, -kier, -kiest
perl — pearl (gem)
perl — purl (knit)
perloin — purloin
perloyn — purloin
perm, -ed, -ing
permananse — permanence
permanence
permanency, -cies
permanent, -ly
permanganate
permeability
permeable
permeate, -ated, -ating
permeation
permiate — permeate

permisabul — permissible
permishun — permission
permissible, -bly
permission
permissive, -ly
permissiveness
permit, -mitted, -mitting
permutation
permute, -muted, -muting
pernicious, -ly
perniciousness
pernickety
pernishus — pernicious
perokside — peroxide
peroration
peroxide, -ided, -iding
perpechual — perpetual
perpechuate — perpetuate
perpendicular, -ly
perpendicularity
perpetrate, -trated, -trating
perpetrater — perpetrator
perpetration
perpetrator
perpetual, -ly
perpetuate, -ated, -ating
perpetuation
perpetuator
perpetuity, -ties
perport — purport
perpose — purpose
perquisite (profit)
perquisite — prerequisite (necessary)
per say — per se
per se
perse — purse
persecushun — persecution
persecute, -cuted, -cuting
persecution
persecutor
persepshun — perception
perseptabul — perceptible
perseve — persevere
perseverance
persevere, -vered, -vering
Persian

persimmon
persist, -ed, -ing
persistence
person
personable, -bly
personage
personal, -ly (private)
  personal   personnel
                      (employees)
personalise, -lised, -lising
personality, -ties
persona non grata
personate, -ated, -ating
  personible   personable
personification
personify, -fied, -fying
personnel (employees)
  personnel   personal
                  (private)
perspective, -ly
  perspeks   perspex
  perspektive   perspective
perspex
perspicacious, -ly
perspicacity
perspicuous, -ly
perspicuousness
perspiration
perspire, -spired, -spiring
persuade, -suaded, -suading
persuader
  persuashun   persuasion
persuasion
persuasive, -ly
  persuit   pursuit
  perswade   persuade
  perswasion   persuasion
pert, -ly
pertness
pertain, -ed, -ing
  pertane   pertain
pertinacious, -ly
pertinacity
pertinent, -ly
perturb, -ed, -ing
perturbable
peruse, -rused, -rusing

pervade, -vaded, -vading
pervasion
pervasive, -ly
perverse, -ly
  pervershun   perversion
perversion
perversity, -ties
pervert, -ed, -ing
perverter
  pervurse   perverse
  pervurshun   perversion
  pervurt   pervert
  pesabul   peaceable
  pesant   peasant
  pesary   pessary
  pese   peace
  pesimism   pessimism
  pesimist   pessimist
pessary, -ries
pessimism
pessimist
pest
pester, -ed, -ing
pesticide
pestilence
  pestilense   pestilence
pestilent, -ly
  pestiside   pesticide
pestle
  pesul   pestle
pet, petted, petting
petal
petard
  peteet   petite
peter, -ed, -ing
  peticoat   petticoat
  petie   petty
  petishun   petition
petite
petition, -ed, -ing
petrel (bird)
  petrel   petrol (fuel)
petrify, -fied, -fying
petrol (fuel)
  petrol   petrel (bird)
petroleum
  petrul   petrel (bird)

petrul petrol (fuel)
petticoat
pettily
pettiness
petty, -tier, -tiest
petulance
petulant, -ly
petunia
pevish peevish
pew
pewter
phalanger
phalanx, -anxes or -anges
phalus phallus
phallic
phallus, phalluses, phalli
phantasm
phantasmagoria
phantom
Pharaoh
pharisaic
pharisee
pharmaceutical, -ly
pharmacist
pharmacy, -cies
pharyngitis
pharynx, pharynges, pharynxes
phase, phased, phasing
pheasant
phenacetin
phenix phoenix
phenol
phenomenal, -ly
phenomenon, -mena
phesant pheasant
phial (vessel)
philander, -ed, -ing
philanderer
philanthropic, -ally
philanthropist
philanthropy, -pies
philarmonic philharmonic
philatelist
philately
philharmonic
Philippines
philosofer philosopher

philosofical philosophical
philosofy philosophy
philosopher
philosophical, -ly
philosophise, -phised, -phising
philosophy, -phies
philter philtre
philtre, -tred, -tring

> For **phis-** words, look
> under **phys-**.

phlegm
phlegmatic, -ally
phlem phlegm
phlox
phobia
phobic
phoenix
phone
phonetic, -ally
phonograf phonograph
phonogram
phonograph
phony, phonier, phoniest
phosfate phosphate
phosforus phosphorus
phosphate
phosphor
phosphorescent
phosphorus
photo, photos
photocopier
photocopy, -pies
photocopy, -copied, -copying
photoelectric
photo-finish
photogenic
photograf photograph
photograph, -graph, -graphing
photographic, -ally
photography
photostat, -stated, -stating
photosynthesis
phrase, phrased, phrasing
phraseology
phrenetic, -ally
phylactery, -teries

physic (medicine)
physical, -ly
physician
physicist
physics
physiognomy, -mies
physiological, -ly
physiology
physiotherapist
physiotherapy
physique
pi (Greek letter)
   pi   pie (food)
pianist
piano, pianos
pianoforte
   piatsa   piazza
piazza
   pibald   piebald
picador
   picancy   piquancy
   picaniny   piccaninny
piccaninny, -nies
piccolo, -los
   pich   pitch
   picinic   picnic
pick, -ed, -ing
pickaxe, -axed, -axing
picket, -ed, -ing
pickle, -led, -ling
pickpocket
pick-up
picnic, -nicked, -nicking
picnicker
pictorial, -ly
picture, -tured, -turing
picturesque
pidgin (talk)
   pidgin   pigeon (bird)
pie (food)
   pie   pi (Greek letter)
piebald
piece, pieced, piecing (part)
   piece   peace (calm)
piecemeal
piecework

pier (wharf)
   pier   peer (look)
pierce, pierced, piercing
   pierse   pierce
piety, -ties
pig, pigged, pigging
pigeon (bird)
   pigeon   pidgin (talk)
pigeonhole, -holed, -holing
pigeon-toed
   pigery   piggery
piggery, -geries
piggyback
pig-headed
   pigiback   piggyback
   pigin   pidgin (talk)
   pigin   pigeon (bird)
pig-iron
piglet
pigment
pigmentation
pigmy, -mies
pigskin
pigstick, -ed, -ing
pigsticker
pigsty, -sties
pigtail
   pigtale   pigtail
   pijamas   pyjamas
pikau
pike, piked, piking
pikelet
pilchard
pile, piled, piling
pile-up
pilfer, -ed, -ing
pilferage
pilferer
   pilferige   pilferage
pilgrim
pilgrimage
   pilgrimige pilgrimage
   pilige   pillage
   pilion   pillion
pill
pillage, -laged, -laging
pillager

pillar
pillbox, -boxes
pillion
pillory, -ries
pillory, -ried, -rying
pillow, pillows
  pilon   pylon
  pilory   pillory
pilot, -ed, -ing
pilotage
  pilow   pillow
  pilyun   pillion
pilsener
pimp, -ed, -ing
pimple
pimply, -plier, -pliest
  pimpul   pimple
pin, pinned, pinning
  pinacle   pinnacle
pinafore
pinball
pince-nez
pincers
pinch, -ed, -ing
pincher
pincushion
pine, pined, pining
pineapple
  pineappul   pineapple
pin-feather
ping, -ed, -ing
ping-pong
pinion, -ed, -ing
pink, -ed, -ing
pinnacle, -cled, -cling
pinpoint, -ed, -ing
pinprick
  pinsers   pincers
pinstripe
pint
pintuck,-ed, -ing
pin-up
  pinyun   pinion
  pionear   pioneer
pioneer, -ed, -ing
pious, -ly
pip, pipped, pipping

pipe, piped, piping
pipedream
pipeline
pipi
pipit
pippin
pipsqueak
piquancy
piquant, -ly
pique, piqued, piquing
piracy
  piramid   pyramid
piranha
  pirasy   piracy
pirate, -rated, -rating
piratical, -ly
  pire   pyre
  pirooet   pirouette
pirouette, -etted, -etting
piscatorial
Pisces
pistachio, -chios
pistil (flower)
pistol (gun)
piston
pit, pitted, pitting
  pitanse   pittance
pitapat, -patted, -patting
pitch, -ed, -ing
pitch-black
pitchblende
pitcher (baseball)
  pitcher   picture (image)
pitchfork, -ed, -ing
pitchi
piteous, -ly
  piter-pater   pitter-patter
pitfall
pith
pithead
pithy, -ier, -iest
pitiable, -ly
  pitiabul   pitiable
pitiful, -fully
pitiless, -ly
pittance
  pittanse   pittance

pitter-patter
pittosporum
pituitary, -taries
pituri
pity, pities
pity, pitied, pitying
   pius   pious
pivot, -ed, -ing
pivotal, -ly
pixie, pixies
pixy, pixies
pizza
pizzicato
placability
placable, -bly
   placabul   placable
placard, -ed, -ing
placate, -cated, -cating
placatory
place, placed, placing (position)
   place   plaice (fish)
placebo, -bos, -boes
placement
placenta, -tas, -tae
placental
placid, -ly
placidity
placket
   plagarism   plagiarism
   plage   plague
plagiarise, -rised, -rising
plagiarism
plagiarist
plague, plagued, plaguing
plaice (fish)
plaid (cloth)
plain, -ly (clear)
   plain   plane (flat)
plain-clothes
plain-spoken
plains wanderer
plaint
plaintiff (sue)
plaintive, -ly (sad)
plait, -ed, -ing (braid)
   plait   plate (dish)
   plaket   placket

plan, planned, planning
plane, planed, planing (flat)
   plane   plain (clear)
planet
planetarium
planetary
plank
plankton
planner
plant, -ed, -ing
plantation
planter
   plantif   plaintiff (sue)
   plantive   plaintive (sad)
plaque
   plase   place (position)
   plase   plaice (fish)
   plasenta   placenta
   plasid   placid
plasma
plaster, -ed, -ing
plasterboard
plasterer
plastic, -ally
   plasticene   plasticine
plasticine
plasticity
   plastisene   plasticine
plate, plated, plating (dish)
   plate   plait (braid)
plateau, -eaus, -eaux
platelet
   plater   platter
platform
   platichude   platitude
platinum
   platipus   platypus
platitude
platitudinous
   plato   plateau
Platonic
platoon
platter
platypus, -puses, -pi
plaudit
plausible, -bly
   plausibul   plausible

play, -ed, -ing
playback
playboy
player
playful, -ly
playground
play-off
   playrite   playwright
playwright
plaza
plea, pleas (request)
plead, -ed, -ing
   pleas   please (satisfy)
pleasant, -ly
pleasantry, -tries
please, pleased, pleasing (satisfy)
pleasurable, -bly
   pleasurabul   pleasurable
pleat, -ed, -ing
   plebean   plebeian
plebeian
plebiscite
   plebisite   plebiscite
plectrum, -tra, -trums
pledge, pledged, pledging
   plee   plea
   pleed   plead
   pleet   pleat
   plege   pledge
plenary, -rily
plenipotentiary, -ries
plenitude
plenteous, -ly
plentiful, -ly
   plentius   plenteous
plenty
   plesant   pleasant
   plese   pleas (requests)
   plese   please (satisfy)
   plesurabul   pleasurable
   plesure   pleasure
plethora
pleurisy
   pli   ply
pliable, -bly
   pliabul   pliable
pliant, -ly

pliers
plight, -ed, -ing
Plimsoll line
plinth
   plite   plight
   pliwood   plywood
plod, plodded, plodding
plodder
   ploi   ploy
plonk, -ed, -ing
   ploomage   plumage
   plootocrasy   plutocracy
   plooviul   pluvial
plop, plopped, plopping
plot, plotted, plotting
plough, -ed, -ing
ploughshare
plover
   plow   plough
ploy
pluck, -ed, -ing
plucky, -ily
plug, plugged, plugging
plum (fruit)
   plum   plumb (test)
plumage
plumb, -ed, -ing (test)
plumber
plumbline
plume, plumed, pluming
   plumige   plumage
   plumline   plumbline
   plummer   plumber
plummet, -ed, -ing
plump, -ed, -ing
plunder, -ed, -ing
plunge, plunged, plunging
plural
pluralism
plurality, -ties
   plurasy   pleurisy
plus
plus-fours
plush
plutocracy, -cies
plutocrat
plutonium

pluvial
ply, plies
ply, plied, plying
plywood
pneumatic, -ally
pneumonia
poach, -ed, -ing
poacher
poch   poach
pock
pocket, -ed, -ing
pocket-book
pocket-knife, -knives
pocket-money
pockmark
pod, podded, podding
poddy
podiatrist
podiatry
podium, -dia
poem
poet
poetess
poetic
poetical, -ly
poetry
pogrom
poignancy
poignant, -ly
poinancy   poignancy
poinant   poignant
poinsettia
point,-ed, -ing
point-blank
pointedly
pointer
pointillism
pointless, -ly
poise, poised, poising
poison, -ed, -ing
poisoner
poisonous, -ly
poke, poked, poking
poker
pokey, pokies (machine)
poky, -kier, -kiest (small)
polar (region)

polar   poler (horse)
polarise, -rised, -rising
polarity
polaroid
pole, poled, poling (stick)
pole   poll (vote)
polemic
polemical, -ly
polen   pollen
poler (horse)
poler   polar (region)
polese   police
police, -liced, -licing
policeman, -men
policewoman, -women
policy, -cies
poligamus   polygamous
poligamy   polygamy
poliglot   polyglot
poligon   polygon
polinate   pollinate
Polineshun   Polynesian
poliomyelitis
polip   polyp
polish, -ed, -ing
polisy   policy
politburo
polite, -ly
politic
polithene   polythene
political, -ly
politician
politicise, -cised, -cising
politicking
politics
politishun   politician
polka, -kaed, -kaing
poll, -ed, -ing (vote)
poll   pole (stick)
pollard
pollen
pollinate, -nated, -nating
pollination
pollster
pollutant
pollute, -luted, -luting
pollution

polo	
polo-neck	
poltegist	poltergeist
poltergeist	
poltise	poultice
poltry	poultry
polushun	pollution
polute	pollute
polyandrous	
polyandry	
polyanthus	
polyester	
polygamist	
polygamous, -ly	
polygamy	
polyglot	
polygon	
Polyneshun	Polynesian
Polynesian	
polyp	
polysaturated	
polythene	
polyunsaturated	
pomander	
pomegranate	
pomel	pommel
Pomeranian	
pommel, -melled, -melling	
pommy, -mies	
pomp	
pompom	
pomposity	
pompous, -ly	
poncho, -chos	
ponder, -ed, -ing	
ponderous, -ly	
ponderus	ponderous
ponie	pony
pontiff	
pontifical, -ly	
pontificate, -cated, -cating	
pontoon	
pony, -nies	
ponytail	
pooch	
poodle	
poodul	poodle

pool, -ed, -ing	
poop, -ed, -ing	
poor, -ly (needy)	
poor	paw (foot)
poor	pore (skin)
poor	pour (flow)
poorhouse	
pop, popped, popping	
popcorn	
pope	
popery	
popet	poppet
popie	poppy
popish, -ly	
poplar (tree)	
poplin	
popourri	potpourri
poppet	
poppy, -pies	
poppycock	
populace	
popular, -ly (known)	
popularise, -rised, -rising	
popularitey	popularity
popularity	
populase	populace
populate, -lated, -lating	
population	
populer	popular
populous, -ly	
populus	populous
popy	poppy
por	paw (foot)
por	poor (needy)
por	pore (skin)
por	pour (flow)
porcelain	
porcelane	porcelain
porch	
porcupine	
pore (skin)	
pore	paw (foot)
pore	poor (needy)
pore	pour (flow)
porfrey	porphyry
poridge	porridge
porige	porridge

pork
porkupine porcupine
pornografy pornography
pornographer
pornographic
pornography
porosity
porous
porphyry, -ries
porpoise, -poises
porpus porpoise
porridge
porselin porcelain
porshun portion
porslin porcelain
port
portable
portal
portend, -ed, -ing
portenshus portentous
portent
portentous, -ly
porter
portfolio, -lios
porthole
portico, -coes, -cos
portion, -ed, -ing
portly, -lier, -liest
portmanteau, -teaus, -teaux
portrait
portraiture
portray, -ed, -ing
portrayal
portret portrait
portul portal
porus porous
poschur posture
pose, posed, posing
poser
poseshun possession
posess possess
posessive possessive
posey posy
posh, -ly
poshun potion
posibility possibility
posibul possible

posishun position
position
positive, -ly
posse
possess, -ed, -ing
possession
possessive, -ly
possessor
possible, -bly
possibility, -ties
possibul possible
possum
post, -ed, -ing
postage
postal
postcard
postcode
postdate, -dated, -dating
poster
posterier posterior
posterior, -ly
posterity
postern
postgraduate
posthaste
posthumous, -ly
posthumus posthumous
postige postage
post-mortem
post-office
postpone, -poned, -poning
postponement
postulant
postulate, -lated, -lating
postumus posthumous
posture, -tured, -turing
posy, -sies
pot, potted, potting
potable
potash
potasium potassium
potassium
potato, -toes
pot-bellied
pot-belly, -lies
potency
potenshul potential

potensy	potency
potent	
potentate	
potential, -ly	
potentiality, -ties	
poter	potter
potery	pottery
pothole	
potion	
potluck	
potpourri, -ris	
pottage	
potter, -ed, -ing	
pottery, -ries	
potty, -ties	
pouch, pouches	
poulterer	
poultice, -ticed, -ticing	
poultise	poultice
poultry	
pounce, pounced, pouncing	
pound, -ed, -ing	
pour, -ed, -ing	
pour	poor (needy)
pour	pore (skin)
pout, -ed, -ing	
poverty	
poverty-stricken	
powch	pouch
powder, -ed, -ing	
powdery	
power, -ed, -ing	
powerful, -ly	
powerhouse	
powerless, -ly	
pownce	pounce
pownd	pound
powt	pout
pow wow, -wowed, -wowing	
pox	
practicable, -bly	
practicabul	practicable
practical, -ly	
practicality	
practice, -ticed, -ticing	
practician	
practise, -tised, -tising	

practishun	practician
practishuner	practitioner
practitioner	
pragmatic, -ally	
pragmatism	
pragmatist	
prairey	prairie
prairie	
praise, praised, praising	
praiseworthy, -thily	
pram	
prance, pranced, prancing	
prandial, -ly	
prang, -ed, -ing	
prank	
pranse	prance
prarey	prairie
prase	praise
prate, prated, prating	
prattle, -tled, -tling	
pratul	prattle
prawn	
pray, -ed, -ing (beg)	
pray	prey (hunt)
prayer	
prayerbook	
preach, -ed, -ing	
preacher	
preamble	
preambul	preamble
prearrange, -ranged, -ranging	
precarious, -ly	
precaution	
precautionary	
precautionry	precautionary
precawshun	precaution
precede, -ceded, -ceding (before)	
precede	proceed (ahead)
precedence	
precedent (law)	
precedent	president (head)
precept	
preceptor	
prech	preach
precinct	

precious, -ly
   precipatation   precipitation
precipice
   precipise   precipice
precipitant, -ly
precipitate, -tated, -tating
precipitation
precipitous, -ly
   precipitus   precipitous
precis (summary)
precise, -ly (exact)
   precishun   precision
precision
preclude, -cluded, -cluding
precocious, -ly
precocity
preconceive, -ceived, -ceiving
   preconcieve   preconceive
   preconsepshun   preconception
preconception
   preconseve   preconceive
   precoshus   precocious
precursor
   predater   predator
predator
predatory
predecessor
   predesessor   predecessor
predestination
predestine, -tined, -tining
predetermination
predetermine, -mined, -mining
predicament
predicate, -cated, -cating
predicative, -ly
predict, -ed, -ing
predictable, -bly
   predictabul   predictable
prediction
predictor
   predilecshun   predilection
predilection
predispose, -posed, -posing
predisposition
predominance
predominant, -ly
predominate, -ated, -ating

pre-eminence
pre-eminent, -ly
pre-empt, -ed, -ing
pre-emptory
preen, -ed, -ing
prefabricate, -cated, -cating
prefabrication
preface, -faced, -facing
prefatory, -rily
prefect
prefecture
prefer, -ferred, -ferring
preferable, -bly
preference
   preferense   preference
   preferenshul   preferential
preferential, -ly
preferment
   prefice   preface
   prefiks   prefix
prefix
pregnancy, -cies
   pregnansy   pregnancy
pregnant, -ly
prehensile
prehistoric, -ally
prejudge, -judged, -judging
prejudgment
prejudice, -diced, -dicing
prejudicial, -ly
   prejudise   prejudice
   prejudishul   prejudicial
prelate
preliminary, -aries
prelude, -luded, -luding
premarital
premature, -ly
premenstrual tension
premier (chief)
premiere (first performance)
premise, -ised, -ising
premises
premium
   premonishun   premonition
premonition
premonitory
prenatal

prene   preen
preoccupation
preoccupy, -pied, -pying
preparation
preparatory, -rily
preparatry   preparatory
prepare, -pared, -paring
preponderance
preponderant, -ly
preposition
preposterous, -ly
prerekwisit   prerequisite
prerequisite (necessary)
prerequisite   perquisite (profit)
prerogative
pres   press
presage, -saged, -saging
prescripshun   prescription
prescription
prescriptive, -ly
presede   precede
presedence   precedence
presedent   precedent
presedent   president
preseed   precede
preseleckshun   preselection
preselect, -ed, -ing
preselection
presence
presense   presence
present, -ed, -ing
presentable, -bly
presentation
presentiment
presently
presept   precept
preservation
preservative
preserve, -served, -serving
presher   pressure
presherise   pressurise
preshus   precious
preside, -sided, -siding
presidency
presidenshul   presidential
presidensy   presidency

president
presidential
presige   presage
presinct   precinct
presipice   precipice
presipis   precipice
presipitate   precipitate
presipitus   precipitous
presise   precise
press, -ed, -ing
press-up
pressure, -sured, -suring
pressurisation
pressurise, -rised, -rising
prest   priest
prestege   prestige
presthood   priesthood
prestige
prestigious, -ly
prestigus   prestigious
presto
presume, -sumed, -suming
presumption
presumptuous, -ly
presumshun   presumption
presumtuus   presumptuous
presuppose, -posed, -posing
presupposition
pretence
pretend, -ed, -ing
pretender
pretense   pretence
pretenshun   pretension
pretenshus   pretentious
pretension
pretentious, -ly
preternatural, -ly
pretext
pretie   pretty
prettily
prettiness
pretty, -tier, -tiest
prety   pretty
pretzel
prevail, -ed, -ing
prevale   prevail
prevalence

prevalense — prevalence
prevalent, -ly
prevaricate, -cated, -cating
prevarication
prevenshun — prevention
prevent, -ed, -ing
preventable, -bly
preventabul — preventable
preventative, -ly
prevention
preventive, -ly
preview, -ed, -ing
previous, -ly
prey, -ed, -ing (hunt)
prey — pray (beg)
pri — pry
price, priced, pricing
priceless, -ly
prick, -ed, -ing
prickle, -led, -ling
prickly, -lier, -liest
prickul — prickle
pride, prided, priding
prie — pry
prier — prior
priery — priory
priest
priesthood
priestly, -lier, -liest
prig
priggish, -ly
prim, primmer, primmest
primacy
prima donna
prima-facie
primary, -ries
primer
primeval, -ly
primitive, -ly
primogenitor
primogeniture
primordial, -ly
primrey — primary
primrose
primula
primus
prince

princedom
princely, -lier, -liest
princess
principal (head)
principality, -ties
principle (law)
principul — principal (head)
prinse — prince
prinsess — princess
prinsipal — principal
prinsipality — principality
print, -ed, -ing
printer
printery, -ries
print-out
prion
prior
priority, -ties
priority-paid
priory, -ries
prise, prised, prising (move)
prise — price (cost)
prise — prize (award)
prism
prismatic, -ally
prison
prisoner
prissy, -ier, -iest
pristeen — pristine
pristine
privacy, -cies
privasy — privacy
privisy — privacy
private, -ly
privateer
privation
privelage — privilege
privet
privie — privy
privilege, -leged, -leging
privy, -vies
prize, prized, prizing (award)
prizm — prism
probability, -ties
probable, -ly
probabul — probable

probate, -bated, -bating
probation
probationer
probe, probed, probing
  probible   probable
probity
problem
problematic, -ally
procedural, -ly
procedure
proceed, -ed, -ing
  proceshun   procession
process, -ed, -ing
procession
processional, -ly
processor
proclaim, -ed, -ing
proclamation
  proclaym   proclaim
procrastinate, -nated, -nating
procrastination
procrastinator
procreate, -ated, -ating
proctor
procurable
  procurabul   procurable
procure, -cured, -curing
procurer
prod, prodded, prodding
prodigal, -ly
prodigality, -ties
prodigious, -ly
  prodigus   prodigious
prodigy, -gies
  prodijus   prodigious
produce, -duced, -ducing
producer
producible
  producshun   production
product
production
productive, -ly
productivity
  produse   produce
  produser   producer
profane, -faned, -faning
profanely

profanity, -ties
  profecy   prophecy (noun)
  profecy   prophesy (verb)
  profer   proffer
  profeser   professor
  profeshunal   professional
  profesor   professor
profess, -ed, -ing
professional, -ly
professionalism
professor
professorial, -ly
  profet   profit (gain)
  profet   prophet (seer)
proffer, -ed, -ing
proficiency, -cies
proficient, -ly
profile, -filed, -filing
  profishency   proficiency
  profishent   proficient
profit, -ed, -ing
profitable, -bly
  profitabul   profitable
profiteer, -ed, -ing
profitless
profligacy
profligate, -ly
pro-forma
profound, -ly
  profownd   profound
profundity, -ties
profuse, -ly
  profushun   profusion
profusion
progenitor
progeny, -nies
prognosis, -noses
prognostic
prognosticate, -cated, -cating
prognostication
program, -grammed, -gramming
programmable
programme
programmer
  progreshun   progression
progress, -ed, -ing

progression
progressive, -ly
prohibishun   prohibition
prohibit, -ed, -ing
prohibition
prohibitive, -ly
projecshun   projection
project, -ed, -ing
projectile
projection
projectionist
projector
proksimate   proximate
proksy   proxy
prolapse, -lapsed, -lapsing
proletarian
proletariat
proliferate, -rated, -rating
prolific, -ally
prolog   prologue
prologue
prolong, -ed, -ing
prolongation
prom
promenade, -naded, -nading
prominence
prominense   prominence
prominent, -ly
promiscuity, -ties
promiscuous, -ly
promiscuus   promiscuous
promise, -mised, -mising
promissory
promontory, -ries
promontry   promontory
promoter
promotion
promp   prompt
prompt, -ed, -ing
prompter
promulgate, -gated, -gating
promulgation
prone
prong, -ed, -ing
pronoun
pronounce, -nounced, -nouncing
pronouncement

pronown   pronoun
pronownse   pronounce
pronto
pronunciation
prood   prude
proof, -ed, -ing
proofread, -read, -reading
proofreader
proon   prune
proove   prove
prop, propped, propping
propaganda
propagate, -gated, -gating
propagation
propagator
propane
propel, -pelled, -pelling
propellant (noun)
propellent (adjective)
propeller
propensity, -ties
proper, -ly
property, -ties
prophecy, cies
prophesy, -sied, -sying
prophet
prophetess
prophetical, -ly
prophilactic   prophylactic
prophylactic
propishiate   propitiate
propishus   propitious
propitiate, -ated, -ating
propitious, -ly
proponent
proporshunal   proportional
proportion
proportional, -ly
proportionate, -ly
proposal
propose, -posed, -posing
proposer
proposishun   proposition
proposition
propound, -ed, -ing
propownd   propound
proprietary

proprieter — proprietor
proprietor
proprietry — proprietary
propriety, -ties
propulsion
pro-rata
prorogue, -rogued, -roguing
prosaic, -ally
proscenium, -nia
proscribe, -scribed, -scribing
proscription
prose
prosecushun — prosecution
prosecute, -cuted, -cuting
prosecution
prosecutor
prosedure — procedure
proseed — proceed
proselite — proselyte
proselyte, -lyted, -lyting
proselytise, -tised, -tising
prosess — process
prosicute — prosecute
prosilite — proselyte
prosilitise — proselytise
prosody
prospect, -ed, -ing
prospective, -ly
prospector
prospectus
prosper, -ed, -ing
prosperity, -ties
prosperous, -ly
prosperus — prosperous
prostate gland
prosthesis, -ses
prostitushen — prostitution
prostitute, -tuted, -tuting
prostitution
prostrate, -trated, -trating
prostration
protagonist
protea
protecshun — protection
protect, -ed, -ing
protection
protectionist

protective, -ly
protector
protectorate
proteen — protein
protégé
protein
protest, -ed, -ing
Protestant
Protestantism
protestation
protocol
proton
prototipe — prototype
prototype
protract, -ed, -ing
protractor
protrood — protrude
protrooshun — protrusion
protrude, -ruded, -ruding
protrusion
protruberance
protruberant, -ly
proud, -ly
provable
prove, proved, proven, proving
provender
proverb
proverbial, -ly
provide, -vided, -viding
providence
providense — providence
provident, -ly
providential, -ly
provider
province
provincial, -ly
provinshul — provincial
provishun — provision
provision
provisional, -ly
proviso
provocation
provocative, -ly
provoke, -voked, -voking
provost
prow
prowd — proud

prowess

prowl, -ed, -ing

proximate, -ly

proximity

proxy, proxies

prozaic   prosaic

prude

prudence

prudense   prudence

prudent, -ly

prudential, -ly

prudish, -ly

prune, pruned, pruning

prunus

prurience

prurient, -ly

Prushan   Prussian

Prussian

pry, pried, prying

psalm

psalmist

psaltery, -teries

pseudo

pseudonym

psyche

psychedelic

psychiatric, -ally

psychiatrist

psychiatry

psychic, -ally

psychoanalyse, -lysed, -lysing

psychoanalysis

psychoanalyst

psychological, -ly

psychologist

psychology, -gies

psychopath

psychopathy

psychosis, -ses

psychosomatic

psychotherapist

pschotherapy

psychotic

> For **psyco-** words, look
> under **psycho-**.

psykey   psyche

psykic   psychic

ptomaine

puberty

pubes

pubescence

pubescent

pubic

publesher   publisher

public, -ly

publican

publication

publicise, -cised, -cising

publicity

publish, -ed, -ing

publisher

publisise   publicise

publisity   publicity

puce

puck

pucka (genuine)

pucker, -ed, -ing (fold)

pudding

puddle, -dled, -dling

puddul   puddle

puding   pudding

puerile, -ly

puerility, -ties

puff, -ed, -ing

puffin

puffy, -fier, -fiest

pufy   puffy

pugilism

pugilist

pugilistic, -ally

pugnacious, -ly

pugnacity

pugnasity   pugnacity

pug-nosed

pukka

pulchritude

pulie   pulley

pulkritude   pulchritude

pull, -ed, -ing

pullet

pulley, -leys

pullover

pulmonary

pulmonry   pulmonary
pulp, -ed, -ing
pulpit
pulpwood
pulpy, -pier, -piest
pulsar
pulsate, -ated, -ating
pulsation
pulsator
pulse, pulsed, pulsing
    pulser   pulsar
pulverise, -rised, -rising
puma
pumice
    pumise   pumice
    pumkin   pumpkin
pummel, -melled, -melling
pump, -ed, -ing
pumpernickel
pumpkin
pun, punned, punning
    punative   punitive
punch, -ed, -ing
punch-drunk
punch-up
punctilious, -ly
    puntilius   punctilious
punctual, -ly
punctuality
punctuate, -ated, -ating
punctuation
puncture, -tured, -turing
pundit
pungency
pungent, -ly
    punie   puny
punish, -ed, -ing
punishable
punishment
punitive, -ly
    pungensy   pungency
    punjent   pungent
punk
punnet
punt, -ed, -ing
punter
puny, -nier, -niest

pup, pupped, pupping
    pupet   puppet
    pupie   puppy
pupil
puppet
puppeteer
puppetry
puppy, -pies
    pur annum   per annum
    puray   puree
    purceive   perceive
purchase, -chased, -chasing
purdah
pure, purer, purest
puree, -reed, -reeing
purgative, -ly
purgatory
    purgatry   purgatory
purge, purged, purging
    purifie   purify
purify, -fied, -fying
    purile   puerile
puritan
puritanical, -ly
puritanism
    puritie   purity
purity
    purje   purge
    purjery   perjury
purl, -ed, -ing (knit)
    purl   pearl (gem)
purloin, -ed, -ing
    puroolense   purulence
purple, -pled, -pling
purport, -ed, -ing
purpose
purposeful, -ly
    purpul   purple
purr, -ed, -ing
purser
pursuant, -ly
pursue, -sued, -suing
pursuit
    pursute   pursuit
purulence
purulent, -ly
    purvay   purvey

purvey, -ed, -ing
purveyor
pus
  puse — puce
push, -ed, -ing
pushbike
push-button
pushover
push-up
pushy
pusillanimous, -ly
pussyfoot
put, put, putting
putative, -ly
  puter — pewter
  putie — putty
putrefaction
putrefy, -fied, -fying
putrescent
putrid, -ly
  putrify — putrefy
putt, -ed, -ing
putter
putty, -ties
putty, puttied, puttying
put-upon
  puty — putty
  puzel — puzzle
puzzle, -zled, -zling
  pye — pi (Greek letter)
  pye — pie (food)
pygmy, -mies
pyjamas
pylon
pyramid
pyramidal, -ly
pyre
pyrex
  pyric — pyrrhic
pyrotechnics
pyrrhic
pythagoras
python
pyx

Qq

qeue   queue
quack, -ed, -ing
quackery, -eries
quad (timber)
quadrangle
  quadrangul   quadrangle
quadrant
  quadrafonic   quadraphonic
quadraphonic
quadrasonic
quadratic
  quadril   quadrille
quadrille
quadrillion
quadriplegia
quadriplegic
quadruped
quadrupedal
quadruple, -pled, -pling
quadruplet
  quadrupul   quadruple
quaff, quaffed, quaffing
quagmire
quail
quaint, -ly
quaintness
quake, quaked, quaking
Quaker
Quakerism
qualification
  qualifi   qualify
qualified
qualifier
qualify, -fied, -fying
qualitative, -ly
quality, -ties
qualm
quandary, -ries

quandong
  quandry   quandary
quango
  quantifi   quantify
quantifiable
quantification
quantify, -fied, -fying
quantitative, -ly
quantity, -ties
quarantine, -tined, -tining
  quarel   quarrel
  quarey   quarry
quark
  quarm   qualm
quarrel, -relled, -relling
quarreller
quarrelsome, -ly
quarry, -ries
quarry, -ried, -rying
quart, quarts
quarter
quarterdeck
quarterly
quartermaster
quartet
quartile
quarto, -tos
quartz (rock)
  quartz   quarts
                (measures)
quash, -ed, -ing
quasi
quatrain
quattrocento
quaver, -ed, -ing
quavery
quay (wharf)
  que   cue (billiards)
  que   queue (line)
queasy, -sier, -siest
queasiness
queen, -ly
queer, -ly
queerness
quell, -ed, -ing
queller
quench, -ed, -ing

quenchable
quenchless
querie   query
querulous, -ly
querulousness
querulus   querulous
query, -ries
query, -ried, -rying
queschun   question
quest, -ed, -ing
quester
question, -ed, -ing
questionable, -bly
questionair   questionnaire
questioner
questionnaire
questyun   question
queue, queued, queuing
quibble, -bled, -bling
quibbler
quibel   quibble
quich   quiche
quiche
quick, -ly
quicken
quickie
quicklime
quickness
quicksand
quicksilver
quickstep
quick-tempered
quick-witted
quid, quid, quids
quid pro quo
quiescence
quiescent, -ly
quiesense   quiescence
quiet, -ly (silent)
quiet   quite (rather)
quieten, -ed, -ing
quietness
quill
quilt
quilted
quince
quinella

quinine
quinse   quince
quinsy, -sies
quintesense   quintessence
quintessence
quintessential
quintet
quintette
quintuple, -pled, -pling
quintuplet
quintupul   quintuple
quip, quipped, quipping
quipster
quire (paper)
quire   choir (sing)
quirk
quish   quiche
quisine   cuisine
quit, quitted or quit, quitting
quite (rather)
quite   quiet (silent)
quits
quitter
quiver, -ed, -ing
quivery
quixotic
quixotism
quiz, quizzes
quiz, quizzed, quizzing
quizzical, -ly
quod (prison)
quod   quad (timber)
quoit
quokka
quorum
quoshent   quotient

> For other quo- words, look
> under **qua-**.

quota
quotation
quote, quoted, quoting
quotient

Rr

rabbi, -bis
rabbinical
rabbit, -bited, -biting
rabbiter
rabble, -bled, -bling
rabblerouser
rabi   rabbi
rabid, -ly
rabies
rabit   rabbit
rabud   rabid
rabul   rabble
raccoon
race, raced, racing
racecorse   racecourse
racecourse
racegoer
racehorse
racer
racetrack
raceway
racial, -ly
racialism
racialist
racism
racist
rack, -ed, -ing
rack-and-pinion
racket, -ed, -ing
racketeer
rackit   racket
raconter   raconteur
raconteur
racquet
racy, -cier, -ciest
radar
raddle, -led, -ling
rade   raid

radeo   radio
radial, -ly
radialogy   radiology
radial-ply
radian
radiance
radianse   radiance
radiant, -ly
radiate, -ated, -ating
radiater   radiator
radiation
radiator
radical, -ly
radicalism
radicul   radical
radii
radio, -dioed, -dioing
radioactive
radioastronomy
radiografy   radiography
radiogram
radiographer
radiography
radiologist
radiology
radiotelephone
radiotherapy
radish
radiul   radial
radium
radius, radii, radiuses
raffia
raffish, -ly
raffle, -led, -ling
raft
rafter
rag, ragged, ragging
ragamuffin
rage, raged, raging
raglan
ragout, -gouted, -gouting
ragtime
raid, -ed, -ing
rail, -ed, -ing
raillery, -ries
railroad
railway

raiment
rain, -ed, -ing (water)
rain   reign (rule)
rain   rein (bridle)
rainbird
rainbow
raincoat
rainfall
rainforest
raise, raised, raising (lift)
raise   rays (beams)
raisin
raison d' être
raisun   raisin
raje   rage
rake, raked, raking
rakish, -ly
rakket   racket
rale   rail
ralie   rally
rally, -lies
rally, -lied, -lying
ram, rammed, ramming
ramble, -bled, -bling
rambler
rambul   ramble
ramification
ramify, -fied, -fying
ramp
rampage, -paged, -paging
rampageous, -ly
rampagius   rampageous
rampant, -ly
rampart
ramrod
ramshackle
ramshackul   ramshackle
ranch
rancher
rancid
rancidity
rancorous, -ly
rancour
rancur   rancour
rancurus   rancorous
random, -ly
randy

rane   rain (water)
rane   reign (rule)
rane   rein (bridle)
range, ranged, ranging
rangefinder
ranger
rangul   wrangle
rank, -ed, -ing
rankle, -kled, -kling
ransack, -ed, -ing
ransid   rancid
ransom, -ed, -ing
ransome   ransom
ransum   ransom
rant, -ed, -ing
rap, rapped, rapping (strike)
rap   wrap (cover)
rapacious, -ly
rapacity
rapashus   rapacious
rapasity   rapacity
rapcher   rapture
rape, raped, raping
rapid, -ly
rapid-fire
rapier
rapine
rapist
rapport
rapprochement
rapsody   rhapsody
rapt (engrossed)
rapt   wrapped
                 (cover)
rapture
rapturous, -ly
rapturus   rapturous
rare, rarer, rarest
rarefacshun   rarefaction
rarefaction
rarefy, -fied, -fying
rarely
raring
rarity, -ties
rasbery   raspberry
rascal
rascality, -ties

rascally
rase, rased, rasing (destroy)
   rase   race (run)
   rase   raise (lift)
rash, -ly
   rashal   racial
   rashalist   racialist
rasher
   rashio   ratio
rashness
   rashul   racial
   rashun   ration
   rashunalise   rationalise
   rasin   raisin
   rasism   racism
   rasist   racist
   raskul   rascal
rasp, -ed, -ing
raspberry, -ries
rat, ratted, ratting
   ratabul   rateable
ratchet
rate, rated, rating
   rateo   ratio
ratepayer
   rath   wrath
rather
ratification
ratify, -fied, -fying
ratio, -tios
ration, -ed, -ing
rational, -ly (reasonable)
rationale (statement)
rationalise, -lised, -lising
rationalism
rationality, -ties
rat-race
rattan
rattle, -tled, -tling
rattlesnake
rattletrap
ratty, -tier, -tiest
   ratul   rattle
raucous, -ly
   raucus   raucous
ravage, -aged, -aging
ravager

rave, raved, raving
ravel, -elled, -elling
raven
   ravene   ravine
ravenous, -ly
   ravige   ravage
ravine
ravioli
ravish, -ed, -ing
raw (uncooked)
   raw   roar (noise)
   rawcus   raucous
rawhide
ray
rayon
rays (beams)
   rays   raise (lift)
   rays   raze (destroy)
raze, razed, razing (destroy)
   razer   razor
razoo
razor
reach, -ed, -ing
   reacktion   reaction
react, -ed, -ing
reaction
reactionary
reactive, -ly
reactor
read, read, reading (book)
   read   red (colour)
   read   reed (plant)
readable, -bly
   readabul   readable
reader
readership
readily
readiness
ready, readied, readying
ready, readier, readiest
ready-made
   reaf   reef
reafforest, -ed, -ing
reafforestation
reagent
   reak   reek (smell)
   reak   wreak (inflict)

real, -ly (true)
  real   reel (wind)
realign, -ed, -ing
realisation
realise, -lised, -lising
realism
realist
realistic, -ally
reality, -ties (fact)
realm
  realter   realtor
realtor
realty (real estate)
ream, reamed, reaming
reap, -ed, -ing
reaper
reappear, -ed, -ing
rear, -ed, -ing
  reargard   rearguard
rearguard
rearmament
reason, -ed, -ing
reasonable, -bly
  reasonabul   reasonable
reassemble, -bled, -bling
  reassembul   reassemble
reassert, -ed, -ing
reassertion
reassess, -ed, -ing
reassessment
reassurance
reassure, -sured, -suring
  reath   wreath
rebate, -bated, -bating
rebel, -belled, -belling
rebellion
rebellious, -ly
  rebelyun   rebellion
  rebild   rebuild
rebound, -ed, -ing
  rebownd   rebound
rebuff, -ed, -ing
rebuild, -built, -building
rebuke, -buked, -buking
rebut, -butted, -butting
  rebutal   rebuttal
rebuttal

recalcitrance
recalcitrant
recall, -ed, -ing
recant, -ed, -ing
recantation
recapitulate, -lated, -lating
recapitulation
recede, -ceded, -ceding
receipt
  receit   receipt
receive, -ceived, -ceiving
receiver
receivership
recent, -ly
  recepe   recipe
  recepshun   reception
  recepshunist   receptionist
receptacle
  receptacul   receptacle
reception
receptionist
receptive, -ly
  receshun   recession
recess, -ed, -ing
recessive, -ly
  rech   retch (vomit)
  rech   wretch (victim)
recidivism
recidivist
  reciept   receipt
  recieve   receive
recipe
recipient
reciprocal, -ly
reciprocate, -cated, -cating
reciprocation
reciprocity
  reciprosity   reciprocity
recital
recitation
recite, -cited, -citing
  reck   wreck
  reckage   wreckage
reckless, -ly
reckon, -ed, -ing
reclaim, -ed, -ing
reclamation

reclassify, -fied, -fying
recline, -clined, -clining
recluse
recognisable, -bly
  recognisabul   recognisable
recognise, -nised, -nising
  recognishun   recognition
recognition
recoil, -ed, -ing
  recolecshun   recollection
recollect, -ed, -ing
recollection
recommend, -ed, -ing
recommendation
reconcile, -ciled, -ciling
reconciliation
recondite
recondition, -ed, -ing
reconnaissance
  reconnoiter   reconnoitre
reconnoitre, -tred, -tring
reconsider, -ed, -ing
  reconsile   reconcile
  reconsiliation   reconciliation
reconstruct, -ed, -ing
reconstruction
  recoop   recoup
record, -ed, -ing
recorder
  recorse   recourse
recount, -ed, -ing
recoup, -ed, -ing
recourse
recover, -ed, -ing
recovery, -eries
  recownt   recount
recreant, -ly
recreation
recriminate, -nated, -nating
recrimination
recriminatory
recruit, -ed, -ing
recruitment
  recrute   recruit
rectangle
  rectangul   rectangle
rectangular, -ly

rectification
rectifier
rectify, -fied, -fying
rectilinear, -ly
  rectilinier   rectilinear
rectitude
rector
rectory, -ries
rectum
recumbency
  recumbensy   recumbency
recumbent, -ly
recuperate, -rated, -rating
recuperation
recuperative
recur, -curred, -curring
recurrence
  recurrense   recurrence
recurrent, -ly
recyclable
  recyclabul   recyclable
recycle, -cycled, -cycling
  recycul   recycle
red, redder, reddest (colour)
  red   read (book)
redbreast
  redbrest   redbreast
redden, -ed, -ing
reddish
  reddy   ready
redeem, -ed, -ing
redeemable, -ably
redeemer
  redempshun   redemption
redemption
redemptive
  reden   redden
  redeploi   redeploy
redeploy, -ed, -ing
redeployment
redevelop, -ed, -ing
redevelopment
red-handed
  redie   ready
redistribute, -buted, -buting
redistribution
redolence

redolent, -ly
redouble, -led, -ling
redoubtable, -bly
redound, -ed, -ing
redoutabul   redoubtable
redress, -ed, -ing
redskin
reduce, -duced, -ducing
reducksun   reduction
reduction
redundancy, -cies
redundansy   redundancy
reduplicate, -cated, -cating
redwood
reed (plant)
reed   read (book)
reedwarbler
reedy, reedier, reediest
reef, -ed, -ing
reefer
reek, -ed, -ing (smell)
reek   wreak (inflict)
reel, -ed, -ing (wind)
reel   real (true)
re-elect, -ed, -ing
re-election
re-entry, -tries
refer, -ferred, -ferring
referee, -reed, -reeing
reference
referense   reference
referendum, -da, -dums
referent
referral
refill, -ed, -ing
refine, -fined, -fining
refinement
refinery, -ries
refleckshun   reflection
reflect, -ed, -ing
reflection
reflector
refleks   reflex
reflex
refloat, -ed, -ing
reform, -ed, -ing
reformation

reformatory, -ries
reformer
refrackshun   refraction
refraction
refractive, -ly
refrain, -ed, -ing
refrence   reference
refresh, -ed, -ing
refresher
refreshment
refrigerant
refrigerate, -rated, -rating
refrigerater   refrigerator
refrigeration
refrigerator
refuel, -elled, -elling
refuge
refugee
refulgence
refulgent, -ly
refund, -ed, -ing
refurbish, -ed, -ing
refusal
refuse, -fused, -fusing
refutation
refute, -futed, -futing
regain, -ed, -ing
regal, -ly (royal)
regale, -galed, -galing (feast)
regalia
regane   regain
regard, -ed, -ing
regardless, -ly
regatta
regeme   regime
regency, -cies
regenerate, -rated, -rating
regeneration
regenerative, -ly
regent
regime
regimen
regiment
regimental
regimentation
region
regional, -ly

regionalism
register, -ed, -ing
registrar
registration
registry, -tries
regon   region
regreshun   regression
regress, -ed, -ing
regression
regressive, -ly
regret, -gretted, -gretting
regretabul   regrettable
regretful, -ly
regrettable, -bly
regualation   regulation
reguard   regard
regular, -ly
regularity
regulate, -lated, -lating
regulation
regulator
regulatory
reguler   regular
regurgitate, -tated, -tating
rehabilitate, -tated, -tating
rehabilitation
rehash, -ed, -ing
rehearsal
rehearse, -hearsed, -hearsing
reherse   rehearse
reign, -ed, -ing (king)
reign   rain (water)
reign   rein (bridle)
reimburse, -bursed, -bursing
reimbursement
rein, -ed, -ing (bridle)
rein   rain (water)
rein   reign (rule)
reincarnation
reindeer, -deer
reinforce, -forced, -forcing
reinforcement
reinstate, -stated, -stating
reiterate, -rated, -rating
reiteration
reiterative, -ly
rejeckshun   rejection

reject, -ed, -ing
rejection
rejeme   regime
rejister   register
rejoice, -joiced, -joicing
rejoin, -ed, -ing
rejoinder
rejoise   rejoice
rejoovenate   rejuvenate
rejuvenate, -nated, -nating
rejuvenation
rekord   record

> For **rekw-** words, look
> under **requ-**.

relaks   relax
relapse, -lapsed, -lapsing
relate, -lated, -lating
relation
relative, -ly
relativity
relax, -ed, -ing
relaxation
relay, -ed, -ing
release, -leased, -leasing
relegate, -gated, -gating
relegation
releif   relief
relent, -ed, -ing
relentless, -ly
relese   release
relevance
relevancy
relevanse   relevance
relevant, -ly
releve   relieve
reli   rely
reliable, -bly
reliability
reliabul   reliable
reliance
reliant
relic
relief
relieve, -lieved, -lieving
religion
religious, -ly

religun religion
religus religious
relinkwish relinquish
relinquish, -ed, -ing
relish, -ed, -ing
relm realm
reluctance
reluctanse reluctance
reluctant,-ly
rely, relied, relying
remain, -ed, -ing
remainder
remains
remand, -ed, -ing
remark, -ed, -ing
remarkable, -bly
remedial, -ly
remedy, -dies
remedy, -died, -dying
remember, -ed, -ing
remembrance
remembranse remembrance
remind, -ed, -ing
reminder
reminisce, -nisced, -niscing
reminiscence
reminiscent, -ly
reminisense reminiscence
reminisent reminiscent
reminiss reminisce
remishun remission
remiss, -ly
remission
remit, -mitted, -mitting
remittance
remnant
remonstrate, -trated, -trating
remonstrative
remooval removal
remoove remove
remorse
remorseful, -ly
remote, remoter, remotest
remotely
removable
removalist
remove, -moved, -moving

remunerate, -rated, -rating
remuneration
remunerative, -ly
ren wren
Renaissance
renal
rench wrench
rend, rent, rending
render, -ed, -ing
rendezvous, -voused, -vousing
rendition
renegade
renege, reneged, reneging
renew, -ed, -ing
renounce, -nounced, -nouncing
renovate, -vated, -vating
renovater renovator
renovation
renovator
renown
renowned
rent, -ed, -ing
rental
rentul rental
renue renew
renunciation
reorganisation
reorganise, -nised, -nising
repair, -ed, -ing
repairer
reparable, -bly
reparation
repartee
repast
repatriate, -ated, -ating
repatriation
repay, -paid, -paying
repeal, -ed, -ing
repeat, -ed, -ing
repeatedly
repeater
repel, -pelled, -pelling
repellant repellent
repellent, -ly
repent, -ed, -ing
repentance
repentanse repentance

repentant, -ly
  repercushun   repercussion
repertoire
repertory, -ries
  repetishus   repetitious
repetition
repetitious, -ly
  repetry   repertory
  repitition   repetition
replace, -placed, -placing
replacement
replay, -played, -playing
replenish, -ed, -ing
replenishment
replete
replica
reply, -plies
reply, -plied, -plying
report, -ed, -ing
reportable
reporter
repose, -posed, -posing
repository, -tories
  repositry   repository
  reposseshun   repossession
repossess, -ed, -ing
repossession
  reprehenshun   reprehension
reprehensible, -bly
reprehension
represent, -ed, -ing
representation
representational
representative, -ly
  represhun   repression
repress, -ed, -ing
  repressabul   repressible
repressible
repression
repressive, -ly
reprieve, -prieved, -prieving
reprimand, -ed, -ing
reprint, -ed, -ing
reprisal
  reprisul   reprisal
reproach, -ed, -ing
reproachable, -bly

reprobate, -bated, -bating
reprobation
  reproch   reproach
reproduce, -duced, -ducing
  reproducshun   reproduction
reproduction
reproof, -ed, -ing
reprove, -proved, -proving
reproval
reptile
reptilian
republic
republican
republicanism
repudiate, -ated, -ating
repudiation
repugnance
  repugnanse   repugnance
repugnant, -ly
repulse, -pulsed, -pulsing
repulsion
repulsive, -ly
reputable, -bly
  reputabul   reputable
reputation
repute, -puted, -puting
request, -ed, -ing
requiem
  requierment   requirement
require, -quired, -quiring
requirement
  requisishun   requisition
requisite
requisition
  rerite   rewrite
  reritten   rewritten
  rerote   rewrote
rescind, -ed, -ing
rescue, -cued, -cuing
rescuer
research, -ed, -ing
researcher
  reseat   receipt
  resede   recede
  reseipt   receipt
resemble, -bled, -bling
  resembul   resemble

resent, -ed, -ing (hurt)
   resent   recent (new)
resentful, -ly
resentment
   resepshun   reception
   reseptacul   receptacle
   reseptive   receptive
   reserch   research
reservation
reserve, -served, -serving
reservoir
   resess   recess
   resesshun   recession
   resession   recession
reset, -set, -setting
   reseve   receive
   resevoir   reservoir
reside, -sided, -siding
residence
   residenshul   residential
resident
residential
   residivision   recidivism
residual, -ly
residuary
residue
resign, -ed, -ing
resignation
resilience
resilient, -ly
resin
   resind   rescind
resinous
   resinus   resinous
   resipe   recipe
   resipient   recipient
   resiprocul   reciprocal
   resiprosity   reciprocity
resist, -ed, -ing
resistance
   resitation   recitation
resistor
   resite   recite
resolute, -ly
resolution
resolve, -solved, -solving
resonance

resonant, -ly
resonate, -nated, -nating
   resorce   resource
resort, -ed, -ing
resound, -ed, -ing
resource
resourceful, -ly
respect, -ed, -ing
respectability, -ties
respectable, -bly
   respectabul   respectable
respectful, -ly
respective, -ly
respiration
respirator
respiratory
   respiratry   respiratory
respite
resplendent, -ly
   responce   response
respond, -ed, -ing
respondent
response
responsibility, -ties
responsible, -bly
responsive, -ly
rest, -ed, -ing (sleep)
   rest   wrest (grab)
   restaration   restoration
restaurant
   resterant   restaurant
restful, -ly
   restitushion   restitution
restitution
restive, -ly
   restle   wrestle
   restler   wrestler
restless, -ly
restoration
restorative
restore, -stored, -storing
restrain, -ed, -ing
restraint
   restricshun   restriction
restrict, -ed, -ing
restriction
restrictive, -ly

restructure, -tured, -turing
result, -ed, -ing
resultant
   resumay   résumé (review)
résumé (review)
resume, -sumed, -suming (take up)
resumption
resurgence
resurgent
resurrect, -ed, -ing
resurrection
resuscitate, -tated, -tating
resuscitation
resuscitator
   resusitation   resuscitation
retail, -ed ,-ing
retain, -ed, -ing
retainer
retaliate, -ated, -ating
retaliation
retard, -ed, -ing
retardation
retch, -ed, -ing (vomit)
   retch   wretch (victim)
retention
retentive, -ly
reticence
reticent, -ly
retina, -nas, -nae
   retinew   retinue
retinue
retire, -tired, -tiring
retirement
   retisent   reticent
   retoric   rhetoric
   retoricul   rhetorical
retort, -ed, -ing
retrace, -traced, -tracing
retract, -ed, -ing
retractable
   retrase   retrace
retread, -treaded, -treading
retreat, -ed, -ing
   retred   retread
   retreive   retrieve
retrench, -ed, -ing
retrenchment

   retribushun   retribution
retribution
retrieve, -trieved, -trieving
retrievable
retrieval
retriever
retroactive, -ly
retrograde, -graded, -grading
   retrogreshun   retrogression
retrogress, -ed, -ing
retrogression
retrogressive, -ly
retro-rocket
retrospect
retrospective, -ly
return, -ed, -ing
reunion
reunite, -nited, -niting
rev, revved, revving
   revalie   reveille
revaluation
revalue, -ued, -uing
   revalueation   revaluation
reveal, -ed, -ing
reveille (bugle call)
revel, -elled, -elling
revelation
reveller (festivity)
revelry, -ries
   revenew   revenue
revenge, -venged, -venging
revenue
reverberate, -rated, -rating
reverberation
reverberatory
revere, -vered, -vering (respect)
reverence
reverend
   reverense   reverence
reverent, -ly
reverie (daydream)
reversal
reverse, -versed, -versing
reversion
revert, -ed, -ing
   revertabul   revertible
revertible

review, -ed, -ing (survey)
review   revue (theatre)
revile, -viled, -viling
revise, -vised, -vising
revishun   revision
revision
revival
revivalism
revive, -vived, -viving
revocation
revoke, -voked, -voking
revolt, -ed, -ing
revolushun   revolution
revolution
revolutionary, -ries
revolutionise, -nised, -nising
revolutionry   revolutionary
revolve, -volved, -volving
revolver
revue (theatre)
revue   review (survey)
revulshun   revulsion
revulsion
reward, -ed, -ing
rhapsodical, -ly
rhapsodise, -dised, -dising
rhapsody, -dies
rhesus
rhetoric
rhetorical, -ly
rheumatic
rheumatism
rheumatoid arthritis
rhinestone
rhino, -nos
rhinoceros, -roses, -ros
rhododendron
rhombus, -buses, -bi
rhubarb
rhyme, rhymed, rhyming (verse)
rhythm
rhythmical, -ly
rib, ribbed, ribbing
ribald
ribaldry
ribbon
rice

rich, -ly
riches
Richter scale
rick, -ed, -ing
rickets
rickety
rickshaw
ricochet, -ed, -ing
ricshore   rickshaw
rid, rid or ridded, ridding
ridance   riddance
riddance
riddle, -dled, -dling
ride, rode, ridden, riding
rider
ridge, ridged, ridging
ridicule, -culed, -culing
ridiculous, -ly
ridiculus   ridiculous
ridul   riddle
rie   rye (grain)
rie   wry (askew)
Riesling
rife
riffraff
rifle, -fled, -fling
rift
riful   rifle
rig, rigged, rigging
right, -ed, -ing (correct)
right   rite (ceremony)
right   write (inscribe)
righteous, -ly
rightful, -ly
right-handed
right-winger
rigid, -ly
rigidity
rigmarole
rigor mortis
rigorous, -ly
rigorus   rigorous
rigour
rig-out
rigul   wriggle
rile, riled, riling
rim, rimmed, rimming (edge)

rime, rimed, riming (frost)
   rime   rhyme (verse)
rind
ring, ringed, ringing (surround)
ring, rang, rung, ringing (bell)
   ring   wring (squeeze)
ringbark, -ed, -ing
ringer
   ringer   wringer
ring-in
ringleader
ringlet
ringtail possum
ringworm
rink
rinse, rinsed, rinsing
riot, -ed, -ing
riotous, -ly
   riotus   riotous
rip, ripped, ripping
ripcord
ripe, riper, ripest
ripen, -ed, -ing
rip-off
ripper
ripple, -pled, -pling
   rippul   ripple

> If the word is not under **ri-**
> look under **re-**.

rip-roaring
rip-tide
rise, rose, risen, rising
risk, -ed, -ing
   riskay   risqué
riskily
risky, -kier, -kiest
risqué
rissole
   rist   wrist
   rit   writ
rite (ceremony)
   rite   right (correct)
   rite   write (inscribe)
   riter   writer
   rithe   writhe
   ritten   written

ritual,-ly
rival, -valled, -valling
rivalry, -ries
river
rivergum
rivet, -ed, -ing
rivulet
   ro   roe (fish)
   ro   row (boat
roach, -ches
road (street)
   road   rode (did ride)
roadblock
roadworthiness
roadworthy
roar, -ed, -ing (noise)
   roar   raw (uncooked)
roast, -ed, -ing
rob, robbed, robbing
robber
robbery, -ries
robe, robed, robing
   robery   robbery
robin
robot
robust, -ly
rock, -ed, -ing
rocker
rockery, -ries
rocket, -ed, -ing
rocketry
rock'n'roll
rock-wallaby
rococo
rod
   rodayo   rodeo
rode (did ride)
   rode   road (street)
rodent
rodeo, -deos
   rodio   rodeo
roe (fish)
   roe   row (boat)
   roge   rogue
   rogish   roguish
rogue, rogued, roguing
roguery, -gueries

roguish,-ly
role (character)
roll, -ed, -ing (turn)
roll bar
rollcall
roller
roller-skate, -skated, -skating
rolling-pin
rollick, -ed, -ing
rollmop
roll-up
roly-poly
Roman Catholic
romance, -manced, -mancing
romantic, -ly
romanticise, -cised, -cising
romanticism
romanticist
Romany, -nies (gipsy)
rombus rhombus
rome roam
romp, -ed, -ing
rondo, -dos
roneo, -ed, -ing
rong wrong
roo (kangaroo)
roo rue (regret)
roodiment rudiment
roof, roofs
roofless
roof-rack
rooful rueful
rooge rouge
rooin ruin
rooinous ruinous
rook, -ed, -ing
rookery, -ries
rookie
rool rule
roolet roulette
room, -ed, -ing
roomatism rheumatism
roomer rumour
roomy, -mier, -miest
roon ruin
roopee rupee
roorul rural

roose ruse
roost, -ed, -ing
rooster
root, -ed, -ing (plant)
root route (way)
ropable
rope, roped, roping
ropeable
ropeway
ropey
ropy, ropier, ropiest
ror roar (noise)
ror raw (uncooked)
rort
rosary, -ries
rosay rosé (wine)
rose, rosed, rosing (flower)
rosé (wine)
rosella
rosemary
rosery rosary
roset rosette
rosette
rosewood
rosie rosy
rosily
rost roast
roster
rostrum, -trums, -tra
rosy, rosier, rosiest
rot, rotted, rotting
rotary
rotate, -tated, -tating
rotation
rote (routine)
rote wrote (did write)
roten rotten
roter rotor
rotisserie
rotor
rotten, -ly
rotund, -ly
rotundity
roudy rowdy
rouge, rouged, rouging
rough, -ly

roughage
roughen, -ed, -ing
roughshod
  rought   wrought
  roulet   roulette
roulette, -letted, -letting
round, -ed, -ing
roundabout
rounders
roundly
round-up
rouse, roused, rousing
rouseabout
rout, routed, routing (defeat)
route (way)
  route   root (plant)
  routeen   routine
routine
rove, roved, roving
rover
row, -ed, -ing (boat)
  row   roe (fish)
  rowdie   rowdy
rowdily
rowdy, -dier, -diest
rowel, -elled, -elling
rowlock
  rownd   round
  rowse   rouse
  rowt   rout
royal, -ly
royalist
royalty, -ties
rub, rubbed, rubbing
rubber
rubbish
rubbishy
rubble
rubella
  ruber   rubber
rubicund
  rubie   ruby
  rubish   rubbish
rubric
  rubul   rubble
ruby, -bies
ruck, -ed, -ing

rucksack
  ruckshun   ruction
ruction
rudder
ruddy, -dier, -diest
rude, ruder, rudest (rough)
  rude   rued (regret)
rudely
rudeness
  ruder   rudder
rudimentary
rudiments
  rudy   ruddy
rue, rued, ruing (regret)
  rued   rude (rough)
rueful, -ly (pity)
  ruf   rough (coarse)
  ruffen   roughen
ruffian
ruffle, -fled, -fling (annoy)
  rufful   ruffle
  rufian   ruffian
  rufige   roughage
  rufle   ruffle
  ruful   rueful
rug, rugged, rugging
rugby
ruin, -ed, -ing (destroy)
  ruin   rune (letter)
ruination
ruinous, -ly
  ruinus   ruinous
rule, ruled, ruling
ruler
rum
  rumatism   rheumatism
rumba
rumble, -bled, -bling
  rumbul   rumble
rumen, -mina
  rumer   rumour
  rumige   rummage
ruminant
ruminate, -nated, -nating
rummage, -maged, -maging
rumour, -ed, -ing
rump

rumple, -pled, -pling
   rumpul   rumple
rumpus
run, ran, run, running
runabout
rune (letter)
   rune   ruin (destroy)
rung (did ring)
   rung   wrung
                    (squeezed)
run-in
runner
runner-up
runny
run-off
run-of-the-mill
run-on
runt
runway
   rupcher   rupture
rupee
rupture, -tured, -turing
rural, -ly
ruse
rush, -ed, -ing
   Rushun   Russian
   rusit   russet
rusk
russet
Russian roulette
rust, -ed, -ing
rustic, -ally
rusticity, -ties
rustle, -tled, -tling
rustproof
rusty, -tier, -tiest
rut, rutted, rutting
ruthless, -ly
rye (grain)
   rye   wry (askew)
rye-grass
   ryme   rhyme
   rythm   rhythm

Ss

Sabath	Sabbath
Sabbath	
sabbatical	
sabbaticul	sabbatical
sabel	sable
saber	sabre
Sabin vaccine	
sable	
sabot	
sabotage, -taged, -taging	
saboteur	
sabre, -bred, -bring	
sabre-toothed	
sac (bag)	
sac	sack (hessian)
sacarin	saccharin
saccharin	
sacerdotal, -ly	
sachay	sachet
sachel	satchel
sachet	
sack, -ed, -ing	
sackarin	saccharin
sackcloth	
sacrament	
sacramental, -ly	
sacred, -ly	
sacredness	
sacrement	sacrament
sacrifice, -ficed, -ficing	
sacrificial, -ly	
sacrifise	sacrifice
sacrifishul	sacrificial
sacriledge	sacrilege
sacrilege	
sacrilegious, -ly	
sacrilige	sacrilege
sacriligus	sacrilegious

sacrosanct	
sad, sadder, saddest	
sadden, -ed, -ing	
saddle, saddled, saddling	
saddleback	
saddler	
saddlery, -ries	
saden	sadden
sadler	saddler
sadlery	saddlery
sadism	
sadist	
sadistic, -ally	
sadul	saddle
safari, -ris	
safe, safer, safest	
safegard	safeguard
safeguard	
safekeeping	
safely	
safety, -ties	
saffire	sapphire
saffron	
safire	sapphire
safron	saffron
saftie	safety
sag, sagged, sagging	
saga	
sagacious, -ly	
sagacity, -ties	
sagasity	sagacity
sagayshus	sagacious
sage, sager, sagest	
Sagittarius	
sago	
said	
sail (boat)	
sail	sale (sold)
sailsman	salesman
sailboard	
sailcloth	
sailor	
sailplane, -planed, -planing	
saint, -ly	
sainted	
sainthood	
saintliness	

sake

sakred	sacred
sakson	Saxon
saksophone	saxophone

salaam
salacious, -ly
salad
salamander
salami

salamy	salami

salaried
salary, -ries (wage)

salary	celery (food)
salasious	salacious

sale (sold)

sale	sail (boat)

saleability
saleable, -ly

saleabul	saleable
salene	saline

salesgirl
saleslady, -dies
salesman, -men
salesmanship
salesroom
saleswoman, -women
saleyard

salie	sally

salience

saliense	salience

salient, -ly
saline
salinity
saliva
salivary
salivate, -vated, -vating
salivation
sallow
sallowish
sally, -lies
sally, -lied, -lying

salm	psalm

> For all other **sall**- words,
> look under **sal-**.

salmon
salmonella

salon

saloobrius	salubrious

saloon

saloot	salute
salow	sallow

salt, -ed, -ing
saltbush
saltcellar

saltery	psaltery
saltseller	saltcellar

salubrious, -ly

salubrius	salubrious
salud	salad

salutary
salutation
salute, -luted, -luting
salvage, -vaged, -vaging (save)

salvage	selvedge (edge)

salvager
salve, salved, salving
salver

salvidge	salvage (save)
salvidge	selvedge (edge)

salvo, -vos, -voes
sal volatile

samantic	semantic

samba
same

samon	salmon

samovar
Samoyed
sampan
sample, -pled, -pling
sampler

sampul	sample

samurai

samuri	samurai
sanatarium	sanitarium

sanatorium, -toriums, -toria

sancshun	sanction

sanctification
sanctify, -fied, -fying
sanctimonious, -ly

sanctimonius	sanctimonious

sanction, -ed, -ing
sanctity, -ties
sanctuary, -ries

sanctum, -tums
sand, -ed, -ing
sandal
sandalwood
sandbag, -bagged, -bagging
sandbank
sandblast, -ed, -ing
sandfly, -flies
sandpaper, -ed, -ing
sandpiper
sandshoe
sandsoap
sandstone
  sandul   sandal
  sandwhich   sandwich
sandwich, -wiches
  sandwitch   sandwich
sane, saner, sanest (not mad)
  sane   seine (net)
sanely
saneness
sang
sangfroid
sanguinary
sanguine, -ly
  sangwin   sanguine
sanitarium, -tariums, -taria
sanitary
sanitation
  sanitorium   sanatorium
sanity
sank

> For all other **sank-** words,
> look under **sanct-**.

sanskrit
Santa Claus
  Santa Klaus   Santa Claus
sap, sapped, sapping
  saper   sapper
sapience
sapiency
sapient, -ly
sapling
sapper
sapphire
  sappling   sapling

sapwood
sarcasm
sarcastic, -ally
  sarcofagus   sarcophagus
sarcophagus, -gi, -guses
  sardeen   sardine
sardine, -dines
sardonic, -ally
  sargent   sergeant
sari
sarong
sarsaparilla
sartorial, -ly
  sary   sari
  saserdotal   sacerdotal
sash
sashay (trip)
  sashay   sachet (bag)
  sashiate   satiate
sassafras
Sassenach
Satan (devil)
Satanic, -ally
Satanism
Satanist
satay
satchel
sate, sated, sating
sateen (cotton)
satellite
  Saten   Satan (devil)
  saten   sateen (cotton)
  saten   satin (silk)
  Saterday   Saturday
  satiabel   satiable
satiable, -ly
satiate, -ated, -ating
satiation
satin (silk)
satinwood
satire (sarcasm)
  satire   satyr (a god)
satiric
satirical, -ly
satirist
  satisfacshun satisfaction
satisfaction

satisfactorily
satisfactory
   satisfactry   satisfactory
   satisfiabul   satisfiable
satisfy, -fied, -fying
saturate, -rated, -rating
saturation
Saturday
Saturn (planet)
   saturn   sauterne (wine)
saturnine, -ly
satyr (a god)
   satyr   satire (sarcasm)
sauce (liquid)
   sauce   source (origin)
saucepan
saucer
   saucerer   sorcerer
   saucery   sorcery
saucily
sauciness
saucy, -cier, -ciest
sauerkraut
sauna
saunter, -ed, -ing
saurian
sausage
   sausy   saucy
sauté, -téed, -téeing
sauterne (wine)
   sauturn   sauterne
savage, savaged, savaging
savagely
savagery, -ries
   savana   savanna
savanna
savant
save, saved, saving
saveloy
saver (keeper)
   saver   savour (taste)
   savier   saviour
   savige   savage
   savigery   savagery
   savigry   savagery
saving
saviour

savoir-faire
savory, -vories (herb)
savour, -ed, -ing (taste)
   savour   saver (keeper)
savoury, -vouries (tasty)
savoy
savvy
saw, sawed, sawing (cut)
   saw   soar (rise)
   saw   sore (hurt)
   sawcer   saucer
   sawcey   saucy
   sawdid   sordid
sawdust
sawmill
   sawna   sauna
   sawnter   saunter
sawpit
   saws   sauce (liquid)
   saws   source (origin)
   sawser   saucer
   sawsey   saucy
saxhorn
   saxofone   saxophone
   saxofonist   saxophonist
Saxon
saxophone
saxophonist
say, said, saying
   sayance   seance
say-so
scab, scabbed, scabbing
scabbard
   scabees   scabies
scabies
scaffold
scaffolding
scalar
scald, -ed, -ing (burn)
   scald   scold (chide)
scale, scaled, scaling
   scaliwag   scallywag
scallop, -ed, -ing
scallywag
scalp, -ed, -ing
scalpel
scalper

scalpul — scalpel
scamp
scamper, -ed, -ing
scan, scanned, scanning
scandal
scandalise, -lised, -lising
scandalmonger
scanner
scanshun — scansion
scansion
scant
scantness
scanty, scantier, scantiest
scapegoat
scapula, -lae
scar, scarred, scarring
scarab
scarce, scarcer, scarcest
scarcely
scarceness
scarcity, -ties
scare, scared, scaring
scarecrow
scaremonger
scarf, scarfs, scarves
scarify, -fied, -fying
scarlet
scarp
scarper
scarsity — scarcity
scary, scarier, scariest
scate — skate
scathing, -ly
scatter, -ed, -ing
scatterbrain
scatty, -tier, -tiest
scavenge, -venged, -venging
scavenger
sceme — scheme
scenario, -narios
scene (view)
scene — seen (to see)
scenery, -neries
scenic, -ally
scent (perfume)
scent — cent (coin)
scent — sent (to send)

scepter — sceptre
sceptic
sceptical, -ly
scepticism
sceptre
scerge — scourge
scermish — skirmish
schedule, -uled, -uling
schematic, -ally
scheme, schemed, scheming
schemer
schism
schismatic
schizofrenia — schizophrenia
schizoid
schizophrenia
schizophrenic
schnapper
schnapps
scholar
scholarly
scholarship
scholastic, -ally
scholasticism
school, -ed, -ing
schoolboy
schoolgirl
schooner
sciatic
sciatica
science
scientific, -ally
scientist
scimitar
scintillate, -lated, -lating
sciolism
scion
scissors
scitsofrenia — schizophrenia
sclerosis, -ses
scoff, -ed, -ing
scolar — scholar
scolarship — scholarship
scolastic — scholastic
scold, -ed, -ing (chide)
scold — scald (burn)
scollop

scone
  scool   school
scoop, -ed, -ing
scooter
scope
scorch, -ed, -ing
score, scored, scoring
scorer
scorn, -ed, -ing
scornful, -ly
Scorpio
scorpion
  scorpiun   scorpion
Scotch
scotch, -ed, -ing
scot-free
Scotsman, -men
Scotswoman, -women
Scottish
scoundrel
  scoundrul   scoundrel
scour, -ed, -ing (scratch)
  scour   scow (barge)
scourge, scourged, scourging
scout, -ed, -ing
scow (barge)
  scow   scour (scratch)
scowl, -ed, -ing
  scowndrel   scoundrel
  scowt   scout
scrabble, -bled, -bling
  scrabbul   scrabble
scrag, scragged, scragging
scraggly, -glier, -gliest
scraggy, -gier, -giest
scram, scrammed, scramming
scramble, -bled, -bling
  scrambul   scramble
scrap, scrapped, scrapping
scrapbook
scrape, scraped, scraping
scraper
scrappily
scrappy, -pier, -piest
  scrapy   scrappy
scratch, -ed, -ing
scrawl, -ed, -ing

scrawny, -nier, -niest
scream, -ed, -ing
screamer
scree
screech, -ed, -ing
screed
screen, -ed, -ing
screenplay
screw, -ed, -ing
screwball
screwdriver
  screwtinise   scrutinise
screwy, screwier, screwiest
scribal (writer)
scribble, -bled, -bling (write)
scribbler
  scribbul   scribble
scribe, scribed, scribing
scrim
  scrimage   scrimmage
scrimmage, -maged, -maging
scrimp, -ed, -ing
scrip (receipt)
  scripcher   scripture
script (handwriting)
scriptural, -ly
Scripture
scrofula
scrofulous, -ly
scroll
  scroo   screw
  scrotem   scrotum
scrotum
scrounge, scrounged, scrounging
scrounger
  scrownge   scrounge
scrub, scrubbed, scrubbing
scrubber
scrubby, -bier, -biest
scruff
scruffy, scruffier, scruffiest
scrum, scrummed, scrumming
  scrumage   scrummage
scrummage
  scrumpshus   scrumptious
scrumptious, -ly
scrumptiousness

scrumshus	scrumptious
scrunch, -ed, -ing	
scruple, -pled, -pling	
scrupul	scruple
scrupulosity	
scrupulous, -ly	
scrupulousness	
scrutinise, -nised, -nising	
scrutiny, -nies	
scuba	
scud, scudded, scudding	
scuff, -ed, -ing	
scuffle, -fled, -fling	
scuful	scuffle
scul	scull (row)
scul	skull (head)
sculery	scullery
scull, -ed, -ing (row)	
scull	skull (head)
scullery, -leries	
scullion	
scullyon	scullion
sculpcher	sculpture
sculpt, -ed, -ing	
sculpter	sculptor
sculptor	
sculptress	
sculptural, -ly	
sculpture, -tured, -turing	
scum, scummed, scumming	
scummy, -mier, -miest	
scungie	scungy
scungy	
scurf	
scurge	scourge
scurie	scurry
scurilus	scurrilous
scurrilous, -ly	
scurrulus	scurrilous
scurry, -ries	
scurry, -ried, -rying	
scurvey	scurvy
scurvily	
scurvy, -vier, -viest	
scury	scurry
scuttel	scuttle
scuttle, -tled, -tling	

scuttlebutt	
scuttul	scuttle
scythe, scythed, scything	
sea (ocean)	
see	see (look)
sea-anemone	
seaboard	
seabord	seaboard
seafarer	
seafaring	
seafood	
seagoing	
seagull	
seahorse	
seal, -ed, -ing	
sealant	
sealer	
sea-level	
sealing (close)	
sealing	ceiling (roof)
seam, -ed, -ing (join)	
seam	seem (appear)
seaman, -men (sailors)	
seamanship	
seamen	semen (seed)
seamstress	
seamy -mier, -miest	
sean	scene (view)
sean	seen (to see)
seance	
seanse	seance
seaplane	
sear, -ed, -ing (burn)	
sear	seer (prophet)
search, -ed, -ing	
searcher	
searchlight	
search-warrant	
sea-scout	
sea-shell	
seashore	
seasickness	
seaside	
season, -ed, -ing	
seasonable, -bly	
seasonabul	seasonable
seasonal, -ly	

seat, -ed, -ing
seawards
seaweed
seaworthiness
seaworthy
sebaceous
  sebashus   sebaceous
  secaters   secateurs
secateurs
secede, -ceded, -ceding
  secesshun   secession
secession
  secetary   secretary
seclude, -cluded, -cluding
  seclushun   seclusion
seclusion
second, -ed, -ing
secondary, -arily
secondary boycott
second-class
second-degree
second-hand
secondly
second-rate
  secondry   secondary
seconds
  secratery   secretary
secrecy, -cies
  secreshun   secretion
  secresy   secrecy
secret, -ly
secretarial
secretariat
  secretariul   secretarial
secretary, -ries
secrete, -creted, -creting
secretion
secretive, -ly
  secretry   secretary
  secshun   section
sect
  sectar   sector
sectarian
sectarianism
section
sectional, -ly
  secter   sector

sector
secular, -ly
secularism
secularist
securable
  securabul   securable
secure, -cured, -curing
security, -ties
  sed   said
  sedament   sediment
sedan
sedate, -dated, -dating
sedation
sedative
sedentary
  sedentery   sedentary
  seder   cedar
sedge
sediment
sedimentary
sedimentation
  sedimentery   sedimentary
  sedishun   sedition
  sedishus   seditious
sedition
seditious, -ly
  seditive   sedative
seduce, -duced, -ducing
seducer
  seducshun   seduction
seduction
seductive, -ly
seductiveness
sedulous
  sedulus   sedulous
see, saw, seen, seeing (look)
  see   sea (ocean)
seed, seeded, seeding (plant)
  seed   cede (yield)
seediness
seedling
seedy, seedier, seediest
  seefarer   seafarer
  seefood   seafood
  seege   siege
  seegull   seagull
seek, sought, seeking

seel	seal
seelant	sealant
seeler	sealer
see-level	sea-level
seeling	ceiling (roof)
seeling	sealing (close)

seem, -ed, -ing (appear)

seem	seam (join)
seeman	seaman (sailor)

seemly, -lier, -liest

seemstress	seamstress
seemy	seamy

seen (to see)

seen	scene (view)
seenery	scenery
seenic	scenic
seenile	senile

seep, -ed, -ing
seepage

seepige	seepage
seequel	sequel

seer (prophet)

seer	sear (burn)
searsucker	seersucker

seersucker
seesaw

seese	cease
seesfire	ceasefire
seeshore	seashore
seesun	season
seet	seat

seethe, seethed, seething

seeweed	seaweed
seeze	seize
seezure	seizure
sege	sedge

segment
segmentation
segregate, -gated, -gating
segregation
segregationist

seige	siege

seine (net)

seine	sane (not mad)
seismagraf	seismograph

seismic
seismograph

seismologist
seismology
seize, seized, seizing
seizure

sekaters	secateurs
sekond	second
sekrete	secrete
seks	sex
sekshun	section
sekstant	sextant
seksual	sexual
seksy	sexy
sekt	sect
sektor	sector
sekular	secular
sekure	secure
sekwel	sequel
sekwense	sequence
sekwin	sequin
Selcius	Celsius

seldom, -ly

selebrate	celebrate
selebrity	celebrity
seleckshun	selection

select, -ed, -ing

selecter	selector

selection
selective, -ly
selectivity
selector

seler	cellar (room)
seler	seller (goods)
selerity	celerity
selery	celery (food)
selery	salary (wage)
selestial	celestial

self, selves
self-addressed
self-aggrandisement
self-assurance
self-centred
self-confessed
self-confidence
self-confident
self-conscious, -ly
self-contained
self-defence

self-denial
self-destruct
self-determination
self-employed
self-evident, -ly
self-fertilisation
self-government
self-image
   self-imidge   self-image
self-important, -ly
self-interest
selfish,-ly
selfishness
selfless, -ly
self-made
self-opinionated
self-pollination
self-possessed
self-raising flour
self-respect
self-righteous, -ly
self-rule
self-sacrifice
self-service
self-sown
self-starter
self-sufficient
self-willed
   selibacy   celibacy
   selibat   celibate
   selibrate   celebrate
sell, sold, selling (goods)
   sell   cell (prison)
seller (goods)
   seller   cellar (room)
   sellofane   cellophane
   sellophane   cellophane
sell-out
   sellullar   cellular
   selluloid   celluloid
   sellulose   cellulose
   sellvage   salvage (save)
   sellvedge   selvedge (edge)
   Selsius   Celsius
   selular   cellular
   seluloid   celluloid
   selulose   cellulose

selvage (edge)
selvedge (edge)
   selvedge   salvage (save)
   semafor   semaphore
semantic
semaphore, -phored, -phoring
semblance
   semblanse   semblance
semen (seed)
   semen   seamen
                 (sailors)
semester
semibreve
   semicercul   semicircle
semicircle
semicircular
semicolon
semiconductor
semidetached
seminal, -ly
seminar
seminary, -aries
   seminery   seminary
semiprecious
   semipreshus   semiprecious
semiquaver
Semite
   semitery   cemetery
Semitic
semitone
semitrailer
semolina
   sena   senna
   senario   scenario
   senat   senate
senate
   senater   senator
senator
senatorial
   senatoriul   senatorial
send, sent, sending
sender
senile
   senilitey   senility
senility
senior
seniority, -ties

senna
  senotaf · · · · · · · cenotaph
  sensability · · · · · sensibility
  sensabul · · · · · · sensible
sensation
sensational, -ly
sensationalise, -ised, -ising
sensationalism
sensationalist
  sensatise · · · · · · sensitise
sense, sensed, sensing
  senser · · · · · · · censer (incense)
  senser · · · · · · · censor (books)
  senser · · · · · · · sensor (device)
  senshual · · · · · · sensual
  senshur · · · · · · censure (blame)
sensible, -bly
sensibility, -ties
  sensibul · · · · · · sensible
sensitise, -tised, -tising
sensitivity, -ties
sensor (device)
  sensor · · · · · · · censer (incense)
  sensor · · · · · · · censor (books)
  sensorey · · · · · · sensory
  sensorious · · · · · censorious
sensory, -orily
sensual, -ly
sensualist
  sensualitey · · · · · sensuality
sensuality, -ties
sensuous, -ly
  sensus · · · · · · · census
sent (to send)
  sent · · · · · · · · cent (money)
  sent · · · · · · · · scent (perfume)
  sentenary · · · · · · centenary
sentence, -tenced, -tencing
  sentenchus · · · · · sententious
  sentennial · · · · · centennial
sententious, -ly
  senter · · · · · · · centre
sentience
sentient, -ly
  sentigrade · · · · · Centigrade
  sentigram · · · · · · centigram
sentiment

sentimental, -ly
sentimentalism
sentimentalist
sentimentality, -ties
  sentimeter · · · · · centimetre
sentinel, -nelled, -nelling
  sentipede · · · · · · centipede
  sentor · · · · · · · centaur
  sentral · · · · · · · central
  sentralise · · · · · centralise
  sentrey · · · · · · · sentry
  sentrifugal · · · · · centrifugal
  sentifuge · · · · · · centrifuge
  sentripetal · · · · · centripetal
sentry, -tries
  sentupul · · · · · · centuple
  senturion · · · · · · centurion
  sentury · · · · · · · century
  senyor · · · · · · · senior
  senyority · · · · · · seniority
sepal
separable, -bly
  separabul · · · · · · separable
separate, -rated, -rating
separately
separation
separationist
separator
  seperabul · · · · · · separable
  seperate · · · · · · separate
  seperation · · · · · separation
  sephalitis · · · · · cephalitis
sepia
sepoy
sepsis
September
septennial, -ly
  septer · · · · · · · sceptre
septet
septic
septicaemia
  septisemia · · · · · septicaemia
septuagenarian
sepulchral, -ly
sepulchre
  sepulchrul · · · · · sepulchral
  sepulker · · · · · · sepulchre

sequel	
sequence	
sequense	sequence
sequenshul	sequential
sequential, -ly	
sequester, -ed, -ing	
sequestration	
sequin	
ser	sir
seraf	seraph
serafic	seraphic
seramic	ceramic
seranade	serenade
serch	search
seremony	ceremony
seraph, -aphs, -aphim	
seraphic, -ally	
serch	search
sere (dry)	
sere	sear (burn)
serebrul	cerebral
sereen	serene
serees	series
serenade, -naded, -nading	
serendipity	
serene, -ly	
serenitey	serenity
serenity, -ties	
seres	series
sereze	cerise
serf (slave)	
serf	surf (sea)
serfdom	
serge (cloth)	
serge	surge (rush)
sergeant	
serial, -ly (part)	
serial	cereal (grain)
serialisation	
serialise, -lised, -lising	
seribelum	cerebellum
seribrul	cerebral
seribrum	cerebrum
series	
serif	
serimonial	ceremonial
serimonius	ceremonious
serimony	ceremony
serious, -ly	
seriousness	
serius	serious
serjent	sergeant
serloin	sirloin
serly	surly
serman	sermon
sermise	surmise
sermon	
sermount	surmount
sername	surname
serpent	
serpentine	
serplice	surplice (gown)
serplus	surplus (extra)
serprise	surprise
serrate, -rated, -rating	
serration	
serry, -ried, -rying	
sertain	certain
sertainty	certainty
sertax	surtax
sertifiabul	certifiable
sertificate	certificate
sertify	certify
sertitude	certitude
serum, sera, serums	
servant	
servay	survey
servaylanse	surveillance
serve, served, serving	
server	
servery, serveries	
servical	cervical
service, -viced, -vicing	
serviceability	
serviceable, -bly	
serviceabul	serviceable
serviceman, -men	
servicewoman, -women	
serviet	serviette
serviette	
serviks	cervix
servile, -ly	
servility	
servitude	

servival	survival
servive	survive
serviver	survivor
servix	cervix
sesame	
sesayshun	cessation
sese	cease
seseed	secede
seseshun	secession
seshun	cession (yield)
seshun	session (period)
sesless	ceaseless
seson	season
sesonabul	seasonable
sesonal	seasonal
sespit	cesspit
sesquicentenary, -ries	
sesseshun	secession
session (period)	
session	cession (yield)
set, set, setting	
setback	
setee	settee
seter	setter
setul	settle
settee	
setter	
settle, -tled, -tling	
settlement	
settler	
settul	settle
set-up	
seudo	pseudo
seudonim	pseudonym
sevear	severe
seven	
seventeen	
seventeenth	
seventh	
Seventh-Day Adventist	
seventieth	
seventy, -ties	
sever, -ed, -ing	
several, -ly	
severance	
severanse	severance
severe, -verer, -verest	

severely	
severitey	severity
severity, -ties	
sew, sewed, sewn, sewing (stitch)	
sew	sow (plant)
sewage	
sewer (drain)	
sewer (stitcher)	
sewer	sower (planter)
sewerage	
sewerige	sewerage
sewige	sewage
sex, -ed, -ing	
sexiness	
sexist	
sextant	
sextet	
sexton	
sexual, -ly	
sexualitey	sexuality
sexuality	
sexy, sexier, sexiest	
sezarian	caesarian
sfere	sphere
sfericul	sperical
sferoid	spheroid
sfincter	sphincter
sfinx	sphinx
sha	shah
shabbily	
shabbiness	
shabby, -bier, -biest	
shaby	shabby
shack	
shackle, -led, -ling	
shackul	shackle
shaddow	shadow
shade, shaded, shading	
shadow, -ed, -ing	
shadowy	
shady, -dier, -diest	
shaft	
shag, shagged, shagging	
shagginess	
shaggy, -gier, -giest	
shagrin	chagrin
shagy	shaggy

shah
  shak   shack
shake, shook, shaken, shaking
shakedown
shaker
Shakespearian
shake-up
  shakey   shaky
shakily
shakiness
shaky, shakier, shakiest
  shal   shall
  shalay   chalet
shale
  shalet   chalet
shall (will)
  shall   shell (cover)
shallot
shallow, -ly
shallowness
sham, shammed, shaming
shamble, -bled, -bling
shambles
  shambul   shamble
shame, shamed, shaming
shamefaced, -ly
shameful, -ly
shameless, -ly
  shampane   champagne
shampoo, -ed, -ing
shamrock
  shamy   chamois
  shandeleer   chandelier
  shandie   shandy
shandy, -dies
shanghai, -haied, -haiing
shank
shan't (shall not)
  shant   shan't
shantung
shanty, -ties
shape, shaped, shaping
shapeliness
shapely, -lier, -liest
  shaperon   chaperone
  sharade   charade
shard

share, shared, sharing
sharebroker
sharefarmer
shareholder
shark
sharkskin
sharp, -ly
sharpen, -ed, -ing
sharpener
sharper
sharpness
sharpshooter
sharpwitted
  shasee   chassis
shashlik
  shater   shatter
  shatow   chateau
shatter, -ed, -ing
shave, shaved, shaven, shaving
shaver
shawl
sheaf, sheaves
shear, sheared, shorn, shearing (cut)
  shear   sheer (thin)
shearer
shearwater
sheath, sheaths
sheathe, sheathed, sheathing
sheave, sheaved, sheaving
shed, shed, shedding
  shedule   schedule
  sheef   sheaf
  sheek   chic (smart)
  sheek   sheik (ruler)
sheen
sheep, sheep
sheep-dip
sheepdog
sheepish, -ly
sheepishness
sheep-run
sheepskin
sheer, -ed, -ing (swerve)
sheer (thin)
  sheer   shear (cut)
sheet, -ed, -ing
  shef   chef

sheik (ruler)
  sheik   shake (move)
sheila
  sheild   shield
shekel
  shel   shell
  shelac   shellac
shelf, shelves
  shelfish   shellfish
shell, -ed, -ing (cover)
she'll (she will)
  shell   she'll
shellac, -lacked, -lacking
shellfish, -fishes, -fish
shell-shocked
shelly, -lier, -liest
shelter, -ed, -ing
shelve, shelved, shelving
shemozzle
shenanigan
she-oak
  sheperd   shepherd
shepherd, -ed, -ing
shepherdess
sherbet
  sherbut   sherbet
  sherie   sherry
sherif (Muslim leader)
sheriff (law man)
sherry, -ries
  shery   sherry
  sheth   sheath
  sheves   sheaves
  shevron   chevron
shibboleth
  shic   chic (smart)
  shic   sheik (ruler)
  shicanery   chicanery
shickered
shied
shield, -ed, -ing
  shiffon   chiffon
shift, -ed, -ing
shiftiness
shiftless, -ly
shifty, -tier, -tiest
  shiling   shilling

shillelagh
shilling
shimmer, -ed, -ing
shimmery
shimmy, -mies
shimmy, -mied, -mying
shin, shinned, shinning
shindig
shine, shone, shined, shining
shiner
  shingel   shingle
shingle, -gled, -gling
shingles
  shinguls   shingles
shiny, shinier, shiniest
ship, shipped, shipping
shipment
  shipreck   shipwreck
  shipright   shipwright
shipshape
shipwreck, -ed, -ing
shipwright
shiralee
shirk, -ed, -ing
shirker
shirr, -ed, -ing
shirt
shirty
shish-kebab
  shivalrey   chivalry
  shivalrus   chivalrous
shiver, -ed, -ing
shivery
  shnaps   schnapps
shoal, -ed, -ing
shock, -ed, -ing
shocker
shod
shoddily
shoddiness
shoddy, -dier, -diest
  shodie   shoddy
  shody   shoddy
shoe, shoes
shoe, shod, shoeing (footwear)
  shoe   shoo (scare)
shoehorn

shoelace
shoemaker
shoeshine
shoestring
  shofer   chauffeur
shogun
  sholder   shoulder
  shole   shoal
shoo, -ed, -ing (scare)
  shoo   shoe (footwear)
  shood   should
shook
shoot, shot, shooting (gun)
  shoot   chute (channel)
shooter
shoot-out
shop, shopped, shopping
shopkeeper
shop-lift, -ed, -ing
shop-lifter
shop-soiled
shop-steward
shore, shored, shoring (sea)
  shore   sure (certain)
  shorely   surely
  shorety   surety
shorn
short, -ly
shortage
shortbread
  shortbred   shortbread
shortcake
short-change, -changed, -changing
short-circuit, -ed, -ing
shortcoming
shorten, -ed, -ing
shortfall
shorthand
  shortidge   shortage
shorts
short-sighted
  short-sited   short-sighted
short-wave
shot
shotgun
shot-put
shot-putter

should
shoulder, -ed, -ing
shoulder-blade
shout, -ed, -ing
shove, -ed, -ing
shovel, -ed, -ing
shoveler (bird)
shoveller (bird), (person)
  shovinism   chauvinism
  shovinist   chauvinist
show, showed, shown, showing
showboat
showdown
shower
showery
showily
showjumper
showjumping
showman, -men
showmanship
show-off
  showt   shout
showy, showier, showiest
shrank
shrapnel
shred, shredded, shredding
shredder
  shreek   shriek
shrew
shrewd, -ly
shrewish, -ly
shriek, -ed, -ing
shrift
shrike
shrill
shrimp
shrine
shrink, shrank, shrunk, shrinking
shrinkage
  shrinkige   shrinkage
shrivel, -elled, -elling
  shroo   shrew
  shrood   shrewd
shroud
  shrowd   shroud
shrub
shrubbery

shrug, shrugged, shrugging
shrunk
shudder, -ed, -ing
   shuffel — shuffle
shuffle, -fled, -fling
shun, shunned, shunning
shunt, -ed, -ing
shunter
   shurbet — sherbert
   shurk — shirk
   shurt — shirt
shush, -ed, -ing
shut, shut, shutting
shutdown
shut-eye
shut-out
   shuttel — shuttle
shutter
shuttle, -tled, -tling
shuttlecock
   shuttul — shuttle
   shuttulcock — shuttlecock
   shutul — shuttle
   shuve — shove
   shuvel — shovel
shy, shied, shying
shy, shyer, shyest
shyly
shyness
shyster
   sianide — cyanide
   siatic — sciatic
   sibernetics — cybernetics
sibilant, -ly
sibling
   sicamore — sycamore
   sicedelic — psychedelic
   siciatry — psychiatry
   sicick — psychic
sick
sicken, -ed, -ing
sickie
sickle
sickliness
sickly, -lier, -liest
   sickul — sickle
   siclamate — cyclamate

   siclamen — cyclamen
   sicle — cycle
   siclic — cyclic
   siclist — cyclist
   siclone — cyclone
   siclotron — cyclotron
   sicoanalise — psychoanalyse
   sicological — psychological
   sicology — psychology
   sicopant — sycophant
   sicopath — psychopath
   sicosis — psychosis
   sicosomatic — psychosomatic
   sicotherapist — psychotherapist
   sicotic — psychotic
   sicul — cycle
side, sided, siding
sideboard
   sidebord — sideboard
sidelight
sideline
   sidelite — sidelight
   sider — cider
sideshow
sidestep, -stepped, -stepping
sidetrack, -ed, -ing
sideways
   sidel — sidle
sidle, -dled, -dling
   sie — sigh
siege, sieged, sieging
sienna
   sience — science
   siense — science
   sientific — scientific
   sientist — scientist
sierra
siesta
sieve, sieved, sieving
   sieze — seize
   sifer — cypher
   sifilis — syphilis
   sifon — syphon
sift, -ed, -ing
   sigar — cigar
   sigaret — cigarette
sigh, -ed, -ing

sight, -ed, -ing (view)
  sight — cite (quote)
  sight — site (place)
sightless, -ly
sightly, -lier, -liest
sightseeing
sightseer
sigma
sign, -ed, -ing (mark)
  sign — sine (maths)
signal, -ed, -ing
signatory, -ries
  signatry — signatory
signature
  signefy — signify
signet (ring)
  signet — cygnet (swan)
significance
  significanse — significance
significant, -ly
signification
  signifie — signify
signify, -fied, -fying
signpost
  signul — signal
sign-writer
  sikedelic — psychedelic
  sikey — psyche
Sikh
  sikiatrist — psychiatrist
  sikiatry — psychiatry
  sikick — psychic
  siksty — sixty
  silabul — syllable
  silabus — syllabus
silage
silence, silenced, silencing
silencer
  silense — silence
silent, -ly
  silestial — celestial
  silf — sylph
silhouette, -etted, -etting
silica
silicon (element)
silicone (synthetic)
silicosis

  silie — silly
  silige — silage
  silinder — cylinder
  silindricul — cylindrical
silk
silken
silkiness
silk-screen
silkworm
silky, -kier, -kiest
silky oak
sill
  sillabul — syllable
silliness
silly, -lier, -liest
silo, -los
  silogism — syllogism
silt, -ed, -ing
  siluet — silhouette
silver, -ed, -ing
silverfish, -fish, -fishes
silverside
silversmith
silvery
  sily — silly
  simbiosis — symbiosis
  simbiotic — symbiotic
  simbol — cymbal (music)
  simbol — symbol (sign)
  simbolicul — symbolical
  simbolise — symbolise
  simbolism — symbolism
  siment — cement
  simer — simmer
  simetry — symmetry
  simfoney — symphony
simian
similar, -ly
similarity, -ties
simile
  similer — similar
simmer, -ed, -ing
  simmetry — symmetry
  simpathetic — sympathetic
  simpathise — sympathise
  simpathy — sympathy
  simpel — simple

simper, -ed, -ing
simple, -pler, -plest
simple interest
simpleton
simplicity, -ties
simplification
simplify, -fied, -fying
   simplisity   simplicity
simplistic, -ally
simply
   simposium   symposium
   simptom   symptom
   simptomatic   symptomatic
   simpul   simple
   simpulton   simpleton
simulate, -lated, -lating
simulation
simulator
simultaneous, -ly
   simultaynius   simultaneous
sin, sinned, sinning
   sinagog   synagogue
   sinamon   cinnamon
since
sincere, -cerer, -cerest
sincerely
sincerity, -ties
   sinchromesh   synchromesh
   sincronise   synchronise
sine (maths)
   sine   sign (mark)
   sine camera   cine camera
sinecure
   sinema   cinema
   sinematograf   cinematograph
   sinepost   signpost
sinew
sinewy
sinful, -ly
sing, sang, sung, singing
singe, singed, singeing
   singel   single
singer
single, -gled, -gling
single-handed
single-minded
singlet

singsong
singular, -ly
singularity, -ties
   singuler   singular
   sinic   cynic
   sinical   cynical
   sinema   cinema
   sinimatograf   cinematograph
   sinisism   cynicism
sinister, -ly
sink, sank, sunk or sunken, sinking
sinker
sinkhole
   sinod   synod
   sinonim   synonym
   sinonimus   synonymous
   sinopsis   synopsis
   sinoptic   synoptic
   sinoshure   cynosure
   sinse   since
   sinsere   sincere
   sinserity   sincerity
   sintax   syntax
   sinthesis   synthesis
   sinthesise   synthesise
   sinthetic   synthetic
   sinue   sinew
sinuous, -ly
sinus, -nuses
sinusitis
   sinuus   sinuous
sip, sipped, sipping
   sipet   sippet
   sipher   cipher
siphon, -ed, -ing
sippet
   sipress   cypress
sir
   sirca   circa
   sircharge   surcharge
sire, sired, siring
siren
   siringe   syringe
sirloin
   sirosis   cirrhosis
   sirup   syrup
   sirus   cirrus

sisal

sise	size
sism	schism
sismic	seismic
sismograf	seismograph
sismologist	seismologist
sissers	scissors

sissy

sist	cyst
sistem	system
sistematic	systematic
sistematise	systematise

sister
sister-in-law, sisters-in-law
sisterly

sistern	cistern

sit, sat, sitting

sitadel	citadel

sitar

sitation	citation

site, sited, siting (place)

site	cite (state)
site	sight (view)
sitely	sightly
siteseeing	sightseeing
siteseer	sightseer
sitey	city
sithe	scythe
sitie	city

sit-in

sitizen	citizen
sitric	citric
sitrus	citrus

sitter
situate, -ated, -ating
situation

sive	sieve
sivere	severe
sivic	civic
sivilian	civilian
sivilisation	civilisation
sivilise	civilise
sivilitey	civility

six
six-shooter
sixteen
sixteenth

sixth, -ly
sixtieth
sixty, -ties
size, sized, sizing
sizeable, -bly

sizeabul	sizeable
sizemic	seismic
sizers	scissors
sizul	sizzle

sizzle, -zled, -zling
sizzler

sizzul	sizzle
skane	skein

skate, skated, skating
skateboard
skater

skedule	schedule
skee	ski
skeem	scheme

skein
skeletal
skeleton

skeletul	skeletal
skematic	schematic
skeme	scheme
skeptic	sceptic
skepticism	scepticism
skepticul	sceptical
skerick	skerrick
skermish	skirmish

skerrick

skert	skirt

sketch, -ed, -ing
sketcher
sketchily
sketchiness
sketchy, sketchier, sketchiest
skew, -ed, -ing
skewer
ski, skis, ski
ski, skied, skiing
skid, skidded, skidding
skiff

skil	skill
skilet	skillet

skilful, -ly
skilfulness

skilite   skylight
skill
skilled
skillet
skillion
skillyun   skillion
skim, skimmed, skimming
skimp, -ed, -ing
skimpily
skimpiness
skimpy, skimpier, skimpiest
skin, skinned, skinning
skin-deep
skindiver
skindiving
skiney   skinny
skinflint
skinhead
skink
skinny, -nier, -niest
skip, skipped, skipping
skiper   skipper
ski-pole
skipper
skirmish
skirt, -ed, -ing
skiscraper   skyscraper
skit (making fun)
skite, skited, skiting (boast)
skitsofrenia   schizophrenia
skittel   skittle
skittish, -ly
skittle, skittled, skittling
skivvy
skol, skolled, skolling
skua
skue   skew
skulk, -ed, -ing
skull (head)
skull   scull (row)
skullcap
skunk

> For all **skw-** words,
> look under **squ-**.

sky, skied or skyed, skying
skydiver

skylark
skylight
skyline
skylite   skylight
skyrocket
skyscraper
slab
slack, -ly
slacken, -ed, -ing
slacks
slag, slagged, slagging
slain
slake, slaked, slaking
slaken   slacken
slalom
slam, slammed, slamming
slander, -ed, -ing
slanderer
slanderous, -ly
slane   slain
slang
slangy
slant, -ed, -ing
slap, slapped, slapping
slapdash
slapstick
slash, -ed, -ing
slasher
slat
slate, slated, slating
slater
slatern   slattern
slather, -ed, -ing
slattern, -ly
slaughter, -ed, -ing
slaughterhouse
Slav
slave, slaved, slaving
slaver
slavish, -ly
slavishness
Slavonic
slawter   slaughter
slay, slew, slain, slaying (kill)
slay   sleigh (sledge)
sleazy, -zier, -ziest
sled, sledded, sledding

sledge
sledge-hammer
sleek, -ly
sleekness
sleep, slept, sleeping
sleeper
sleepily
sleepiness
sleepless, -ly
sleep-out
sleepy, sleepier, sleepiest
sleet
sleeve
sleeved
slege   sledge
sleigh (sledge)
sleight (skill)
sleight   slight (small)
slender, -ly
slept
sleuth
slew
sli   sly
slice, sliced, slicing
slick, -ly
slide, slid, sliding
slight, -ly (small)
slight   sleight (skill)
slim, slimmed, slimming
slim, slimmer, slimmest
slime
slimily
sliminess
slimy, slimier, slimiest
sling, slung, slinging
slink, slunk, slinking
slinky, slinkier, slinkiest
slip, slipped, slipping
sliper   slipper
slipnot   slipknot
slipper
slippery, -perier, -periest
sliprale   sliprail
sliprail
slipshod
slip-stitch

slipstream
slipway
slise   slice
slit, slit, slitting
slite   slight
slither, -ed, -ing
sliver
slo   sloe (fruit)
slo   slow (not fast)
slob
slobber, -ed, -ing
slobbery
sloe (fruit)
sloe   slow (not fast)
slog, slogged, slogging
slogan
sloop
sloose   sluice
slooth   sleuth
slop, slopped, slopping
slope, sloped, sloping
slopily   sloppily
sloppiness
sloppily
sloppy, -pier, -piest
slopy   sloppy
slosh, -ed, -ing
slot, slotted, slotting
sloth
slothful, -ly
slouch, -ed, -ing
slough (skin)
sloven, -ly
slovenliness
slow, -ed, -ing (not fast)
slow   sloe (fruit)
slow   slough (skin)
slowch   slouch
slowcoach
slow-motion
sludge
sludgy, sludgier, sludgiest
slue   slew
sluff   slough
sluggard
sluggardly
sluggish, -ly

sluice, sluiced, sluicing
slum, slummed, slumming
slumber, -ed, -ing
slump, -ed, -ing
slung
slunk
slur, slurred, slurring
   slurie   slurry
slurp, -ed, -ing
slurry
slush
slushy, -shier, -shiest
slut
sluttish, -ly
sly, slyer, slyest or slier, sliest
slyly
slyness
smack, -ed, -ing
small
smallgoods
smallpox
small-time
smarmy
smart, -ed, -ing
smart, smarter, smartest
smart alec
smarten, -ed, -ing
smartly
smash, -ed, -ing
smasher
smattering
smear, -ed, -ing
   smeer   smear
smell, smelled or smelt, smelling
smelly, smellier, smelliest
smelter
smidgin
smile, smiled, smiling
smirch, -ed, -ing
smirk, -ed, -ing
smite, smote, smiting
smith
smithereens
   smithey   smithy
smithy, smithies
smitten
smock, -ed, -ing

smog
smoggy, smoggier, smoggiest
   smogy   smoggy
smoke, smoked, smoking
smoke-bush
smoker
smokescreen
smokestack
smoko
smoky, smokier, smokiest
   smolder   smoulder
smooch, -ed, -ing
smoodge, smoodged, smoodging
smooth, -ed, -ing
smoothly
smoothness
smorgasbord
smother, -ed, -ing
smoulder, -ed, -ing
smudge, smudged, smudging
smug, smugger, smuggest
   smuge   smudge
smuggle, smuggled, smuggling
smuggler
   smuggul   smuggle
   smugle   smuggle
smugly
   smurch   smirch
   smurk   smirk
smut
smuttily
smuttiness
smutty, smuttier, smuttiest
   smuty   smutty
snack
snaffle, -fled, -fling
   snafful   snaffle
snag, snagged, snagging
snagger
snail
snake, snaked, snaking
snakebite
snaky, snakier, snakiest
   snale   snail
snap, snapped, snapping
snapdragon
   snaper   snapper

snapper
snappily
snappiness
snappy, -pier, -piest
snapshot
  snapy   snappy
snare, snared, snaring
snarl, -ed, -ing
snatch, -ed, -ing
sneak, -ed, -ing
sneaker
  sneek   sneak
  sneeker   sneaker
sneer, -ed, -ing
sneeze, sneezed, sneezing
snib, snibbed, snibbing
snick, -ed, -ing
snicker, -ed, -ing
snide
  snif   sniff
  snifel   sniffle
sniff, -ed, -ing
sniffle, -fled, -fling
  snifful   sniffle
  sniger   snigger
snigger, -ed, -ing
snip, snipped, snipping (cut)
snipe, sniped, sniping (shoot)
sniper
  snipet   snippet
snippet
snitch, -ed, -ing
snivel, -elled, -elling
sniveller
  snivul   snivel
snob
snobbery
snobbish, -ly
snood
snook
snooker, -ed, -ing
snoop, -ed, -ing
snoopy
snooze, snoozed, snoozing
snore, snored, snoring
snorkel
  snorkle   snorkel

  snorkul   snorkel
snort, -ed, -ing
snout
snow, -ed, -ing
snowball
  snowey   snowy
snowflake
snow job
snowline
snowman, -men
snowplough
snowshoe, -shoed, -shoeing
  snowt   snout
snowy, snowier, snowiest
snub, snubbed, snubbing
snuff, -ed, -ing
snuffle, -fled, -fling
snug, snugger, snuggest
snuggle, -gled, -gling
so (in this way)
  so   sew (stitch)
  so   sow (pig, plant)
soak, -ed, -ing
so-and-so
soap, -ed, -ing
soapbox
soapie
soap opera
  soappy   soapy
soapstone
soapy, soapier, soapiest
soar, -ed, -ing (fly)
  soar   sore (hurt)
sob, sobbed, sobbing
sober, -ed, -ing
sobriety
  sobrikay   sobriquet
sobriquet
so-called
soccer
sociability
sociable, -bly
  sociabul   sociable
social, -ly
socialisation
socialise, -lised, -lising
socialism

socialist
socialistic, -ally
socialite
society, -ties
socioeconomic, -ally
sociologist
sociology
   sociul   social
sock, -ed, -ing
   socker   soccer
socket
   sockit   socket
sockeye
sod
soda
soda-water
sodden
   soden   sodden
sodium
sodomite
sodomy
sofa
   sofar   sofa
   sofen   soften
   sofism   sophism
   sofist   sophist
   sofisticate   sophisticate
   sofistication   sophistication
   sofistry   sophistry
soft, -ly
softball
soften, -ed, -ing
soft-pedal, -alled, -alling
soft-soap
software
   softwear   software
soggily
sogginess
soggy, -gier, -giest
   sogie   soggy
   sogy   soggy
   soia   soya
soil, -ed, -ing
   soiray   soiree
soiree
   soiya   soya
   sojern   sojourn

sojourn, -ed, -ing
   soke   soak
solace, -aced, -acing
solar
   solareum   solarium
solarium, -laria
   solass   solace
   solatude   solitude
sold
solder, -ed, -ing
soldier, -ed, -ing
soldierly
sole (shoe)
   sole   soul (spirit)
solecism
   soled   solid
   soleful   soulful
   solem   solemn
solemn, -ly
solemnisation
solemnise, -nised, -nising
   solemnitey.   solemnity
solemnity, -ties
solenoid
   soler   solar
   solesism   solecism
solfa, -faed, -faing
   solger   soldier
solicit, -ed, -ing
solicitation
   soliciter   solicitor
solicitor
solicitous, -ly
solicitude
   solicitus   solicitous
solid, -ly
solidarity, -ties
   solidifi   solidify
solidification
solidify, -fied, -fying
solid-state
   solilokwy   soliloquy
soliloquy, -quies
   solisit   solicit
   solisitor   solicitor
   solisitus   solicitous
solitaire

solitary, -taries
solitude
  soljer — soldier

> For **soll-** words,
> look under **sol-**.

solo, -los
soloist
solstice
  solstiss — solstice
solubility, -ties
soluble, -bly
  solubul — soluble
  solushun — solution
solution
solvable
solve, solved, solving
solvency
  solvensy — solvency
solvent
  somber — sombre
  sombraro — sombrero
sombre, -ly
sombrero
some (few)
  some — sum (total)
somebody, -bodies
somehow
someone
  somersalt — somersault
somersault
something
sometime
somewhat
somewhere
somnambulism
somnolence
  somnolense — somnolence
son (boy)
  son — sun (star)
sonar
sonata
  soner — sonar
song
songster
songstress
sonic

sonic boom
  sonick — sonic
son-in-law, sons-in-law
sonnet
sonny, -nies
sonorous, -ly
  sonorus — sonorous
  soo — sue
  soocher — suture
  soocrose — sucrose
  sooet — suet
  sooflay — souffle
sook
sooky
soon
  soop — soup
soot (chimney)
  soot — suit (clothes)
sooth (truth)
soothe, soothed, soothing (calm)
soothsayer
  soovenir — souvenir
sop, sopped, sopping
  sope — soap
sophism
sophist
sophisticate, -cated, -cating
sophistication
sophistry, -ries
soporific
sopping
soppy, -pier, -piest
soprano, -pranos, -prani
sorbet
  sorce — sauce (liquid)
  sorce — source (origin)
sorcerer
sorceress
sorcery, -ceries
  sord — sword
sordid, -ly
  sordust — sawdust
sore, sorer, sorest (hurt)
  sore — saw (cut)
  sore — soar (rise)
  sorel — sorrel
  sorey — sorry

sorghum
  sorgum — sorghum
  sorie — sorry
  sorna — sauna
  sornter — saunter
sorority, -ties
  sorow — sorrow
sorrel
sorrow
sorrowful, -ly
sorry, -rier, -riest
sort (type)
  sort — sought (looked)
  sortee — sortie
sortie, -tied, -tieing
  soshable — sociable
  soshal — social
  soshalise — socialise
  sosietey — society
  sosige — sausage
so-so
sot
  soto vochay — sotto voce
sotto voce
soufflé
sough (rustling sound)
  sough — sow (pig)
sought (looked)
soul (spirit)
  soul — sole (shoe)
sound, -ed, -ing
soundbox
sounding-board
soundproof
soundtrack
soundwave
soup
sour, -ed, -ing
source (origin)
  source — sauce (liquid)
souse, soused, sousing
south
south-east
south-easter
south-eastern
southerly
southern

Southern Cross
southward, -ly
south-west
south-wester
south-western
souvenir
sovereign
sovereignty, -ties
  soverin — sovereign
soviet
  sovrenty — sovereignty
sow, sowed, sowing (pig, plant)
  sow — sew (stitch)
sown (planted)
  sown — sewn (stitched)
  sownd — sound
  sowr — sour
  sowth — south
soy
soya
spa
space, spaced, spacing
spaceship
spacious, -ly
spade, spaded, spading
spadework
  spagetti — spaghetti
spaghetti
span, spanned, spanning
  spaner — spanner
spangle, -gled, -gling
  spangul — spangle
Spaniard
spaniel
spank, -ed, -ing
spanner
  Spanyard — Spaniard
  spanyel — spaniel
spar, sparred, sparring (fight)
spare, spared, sparing (extra)
spark, -ed, -ing
sparkle, -kled, -kling
sparkler
  sparkul — sparkle
  sparow — sparrow
sparrow
sparrowhawk

sparse, sparser, sparsest
sparsity
Spartan
  spase   space
  spashus   spacious
spasm
spasmodic, -ally
spastic, -ally
spat (did spit)
  spatal   spatial
spate (sudden)
spatial, -ly
spatter, -ed, -ing
spatula
spawn, -ed, -ing
spay, -ed, -ing
speak, spoke, spoken, speaking
speakeasy, -easies
speaker
spear, -ed, -ing
spearmint
spec (gamble)
  spec   speck (spot)
special, -ly
specialisation
specialise, -lised, -lising
specialist
speciality, -ties
specialty, -ties
species, -cies
specific, -ly
specification
specify, -fied, -fying
specimen
specious, -ly
speck, -ed, -ing (spot)
  speck   spec (gamble)
speckle, -kled, -kling
spectacle
  spectacul   spectacle
spectacular, -ly
spectator
  specter   spectre
spectre
spectroscope
spectrum, -tra
speculate, -lated, -lating

speculation
speculator
speech
speed, sped, speeding
speedometer
speedway
  speek   speak
  speer   spear
  spekul   speckle
  spel   spell
spell, spelt or spelled, spelling
spellbound
spencer
spend, spent, spending
spendthrift
sperm
  spern   spurn
  spert   spurt
  speshal   special
  speshalist   specialist
  speshus   specious
  spesify   specify
  spesimen   specimen
spew, -ed, -ing
sphere
spherical, -ly
spheroid
sphinx
  spi   spy
spice, spiced, spicing
spick-and-span
spicy, spicier, spiciest
spider
spidery
spiel, -ed, -ing
spigot
spike, spiked, spiking
spill, spilt or spilled, spilling
spillage
  spillige   spillage
spin, spun, spinning
spina bifida
spinach
  spinaker   spinnaker
spinal
spindle, -dled, -dling
spin-dry, -dried, -drying

spine
spinifex
   spinige   spinach
spinnaker
spinner
spin-off
spinster
spiny, spinier, spiniest
spiral, -ralled, -ralling
spire
   spirel   spiral
   spirichual   spiritual
   spirichualist   spiritualist
spirit, -ed, -ing
spiritual, -ly
spiritualism
spiritualist
spirituality, -ties
   spise   spice
   spisy   spicy
spit, spat, spitting
spite, spited, spiting
spiteful, -ly
spitfire
spittle
spittoon
   spittul   spittle
spiv
splash, -ed, -ing
splashdown
splatter, -ed, -ing
splay, -ed, -ing
spleen
   splender   splendour
splendid, -ly
splendour
splice, spliced, splicing
splicer
splint
splinter, -ed, -ing
   splise   splice
split, split, splitting
split-level
splurge, splurged, splurging
splutter, -ed, -ing
spoil, spoilt, spoiling
spoilage

spoilsport
spoke
spoken
spokesperson
sponge, sponged, sponging
sponger
spongy, -gier, -giest
   sponser   sponsor
sponsor, -ed, -ing
sponsorship
spontaneity, -ties
spontaneous, -ly
   sponteneity   spontaneity
spoof, -ed, -ing
spook, -ed, -ing
spool
spoon, -ed, -ing
spoonbill
spoonerism
spoon-feed, -fed, -feeding
spoor (trail)
   spoor   spore (germ)
sporadic, -ally
spore, spored, sporing (germ)
   spore   spoor (trail)
sporran
sport, -ed, -ing
sportive, -ly
sportsman, -men
sportswoman, -women
spot, spotted, spotting
spotlight, -ed, -ing
   spotlite   spotlight
spouse
spout, -ed, -ing
   spowse   spouse
   spowt   spout
sprain, -ed, -ing
   sprane   sprain
sprang
sprat
sprawl, -ed, -ing
spray, -ed, -ing
spread, spread, spreading
spread-eagle, -gled, -gling
   spred   spread
spree

sprie   spry
sprightly, -lier, -liest
spring, sprang, sprung, springing
springboard
springbok, -boks
spring-clean, -ed, -ing
spring-loaded
springy, -gier, -giest
sprinkle, -kled, -kling
sprinkler
sprinkul   sprinkle
sprint, -ed, -ing
sprit (pole)
sprite, -ly (elf)
sprocket
sproose   spruce
sprout, -ed, -ing
sprowt   sprout
spruce, spruced, sprucing
spruce, sprucer, sprucest
sprung
spry, spryer, spryest
spud, spudded, spudding
spume, spumed, spuming
spun
spunge   sponge
spunk
spunky, spunkier, spunkiest
spur, spurred, spurring
spurious, -ly
spurius   spurious
spurm   sperm
spurn, -ed, -ing
spurt, -ed, -ing
sputnik
sputter, -ed, -ing
sputum, sputa
spy, spies
spy, spied, spying
squabble, -bled, -bling
squabul   squabble
squad
squadron
squalid, -ly
squall, -ed, -ing
squalor
squander, -ed, -ing

square, squared, squaring
squarely
square-rigged
squash, -ed, -ing
squat, squatted, squatting
squatter
squattocracy
squaw
squawk, -ed, -ing
squeak, -ed, -ing
squeal, -ed, -ing
squeamish, -ly
squeeze, squeezed, squeezing
squelch, -ed, -ing
squib, squibbed, squibbing
squid, squids, squid
squiggle, -gled, -gling
squiggly
squiggul   squiggle
squint, -ed, -ing
squire, squired, squiring
squirm, -ed, -ing
squirrel
squirt, -ed, -ing
squiz, -ed, -ing
squod   squad
squodron   squadron
squolid   squalid
squonder   squander
squosh   squash
squot   squat
stab, stabbed, stabbing
stabilisation
stabilise, -lised, -lising
stabiliser
stability, -ties
stable, -bled, -bling
stabul   stable
staccato
stack, -ed, -ing
stadium, -dia, -diums
staf   staff
staff, -ed, -ing
stag
stage, staged, staging
stagecoach
stager   stagger

stagflation
stagger, -ed, -ing
staghorn
stagnant, -ly
stagnate, -nated, -nating
stagnation
staid, -ly (calm)
   staid   stayed
                     (stopped)
   staidium   stadium
stain, -ed, -ing
stainless, -ly
stair (step)
   stair   stare (look at)
staircase
stairwell
stake, staked, staking (post)
   stake   steak (meat)
stalactite
stalagmite
stale, staled, staling
stale, staler, stalest
stalemate, -mated, -mating
   stalion   stallion
stalk, -ed, -ing (hunt)
   stalk   stork (bird)
stall, -ed, -ing
stallion
stalwart, -ly
   stalwert   stalwart
stamen
   stamena   stamina
   stamer   stammer
stamina
stammer, -ed, -ing
stamp, -ed, -ing
stampede, -peded, -peding
stance
stanchion
   stanchun   stanchion
stand, stood, standing
standard
standardise, -dised, -dising
stand-by
   standerd   standard
stand-in
stand-offish, -ly

standstill
   stane   stain
stank
   stanse   stance
stanza
staple, -pled, -pling
stapler
   stapul   staple
star, starred, starring
starboard
   starbord   starboard
starch, -ed, -ing
star-crossed
stardom
stare, stared, staring (look at)
   stare   stair (step)
starfish, -fishes, -fish
stargaze, -gazed, -gazing
stargazer
stark, -ly
starkers
starling
start, -ed, -ing
   startch   starch
starter
startle, -tled, -tling
starvation
starve, starved, starving
stash, -ed, -ing
   stashun   station
   stashunry   stationary
   stashunry   stationery
state, stated, stating
stateliness
stately, -lier, -liest
statement
stateroom
statesman, -men
stateswoman, -women
static, -ally
station, -ed, -ing
stationary (still)
stationer (sells paper)
stationery (paper)
statistical, -ly
statistician
statistics

statistishun statistician
stattic static
statuary, -aries (statues)
statue
statuesk statuesque
statuesque, -ly
stature
status
status quo
statute
statutory (law)
statutry statutory
staunch, -ed, -ing
stave, staved, staving
stawk stalk
stay, stayed, staying
stead
steadfast, -ly
steadily
steady, steadied, steadying
steady, steadier, steadiest
steak (meat)
steak stake (post)
steal, stole, stolen, stealing (rob)
steal steel (metal)
stealth
stealthily
stealthy, -thier, -thiest
steam, -ed, -ing
steam-engine
steamer
steamroller
sted stead
stedfast steadfast
stedy steady
steed
steel, -ed, -ing (metal)
steel steal (rob)
steely
steep, -ed, -ing
steeple
steeplechase
steepul steeple
steer, -ed, -ing
steerage
steerige steerage
steersman, -men

stelth stealth
stem, stemmed, stemming
stench
stencil, -cilled, -cilling
stenografer stenographer
stenografy stenography
stenographer
stenography
stensil stencil
step, stepped, stepping, (pace)
stepladder
steppe (plain)
stereo, stereos
stereogram
stereophonic
stereotype, -typed, -typing
sterile, -ly
sterilisation
sterilise, -lised, -lising
steriliser
sterio stereo
steriofonic stereophonic
steriotype stereotype
sterling
stern, -ly
sternum
stethoscope
stetson
stevedore, -dored, -doring
stew, -ed, -ing
steward
stewardess
sti sty
stich stitch
stick, stuck, sticking
sticker
stickler
stick-up
sticky, stickier, stickiest
stickybeak
stif stiff
stifen stiffen
stiff
stiffen, -ed, -ing
stiffener
stifle, -fled, -fling
stiful stifle

stigma, -mas, -mata
stigmatise, -tised, -tising
  stikler   stickler
  stil   still
stile (steps)
  stile   style (type)
stiletto, -tos
  stilish   stylish
  stilist   stylist
still, -ed, -ing
stillbirth
stillborn
still-life
stilt
stilted, -ly
stilton
  stilus   stylus
  stimie   stymie
stimulant
stimulate, -lated, -lating
stimulation
stimulator
stimulus, -li, -luses
sting, stung, stinging
stingray
stingy, -gier, -giest
stink, stank, stunk, stinking
stinker
stinkhorn
stinkpot
stint, -ed, -ing
stipend
stipendiary, -ries
stipple, -pled, -pling
  stipul   stipple
stipulate, -lated, -lating
stipulation
stir, stirred, stirring
  stirling   sterling
stirrup
  stirup   stirrup
stitch, -ed, -ing
stoat
stock, -ed, -ing
stockade, -aded, -ading
stockbroker
stock-car

stocking
stockman, -men
stockpile, -piled, -piling
stocktaking
stockwhip
stocky, -kier, -kiest
stodgily
stodgy, -gier, -giest
  stogy   stodgy
stoical, -ly
stoicism
  stoisism   stoicism
stoke, stoked, stoking
stoker
stole
stolen
stolid, -ly
stoma, stomata
stomach
stomach-ache
  stomick   stomach
stone, stoned, stoning
stonefish
stonemason
stoneware
stony, stonier, stoniest
stood
stooge, stooged, stooging
stool
stoop, stooped, stooping
stop, stopped, stopping
stopcock
stope, stoped, stoping
stopgap
stoppage
stopper
stopwatch
store, stored, storing
storey (floor)
  storey   story (tale)
  storie   storey (floor)
  storie   story (tale)
  storige   storage
stork (bird)
  stork   stalk (hunt)
storm, -ed, -ing
stormily

stormy, -mier, -miest
story, -ries (tale)
   story   storey (floor)
stout, -ly
stove, stoved, stoving
stow, -ed, -ing
stowaway
   stowt   stout
straddle, -dled, -dling
   straf   strafe
strafe, strafed, strafing
straggle, -gled, -gling
straggler
straight (line)
   straight   strait (passage)
straightaway
straighten, -ed, -ing
straightforward, -ly
strain, -ed, -ing
strainer
strait (passage)
   strait   straight (line)
straiten
straitjacket
straitlaced
strand
   strane   strain
strange, stranger, strangest
strangle, -gled, -gling
strangler
stranglehold
   strangul   strangle
strangulate, -lated, -lating
strangulation
strap, strapped, strapping
strapper
strasbourg
strata
stratagem
strata title
   strate   straight (line)
   strate   strait (passage)
   strategie   strategy
strategic, -ally
strategist
strategy, -gies
stratification

stratify, -fied, -fying
   stratigem   stratagem
   stratosfere   stratosphere
stratosphere
stratum, strata
straw
   strawberie   strawberry
strawberry, -ries
stray, -ed, -ing
streak, -ed, -ing
streaky, streakier, streakiest
stream, -ed, -ing
streamer
streamline, -lined, -lining
   streek   streak
   streem   stream
street
strength
strengthen, -ed, -ing
strenuous, -ly
   strenuus   strenuous
streptomycin
stress, -ed, -ing
stretch, -ed, -ing
stretcher
strew, strewed, strewn, strewing
striate, -ated, -ating
striation
   strick   strict
stricken
strict, -ly
stricture
stride, strode, striding
stridence
strident, -ly
strife
strike, struck, stricken, striking
strikebound
strikebreaker
   striknun   strychnine
strine
string, strung, stringing
stringency
   stringensy   stringency
stringent, -ly
stringer
stringy, -gier, -giest

strip, stripped, stripping
stripe, striped, striping
stripling
stripper
striptease
strive, strove, striven, striving
strobe
stroboscope
strode
stroke, stroked, stroking
stroll, -ed, -ing
stroller
strong, -ly
stronghold
stroo   strew
strop, stropped, stropping
stroppie   stroppy
stroppy, stroppier, stroppiest
strove
struck
struckcher   structure
structure, -tured, -turing
strudel
struggle, -gled, -gling
struggler
strugul   struggle
strum, strummed, strumming
strummer
strumpet
strung
strut, strutted, strutting
strychnine
stu   stew
stuard   steward
stub, stubbed, stubbing
stubble
stubbly
stubborn, -ly
stuben   stubborn
stucco, -coes, -cos
stuck-up
stud, studded, studding
student
studie   study
studied
studio, -dios
studious, -ly

studius   studious
study, studies
study, studied, studying
stuf   stuff
stuff, -ed, -ing
stuffily
stuffy, -fier, -fiest
stufy   stuffy
stuko   stucco
stultifie   stultify
stultify, -fied, -fying
stumble, -bled, -bling
stumbul   stumble
stump, -ed, -ing
stump-jump plough
stun, stunned, stunning
stunner
stunt, -ed, -ing
stuntman, -men
stupefie   stupefy
stupefy, -fied, -fying
stupendous, -ly
stupendus   stupendous
stupid, -ly
stupidity, -ties
stupify   stupefy
stupor
sturdie   sturdy
sturdily
sturdy, -dier, -diest
sturgeon
sturgun   sturgeon
sturling   sterling
sturn   stern
stuter   stutter
stutter, -ed, -ing
stutterer
stuward   steward
St Vitus dance
sty, sties
style (type)
style   stile (steps)
stylish, -ly
stylist
stylistic, -ally
stymie, -mied, -mieing
styptic

suage / sewage
suave, -ly
suavity, -ties
sub, subbed, subbing
subaltern
subcomitee / subcommittee
subcommittee
subconscious, -ly
subconshus / subconscious
subcontinent
subcontract, -ed, -ing
subcontractor
subculture
subcutaneous, -ly
subdivide, -vided, -viding
subdivishun / subdivision
subdivision
subdue, -dued, -duing
subeditor
suberb / suburb
suberban / suburban
subgigate / subjugate
subgroup
subheading
subjecshun / subjection
subject, -ed, -ing
subjection
subjective, -ly
subjectivity
sub judice
subjugate, -gated, -gating
subjugation
subjunctive
sublimate, -mated, -mating
sublimation
sublime, -limed, -liming
subliminal, -ly
sublimity, -ties
sublimminal / subliminal
submarine
submerge, -merged, -merging
submishun / submission
submission
submissive, -ly
submit, -mitted, -mitting
submurge / submerge
subnormal, -ly

subordinate, -nated, -nating
subordination
suborn, -ed, -ing
subpena / subpoena
subpoena, -naed, -naing
subscribe, -ribed, -ribing
subscriber
subscription
subsection
subsekwent / subsequent
subsequent, -ly
subservience
subservient, -ly
subset
subside, -sided, -siding
subsidence
subsidie / subsidy
subsidise, -dised, -dising
subsidy, -dies
subsist, -ed, -ing
subsistence
subsistense / subsistence
subsistent, -ly
subsoil
substance
substandard
substanshul / substantial
substantial, -ly
substantiate, -ated, -ating
substation
substitute, -tuted, -tuting
subtefuge / subterfuge
subterfuge
subterranean
subtitle, -tled, -tling
subtitul / subtitle
subtle, -tly
subtlety, -ties
subtracshun / subtraction
subtraction
subtropical
suburb
suburban
suburbia
subversion
subversive
subvert, -ed, -ing

subway
succeed, -ed, -ing
success
successful, -ly
succession
successive, -ly
successor
succinct, -ly
succour, -ed, -ing (aid)
succulent, -ly
succumb, -ed, -ing
such
   suchure   suture
suck, -ed, -ing
sucker (dupe)
   suckshun   suction
   suckulent   succulent
   suckum   succumb
sucrose
   sucsede   succeed
   sucseshun   succession
   sucses   success
   sucseser   successor
   sucsesful   successful
   sucsint   succinct
suction
sudden, -ly
suds
sue, sued, suing
suede
   suer   sewer
suet (meat)
   sufer   suffer
suffer, -ed, -ing
sufferance
   sufferanse   sufferance
suffice, -ficed, -ficing
sufficiency
sufficient, -ly
   suffiks   suffix
   suffishensy   sufficiency
suffix
suffocate, -cated, -cating
suffocation
suffrage
suffragette
suffuse, -fused, -fusing

suffusion
   sufocashun   suffocation
   sufocate   suffocate
   sufrajet   suffragette
   sufrance   sufferance
   sufrige   suffrage
   sufuse   suffuse
sugar
sugary
   sugeschun   suggestion
   sugest   suggest
suggest, -ed, -ing
suggestive, -ly
suicidal
suicide, -cided, -ciding
   suiside   suicide
suit, -ed, -ing (clothes)
   suit   suet (meat)
suitability
suitable, -bly
suitcase
suite (rooms)
   suiter   suitor
suitor
sulk, -ed, -ing
sulky, sulkier, sulkiest
sullage
sullen, -ly
sully, -lied, -lying
sulphur
sulphuric
sultan
sultana
   sultrie   sultry
sultriness
sultry, -trier, -triest
sum, summed, summing (total)
   sum   some (few)
   sumbody   somebody
   sumhow   somehow
   summarine   submarine
summarise, -rised, -rising
summary, -ries (short)
   summary   summery
                  (warm)
summation
summer

summerhouse
summerise summarise
summery (warm)
summery summary
(short)
summit
summon, -ed, -ing (call)
summons, -monses (court)
sumo
sums
sump
sumptuous, -ly
sun, sunned, sunning (star)
sun son (boy)
sun inlaw son-in-law
sunbake, -baked, -baking
sunburn, -ed, -ing
sundae (ice-cream)
Sunday (day)
sundeck
sunder, -ed, -ing
sundial
sundown
sundowner
sundries
sundry, -rily
sunfish, -fishes, -fish
sunflower
sung
sunglasses
sunk
sunken
sunlamp
sunny, -nier, -niest
sunshine
sunspot
sunstroke
suntan, -tanned, -tanning
sup, supped, supping
super
superannuate, -ated, -ating
superannuation
superb, -ly
supercharge, -charged, -charging
supercilious, -ly
superficial, -ly
superfishul superficial

superfluity, -ties
superfluous, -ly
superfosfate superphosphate
superhuman, -ly
superimpose, -posed, -posing
superintendent
superior, -ly
superiority
superlative, -ly
superman, -men
supermarket
supernatural, -ly
supernumerary, -aries
superphosphate
superpower
supersaturate, -rated, -rating
supersede, -seded, -seding
supersonic
superstructure
supervise, -vised, -vising
supervishun supervision
supervision
supervisor
supervisory
supervisry supervisory
supine, -ly
suple supple
suplement supplement
suport support
suposition supposition
supper
supplant, -ed, -ing
supple, -pler, -plest
supplement
supplementation
supplementary
suppliant, -ly
supplier
supply, -plied, -plying
support, -ed, -ing
supporter
supposable, -bly
supposabul supposable
suppose, -posed, -posing
supposition
suppository, -ries
suppress, -ed, -ing

suppression
suppressive
suppurate, -rated, -rating
suppuration
supremacy
  supremasy   supremacy
supreme, -ly
  supres   suppress
  supreshun   suppression
  suprintend   superintend
  supul   supple
  sur   sir
surcharge, -charged, -charging
surcingle

> For other **surc-** words,
> look under **circ-**.

sure, -ly (certain)
  sure   shore (sea)
  sureptishus   surreptitious
surety, -ties
surf, -ed, -ing (sea)
  surf   serf (slave)
surface, -faced, -facing
surfboard
  surfeet   surfeit
surfeit, -ed, -ing
surfer
surfie
  surfis   surface
surge, surged, surging
  surgen   surgeon
surgeon
surgery, -geries
surgical, -ly
surly, -lier, -liest
  surly   surely
surmise, -mised, -mising
surmount, -ed, -ing
surname
  surogat   surrogate
surpass, -ed, -ing
surplice (garment)
  surplis   surplice
surplus (extra)
surprise, -prised, -prising
surrealism

surrealist
surrender, -ed, -ing
  surreptishus   surreptitious
surreptitious, -ly
surrogate
surround, -ed, -ing
  surtaks   surtax
surtax
surveillance
survey, -veys
surveyor
survival
survive, -vived, -viving
survivor
susceptibility
susceptible, -bly
suspect, -ed, -ing
suspend, -ed, -ing
suspender
suspense
suspicion
suspicious, -ly
  suspishun   suspicion
sustain, -ed, -ing
  sustayn   sustain
sustenance
  sustenanse   sustenance
  sut   soot
  sutable   suitable
  suter   suitor
  suthen   southern
  sutlety   subtlety
  sutul   subtle
suture, -tured, -turing
swab, swabbed, swabbing
swaddle, -dled, -dling
  swade   suede
swag
swagger, swaggered, swaggering
swagman, -men
swain
swallow, -ed, -ing
swam
swamp, -ed, -ing
swampy, -pier, -piest
swan
swank, -ed, -ing

swap, swapped, swapping
sware   swear
swarm, -ed, -ing
swarthy, -thier, -thiest
swashbuckler
swastika
swat, swatted, swatting
swathe, swathed, swathing
sway, -ed, -ing
swear, swore, sworn, swearing
sweat, -ed, -ing
sweater
sweatshop
swede
sweep, swept, sweeping
sweeper
sweepstake
sweet, -ly (taste)
sweet   suite (rooms)
sweetbread
sweeten, -ed, -ing
sweetener
sweethart   sweetheart
sweetheart
swell, swelled, swollen, swelling
swelter, -ed, -ing
swerve, swerved, swerving
swet   sweat
sweter   sweater
swich   switch
swift, -ly
swill, -ed, -ing
swim, swam, swum, swimming
swimmer
swimsuit
swindle, -dled, -dling
swindul   swindle
swine
swing, swung, swinging
swipe, swiped, swiping
swirl, -ed, -ing
swish, -ed, -ing
switch, -ed, -ing
switchboard
swivel, -elled, -elling
swob   swab
swollen

swollow   swallow
swomp   swamp
swoon, -ed, -ing
swoop, -ed, -ing
sword
swordfish
sworm   swarm
sworn
swot, swotted, swotting
swum
swurl   swirl
swurve   swerve
syanide   cyanide
sybarite
sybaritic, -ally
sycamore
sycedelic   psychedelic
syche   psyche
syciatrist   psychiatrist
syciatry   psychiatry
sycick   psychic
syclone   cyclone
sycoanalise   psychoanalyse
sycoanalisis   psychoanalysis
sycofant   sycophant
sycological   psychological
sycologist   psychologist
sycology   psychology
sycophant
sycophantic, -ally
sycosis   psychosis
sycotherapist   psychotherapist
sycotherapy   psychotherapy
sycotic   psychotic
Sydney
Sydneysider
syfilis   syphilis
sygnet   cygnet
sylable   syllable
sylf   sylph
sylinder   cylinder
syllabic, -ally
syllable
syllabus, -buses, -bi
syllogise, -gised, -gising
syllogism
syllogistic, -ally

sylph
sylvan
  sylvun   sylvan
symbiosis
symbiotic, -ally
symbol (sign)
  symbol   cymbal (music)
symbolic, -ally
symbolise, -lised, -lising
symbolism
symbolist
  symfony   symphony
symmetrical, -ly
symmetry, -tries
sympathetic, -ally
  sympathey   sympathy
sympathise, -ised, -ising
sympathiser
symphonic
symphony, -nies
symposium, -siums, -sia
symptom
symptomatic
  synagog   synagogue
synagogue
  synanym   synonym
synchromesh
synchronisation
synchronise, -nised, -nising
synchronous, -ly
  synchronus synchronous
syncopate, -pated, -pating
syncopation
syndical
syndicalism
syndicate, -cated, -cating
syndication
syndrome
  synic   cynic
  synical   cynical
synod
synodal
  synonimus synonymous
synonym
synonymous, -ly
synopsis, -ses
synoptic, -ally

syntactical, -ly
  syntaks   syntax
syntax
synthesis, -ses
synthesise, -ised, -ising
synthesiser
synthetic, -ally
  sypher   cipher
syphilis
syphilitic
syphon, -ed, -ing
syringe, -ringed, -ringing
syrup
syrupy
system
systematic
systematical, -ly
systematisation
systematise, -tised, -tising
systemic, -ally
systole
  sythe   scythe
Szechuan
Szechwan

Tt

tab, tabbed, tabbing
tabacco — tobacco
tabard
tabasco
tabasko — tabasco
tabby, -bies
tabel — table
tabie — tabby
table, -bled, -bling
tableau, -leaux, -leaus
tablespoon
tablespoonful, -fuls
tablet
tablit — tablet
tablo — tableau
tabloid
tabloyd — tabloid
taboo, -boos
taboo, -booed, -booing
tabul — table
tabular
tabulate, -lated, -lating
tabulation
taby — tabby
tachometer
tacit, -ly
taciturn
tack, -ed, -ing
tackie — tacky
tackle, -led, -ling
tackler
tackometer — tachometer
tackul — tackle
tacky, -kier, -kiest
taco
tact
tactic
tactical, -ly

tactician
tactics
tactile
tactyle — tactile
tadpole
taffeta
tafita — taffeta
tag, tagged, tagging
tail (end)
tail — tale (story)
tailgate
tailor, -ed, -ing
tailor-made
taint, -ed, -ing
taipan
take, took, taken, taking
takeover
taks — tax
taksation — taxation
taksi — taxi
talc
talcum powder
tale (story)
tale — tail (end)
talent
talented
talie — tally
talisman, -mans
talk, -ed, -ing
talk — talc
talkative, -ly
talkback
tall
tallboy
tallow
tallowwood
tally, -lies (score)
tally, -lied, -lying (score)
tally — telly (T.V.)
Talmud
talon
talor — tailor
talow — tallow
tamale
tamarind
tamborine — tambourine
tambourine

tame, tamed, taming
tame, tamer, tamest
tameable
tam-o'-shanter
tamper, -ed, -ing
tampon
tan, tanned, tanning
tanbark
tandem
tang
   tangenshul   tangential
tangent
tangential, -ly
tangerine
tangible, -bly
   tangibul   tangible
tangle, -gled, -gling
tango, -gos
tango, -goed, -going
   tangul   tangle
   tanjent   tangent
tank
tankard
tanker
tannin
tantalise, -lised, -lising
tantamount
   tantamownt   tantamount
tantrum
tap, tapped, tapping
tap-dancing
tape, taped, taping
taper, -ed, -ing
tape-recorder
tapestry, -tries
tapeworm
tapioca
   tapistry   tapestry
tappet
taproot
tar, tarred, tarring
tarantella (dance)
tarantula (spider)
   tardie   tardy
tardily
tardy, -dier, -diest
tare (weight)

   tare   tear (rip)
target
   targit   target
   tarie   tarry
   tarif   tariff
tariff
tarmac
tarnation
tarnish, -ed, -ing
tarot
   tarow   tarot
tarpaulin
   tarpollun   tarpaulin
tarragon
   tarrif   tariff
tarry, ries
tarry, -ried, -rying
tartan
tartar
tartare sauce
   tarter   tartar
tartily
tarty
   tasit   tacit
   tasiturn   taciturn
task
taskmaster
tassel, tasselled, tasselling
   tassul   tassel
taste, tasted, tasting
tastebud
tasteful, -ly
tasty, -tier, -tiest
   tatoo   tattoo
tattle, -led, -ling
tattoo, -toos
tattoo, -tooed, -tooing
   tattul   tattle
tatty
   taudry   tawdry
taught (teach)
   taught   taut (tight)
   taught   tort (law)
taunt, -ed, -ing
Taurus
taut, -ly (tight)
   taut   taught (teach)

taut	tort (law)
tautological, -ly	
tautology, -gies	
taven	tavern
tavern	
tawdrily	
tawdry, -drier, -driest	
tawny, -nier, -niest	
tax, taxed, taxing	
taxable	
taxabul	taxable
taxation	
tax-deductible	
taxi, taxis	
taxi, taxied, taxiing	
taxicab	
taxidermy	
taxie	taxi
taxonomy, -mies	
tea (drink)	
tea	tee (golf)
teach, taught, teaching	
teachable, -ably	
teachabul	teachable
teacher	
tea-chest	
teacup	
teal	
team, -ed, -ing (group)	
team	teem (rain)
teamster	
teapot	
tear (crying)	
tear, tore, torn, tearing (rip)	
tear	tare (weight)
tear	tier (row)
tearful, -ly	
tearjerker	
tease, teased, teasing	
teaspoon	
teat	
teath	teeth (noun)
teathe	teethe
tea-tree	
tech	teach
techer	teacher
technical, -ly	

technicality, -ties	
technician	
technicolour	
technique	
technocracy	
technological, -ly	
technologist	
technology	
tecneek	technique
tecnical	technical
tecnicality	technicality
tecnishun	technician
tecnocrasy	technocracy
tecnology	technology
tedious, -ly	
tee, teed, teeing (golf)	
tee	tea (drink)
teech	teach
teek	teak
teel	teal
teem, -ed, -ing (rain)	
teem	team (group)
teenager	
teese	tease
tee-shirt	
teet	teat
teeter, -ed, -ing	
teeth (noun)	
teethe, teethed, teething	
teetotal, -ly	
teetotaller	
teflon	
tekneek	technique
teknical	technical
teknicality	technicality
teknicolor	technicolour
teknishun	technician
teknocrasy	technocracy
teknology	technology
tekst	text
tekstile	textile
teksture	texture
telecast, -ed, -ing	
telecommunication	
telefone	telephone
telefonist	telephonist
telefoto	telephoto

telegraf	telegraph	temporal, -ly	
telegram		temporarily	
telegraphic		temporary	
telegraphist		temporise, -rised, -rising	
telegraphy		tempory	temporary
teleks	telex	temprament	temperament
telepathic		tempratcher	temperature
telepathist		tempremental	temperamental
telepathy		tempt, -ed, -ing	
telephone, -phoned, -phoning		temptation	
telephonic, -ally		tempter	
telephonist		temtation	temptation
telephoto lens		tenable, -bly	
teleprinter		tenabul	tenable
telescope, -coped, -coping		tenacious, -ly	
televise, -vised, -vising		tenancy	
televishun	television	tenansy	tenancy
television		tenant	
telex		tend, -ed, -ing	
telifone	telephone	tendency, -cies	
telifonist	telephonist	tendenshus	tendentious
teligram	telegram	tendentious, -ly	
teliphoto	telephoto	tender, -ed, -ing	
teliscope	telescope	tenderfoot, -foots, -feet	
telivise	televise	tenderly	
telivishun	television	tendon	
tell, told, telling		tendril	
teller		tenement	
telltale		tenet	
telly, tellies (T.V.)		teniment	tenement
temerity		tenis	tennis
temper, -ed, -ing		tennis	
tempera		tenon	
temperament		tenor	
temperamental, -ly		tenpin bowling	
temperance		tense, tensed, tensing	
temperanse	temperance	tense, tenser, tensest	
temperate, -ly		tenshun	tension
Temperate Zone		tension	
temperature		tent	
tempest		tentacle	
tempestuous, -ly		tentative, -ly	
tempestuus	tempestuous	tenterhook	
template		tenth	
temple		tenuous, -ly	
templut	template	tenure	
tempo, -pos		tenuus	tenuous

tenyer	tenure
tepee	
tepid, -ly	
teracota	terracotta
terain	terrain
terarium	terrarium
terazo	terrazzo
terban	turban
terbid	turbid
terbine	turbine
terbo	turbo
terbulent	turbulent
terf	turf
tergid	turgid
teribul	terrible
terier	terrier
terific	terrific
terifie	terrify
teritry	territory
terjid	turgid
terkey	turkey
terkwoise	turquoise
term	
termagant	
terminable, -ly	
terminabul	terminable
terminal, -ally	
terminate, -nated, -nating	
termination	
terminology, -gies	
terminus, -ni, -nuses	
termite	
termoil	turmoil
tern (bird)	
tern	turn (move)
ternip	turnip
teror	terror
terorist	terrorist
terpentine	turpentine
terpitude	turpitude
terrace, -raced, -racing	
terracotta	
terrain	
terrarium, -rariums, -raria	
terrazzo	
terrestrial, -ly	
terrible, -bly	

terribul	terrible
terrier	
terrific, -ally	
terrify, -fied, -fying	
terrine	
territorial, -ly	
territory, -ries	
terror	
terrorise, -rised, -rising	
terrorism	
terrorist	
terse, terser, tersest	
tersely	
tertiary, -ries	
tertle	turtle
terylene	
teselate	tessellate
teselation	tessellation
tespoon	teaspoon
tessellate, -ated, -ating	
tessellation	
test, -ed, -ing	
testament	
testicle	
testicul	testicle
testifie	testify
testify, -fied, -fying	
testimonial	
testimony, -nies	
testis, testes	
test-tube	
testy, -tier, -tiest	
tetanus	
tete-a-tete	
tether, -ed, -ing	
tetragon	
tetrahedron, -drons, -dra	
texchur	texture
text	
textbook	
textile	
textual, -ly	
texture, -tured, -turing	
thach	thatch
thalidomide	
than	
thank, -ed, -ing	

thankful, -ly
thankless, -ly
thanksgiving
that, those
that's (that is)
   thats   that's
thatch, -ed, -ing
thaw, -ed, -ing
   thay   they
   theater   theatre
theatre
theatrical, -ly
theft
their (possessive)
   their   there (at that place)
theirs (possessive)
   theirs   there's (there is)
theism
theist
theistic, -ally
   theif   thief
   theives   thieves
   theiving   thieving
thematic, -ally
theme
themselves
then
thence
   thense   thence
theocracy, -cies
   theocrasy   theocracy
theocrat
theodolite
theological, -ly
theologian
theology, -gies
   theolojun   theologian
theorem
theoretic
theoretical, -ly
theorise, -rised, -rising
theorist
   theorm   theorem
theory, -ries
   theosofie   theosophy

theosophical, -ly
theosophist
theosophy
therapeutic, -ally
   therapey   therapy
therapist
therapy, -pies
   therd   third
there (at that place)
   there   their (possessive)
   there   they're (they are)
thereabouts
thereby
therefore
   therem   theorem
therein
thereof
thereon
there's (there is)
   theres   theirs (possessive)
   theres   there's (there is)
   theretic   theoretic
   thereticul theoretical
   therey   theory
thereupon
therewith
   therise   theorise
   therist   theorist
therm
thermal, -ly
thermodynamic, -ally
thermometer
thermometrical,-ly
thermonuclear
thermoplastic
thermos
thermostat
thermostatic, -ally
   Thersday   Thursday
   therst   thirst
   thersty   thirsty
   therteen   thirteen
   therty   thirty

thesaurus, -sauri
these
thesis, -ses
   thesorus   thesaurus
Thespian
they'd (they had)
   theyd   they'd
they'll (they will)
   theyll   they'll
they're (they are)
   theyre   they're
they've (they have)
   theyve   they've
   thi   thigh
thick, -ly
thicken, -ed, -ing
thickener
thicket
thickhead
thickness
thickset
thickskinned
thief, thieves
thieve, thieved, thieving
thievish, -ly
thigh
thimble
   thimbul   thimble
   thime   thyme
thin, thinned, thinning
thin, thinner, thinnest
thine
   thiner   thinner
thing
thingamajig
think, thought, thinking
think-tank
thinly
thinner
thinness
third, -ly
third-degree
   thirm   therm
   thiroid   thyroid
thirst, -ed, -ing
thirstily
thirsty, -tier, -tiest

thirteen
thirteenth
   thirtie   thirty
thirtieth
thirty, -ties
this, these
   thisis   thesis
   thisle   thistle
   thisorus   thesaurus
thistle
thistledown
   thisul   thistle
   thitha   thither
thither
   tho   though
thong
   thor   thaw
   thoraks   thorax
thorax, thoraces, thoraxes
thorn
thorny, -nier, -niest
thorough, -ly (absolute)
   thorough   through (pass)
thoroughbred
thoroughfare
   thort   thought
those
thou (you)
though (but)
thought (did think)
thoughtful, -ly
thoughtless, -ly
thousand
thousandth
   thowsand   thousand
thrall
thrash, -ed, -ing
thread, -ed, -ing
threat
threaten, -ed, -ing
   thred   thread
three
three-dimensional
threepence
three-quarter
threesome
thresh, -ed, -ing

threshold
   thret — threat
threw (did throw)
   threw — through (between)
   threwout — throughout
thrice
thrift
thrifty, -tier, -tiest
thrill, -ed, -ing
thriller
thrips, thrips
   thrise — thrice
thrive, throve, thrived, thriving
thro' (through)
throat
throb, throbbed, throbbing
throe (spasm)
   throe — throw (toss)
thrombosis, -oses
throne (chair)
   throne — thrown (tossed)
throng, -ed, -ing
   throo — threw (tossed)
   throo — through (between)
   throte — throat
throttle, -tled, -tling
   throttul — throttle
through (pass)
   through — thorough (absolute)
   through — threw (tossed)
throughout
throve
throw, threw, thrown, throwing (toss)
   throw — throe (spasm)
throwaway society
thrown (tossed)
   thrown — throne (chair)
thrum, thrummed, thrumming
thrush
thrust, thrust, thrusting
thud, thudded, thudding
thug
thuggery
thuggish, -ly

   thum — thumb
thumb, -ed, -ing
thump, -ed, -ing
thunder, -ed, -ing
thunderbolt
thunderclap
thunderous, -ly
thunderstruck
thundery
   thundrus — thunderous
   thurer — thorough
   thurerbred — thoroughbred
   thurerfare — thoroughfare

> For **thurm-** words, look under **therm-**.

Thursday
   thurst — thirst
   thurteen — thirteen
   thurty — thirty
thus
thwart, -ed, -ing
   thwort — thwart
thyme (plant)
thyroid
tiara
tibia, tibiae, tibias
tic (twitch)
tick, -ed, -ing (sound)
ticker
ticket
tickle, -led, -ling
ticklish
   tickul — tickle
   ticoon — tycoon
tic-tac
tidal
tiddler
tiddlywinks
tide, tided, tiding (ocean)
   tide — tied (bound)
   tidie — tidy
tidily
tidings
   tidul — tidal
tidy, tidied, tidying
tidy, tidier, tidiest

tie, tied, tying
tier, (row)

tier	tear (crying)
tier	tire (weary)
tier	tyre (wheel)
tif	tiff

tiff
tiffin

tifoid	typhoid
tifoon	typhoon
tifus	typhus

tiger

tigeress	tigress

tight, -ly
tighten, -ed, -ing
tightrope
tights
tigress
tiki
tile, tiled, tiling
till, -ed, -ing
tiller
tilt, -ed, -ing
timber, -ed, -ing (wood)
timbre (sound)
timbrel

timbrul	timbrel

time, timed, timing (clock)

time	thyme (plant)

timekeeper
timeless, -ly
timely, -lier, -liest
timepiece
timetable
timid, -ly
timidity
timorous, -ly

timorus	timorous

timpano, -ni
tin, tinned, tinning

tinchur	tincture

tincture, -tured, -turing
tinder
tinderbox
tine
tinea
tinge, tinged, tingeing

tingle, tingled, tingling

tingul	tingle
tinie	tiny

tinker, -ed, -ing
tinkle, -led, -ling

tinkture	tincture
tinkul	tinkle

tinny, -nier, -niest
tin-pot
tinsel, -selled, -selling
tinselly

tinsul	tinsel

tint, -ed, -ing
tintack
tiny, tinier, tiniest
tip, tipped, tipping

tipe	type
tipewriter	typewriter
tipical	typical
tipify	typify
tipist	typist
tipografy	typography

tipple, -led, -ling
tipsily
tipsy, -sier, -siest
tiptoe, -toed, -toeing
tiptop

tipul	tipple

tirade

tiranical	tyrannical
tiranise	tyrannise
tirant	tyrant
tiranus	tyrannous
tirany	tyranny

tire, tired, tiring (weary)

tire	tier (row)
tire	tyre (wheel)

tiresome

tiresum	tiresome

'tis (it is)

tis	'tis (it is)
tis	tizz (anxiety)
tishoo	tissue

tissue, -sued, -suing
tit
titan
titanic

titavation | titivation
titbit |
tite | tight
titen | tighten
tites | tights
tithe, tithed, tithing |
titian |
titillate, -lated, -lating |
titillation |
titivate, -vated, -vating |
titivation |
title, -tled, -tling (name) |
titrate, -trated, -trating |
titter, -ed, -ing |
tittillate | titillate
tittle (dot) |
tittle-tattle, -tled, -tling |
titul | title
titular |
tizz (anxiety) |
to (towards) |
to | too (also)
to | two (number)
toad |
toadfish |
toadstool |
toady, toadies |
toady, toadied, toadying |
toast, -ed, -ing |
toaster |
toastmaster |
toastmistress |
tobacco |
tobacconist |
tobaco | tobacco
tobogan | toboggan
toboggan |
tobogganist |
tocsic | toxic
tocsin (alarm) |
tocsin | toxin (poison)
today |
toddle, -dled, -dling |
toddler |
toddy, -dies |
tode | toad
todler | toddler

todstool | toadstool
todul | toddle
tody | toddy
toe, toed, toeing (foot) |
toe | tow (pull)
toey |
tofee | toffee
toff |
toffee (sweet) |
toffy (rich) |
tog, togged, togging |
together |
togetherness |
toggle, -gled, -gling |
toggul | toggle
toheroa |
toi | toy
toil, -ed, -ing |
toilet |
toiletrain | toilet-train
toiletry, -tries |
toilet-train |
token |
toksic | toxic
toksin | tocsin (alarm)
toksin | toxin (poison)
tol | toll
told |
tole | toll
tolerable, -bly |
tolerance |
toleranse | tolerance
tolerant, -ly |
tolerate, -rated, -rating |
tolerense | tolerance
toll, -ed, -ing |
tolrabul | tolerable
tomahawk |
tomahork | tomahawk
tomarto | tomato
tomato, -toes |
tomb |
tomboy |
tombstone |
tome |
tomfoolery |
tomorow | tomorrow

tomorrer	tomorrow
tomorrow	
ton	
tonal, -ly	
tongs	
tongue, tongued, tonguing	
tongue-tied	
tongue-twister	
tonic	
tonight	
tonite	tonight
tonnage	
tonne	
tonnige	tonnage
tonsher	tonsure
tonsil	
tonsillectomy, -mies	
tonsillitis	
tonsure, -sured, -suring	
too (also)	
too	to (towards)
too	two (number)
took	
tool, -ed, -ing	
toom	tomb
toomstone	tombstone
toon	tune
toor	tour
toot, -ed, -ing	
tooth, teeth	
toothache	
toothake	toothache
toothbrush, -brushes	
toothcomb	
toothless	
toothpaste	
toothy, -thier, -thiest	
tootle, -tled, -tling	
tootul	tootle
top, topped, topping	
topas	topaz
topaz	
topic	
topical, -ly	
topknot	
topless, -ly	
topmast	

topografer	topographer
topografy	topography
topper	
topple, -pled, -pling	
toppul	topple
topsail	
topside	
topsoil	
topsy-turvy	
tor (hill)	
tor	tore (ripped)
tor	tour (trip)
torch	
torcher	torture
torchlight	
torchlite	torchlight
tore (ripped)	
tore	tour (trip)
toreador	
torent	torrent
torid	torrid
torism	tourism
torment, -ed, -ing	
tormenter	tormentor
tormentor	
torn	
tornado, -does, -dos	
tornament	tournament
torney	tawny
tornt	taunt
torpedo, -does	
torpedo, -doed, -doing	
torper	torpor
torpid, -ly	
torpidity	
torpor	
torque	
torrenshul	torrential
torrent	
torrential, -ly	
torrid, -ly	
torshun	torsion
torsion, -ally	
torso, -sos	
tort (law)	
tort	taught (teach)
tort	taut (tight)

tortilla
tortoise
tortoiseshell
tortology — tautology
tortuous, -ly
torture, -tured, -turing
torturer
tortus — tortoise
tortuus — tortuous
toss, tossed, tossing
toss-up
tost — toast
tot, totted, totting
total, -talled, -talling
totalisator
totalitarianism
totality, -ties
totally
tote, toted, toting
totem
toter — totter
totter, -ed, -ing
tottery
totul — total
touch, -ed, -ing (feel)
touchdown
touché (good point)
touchily
touchline
touchstone
touch-type, -typed, -typing
touchy, -chier, -chiest
tough, -ly
toughen, -ed, -ing
toupee
tour, -ed, -ing (trip)
tour — tor (hill)
tour — tore (ripped)
tourer
tourism
tourist
tournament
tournikay — tourniquet
tourniquet
tousle, -sled, -sling
tout, -ed, -ing
tow, -ed, -ing (pull)

tow — toe (foot)
toward
towards
towel, -elled, -elling
tower, -ed, -ing
towl — towel
town
town-planner
township
towring — towering
towsl — tousle
towt — tout
toxic, -ally
toxicity
toxin (poison)
toxin — tocsin (alarm)
toy, -ed, -ing
toyl — toil
toylet — toilet
trace, traced, tracing
tracer
tracery, -ries
trachea, tracheae
trachoma
track, -ed, -ing
trackshun — traction
tracksuit
tract
tractable, -bly
tracter — tractor
traction
tractor
trade, traded, trading
trade-in
trademark
trader
tradesman, -men
tradeswoman, -women
tradishun — tradition
tradition
traditional, -ly
traduce, -duced, -ducing
traducer
traduse — traduce
traffic, -ficked, -ficking
trafficable
trafficator

trafficker
trafic   traffic
tragedian
tragedienne
tragedy, -dies
tragic
tragical, -ly
tragicomedy, -dies
trail, -ed, -ing
trailblazer
trailer
train, -ed, -ing
trainee
trainer
traipse, traipsed, traipsing
trait
traiter   traitor
traitor
traitorous, -ly
traitrous   traitorous
trajectory, -ries
trajectry   trajectory
trajedy   tragedy
trakia   trachea
trakshun   traction
tram, trammed, tramming
tramcar
tramline
trammel, -melled, -melling
tramp, -ed, -ing
trample, -pled, -pling
trampoline, -lined, -lining
trampul   trample
tramul   trammel
trance, tranced, trancing
trane   train
trankwil   tranquil
trankwility   tranquillity
tranquil, -ly
tranquilliser
tranquillity
transact, -ed, -ing
transaction
transactor
transceiver
transcend, -ed, -ing
transcendent

transcendental, -ally
transcribe, -scribed, -scribing
transducer
transe   trance
transend   transcend
transept
transfer, -ferred, -ferring
transferal
transference
transfigure, -ured, -uring
transfiks   transfix
transfix, -ed, -ing
transform, -ed, -ing
transformation
transformer
transfuse, -fused, -fusing
transfusion
transgress, -ed, -ing
transgression
transgressor
transient, -ly
transishun   transition
transister   transistor
transistor
transit, -sited, -siting
transition
transitional, -ly
transitory
translate, -lated, -lating
translation
translator
translucent, -ly
transmigrate, -grated, -grating
transmigration
transmigratory
transmishun   transmission
transmission
transmit, -mitted, -mitting
transmitter
transom
transparency, -cies
transparensy   transparency
transparent, -ly
transperant   transparent
transpire, -spired, -spiring
transplant, -ed, -ing
transplantation

transport, -ed, -ing
transporter
transportation
transpose, -posed, -posing
transsexual
transversal, -ly
transverse, -versed, -versing
transvestism
transvestite
trap, trapped, trapping
trapdoor
trapeze
trapezium, -zuims, -zia
trapper
trappings
   trapse   traipse
   trase   trace
trash
trashy, trashier, trashiest
   trate   trait
   trater   traitor
   traterus   traitorous
trauma, -mata, -mas
traumatic
travail, -ed, -ing (labour)
   travale   travail
travel, -elled, -elling (tour)
traveller
   travelog   travelogue
travelogue
traverse, -versed, -versing
travesty, -ties
travesty, -tied, -tying
trawl, -ed, -ing
trawler
   trawma   trauma
   trawmatic   traumatic
treacherous, -ly
treachery, -eries
treacle
tread, trod, trodden, treading
treadle, -dled, -dling
treadmill
treason
treasonable, -bly
treasonous, -ly
   treasonus   treasonous

treasure, -ured, -uring
treasurer
treasure-trove
treasury, -uries
treat, -ed, -ing
treatable
treatise
   treatiss   treatise
treatment
treaty, -ties
treble, -bled, -bling
   trebul   treble
   trecherus   treacherous
   trechery   treachery
   tred   tread
tree
   treecul   treacle
   treet   treat
   treetis   treatise
   treetment   treatment
   treety   treaty
trefoil
trek, trekked, trekking
trekker
trellis
tremble, -bled, -bling
trembly, -blier, -bliest
   trembul   tremble
tremendous, -ly
   tremendus   tremendous
   tremer   tremor
tremolo, -los
tremor
tremulous, -ly
   tremulus   tremulous
trench, -ed, -ing
trenchant, -ly
trend
trendiness
trendy, -dier, -diest
   treo   trio
trepidation
   treshure   treasure
   treshury   treasury
   treson   treason
trespass, -ed, -ing
trespasser

tress
   tressul   trestle
trestle
trevally
   tri   try
triad
trial
   triangel   triangle
triangle
   triangul   triangle
triangular, -ly
tribal, -ly
tribalism
tribe
   tribul   tribal
tribulation
tribunal
tribune
tributary, -ries
tribute
   tributry   tributary
trice, triced, tricing
triceps
trick,-ed, -ing
trickery, -eries
trickle, -led, -ling
trickster
tricky, -kier, -kiest
tricolour
tricycle
trident
tried
   triel   trial
triennial, -ly
triennium, -enniums, -ennia
trifecta
trifle, trifled, trifling
trifler
   triful   trifle
trigger, -ed, -ing
trigonometrical, -ly
trigonometry
trilby, -bies
trillion
trilogy, -gies
trim, trimmed, trimming
trim, trimmer, trimmest

trimaran
trimester
trimmer
trinity, -ties
trinket
trio, trios
trip, tripped, tripping
tripartite
tripe
triple, -pled, -pling
triplet
triplicate, -cated, -cating
tripod
   tripple   triple
   triptick   triptych
triptych
   tripul   triple
   trise   trice
   trisicul   tricycle
trite, triter, tritest
tritely
   triumf   triumph
triumph
triumphal
triumphant, -ly
trivia
trivial, -ly
triviality, -ties
trod
trodden
   troff   trough
   trofy   trophy
troglodyte
troika
   trolie   trolley
troll, -ed, -ing
trolley, -leys
trollop
   trolop   trollop
   troly   trolley
trombone
trombonist
   troo   true
   trooant   truant
   trooly   truly
troop, -ed, -ing (soldier)
   troop   troupe (band)

trooper
  troos   truce
  trooth   truth
  troothful   truthful
trophy, -phies
tropic
tropical, -ly
  trorma   trauma
  trormatic   traumatic
trot, trotted, trotting
troth
trotter
troubadour
trouble, -bled, -bling
troublemaker
troublesome, -ly
troubleshooter
trough
trounce, trounced, trouncing
troupe (band)
trousers
trousseau, -seaux, -seaus
trout
trowel, -elled, -elling
  trownce   trounce
  trowsers   trousers
  trowt   trout
truancy
  truansy   truancy
truant
  trubul   trouble
truce
truck, -ed, -ing
truckie
truculence
  truculense   truculence
truculent, -ly
trudge, trudged, trudging
true, truer, truest
true-blue
  truf   trough
truffle
  truful   truffle
  truge   trudge
truism
  trulie   truly
trump, -ed, -ing

trumpery, -ries
trumpet
trumpeter
truncate, -cated, -cating
truncheon
  trunchon   truncheon
trundle, -dled, -dling
  trundul   trundle
trunk
  truseau   trousseau
truss, -ed, -ing
trust, -ed, -ing
trustee
trustful, -ly
  trustwerthy   trustworthy
trustworthy
trusty, trustier, trustiest
truth
truthful, -ly
try, tries
try, tried, trying
  tryce   trice
  trycycle   tricycle
  trype   tripe
tryst
  tryte   trite
  tryumph   triumph
tsar
T-shirt
tuan
tub, tubbed, tubbing
tuba, -bas, -bae (instrument)
tubby, -bier, -biest
tube, tubed, tubing
tuber (plant)
tuberculosis
tuberculous
tubular
  tuch   touch
  tuchy   touchy
tuck, -ed, -ing
tucker
Tuesday
  tuf   tough
  tuffen   toughen
tuffet
tuft, -ed, -ing

tug, tugged, tugging
tugboat
   tuishun — tuition
tuition
   tuk — tuck
   tuksedo — tuxedo
tulip
tulle
tumble, -bled, -bling
tumbler
tumbleweed
   tumbul — tumble
   tumer — tumour
tumescent
tumour
tumult
tumultuous, -ly
   tumultuus — tumultuous
tuna (fish)
tundra
tune, tuned, tuning
tuneful, -ly
tuner (radio)
   tung — tongue
tungsten
tunic
   tunige — tonnage
tunnel, -nelled, -nelling
   tunnul — tunnel
turban
turbid, -ly
turbine
turbojet
turboprop
turbot, -bots, -bot
turbulence
   turbulense — turbulence
turbulent, -ly
tureen
   turet — turret
turf, turfs, turves
turgid, -ly
turgidity
   turjid — turgid
turkey, -keys
Turkish
   turkwoise — turquoise

   turm — term
turmeric
   turminabul — terminable
   turminal — terminal
   turminate — terminate
   turminus — terminus
   turmite — termite
turmoil
turn, -ed, -ing (rotate)
   turn — tern (bird)
turncoat
   turnikay — tourniquet
   turniket — tourniquet
turnip
turnout
turnover
turnstile
turntable
turpentine
turpitude
turquoise
turret
   turse — terse
   turshury — tertiary
turtle
turtledove
turtleneck
   turtul — turtle
   Tusday — Tuesday
tusk, -ed, -ing
tussle, -sled, -sling
tussock
   tusul — tussle
tutelage
   tutelige — tutelage
   tuter — tutor
tutor
tutorial
   tutoriul — tutorial
tutu
tuxedo, -dos
twaddle, -dled, -dling
twain
twang
twangy
tweak, -ed, -ing
tweed

tweek   tweak
tweet
tweeter
tweezers
twelfth
   twelth   twelfth
twelve
twentieth
twenty, -ties
twice
   twich   twitch
twiddle, -dled, -dling
   twidul   twiddle
twig, twigged, twigging
twiggy
twilight
   twilite   twilight
twill (fabric)
'twill (it will)
   twill   'twill (it will)
twin, twinned, twinning
twine, twined, twining
twinge, twinged, twinging
twinkle, -kled, -kling
   twinkul   twinkle
twin-set
twirl, -ed, -ing
twist, -ed, -ing
twitch, -ed, -ing
twitcher
twitchy
twitter, -ed, -ing
two (number)
   two   to (towards)
   two   too (also)
two-dimensional
two-faced
twopence
twostep
two-time, -timed, -timing
two-tooth
'twould (it would)
   twould   'twould
two-up
   twurl   twirl
tycoon
   tyfoid   typhoid

   tyfoon   typhoon
   tyfus   typhus
tympanic
tympanum, -nums, -na
type, typed, typing
typecast, -cast, -casting
typeface
typescript
typeset, -set, -setting
typesetter
typewriter
typhoid
typhoon
typhus
typical, -ly
typify, -fied, -fying
typist
typographical, -ally
typography
   tyranical   tyrannical
tyrannical, -ly
tyrannise, -nised, -nising
tyranny, -nies
tyrant
   tyrany   tyranny
tyre (wheel)
   tyre   tire (weary)
tyro, -ros
tzar

Uu

ubikwity   ubiquity
ubiquitous, -ly
ubiquity
U-boat
   ubote   U-boat
   uda   udder
udder
ufologist
   ug   ugh
ug boot
ugh
   uglee   ugly
ugliness
ugly, -lier, -liest
ugly duckling
ukelele
ukulele
ulcer
ulcerate, -rated, -rating
ulceration
ulcerous, -ly
ullage, ullaged, ullaging
   ulsa   ulcer
   ulserate   ulcerate
   ulserayshun   ulceration
   ulserus   ulcerous
   ultamatum   ultimatum
   ulteeria   ulterior
   ultemo   ultimo
ulterior, -ly
ultimate, -ly
ultimatum, -tums, -ta
   ultimit   ultimate
ultimo
ultra
   ultramareen   ultramarine
ultramarine
ultrasound

ultraviolet
ululate, -lated, -lating
umber
   umberella   umbrella
umbilical cord
umbilicus, -bilici
umbra, -brae
umbrage
umbrageous, -ly
umbrella
   umbridge   umbrage
umpire, -pired, -piring
   umpyre   umpire
umpteen
umpteenth
unable
   unabul   unable
unaccompanied
unaccountable, -bly
unaccustomed
   unacustumed   unaccustomed
   unakumpneed   unaccompanied
unanimity
unanimous, -ly
   unanimus   unanimous
unapproachable, -bly
   unaprochibul   unapproachable
unassuming, -ly
unattached
unattended
   unatural   unnatural
unavailing, -ly
   unavaleing   unavailing
unaware
unawares
   unawear   unaware
unbalance, -anced, -ancing
unbecoming, -ly
   unbecuming   unbecoming
unbeknown
unbeknownst
   unbeleif   unbelief
   unbeleiver   unbeliever
   unbeleiving   unbelieving
unbelief
unbeliever
unbelieving, -ly

unbend, -bent or -bended, -bending
  unbenown   unbeknown
unblinking, -ly
unblushing, -ly
unborn
unbosom, -ed, -ing
unbounded, -ly
  unbownded   unbounded
  unbrideld   unbridled
unbridled
unburden, -ed, -ing
uncalled-for
uncanny, -nily
unceremonious, -ly
uncertain, -ly
uncharitable, -ly
uncharted
uncircumcised
uncle
unclean, -ly
uncomfortable, -ly
  unconfortibul   uncomfortable
uncommon, -ly
uncommunicative, -ly
  uncomon   uncommon
uncompromising, -ly
unconcerned, -ly
  uncondishunal   unconditional
unconditional, -ly
unconnected, -ly
unconscionable, -bly
unconscious, -ly
  unconshunibul unconscionable
  unconshus   unconscious
unconstitutional, -ly
unconventional, -ly
  uncooth   uncouth
uncouth, -ly
uncover, -ed, -ing
unction
unctuous, -ly
  uncumftibul   uncomfortable
uncut
  uncuver   uncover
undaunted
undecided
undefined

undemonstrative, -ly
undeniable, -bly
  undeniabul   undeniable
under
under-age
underarm
undercarriage
  undercarridge undercarriage
  underclose   underclothes
underclothes
undercoat
  undercote   undercoat
undercover
  undercurent   undercurrent
undercurrent
undercut, -cut, -cutting
  undercuver   undercover
underdeveloped
underdeveloping
underdevelopment
  underdevelopt underdeveloped
underdog
underdone
  underdun   underdone
  underestamate underestimate
underestimate, -mated, -mating
underexpose, -exposed, -exposing
  underexposhur underexposure
underexposure
  underexpows   underexpose
underfoot
undergo, -went, -gone, -going
undergraduate
  undergrajuate undergraduate
  undergroth   undergrowth
underground
undergrowth
underhand
  underite   underwrite
underlay, -laid, -laying
underlie, -lay, -lain, -lying
  underlieing   underlying
underline, -lined, -lining
underling
  underly   underlie
underlying
undermine, -mined, -mining

underneath
  underneeth   underneath
undernourish, -ed, -ing
  undernurish   undernourish
underpants
underpass
underpin, -pinned, -pinning
underplay, -played, -playing
underprivileged
underproof
  underprufe   underproof
  underscaw   underscore
underscore, -scored, -scoring
undersecretary, -taries
undersell, -sold, -selling
undershot
undersign
  undersine   undersign
understand, -stood, -standing
understanding
  understait   understate
understate, -stated, -stating
understatement
  understayt   understate
understood
understudy, -studied, -studying
  undertaik   undertake
  undertaiker   undertaker
undertake, -took, -taken, -taking
undertaker
under-the-counter
  undertoan   undertone
  undertoe   undertow
undertone
undertow
  underware   underwear
underwear
underworld
underwrite, -written, -writing
undesirable, -bly
  undesiribul   undesirable
undeveloped
  undevelupt   undeveloped
  undew   undue
  undewlate   undulate
  undewly   unduly
undo, -did, -done, -doing

  undoo   undo
undoubted, -ly
  undowted   undoubted
undress, -dressed, -dressing
undue
undulate, -lated, -lating
undulation
undulatory
unduly
  undur   under
undying
  undyou   undue
unearned
unearned income
unearth, -ed, -ing
unearthly
uneasily
uneasiness
uneasy, -easier, -easiest
  unecessary   unnecessary
uneducated
  uneekwell   unequal
  uneesy   uneasy
  uneeven   uneven
  unekwivacal   unequivocal
unemployed
unemployment
unequal, -ly
  uneque   unique
unequivocal, -ly
unerring, -ly
  unesesary   unnecessary
uneven, -ly
unevenness
unfailing, -ly
unfair, -ly
  unfaling   unfailing
  unfare   unfair
unfamiliar, -ly
unfamiliarity
unfeeling, -ly
  unfemilyer   unfamiliar
unfinished
unfit, -fitted, -fitting
unflagging, -ly
  unflapibul   unflappable
unflappable, -bly

unfold, -ed, -ing
unforchinate — unfortunate
unforeseen
unforgettable
unformed
unforsean — unforeseen
unfortunate, -ly
unfounded, -ly
unfowld — unfold
unfownded — unfounded
unfrock, -ed, -ing
unfurl, -ed, -ing
ungainliness
ungainly
unganely — ungainly
ungarded — unguarded
ungodliness
ungodly
ungracious, -ly
ungrashus — ungracious
unguarded, -ly
unguent
ungulate
unhappily
unhappiness
unhappy, -pier, -piest
unhealthily
unhealthiness
unhealthy, -thier, -thiest
unheard-of
unhelthy — unhealthy
unherdoff — unheard-of
unhinge, -hinged, -hinging
unhinj — unhinge
unholey — unholy
unholy, -lier, -liest
unholesum — unwholesome
uni
unicameral
unicellular
uniceluler — unicellular
unicorn
unidirechunal — unidirectional
unifacation — unification
unification
uniform, -ly
uniformity, -ties

unify, -fied, -fying
unike — unique
unilateral, -ly
unilatrel — unilateral
unimaginable, -ably
unimaginabul — unimaginable
unimpeachable, -ably
unimpeechibul — unimpeachable
unimployed — unemployed
unimprooved — unimproved
unimproved
uninhibited
uninspired
uninspiring
union
union card
unionisation
unionise, -nised, -nising
unionist
unionistic
Union Jack
unique, -ly
uniqueness
unirve — unnerve
unisex
unisexual, -ly
unisexuality
unison
unit
Unitarian
Unitarianism
unitary
unite, united, uniting
unit trust
unity, -ties
universal, -ly
universal suffrage
universe
university, -ties
unkempt
unkemt — unkempt
unkind, -ly
unkined — unkind
unkle — uncle
unknit, -knitted, -knitting
unknown
unlawful, -ly

unlearned, -ly	
unlearnt	
unleash, -ed, -ing	
unleavened	
unleesh	unleash
unlerned	unlearned
unlernt	unlearnt
unles	unless
unless	
unlettered	
unlike	
unlikelihood	
unlikely	
unlikelyhood	unlikelihood
unlimited	
unlisted	
unload, -ed, -ing	
unlode	unload
unlooked-for	
unluckily	
unluckiness	
unlucky	
unluckyly	unluckily
unmake, -made, -making	
unmanageable, -bly	
unmanagebul	unmanageable
unmanliness	
unmanly	
unmannerliness	
unmannerly	
unmenchunabul	unmentionable
unmentionable, -bly	
unmistakable, -bly	
unmistakabul	unmistakable
unmitigated, -ly	
unmooved	unmoved
unmoved	
unnatural, -ly	
unnecessary, -rily	
unnerve, -nerved, -nerving	
unnesesarily	unnecessarily
unnesesary	unnecessary
unobtrusif	unobtrusive
unobtrusive, -ly	
unofficial, -ly	
unofishel	unofficial
unorganised	

unorgenized	unorganised
unpalatable, -bly	
unpalatabul	unpalatable
unparaleled	unparalleled
unparalleled	
unparraleled	unparalleled
unpicked	
unplaced	
unplaised	unplaced
unpolished	
unpopular, -ly	
unpopularity	
unpopuler	unpopular
unprecedented, -ly	
unpresidented	unprecedented
unprincipled	
unprinsipled	unprincipled
unprintable	
unprintibul	unprintable
unprofeshunel	unprofessional
unprofessional, -ly	
unproffessinal	unprofessional
unkwalified	unqualified
unqualified	
unquestionable, -bly	
unquestionibul	unquestionable
unravel, -elled, -elling	
unravell	unravel
unreal, -ly	
unrealistic, -ally	
unreckonized	unrecognised
unredeamed	unredeemed
unredeemed	
unreel	unreal
unreelistic	unrealistic
unreesenibul	unreasonable
unrekwited	unrequited
unrelaited	unrelated
unrelated	
unrelenting, -ly	
unreleived	unrelieved
unrelieved	
unremiting	unremitting
unrepeatable, -bly	
unrepeetibul	unrepeatable
unrequited, -ly	
unrest	

unrivalled
  unriveled   unrivalled
  unrooly   unruly
unruffled
  unrufled   unruffled
unruly
unsafe, -ly
  unsaif   unsafe
  unsaterated   unsaturated
unsaturated
  unsavery   unsavoury
unsavoury
unscathed
unschooled
unscrew, -ed, -ing
unscrupulous
  unskru   unscrew
  unskuled   unschooled
unseasonable, -bly
unseat, -seated, -seating
  unseesenibul   unseasonable
  unseet   unseat
unsecured
  unsecurred   unsecured
unseemliness
unseemly
  unseemlynes   unseemliness
unseen
unselfish, -ly
  unsellfish   unselfish
unserviceable
  unservisabul   unserviceable
  unsetled   unsettled
unsettled
unshakable, -bly
unshakeable, -bly
  unshakibul   unshakeable
  unshore   unsure
unsightly
  unsitely   unsightly
  unskild   unskilled
unskilled
unsociability
unsociable, -bly
unsolicited
  unsolisited   unsolicited
  unsoshabul   unsociable

unsound, -ly
  unsownd   unsound
unspeakable, -bly
  unspeekabul   unspeakable
unspoilt
  unspoylt   unspoilt
unstable, -bly
  unstabul   unstable
unsteady, -dily
  unstedie   unsteady
unstructured
  unstruxured   unstructured
unstudied
  unstudyed   unstudied
  unsubstanshul   unsubstantial
unsubstantial, -ly
unsung
unsure
unswerving, -ly
  unswurving   unswerving
  untangel   untangle
untangle, -gled, -gling
untapped
untenable, -bly
unthinkable, -bly
  unthinkabul   unthinkable
unthinking, -ly
  untidie   untidy
untidiness
untidy, -died, -dying
untidy, -dier, -diest
untie, -tied, -tying
until
  untill   until
untimely
unto
  untoo   unto
untold
untouchable
  untouchabul   untouchable
  untooward   untoward
untoward, -ly
  untroo   untrue
  untrooth   untruth
untrue
untruth
unturned

unushual	unusual	upholster, -ed, -ing	
unusual, -ly		upholsterer	
unutterable, -bly		upholstery, -ries	
unutterabul	unutterable	upill	uphill
unvale	unveil	upkeep	
unveil, -ed, -ing		uplift	
unvoiced		up-market	
unvoised	unvoiced	upold	uphold
unwarented	unwarranted	upolster	upholster
unwarranted		upon	
unweeldy	unwieldy	upper	
unwelcome, -ly		upper case	
unwellcum	unwelcome	upper chamber	
unwholesome, -ly		uppercut	
unwieldiness		upper hand	
unwieldy		upper house	
unwiling	unwilling	uppermost	
unwilling, -ly		upright	
unwillingness		uprising	
unwind, -wound, -winding		uprite	upright
unwined	unwind	uproar	
unwitting, -ly		uproarious, -ly	
unworldliness		uproot, -ed, -ing	
unworldly		uprore	uproar
unworthily		upset, -set, -setting	
unworthiness		upshot	
unworthy		upside down	
unwritten		upstage, -staged, -staging	
up, upped, upping		upstairs	
up-and-coming		upstaje	upstage
up-beat		upstanding	
upbrade	upbraid	upsurge, -surged, -surging	
upbraid, -ed, -ing		upsurje	upsurge
upbringing		upswing, -swung, -swinging	
up-country		uptaik	uptake
updait	update	uptake	
update, -dated, -dating		up-tempo	
upeld	upheld	uptight	
uper	upper	uptite	uptight
up-end, -ended, -ending		up-to-date	
upgrade, -graded, -grading		up-too-date	up-to-date
upgraid	upgrade	upturn, -ed, -ing	
upheaval		upward, -ly	
upheevul	upheaval	upwards	
upheld		upwood	upward
uphill		uranic	
uphold, -held, -holding		uranium	

Uranus
urban (town)
urbane, -ly (civilised)
urbanity, -ties
urchin
urea
   urear   urea
ureter
urethra, -thrae, -thras
urethral
urge, urged, urging
urgency
urgent, -ly
urinal
urinary
urinate, -nated, -nating
urination
urine
   urinel   urinal
urinous
   urj   urge
   urjensy   urgency
   urjent   urgent
urn (jug)
   urn   earn (gain)
urogenital
   urojenital   urogenital
urology
   urolojy   urology
ursine
usability
usable
usableness
   usabul   usable
usage
   usaje   usage
use, used, using
useable
   useabul   useable
used
useful, -ly
usefulness
useless, -ly
uselessness
usher
usherette
usual, -ly

   ushuel   usual
   ushuelly   usually
usurp, usurped, usurping
usurpation
usurper
usury, -ries
   utalisation utilisation
ute
utensil
   utensle   utensil
uterine
uterus, uteri
utilisation
utilise, -lised, -lising
utilitarian
utilitarianism
utility, -ties
utmost
utopia
utopian
utopianism
   utta   utter
utter, uttered, uttering
utterly
uttermost
U-turn
   uttur   utter
   uturus   uterus
uvula, -las, -lae
uxorious, -ly
uxoriousness

Vv

vacancy, -cies
  vacansy   vacancy
vacant, -ly
vacate, -cated, -cating
vacation
vaccinate, -nated, -nating
vaccination
vaccine
  vaccuum   vacuum
  vacency   vacancy
vacillate, -lated, -lating
  vacseen   vaccine
  vacsinate   vaccinate
  vacsination   vaccination
  vacsine   vaccine
vacuity, -ties
vacuous, -ly
vacuum
vacuum-packed
vacuum-sealed
  vacuus   vacuous
vagabond
vagary, -ries
vagarious
  vagarius   vagarious
  vage   vague
vagina, -nas, -nae
vaginal
vagrancy, -cies
  vagransy   vagrancy
vagrant, -ly
vague, vaguer, vaguest
vaguely
  vail   vale (valley)
  vail   veil (cover)
vain, -ly (proud)
  vain   vane (blade)
  vain   vein (blood)

vainglorious, -ly
  vainglorius   vainglorious
vainglory
  vajina   vagina
  valadation   validation
  valantine   valentine
  valay   valet
vale (valley)
  vale   veil (cover)
  valedicshun   valediction
valediction
valedictory
  valedictry   valedictory
valentine
  valer   valour
  valerus   valorous
  valese   valise
valet, -leted, -leting
valiant, -ly
valid, -ly
validate, -dated, -dating
validation
validity, -ties
valise
valley, -leys
  valor   valour
valorous, -ly
  valorus   valorous
valour
valuable, -bly
valuation
value, -ued, -uing
valuer
valve, valved, valving
valvular
  valy   valley
  valyu   value
  valyubul   valuable
  valyuless   valueless
vamoose, -moosed, -moosing
vamp, -ed, -ing
vampire
van
vandal
vandalism
  vandul   vandal
vane (blade)

vane — vain (proud)
vane — vein (blood)
vaneer — veneer
vangard — vanguard
vanglorius — vainglorious
vanguard
vanilla
vanish, -ed, -ing
vanity, -ties
vankwish — vanquish
vanquish, -ed, -ing
vantage
vapid, -ly
vaporise, -rised, -rising
vaporiser
vaporous, -ly
vapour
variability
variable, -bly
variabul — variable
variance
varianse — variance
variant
variation
varicolored — varicoloured
varicoloured
varicose
varied
variegate, -gated, -gating
varietal, -ly
variety, -ties
various, -ly
varius — various
varnish, -ed, -ing
vary, varied, varying
vascular, -ly
vase
vasectomy, -mies
vaseline
vasillate — vacillate
vast, -ly
vat, vatted, vatting
Vatican
vaudavil — vaudeville
vaudeville
vault, -ed, -ing
vaunt, -ed, -ing

veal
vector
veel — veal
veemense — vehemence
veement — vehement
veer, -ed, -ing
vegatation — vegetation
vegetable
vegetabul — vegetable
vegetarian
vegetarianism
vegetate, -tated, -tating
vegetation
vegetative, -ly
vegtabul — vegetable
vehemence
vehement, -ly
vehicle
vehicular
veicular — vehicular
veil, -ed, -ing (cover)
veil — vale (valley)
vein (blood)
vein — vain (proud)
vein — vane (blade)
veks — vex
veksashus — vexatious
vektor — vector
Velcro
veldt
vellum
velocipede
velocity, -ties
velodrome
veloor — velour
velour
velum — vellum
velt — veldt
velvet
velveteen
velvety
venal, -ly
venality, -ties
vend, -ed, -ing
vender — vendor
vendetta
vendor

veneer
venerability
venerable, -bly
   venerabul   venerable
venerate, -rated, -rating
veneration
venereal
   venerial   venereal
venetian blind
   venew   venue
vengeance
vengeful, -ly
   vengense   vengeance
venial, -ly
venison
venom
venomous, -ly
   venomus   venomous
venous (of veins)
   venous   Venus (planet)
vent, -ed, -ing
   ventalation   ventilation
ventilate, -lated, -lating
ventilation
ventilator
ventral, -ly
ventricle
   ventricul   ventricle
   ventrilokwism   ventriloquism
ventriloquism
ventriloquist
venture, -tured, -turing
venturer
venturesome, -ly
venturous, -ly
   venturus   venturous
venue
Venus (planet)
   venus   venous (of veins)
veracious, -ly (honest)
   veracious   voracious (greedy)
veracity, -ties
veranda
   verashus   veracious
   verasity   veracity

verb
verbal, -balled, -balling
verbalise, -lised, -lising
verbally
verbatim
   verbel   verbal
verbena
verbiage
   verbige   verbiage
verbose, -ly
verbosity
verdant, -ly
verdict
verdure
verdurous
verge, verged, verging
verger
   vergin   virgin
   verie   vary
verifiable, -bly
verification
   verifie   verify
verify, -fied, -fying
verily
verisimilitude
veritable, -bly
vermicelli
vermilion
vermin
verminous, -ly
vermouth
vernacular, -ly
vernal, -ly
vernier
versatile, -ly
versatility
verse, verses (poem)
   verses   versus (against)
versification
versify, -fied, -fying
version
versus (against)
   versus   verses (poems)
vertebra, -brae
vertebrate
   verteks   vertex
vertex, -tices

vertical, -ly
vertiginous, -ly
   vertiginus   vertiginous
vertigo, -goes
verve
very, -rier, -riest
   vesa   visa
vespers
vessel
vest, -ed, -ing
vestal
   vestibul   vestibule
vestibule
vestige
vestigial, -ly
vestment
   vestrie   vestry
vestry, -tries
   vestul   vestal
vesture, -tured, -turing
vet, vetted, vetting
   vetenary   veterinary
   vetenry   veterinary
veteran
veterinary, -ries
veto, -toes
veto, -toed, -toing
vex, -ed, -ing
vexation
vexatious, -ly
   veza   visa
   vi   vie
via
viability
viable, -bly
   viabul   viable
viaduct
vial (tube)
   vial   vile (bad)
   vialate   violate
   vialin   violin
viand
viaticum, -ca, -cums
vibes
vibrant, -ly
vibrate, -brated, -brating
vibration

   vibrater   vibrator
vibrator
viburnum
vicar
vicarage
   vicarige   vicarage
vicarious, -ly
   vicarius   vicarious
vice
vice-chairman, -men
vice-chancellor
vice-president
   vicer   vicar
viceregal, -ly
   viceroi   viceroy
viceroy
vice versa
vicinity, -ties
vicious, -ly (evil)
   vicious   viscous (thick)
vicissitude
   vicount   viscount
   victer   victor
victim
victimisation
victimise, -mised, -mising
victor
Victorian
victorious, -ly
   victorius   victorious
victory, -ries
victual, -ualled, -ualling
victualler
video
videophone
videotape, -taped, -taping
   vidio   video
vie, vied, vying
   vieing   vying
Vietnamese, -ese
view, -ed, -ing
viewer
viewfinder
viewpoint
   viger   vigour
vigil
vigilance

vigilanse — vigilance
vigilant, -ly (watchful)
vigilante (law enforcer)
vigneron
vignette, -gnetted, -gnetting
vigoro
vigorous, -ly
vigorus — vigorous
vigour
viksen — vixen
vilafication — vilification
vilain — villain
vile, viler, vilest (bad)
vile — vial (tube)
vilely
vilification
vilifie — vilify
vilifier
vilify, -fied, -fying
vilige — village
villa
village
villager
villain
villainous, -ly
villainy, -nies
villanus — villainous
vim
vinaigrette
vindicate, -cated, -cating
vindication
vindictive, -ly
vine
vinegar
vinegary
vineyard
vinigar — vinegar
vino
vintage, -taged, -taging
vintige — vintage
vinul — vinyl
vinyl
viola
violate, -lated, -lating
violation
violator
violence

violense — violence
violent, -ly
violet
violin
viper
viperous, -ly
viperus — viperous
virago, -goes, -gos
viral
virgin
virginal, -ly
virginity
Virgo
virile
virility, -ties
virtual, -ly
virtue
virtuoso
virtuous, -ly
virtuus — virtuous
virulence
virulense — virulence
virulent, -ly
virus, viruses
visa, -saed, -saing
visage
vis-a-vis
viscera
viscosity
viscount
viscountess
viscous, -ly, (thick)
viscous — vicious (evil)
viscuus — viscous (thick)
vise — vice
vise-chairman — vice-chairman
vise-president — vice-president
visera — viscera
viseregal — viceregal
viseversa — vice versa
vishiate — vitiate
vishun — vision
vishunry — visionary
vishus — vicious (evil)
visibility, -ties
visible, -bly
visibul — visible

visinity — vicinity
vision
visionary, -ries
visionry — visionary
visissitude — vicissitude
visit, -ed, -ing
visitant
visitation
visiter — visitor
visitor
viskosity — viscosity
vista
visual, -ly
visualise, -lised, -lising
visuul — visual
visuulise — visualise
vital, -ly
vitality, -ties
vitamin
vitel — vital
vitiate, -ated, -ating
viticulture
vitreous, -ly
vitrification
vitrifie — vitrify
vitrify, -fied, -fying
vitriol
vitriolic
vituperate, -rated, -rating
viul — vial (tube)
viul — vile (bad)
vivacious, -ly
vivasious — vivacious
viva voce
vivid, -ly
vivisecshun — vivisection
vivisect, -ed, -ing
vivisection
vivisectionist
vixen
vocabulary, -ries
vocal, -ly
vocalisation
vocalise, -lised, -lising
vocalist
vocation
vocational, -ly

vociferous, -ly
vociferus — vociferous
vodka
voge — vogue
vogue
voice, voiced, voicing
void, -ed, -ing
voiige — voyage
voile
voise — voice
volatile
volatility
volcanic, -ally
volcano, -noes, -nos
voley — volley
volishun — volition
volition
volley, -leys
volley, -ed, -ing
volleyball
volt
voltage
voltaic
voltmeter
voluble, -bly
volubul — voluble
volume
volumetric, -ally
voluminous, -ly
voluminus — voluminous
voluntarily
voluntary, -taries
volunteer, -ed, -ing
voluptuous, -ly
voluptuus — voluptuous
vomit, -ed, -ing
voodoo, -doos
voodoo, -dooed, -dooing
voodooism
voracious, -ly (greedy)
voracious — veracious (honest)
voracity
vorasious — voracious
vortex, -texes, -tices
vortical, -ly
vosiferus — vociferous

votary, -ries
vote, voted, voting
voter
votive, -ly
vouch, -ed, -ing
voucher
vouchsafe, -safed, -safing
vow, -ed, -ing
   vowch   vouch
   vowcher   voucher
vowel
   vowul   vowel
voyage, -aged, -aging
voyager
   voyd   void
voyeur
voyeurism
   voyse   voice
   vue   view
vulcanise, -nised, -nising
vulcanism
vulcanite
   vulcher   vulture
vulgar, -ly
vulgarism
vulgarity, -ties
vulnerability
vulnerable, -bly
   vulnerabul   vulnerable
vulpine
vulture
vulva, -vae, -vas
   vurb   verb
   vurchoo   virtue
   vurchual   virtual
   vurchuus   virtuous
   vurgin   virgin
   vurtue   virtue
   vurtuous   virtuous
   vye   vie

wan

Ww

wack   whack
wad, wadded, wadding
waddle, -dled, -dling
waddy, -dies (club)
  waddy   wadi (channel)
wade, waded, wading
wader
wadi, -dies (channel)
  wadi   waddy (club)
  wadle   waddle
  wadul   waddle
  wafe   waif
wafer
wafery
waffle, -fled, -fling
  waful   waffle
wag, wagged, wagging
wage, waged, waging
wager
waggish, -ly
waggle, -gled, -gling
waggly
wagon
wagtail
  wagul   waggle
wahine
waif
wail, wailed, wailing (cry)
  wail   wale (welt)
  wail   whale
                        (mammal)
wainscot, -scotted, -scotting
wainwright
waipiro
waist (body)
  waist   waste
                        (squander)
waistband

waistcoat
waistline
wait (stay)
  wait   weight
                        (amount)
waiter
  waitey   weighty
waitress
waive, waived, waiving (forgo)
  waive   wave (ocean)
waiver (law)
  waiver   waver (sway)
wake, woke, woken, waking
wakeful, -ly
waken, -ened, -ening
  waks   wax
  walabey   wallaby
wale, waled, waling (welt)
  wale   wail (cry)
  wale   whale
                        (mammal)
walk, -ed, -ing
walkabout
walkathon
walker
walkie-talkie
walkout
walkover
wall
wallaby, -bies
wallaroo
wallet
walleyed
wallflower
wallop, -ed, -ing
wallow, -ed, -ing
wallpaper
wall-to-wall
walnut
  walop   wallop
  walow   wallow
walrus, -ruses
  walts   waltz
waltz, -ed, -ing
wampum
wan, wanner, wannest (pale)
  wan   won (win)

wand
wanda (ghost)
wander, -ed, -ing (walk)
   wander   wonder (think)
wanderer
wanderlust
wane, waned, waning
wangle, -gled, -gling
wangler
   wangul   wangle
want, -ed, -ing
wanton, -ly (lewd)
   wanton   won ton
                        (dough)
war, warred, warring
   warant   warrant
   warantee   warranty
waratah
warble, -bled, -bling
warbler
war cry
ward
warden
wardress
wardrobe
ware (goods)
   ware   wear (cover)
   ware   where (place)
warehouse
   warehowse   warehouse
   warey   wary
   warf   wharf
warfare
warhead
warily
wariness
   warior   warrior
warlike
warlock
warm, -ed, -ing
warm-blooded
warmonger
warmongering
warmth
warn, -ed, -ing (signal)
   warn   worn (tired)
warp, -ed, -ing

warrant, -ed, -ing
warrant officer
warrantor
warranty, -ties
warren
warrigal
warrior
wart (lump)
   wart   wort (plant)
wart-hog
   warves   wharves
wary, warier, wariest
was
wash, -ed, -ing
washboard
washer
washing soda
wash-out
wasn't (was not)
   wasnt   wasn't
wasp
waspish, -ly
wassail
wassailer
wastage
waste, wasted, wasting (squander)
   waste   waist (body)
wasteful, -ly
wasteland
wastrel
   wat   watt (power)
   wat   what (question)
watch, -ed, -ing
watchdog
watchful, -ly
watchman, -men
watchword
   wate   wait (stay)
   wate   weight
                        (measure)
water, -ed, -ing
waterbed
water-buffalo
water-closet
watercolour
watercolourist
water-column

watercourse
watercress
waterfall
waterfowl
waterfront
waterfrontage
watergate
waterhole
watering-can
watering hole
waterlily
waterlog, -logged, -logging
waterloo
watermark
watermelon
water-pistol
water-polo
waterproof
water-rat
water-repellent
watershed
water-ski, -ski'd or skied, -skiing
watertable
watertight
  watertite   watertight
water-tower
water-vapour
waterway
waterwheel
waterworks
watery
  watige   wattage
watt (power)
  watt   what (question)
wattage
wattle, -tled, -tling
wattlebird
wave, waved, waving (ocean)
  wave   waive (forgo)
waveband
wavefront
wavelength
waver, wavered, wavering (sway)
  waver   waiver (law)
wavily
waviness
wavy, -vier, -viest

wax, waxed or waxen, waxing
waxen
  waxflour   waxflower
waxflower
waxplant
waxwork
way (method)
  way   weigh (amount)
  way   whey (liquid)
waybill
wayfarer
waylay, -laid, -laying
way-out
wayward, -ly
  waywerd   wayward
we (us)
  we   wee (little)
weak, -ly (feeble)
  weak   week (time)
weaken, -ed,-ing
weakling
weakly, -lier, -liest (feebly)
  weakly   weekly (time)
weal (hurt)
  weal   wheel (disc)
wealth, -ily
wealth tax
wealthy, -thier, -thiest
wean, -ed, -ing
weaner
weapon
wear, wore, worn, wearing (cover)
  wear   ware (goods)
  wear   where (place)
  wearey   weary
wearisome, -ly
weary, -rier, -riest
weary, -ried, -rying
weasel
  weat   wheat
weather, -ed, -ing (rain)
  weather   wether (geld)
  weather   whether (if)
weatherboard
weathercock
weathervane
weave, wove or weaved, weaving

weave	we've (we have)
web, webbed, webbing	
webfoot, -feet	
webfooted	
wed, wedded or wed, wedding (join)	
we'd	
wed	we'd (we had)
Wedensday	Wednesday
wedge, wedged, wedging	
wedge-tailed eagle	
wedgie	
wedlock	
Wednesday	
wee, weer, weest (small)	
weed, weeded, weeding	
weediness	
weedul	wheedle
weedy, -dier, -diest	
week (time)	
week	weak (feeble)
weekday	
weeken	weaken
weekend	
weekender	
weekling	weakling
weekly, -lies (time)	
weekly	weakly (feebly)
weel	weal (hurt)
weel	wheel (disc)
weelbarow	wheelbarrow
weeld	wield
ween	wean
weep, wept, weeping	
weeping willow	
weet	wheat
weevil	
weeze	wheeze
weft	
wege	wedge
weigh, -ed, -ing	
weight, -ily	
weightiness	
weightlessness	
weighty, -tier, -tiest	
weild	wield
weir (dam)	
weird, -ly	

weja	ouija
welch, -ed, -ing	
welcher	
welcome, -comed, -coming	
weld, -ed, -ing	
welder	
welfare	
welfare state	
well, better, best	
we'll (we will)	
well-appointed	
well-balanced	
well-being	
well-born	
well-bred	
well-connected	
well-disposed	
well-grounded	
well-heeled	
well-informed	
well-known	
well-meaning	
well-off	
well-preserved	
well-read	
well-rounded	
well-to-do	
welsh, -ed, -ing	
welt	
welter	
welth	wealth
wen (swelling)	
wen	when (at what time)
wench	
wend, wended, wending	
wenever	whenever
Wensday	Wednesday
went	
wepon	weapon
wept	
wer	weir (dam)
werd	weird
were (was)	
were	where (place)
we're (we are)	
were	we're (we are)

wereabouts — whereabouts
wereas — whereas
werefore — wherefore
weren't (were not)
werent — weren't
weresoever — wheresoever
wereupon — whereupon
werever — wherever
werewithal — wherewithal
werewolf, -wolves
werey — weary
werisum — wearisome
werk — work

> For other **werk-** words,
> look under **work-**.

werld — world

> For other **werl-** words,
> look under **worl-**.

werm — worm

> For other **wer-** words,
> look under **wor-**.

Wesleyan
west
West End
westerly, -lies
western
westerner
Westernise, -nised, -nising
westernmost
Westminster system
westward
westwardly
westwards
wet, wetted, wetting (soak)
wet, wetter, wettest
wet — whet (sharpen)
wether, -ed, -ing (geld)
wether — weather (rain)
wether — whether (if)
wetherboard — weatherboard
wethercock — weathercock
wethervane — weathervane
wetsuit
wettex

we've (we have)
weve — weave (cloth)
weve — we've (we have)
weevel — weevil
whack, whacked, whacking
whacko
whale, whales (mammal)
whale, whaled, whaling
whaleboat
whalebone
whaler
whaler shark
wham, whammed, whamming
wharf, wharves, wharfs
wharfey — wharfie
wharfie
what (question)
what — watt (energy)
whata
what-d'ye-call-it
whatever
whatnot
whatsoever
wheat
wheat germ
wheatmeal
whedul — wheedle
wheedle, -dled, -dling
wheel (disc)
wheel — weal (hurt)
wheelbarrow
wheelchair
wheeler-dealer
wheet — wheat
wheeze, wheezed, wheezing
wheezy, -zier, -ziest
whelk
whelp
when
whenever
where (place)
where — ware (goods)
where — wear (cover)
whereabouts
whereas
wherefore
wheresoever

whereupon
wherever
wherewithal
   wherl — whirl (spin)
   wherl — whorl (circle)
wherry, -ries
whet, whetted, whetting (sharpen)
   whet — wet (soak)
whether (if)
   whether — weather (rain)
   whether — wether (geld)
whew
whey (liquid)
   whey — way (method)
   whey — weigh (measure)
which (what)
   which — witch (magic)
whichever
whiff
whiffle, -fled, -fling
while, whiled, whiling (time)
   while — wile (trick)
whilst
whim
whimper, -ed, -ing
whimsey, -sies
whimsical, -ally
whimsicality, -ties
whimsy, -sies
whine, whined, whining (complain)
   whine — wine (grape juice)
whinge, whinged, whingeing
whinny, -nies
whinny, -nied, -nying
whip, whipped, whipping
whipbird
whipcord
whiplash
whippersnapper
whippet
whipping boy
whip-round
whirl (spin)
   whirl — whorl (circle)
whirligig

whirlpool
whirlwind
whirr, whirred, whirring
whisk, whisked, whisking
whisker
whiskey, -keys (U.S., Irish)
whisky, -kies (Scotch, Canadian)
whisper, -ed, -ing
whist
whistle, -tled, -tling
whistler
   whisul — whistle
whit (jot)
   whit — wit (humour)
white, whiter, whitest
whitebait, -bait
whitecap
white-collar
white-elephant
white ensign
white-eye
whitefish, -fishes, -fish
white flag
white lie
white light
white pointer
white slave
whitewash
whither (where)
   whither — wither (shrivel)
whiting
whitlow
whittle, -tled, -tling
   whitul — whittle
whiz, whizzed, whizzing
who
whoa (stop)
   whoa — woe (sorrow)
who'd (who would)
   whod — who'd
whodunit
whoever
whole (all)
   whole — hole (opening)
wholegrain
wholehearted
wholemeal

whole number
wholesale, -saled, -saling
wholesome, -ly
who'll (who will)

~~wholl~~ who'll

wholly (entirely)

~~wholly~~ holy (good)

whom

~~whom~~ womb (uterus)

whoop (cry)

~~whoop~~ hoop (ring)

whoopee
whooping cough
whoops
whoops-a-daisy
whoosh
whop, whopped, whopping
whopper
whore, whored, whoring

~~whore~~ who're

who're (who are)
whorl (circle)

~~whorl~~ whirl (spin)

whorled
who's (who has)

~~whos~~ who's

whose (possessive)
whosoever

~~whur~~ whirr
~~whurl~~ whirl (spin)
~~whurl~~ whorl (circle)

who've (who have)

~~whove~~ who've

why, whys

~~wich~~ which
(question)

~~wich~~ witch (magic)

wick
wicked, -ly
wickedness
wicker
wickerwork
wicket
wicket-keeper
wide, wider, widest
wide-angle
widely

widen, -ed, -ing
widespread
widgie
widow, -ed, -ing
widower
width
wield

~~wierd~~ weird

wife, wives
wig, wigged, wigging
wiggle, -gled, -gling
wiggly

~~wiggul~~ wiggle

wigwam
wilco
wild, -ly
wildcat, -catted, -catting
wildcat strike
wilderness
wildfire
wild flower
wildfowl
wild-goose chase
wildlife
Wild West
wile (trick)

~~wile~~ while (time)

wilful, -ly
wiliness
will, willed, willing
willingness
will-o'-the-wisp
willow
willowy
willpower
willy-nilly

~~wilst~~ whilst

wilt, wilted, wilting
wily, -lier, -liest

~~wim~~ whim
~~wimen~~ women

> For other wi- words,
> look under **whi-**.

wimple, -pled, -pling
win, won, winning
wince, winced, wincing

winch, winched, winching
wind, -ed, -ing (air)
wind, wound, winding (turn)
windbag
windbreak
windcheater
winder
windfall
wind gauge
windjammer
windlass
windmill
window
window-dressing
window-shop, -shopped, -shopping
windpipe
windrow
windscreen
windsock
windsurf, -ed, -ing
windsurfer
wind-tunnel
windvane
windward
windy, windier, windiest
wine, wined, wining (grape juice)

wine	whine
	(complain)

wing, winged, winging
winger
wingspan
wingspread
wink, -ed, -ing
winkle, -kled, -kling
winnings
winnow, -ed, -ing
winnower
winsome, -ly
winsomeness
winter
wintery
wintry

wip	whip

For other **wip-** words,
look under **whip-**.

wipe, wiped, wiping

wipe-out
wiper
wire, wired, wiring
wireless
wirrah

wirl	whirl (spin)
wirl	whorl (circle)
wirr	whirr

wiry, wirier, wiriest
wisdom
wisdom tooth, -teeth
wise, wiser, wisest
wisecrack
wisecracker
wish, wished, wishing
wishbone
wishful, -ly
wishy-washy

wisk	whisk

For other **wis-** words,
look under **whis-**.

wisp, wisped, wisping
wisteria
wistful, -ly
wistfulness
wit (humour)

wit	whit (jot)

For other **wit-** words,
look under **whit-**.

witch (magic)

witch	which
	(question)

witchcraft
witchdoctor
witchetty grub
witch-hunt
witch-hunting
with
withdraw, -drew, -drawn, -drawing
withdrawal
withdrawal sympton
withdrawn

withdroo	withdrew

wither, -ed, -ing (shrivel)

wither	whither (where)

withers
withhold, -held, -holding
withholder
within
   withold   withhold
without
withstand, -stood, -standing
witness, -ed, -ing
witticism
   wittisism   witticism
witty, -tier, -tiest
wives
   wiz   whiz
wizard
wizened
   wo   whoa (stop)
   wo   woe (sorrow)
wobbegong
wobble, -bled, -bling
wobble board
   woble   wobble
   wobul   wobble
   wod   wad
   wodle   waddle
   wodul   waddle
woe (sorrow)
   woe   whoa (stop)
woebegone
woeful, -ly
   woft   waft
   woful   woeful
   wolet   wallet
wok
wolf, wolves
wolfish, -ly
wolfhound
wolfram
wolf spider
wolf-whistle, -led, -ling
   wolop   wallop
   wolow   wallow
wolves
   wom   womb
woman, women
womanise, -nised, -nising
womaniser
womanish, -ly

womanly
womb
wombat
women
women's lib
women's liberation
womera
won (win)
   won   one (number)
wonder, -ed, -ing (think)
   wonder   wander (walk)
wonderful, -ly
wonderland
wonderment
wondrous, -ly
   wondrus   wondrous
wonky, wonkier, wonkiest
wont (accustomed)
   wont   want (need)
   wont   won't (will not)
won't (will not)
won ton (dough)
   wonton   wanton (lewd)
woo, wooed, wooing
wood (timber)
   wood   would (will)
woodblock
woodcarving
woodchip
woodchuck
woodcut
wooden, -ly
woodenness
woodwind
woodwork
woody, woodier, woodiest
wooer
woof, -ed, -ing
woofer
wool
wool classer
wool classing
woolclip
   woolen   woollen
   woolf   wolf
wool-gatherer
wool-gathering

woolgrower
wool-growing
woollen
woollies
woolly, -lier, -liest
woolshed
wool-stapler
wool-stapling
woom   womb
wooman   woman
woomera
woond   wound
woozily
wooziness
woozy
wop   whop (hit)
wor   war
worble   warble
worbul   warble
word, worded, wording
worden   warden
wordily
wordiness
wordless, -ly
word processor
wordrobe   wardrobe
wordy, -dier, -diest
wore
worf   wharf
worfair   warfare
work, worked, working
workable
workaday
workaholic
workbench
workbox
worker
work force
workhorse
workhouse
working capital
working class, -classes
working model
working party, -parties
workman, -men
work-out
works committee

workshop
work-to-rule
worl   whirl (spin)
worl   whorl (circle)
world (earth)
world   whirled (spun)
world-class
worldliness
worldly, -lier, -liest
worm, wormed, worming
worm   warm (heat)
wormhole
wormwood
wormy, wormier, wormiest
worn (tired)
worn   warn (signal)
worn-out
worp   warp
worrier
worrisome
worry, -ries
worry, -ried, -rying
worse
worsen, -ed, -ing
worship, -shipped, -shipping
worshipper
worst
worsted
wort (plant)
wort   wart (lump)
worth
worthily
worthiness
worthless, -ly
worthwhile
worthy, -thier, -thiest
wos   was

> For other **wo-** words,
> look under **wa-**.

would (will)
would   wood (timber)
would-be
wouldn't (would not)
wouldnt   wouldn't
wound, wounded, wounding (injure)
wove

woven
wowser
wrack (seaweed)
wraith
wrangle, -gled, -gling
wrangler
   wrangul   wrangle
wrap, wrapped or wrapt, wrapping
wrapper
wrath
wrathful, -ly
wreak, -ed, -ing
wreath, wreaths (flowers)
wreathe, -thed, -thing (encircle)
wreck, -ed, -ing
wreckage
wrecker
   wrek   wreck
wren
wrench, -ed, -ing
wrest, wrested, wresting
wrestle, -tled, -tling
wrestler
wretch
wretched, -ly
   wri   wry
wrick, wricked, wricking
wriggle, -gled, -gling
wriggler
wriggly
   wrigul   wriggle
wright (worker)
wring, wrung, wringing
wringer
wrinkle, -kled, -kling
wrinkly
   wrinkul   wrinkle
wrist
wristpin
wristwatch
writ
write, wrote, written, writing
   write   right (true)
   write   rite (ceremony)
   write   wright (worker)
write-off, written-off, writing-off
writer

writhe, writhed, writhing
written
wrong
wrongdoing
wroth
wrought
wrought iron
wrung
wry, wrier, wriest
   wun   one (number)
   wun   won (win)
   wunce   once
   wunder   wonder
   wunse   once
   wur   whirr
   wurl   whirl (spin)
   wurl   whorl (circle)
wurley
wurlitzer
wurrung
wurrup
wye, wyes

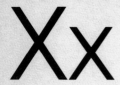

X-axis
X chromosome
 X cromosome   X chromosome
 xenofobia   xenophobia
xenophobe
xenophobia
xenophobic
 xerograf   xerograph
 xerografic   xerographic
 xerografy   xerography
xerograph
xerographic
xerography
 xeroks   xerox
xerox
Xmas
X-ray
X-ray tube
xylocarp
 xylofone   xylophone
 xylograf   xylograph
 xylografer   xylographer
 xylografic   xylographic
 xylografy   xylography
xylograph
xylographer
xylographic
xylography
xyloid
xylophagous
xylophone
xylophonic
xylophonist

y	why
yabber	
yabbie	yabby
yabby, yabbies	
yacht	
yachting	
yack	yak
yahoo	
yahweh	
yak, yakked, yakking	
yakka	
yam	
yandie	yandy
yandy	
Yang	
yank, yanked, yanking (pull)	
Yank (American)	
yap, yapped, yapping	
yard	
yardarm	
yardstick	
yarmelke	
yarmulke	
yarn, -ed, -ing	
yarran	
yaw, -ed, -ing	
yaw	yore (long ago)
yaw	your
yaw	you're (you are)
yawl	
yawn, -ed, -ing	
yaws (disease)	
yaws	yours
Y-axis	
yay	yea
Y chromosome	
Y cromosome	Y chromosome
ye	

yea	
yeah	
yeald	yield
year	
yearbook	
yearling	
yearly, -lies	
yearn, -ed, -ing	
yeast	
yeasty, yeastier, yeastiest	
yeeld	yield
yeer	year
yeest	yeast
yell, -ed, -ing	
yellow	
yellowcake	
yellowish	
yellow pages	
yellow peril	
yelosih	yellowish
yelow	yellow
yelp, -ed, -ing	
yen, yenned, yenning	
yeoman, -men	
yern	yearn
yes, yeses	
yes-man, -men	
yesterday	
yesteryear	
yet	
yeti	
yety	yeti
yew (tree)	
yew	ewe (sheep)
yew	you (person)
yewse	use
yewshual	usual
yewshuul	usual
yewsual	usual
yewsuul	usual

> For other **ye-** words,
> look under **u-**.

Yiddish
yield, yielded, yielding
Yin
yippee

yob
yodel, -delled, -delling
yodeller

yodle	yodel
yodul	yodel

yoga

yogert	yoghourt
yogert	yoghurt
yogert	yogurt

yoghourt
yoghurt
yogurt
yogi, -gis
yogism
yoicks
yoke, yoked, yoking (frame)

yoke	yolk (egg)

yokel

yokle	yokel
yokul	yokel

yolk (egg)

yoman	yeoman

Yom Kippur
yonder
yoo-hoo
yore (long ago)

yore	yaw (move)
yore	your
yore	you're (you are)
yors	yours

yorker
Yorkshire pudding

yot	yacht

you (person)

you	ewe (sheep)
you	yew (tree)

you'd (you would)

youd	you'd

you'll (you will)

youll	you'll

young
youngster
your (possessive)

your	yaw (move)
your	yore (long ago)
your	you're (you are)

you're (you are)

youre	you're

yours
yourself, -selves
youth, youths
youthful, -ly
you've (you have)

youve	you've
yowey	yowie

yowie
yowl, yowled, yowling
yoyo, -yos
yuan

yuckey	yucky, yukky
yuckie	yucky, yukky

yucky, yuckier, yuckiest
yuk
yukky, yukkier, yukkiest
yule (Christmas)

yule	you'll (you will)

yummy, yummier, yummiest

yung	young
yungster	youngster
yurn	yearn
yuse	use
yuseful	useful
yusual	usual
yusuul	usual
yutensle	utensil
yutensul	utensil
yuterine	uterine
yuteris	uterus
yuterus	uterus
yuth	youth
yutilise	utilise
yutopia	utopia

> For other **yu-** words,
> look under **u-**.

Zz

zabaglione
zany, -nier, -niest
zap, zapped, zapping
   zar   tsar
zeal
zealot
zealotry
zealous, -ly
zebra
zebra crossing
zebu
   zeel   zeal
   zefer   zephyr
   zelot   zealot
   zelous   zealous
Zen
zenith
zenithal
   zenofobia   xenophobia
   zenophobia   xenophobia
   zepher   zephyr
zephyr
   zeplen   zeppelin
zeppelin
   zercon   zircon
zero, -ros
zero, -roed, -roing
   zeroks   xerox
zero population growth
   zerox   xerox
zest
zestful, -ly
   zigote   zygote
zigzag, -zagged, -zagging
zilch
zillion
   zilofone   xylophone
   zilophone   xylophone

zinc
zing
   zink   zinc
zinnia
Zion
Zionism
Zionist
Zionistic
zip, zipped, zipping
zip-fastener
zipper
zippy, -pier, -piest
zircon
zirconium
zither
zodiac
zodiacal
zombie, -bies
zombiism
   zomby   zombie
zone, zoned, zoning
zonk, zonked, zonking
zoo
   zoochiney   zucchini
   zoochini   zucchini
   zoologey   zoology
zoological, -ly
zoologist
zoology, -gies
zoom, zoomed, zooming
zot, zotted, zotting
zucchini, zucchini, zucchinis
Zulu, -lus, -lu
Zuni, -nis, -ni
zwieback
zygote